*Fourth Edition*

# Educational Administration and Organizational Behavior

**E. Mark Hanson**
*University of California at Riverside*

**Allyn and Bacon**
*Boston   London   Toronto   Sydney   Tokyo   Singapore*

Series Editor: Ray Short
Series Editorial Assistant: Christine Shaw
Marketing Manager: Kathy Hunter
Manufacturing Buyer: Aloka Rathnam
Cover Administrator: Suzanne Harbison
Editorial-Production Service: Electronic Publishing Services Inc.

Copyright © 1996, 1991, 1985, 1979 by Allyn and Bacon
A Simon & Schuster Company
Needham Heights, Massachusetts 02194

**Library of Congress Cataloging-in-Publication Data**
Hanson, E. Mark, 1938—
   Educational administration and organizational behavior / E. Mark Hanson.—4th ed.
     p. cm.
   Includes bibliographical references and indexes.
   ISBN 0-205-18881-8
   1. School management and organization—United States.   I. Title.
LB2805.H297  1995
371.2—dc20                                  95-692
                                             CIP

Printed in the United States of America
10 9 8 7 6 5 4         99

*In memory*
*Ernest M. Hanson,*
*Ruth K. Hanson, and*
*Martha Peláez de Duque*

*Special thanks to*
*Adelle, Muriel, David, and Rodney*

# Contents

# *Preface*

Anyone reading about American public education in the daily press might assume that in recent years our schools have become wholly owned subsidiaries of the Barnum and Bailey Circus. This is partly because more than at any other time in our nation's history, schools have become a pawn in a battle to redefine the course of America. Schools are constantly being subjected to analyses from the ideological left and right, the ill-informed, and more than a few weirdos. The intent is usually to draw others to a singular cause based on a particular point of view.

This rush-to-judgment approach to analysis, however, does little to provide intellectually honest solutions to the complex problems that impact on the quality of education of our nation's youth.

The eminent scholar James G. March once wrote that "to describe American public school administration quickly is to describe it badly." The challenge of the 1990s requires that American education be better than ever before, leaving little room for the anesthesia of ignorance born of "quick and dirty" analysis. Anyone who reads this book will agree, I hope, that these sins were not committed here.

In all four editions of this book, a special attempt was made to establish a meaningful link between the "ivory tower" and the "firing line." A firing line without an ivory tower is a system that simply reproduces itself and all its problems without a sense of where it is now and the possible paths before it. An ivory tower without a firing line is little more than an exercise in spinning wheels. We tend to forget that virtually everything we do is related to some cause and effect relationship squirreled away in the back of our minds, whether it be the way we brush our teeth of the way we hire personnel. Without linking practice to some theoretical framework we become random in our behavior, and that leads us nowhere fast.

Consequently, for those who argue that they only want so-called practical knowledge about running an educational system, my response is that there is nothing more practical than understanding how an educational organization works within the context of theory and practice. Only then can something be done to make it work better.

## Plan for the Text

Specifically, this book has six basic objectives. First, it describes and critiques concepts, analytical tools, case material, and organizational theory from the public and business administration sectors and the educational administration sector. Although the educational system is unique among organizations, I believe that materials found in other management sectors are at times more advanced and can provide a wealth of insight into many issues in the educational administration field.

Second, this book is written within the framework of the social and behavioral sciences. It is not prescriptive and does not stress "cookbook" responses to complex issues. Rather, analytical thinking is the requirement of the day.

Third, it presents the notion that the field of educational administration tends to be configured around three holistic conceptual frameworks. These three models—the classical hierarchical model, the social systems model, and the open system model—say a great deal about how organizations function. Because the basic assumptions about management behavior underlying each of these three models are quite distinct, different people operating with different conceptual frameworks perceive and attack different problems by different means. This book intends to provide a comprehensive grounding in all three conceptual frameworks that will permit a more expansive analysis of educational possibilities and problems, and thus promote positive educational development.

Fourth, the key processes of communication, leadership, motivation, conflict and organizational change are analyzed in terms of how they influence educational systems. The book also contains a section on the international context of educational management. It emphasizes the economic, political, demographic, and social conditions that significantly influence schooling as well as how education is managed in Third World countries. This type of information can be important because these countries are producing the great migrations of the world and thereby influencing school enrollment throughout much of America.

Finally, I wanted to write a book that wouldn't be a crashing bore to read or filled with academic gibberish. Colleagues and students who have read the material tell me that for the most part I have succeeded.

An ancient saying reminds us, "When you drink the water, remember who dug the well." Many generations of academicians and practitioners provided the scholarship that gave intellectual life to this text. To them I owe my greatest debt.

$C\ h\ a\ p\ t\ e\ r$ *1*

# Organizational Behavior in Schools

## *An Overview*

Schools are perhaps the most complex of all our social inventions. Like other formal organizations, the school must deal with the tasks of structuring, managing, and giving direction to a complex mix of human and material resources. Unlike most other formal organizations, the school has a human product that gives rise to unique problems of organization and management. Because virtually everyone—parents, taxpayers, legislators, teachers—is considered a stockholder in the school, the processes of school governance become exceedingly complex.

As we try to understand the operations of schools, we typically turn to the teachings of the social and behavioral sciences. In doing so, Hodgkinson reminds us that "administration . . . has never laid any claims to conceptual purity; it is an applied discipline, its paradigms and theoretical underpinnings borrowed from elsewhere."[1] In recent years some of our most significant contributions to the field of management have come from engineering, political science, and biology.

Thomas Sergiovanni writes that because the field of educational administration has adopted so many of its ideas and so much conceptual knowledge from other disciplines, it has become essentially characterless "with no identity of its own, with little or no sense of what it is, what it means, where it is going, or even why it exists."[2] However, borrowing theory from other fields is not necessarily bad; the problems arise when borrowed material is not closely woven into the practice of educational administration.

Considerable dialogue about the link between theory and practice has always surrounded the field of educational administration. Donald Willower writes that "to separate science from school life is a serious error because the subject matter of social science used reflectively by a savvy administrator can drive school improvement and enhance student learning."[3] It never ceases to amaze me when graduate students stress that they want practical knowledge while having little or no interest in theory. What they seem to mean by that observation is that they are interested in learning the "nuts and bolts" skills, tools, and information that will assist them in running their schools on a day-to-day basis.

In a related context, Lee Iacocca, former president of Chrysler Corporation, reflects in his biography on the nuts and bolts of his own academic training.

> In addition to all the engineering and business courses, I also studied four years of psychology and abnormal psychology at Lehigh. I'm not being facetious when I say that these were probably the most valuable courses of my college career. It makes for a bad pun, but it's true: I've applied more of those courses in dealing with the nuts I've met in the corporate world than all the engineering courses in dealing with the nuts (and bolts) of automobiles.

Iacocca recalls one particularly valuable academic experience that took place in a psychiatric hospital.

> The focus of the course was nothing less than the fundamentals of human behavior. What motivates that guy? How did this woman develop her problems? What makes Sammy run? What led Joe over there to act like an adolescent at the age of Fifty. . . .
>
> As a result of this training, I learned to figure people out pretty quickly. To this day, I can usually tell a fair amount about somebody from our first meeting. That's an important skill to have, because the most important thing a manager can do is hire the right people.[4]

With this thought in mind, I have often asked gatherings of distinguished educators to list 10 of the most critical educational problems facing U.S. schools today. I do not recall a single instance when someone suggested that a major problem facing our schools today is that we do not have enough practical, nuts and bolts information about how to run schools on a day-to-day basis.

The theory this book presents is linked directly to searching for a better understanding of how educational systems work and how to make those systems more effective instruments for carrying out their missions in society. What could be more practical than that?

## Purpose and Organization of This Book

This book will examine and analyze the following management processes that are central to directing educational organizations: leadership, motivation, communication, conflict management, change, and situational (contingency) techniques. A final chapter examines educational management in an international context, particularly in Third World countries.

In addition, there are certain unifying perspectives (sometimes called conceptual frameworks, models, lenses, or optics) that tend to capture and focus our thinking, as a magnifying glass can capture and focus light.

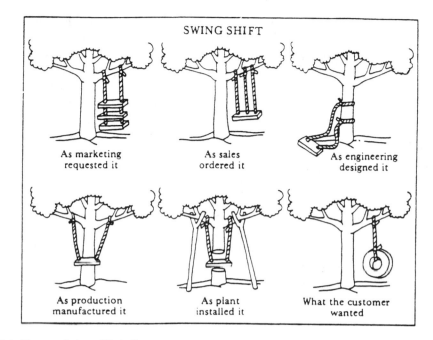

SWING SHIFT

As marketing
requested it

As sales
ordered it

As engineering
designed it

As production
manufactured it

As plant
installed it

What the customer
wanted

Reprinted by permission of Parts Pups.

Our reactions to situations in organizations are determined largely by these varying perspectives—not necessarily by objective reality. The conceptual perspective we
carry around in our heads can lead to a situation Weick refers to as "believing is seeing."[5] That is, we see what we tend to believe already exists and we screen out the rest.[6]
Behavior, like beauty, is in the eye of the beholder.

The book develops three major conceptual frameworks (perspectives) that have
important implications for schools. These frameworks depict educational organizations
as bureaucracies, sociopolitical systems, and open systems. The management processes of each will be analyzed in terms of how administrators who hold differing perspectives on the functions of educational organizations typically attend to them.

The primary objective of this book is to enhance insight into human behavior
within organizations in order to promote greater skill in governing schools. *Governance* is defined here as control over decision-making processes. In recent years, the
study of decision making has become central to the thinking of educational administrators because "all other functions of administration can best be interpreted in terms
of the decision-making process."[7] The concept of *decision* is defined as "all judgments
that affect a course of action. The concept of *decision-making process* is therefore construed to mean not only the decision but also the acts necessary to put the decision
into operation and so actually affect the course of action of an enterprise."[8]

There is much empirical research and scholarly writing on decision making.[9] Most
of the writings, as they reflect on organizations, find their conceptual roots in one of
three basic bodies of theory that offer explanations about how organizations should
or do work. These theories are identified in the management literature as *classical*

*organization theory, social system theory* (sometimes called sociopolitical group theory), and *open system theory*. These conceptual models (sometimes depicted as schools of thought or traditions) are often referred to as holistic, because they explain a wide range of phenomena and possess a visible unity and inherent logic on the ordering of organizational events. The models have contradictory basic assumptions about what draws and holds people together and how people work collaboratively to achieve a set of goals.

Case studies of governance and decision making, which draw close relationships between empirical data and the bodies of theory under discussion, will be presented. In addition, several brief teaching cases will be presented for student analysis.

## Conceptual Frameworks and School Organization

The behavior of educational officials differs according to which pair of conceptual eyeglasses they put on. Unfortunately, most educators have been taught to believe that only one model can apply to the schools—a model derived from classical organization theory.

### Classical Organization Theory

As Figure 1.1 illustrates, all three bodies of theory are represented in contemporary management thinking, although they entered the mainstream of thought at different

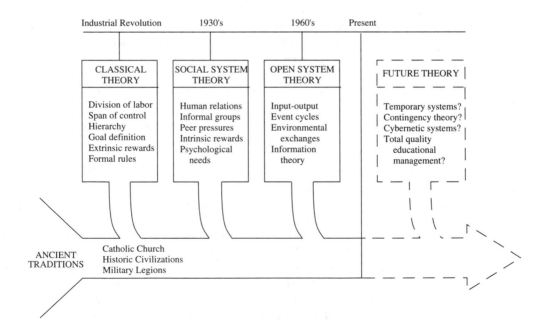

**FIGURE 1.1  The Evolution of Organization Theory**
Adapted from Billy Hodge and Herbert Johnson, *Management and Organizational Behavior: A Multidimensional Approach* (New York: John Wiley & Sons, 1970), p. 19.

historical periods. The pioneer writers obviously did not invent the phenomena they wrote about. When Max Weber (1864–1920) began writing at the turn of the century about what he termed *bureaucracy,* elements of that bureaucracy had been present in descriptions of organized life dating back to ancient Rome and China.

Most classical thinkers such as Max Weber (a German sociologist), Henri Fayol (a French industrialist), and Frederick Taylor (an American industrial engineer), lived through the industrial revolution as it went through its most fervent stages around the turn of the twentieth century. As they watched the rapidly growing technology of mass production collide with the traditional patterns of management (which were designed for simpler societies), they clearly saw the resulting wasteful and appalling inefficiency.

As the classical theorists began to examine the problems of management erupting in the production centers of society, they shaped notions about organizations that were intended to resolve many of the administrative ills. Many of the classical theorists' ideas on work and management were defined as universal scientific principles. If these principles were applied in almost any organizational setting, it was argued, the result would be the efficient use of time, materials, and personnel.

In brief, the classical theorists believed that applying the bureaucratic structure and processes of organizational control would promote rational, efficient, and disciplined behavior, and make possible the achievement of well-defined goals. Efficiency, then, is achieved by arranging positions within an organization according to hierarchy and jurisdiction and by placing power at the top of a clear chain of command. Scientific procedures are used to determine the best way of performing a task, and then rules are written that require workers to perform in a prescribed manner. Experts are hired for defined roles and are grouped according to task specialization. Using rationally defined structures and processes such as these, a scientifically ordered flow of work can be carried out with maximum efficiency.

The conceptual model distilled from classical theory had a great impact on the practice and study of organizational life. It quickly spilled over the boundaries of industry and was incorporated into the practice of management in all sectors of society, including the schools.

## Social Systems Theory

Within the classical theory framework, the individual worker was conceived of as an object, a part of the bureaucratic machine. Preparing the work environment for maximizing labor efficiency was like applying precepts from the physical sciences to the human domain of work. Within this context, Elton Mayo, who was a professor of industrial research at the Harvard School of Business, began his famous study at the Hawthorne Works of the Western Electric Company in Chicago in the 1920s.[10]

Mayo and his associates set out to study the effects of illumination on worker productivity in order to generate scientific principles that would lead to greater efficiency. The most important finding of these experiments, however, was the discovery of the impact that social-psychological variables within the worker group had on the processes of production. The discovery that workers could control the production process to a considerable degree, independent of the demands of management, shattered many of the precepts central to classical theory. A new era of organization theory was entered into. This domain of thought is sometimes referred to as *social systems theory* and at other times *sociopolitical group theory.* In this text the two terms will be used interchangeably.

Classical management theory taught that the needs of the organization and the needs of the worker coincided because if the company prospered, the worker would prosper also. However, as an awareness of the basic differences between the needs of the individual (or his or her work group) and the needs of the organization grew, and as worker groups became more sophisticated in the subrosa skills of manipulating the production process, management technology gave birth to the "human relations philosophy" as a means of reducing conflict. The argument went that by being considerate, using democratic procedures whenever possible, and maintaining open lines of communication, management and workers could talk over their respective problems and resolve them in a friendly, congenial way.

Not unlike the classical theory of the previous generation, the human relations orientation to the problems of managerial control spread quickly to other sectors of society, including the schools. The social upheaval caused by the Depression and the turmoil of World War II created a receptive climate for this new administrative theory. The enthusiasm for the human relations orientation dampened considerably after the 1950s because many worker organizations came to view it as only another management tactic designed to pacify, and thereby control, the workers' actions.

However, the study of behavior in social system settings intensified, and a greater sophistication developed about how and why group members behave as they do under given conditions. In time a natural social systems orientation to the analysis of behavior evolved in the literature as an alternative to the "rational" systems approach.[11] The natural social systems orientation attempts to take into account how people *do* behave in organizations rather than how they *should* behave. Stephen Vincent Benét has provided an insightful illustration of the trials of attempting to take a rational plan off the drawing board and send it into the real (natural) world. Benét contrasts the military blueprint with military action.

> *If you take a flat map*
> *And move wooden blocks upon it strategically,*
> *The thing looks well, the blocks behave as they should.*
> *The science of war is moving live men like blocks.*
> *And getting the blocks into place at a fixed moment.*
> *But it takes time to mold your men into blocks.*
> *And flat maps turn into country where creeks and gullies*
> *Hamper your wooden squares. They stick in the brush,*
> *They are tired and rest, they straggle after ripe blackberries,*
> *And you cannot lift them up in your hand and move them.*[12]

Ronald Corwin comments on school operations within the framework of a natural systems model.

1. Members in different parts of an organization (math teachers, coaches, or janitors) often place the interests and objectives of their own unit above those prescribed for the overall organization.

2. One's status and activity in an organization take on value as ends in themselves (indeed, salary schedules for teaches are based on their seniority, independent of demonstrated contributions to explicit goals).
3. The official goals tend to become distorted and neglected as the organization strains to survive or expand.
4. Decisions are the outcomes of bargaining and compromise among competing subgroups.
5. No one group has sufficient information or power to compel a high degree of coordination among the subgroups.[13]

The conceptual perspective of the natural social systems model suggests that an organization consists of a collection of groups (social systems) that collaborate to achieve system goals on some occasions and, on other occasions, that cooperate to accomplish the goals of their own groups. Coalitions among subgroups within an organization (e.g., English teachers, history teachers, and science teachers) form to provide power bases upon which action can be taken (e.g., "Let's all vote to reject writing behavioral objectives"). Within the social systems framework the study of formal and informal power is one of several critical variables used to identify and analyze the processes of organizational governance.

## Open System Theory

During the 1960s, another strand of thought developed which originated in the new technostructure of society. The earlier two traditions of classical and social systems theory tend to view organizational life as a *closed system*, that is, as isolated from the surrounding environment.[14] *Open system theory* conceives of an organization as a set of interrelated parts that interact with the environment almost as a living creature does. The organization trades with its environment. It receives inputs such as human and material resources, values, community expectations, and societal demands; transforms them through a production process (e.g., classroom activities); and exports the product (e.g., graduates, new knowledge, revised value sets) into the environment (e.g., business, military, home, college) with value added. The organization receives a return (e.g., community financial support) for its efforts so it can survive (and hopefully prosper). The cycle then begins once again.

Within the systems theory context, the organization is perceived as consisting of cycles of events, which interlock through exporting and importing with other organizations, which are also made up of cycles of events. Management is very complex because the leadership has almost no control over the shifting conditions in the environment (e.g., new laws, demographic shifts, political climate, market for graduates) on the input or the output side of the equation. Control of the production process is also complex because the various subsystems of the organization (e.g., athletic department or minority group students) also are shaped by event cycles that are programmed by values, expectations, traditions, and vested interests. Changing these internal subgroups and their event cycles is a difficult task. The manager attempts to stream the cycles together so that minimum conflict and waste are generated.

Through the perspective of open system theory, a new logic on issues of organizational governance has emerged. It emphasizes the relationship of the organization with its surrounding environment, and thus places a premium on planning and pro-gramming for events that cannot be controlled directly. The key to making an open system work effectively and efficiently is its ability to gather, process, and utilize information.[15]

## Implications of Organization Models for Educational Decision Making

Thus far the essence of three organizational models has been illustrated, all three of which are used to shape decision making in contemporary society. Chapters Two, Three, and Five of this book make a comprehensive examination of these models and the ways in which they influence contemporary education. Chapter Four is an ethno-graphic study of school systems as they reflect characteristics of the bureaucratic, social system, and open system models. Chapter Six examines a relatively new orientation, which argues that the key to understanding management behavior is to understand the nature of the changing situations managers must face. As the situations change, so must the styles of management.

The discussions of leadership, motivation, communication, educational marketing, conflict and stress, and organizational change, found respectively in Chapters, Seven, Eight, Nine, Ten, Eleven, and Twelve, bring together current thinking on the problems and possibilities associated with each process.

In the process of leadership, for example, if the members of a board of education conceive of the school district from a classical organization perspective, they will prob-ably search for a superintendent who talks about "going by the book" and "running a tight ship"; who insists on disciplined obedience to policy, as enforced through the chain of command; who considers himself or herself to have ultimate authority and responsibility over everything that goes on in the school district; and who displays what the military refers to as "command presence."

If the same members of the board of education view the school from the per-spective of social systems theory, they probably will search for a skilled politico who can maximize the productivity of sometimes conflicting and hostile subgroups in the school community. Controlled strategies of compromising, bargaining, retreating, and charging would be expected of a superintendent viewing management from a social systems perspective.

Finally, if school board members maintain an open system perspective, they may look for a superintendent who is concerned with comprehensive planning so that the use of people and resources will be maximized. In this instance, the leader's informa-tion network inside and outside the school system is such that he or she can antici-pate, as much as humanly possible, the development of events before the system finds itself caught up in them. The elimination of crisis management—simply moving from crisis to crisis, trying to put out fires before they become infernos—is a major inten-tion of this administrative perspective.

Indeed, as any administrator is aware, understanding and responding to issues, needs, and problems before they get out of control is a critical part of the job. Unfor-tunately, it is exactly in this area that so many school leaders take their biggest hit. In response to this necessity, Chapter Ten examines the use of private sector marketing techniques as a means of strengthening school-community communication.

Chapter Twelve deals with the what, how, why, and when issues associated with the processes of change. The educational institution has been almost possessed by the idea of change in recent years. An innovation tends to enter the field like the magnificent bull elephant trumpeting his arrival for all to hear. More than a few observers, however, are beginning to take note that he also arrives defecating copiously over much of the path he has trod. I suppose the moral of this is not to ignore his presence but to be careful where you step.

This book concludes with a chapter on educational management internationally, particularly in Third World countries. Hopefully, American educators can benefit by knowing something about the educational systems of developing countries where so many of our newly arrived immigrant students began their schooling.

## Obscured Situations and Limited Perspectives

Reflecting on the complex problems of decision making, March and Simon write:

> The organization and social environment in which the decision maker finds himself determines what consequences he will anticipate, what ones he will not; what alternatives he will consider, what ones he will ignore. In a theory of organization these variables cannot be treated as unexplained independent factors, but must themselves be determined and predicted by the theory. . . . Choice is always exercised with respect to a limited, approximate, simplified "model" of the real situation . . . the chooser's . . . "definition of the situation."[16]

In light of this observation, it becomes clear why this book does not promise prescriptions for the problems found in the schools. For decades writers in the field have tried to prescribe solutions to just about every experience common to the schools, and often as not the wrong people tried to apply the wrong solution to the wrong problem. If we have learned anything in the past 50 years, it is that just because it worked for me up in Thrasher County is no reason it will work for you in Thornton Township.

As March and Simon point out, a situation demanding a decision is often fogged not only because the decision maker cannot see all the conditions involved, but also because he or she sees the situation through a limited perspective. Providing decision makers with concepts and theoretical frameworks that aid them in determining what to look for and in diagnosing and analyzing what they see will make them more effective decision makers. That is the objective of this book.

## Conclusion

The story is told of a transcontinental hot-air balloon race in which the pilot of one of the huge air bags got lost over a western state during a storm. When the skies finally cleared, he spotted a lone farmer sitting on a wooden fence. Drifting overhead, the pilot called down, "Where am I?"

The farmer looked up, appraised the situation and yelled back, "You're in a hot-air balloon!"

Taken aback briefly, the pilot rephrased the question. "What is my location?"

The farmer called up. "You're over my field!"

Undaunted, the pilot tried once more. "Is there a city near here?"

"Yes!" called back the farmer as he watched the balloon drift off in the distance.

This brief story illustrates how a simple human encounter can be confounded by any number of barriers, such as communication, values, life-styles, expectations, differing perspectives, and so forth.

Given this simple situation, consider the possibilities of confusion when one is dealing with hundreds of people in a complex organization. The many and varied problems can be formidable. As this chapter points out, however, the problems can be dealt with intelligently if one learns how to think about them analytically, using a variety of perspectives.

The brief case that follows is intended to illustrate the complexities of making a decision when choice depends on perspective.

## An Ancient Tale

Long ago in an ancient kingdom there lived a princess who was very young and very beautiful. The princess, recently married, lived in a large and luxurious castle with her husband, a powerful and wealthy lord. The young princess was not content, however, to sit and eat strawberries by herself while her husband took frequent and long journeys to neighboring kingdoms. She felt neglected and soon became quite unhappy. One day, while she was alone in the castle gardens, a handsome vagabond rode out of the forest bordering the castle. He spied the beautiful princess, quickly won her heart, and carried her away with him.

Following a day of dalliance, the young princess found herself ruthlessly abandoned by the vagabond. She then discovered that the only way back to the castle led through the bewitched forest of the wicked sorcerer. Fearing to venture into the forest unaccompanied, she sought out her kind and wise godfather. She explained her plight, begged forgiveness of the godfather, and asked his assistance in returning home before her husband returned. The godfather, however, surprised and shocked at her behavior, refused forgiveness and denied her any assistance.

Discouraged but still determined, the princess disguised her identity and sought the help of the most noble of all the kingdom's knights. After hearing the sad story, the knight pledged his unfailing aid—for a modest fee. But alas, the princess had no money and the knight rode away to save other damsels.

The beautiful princess had no one else from whom she might seek help, and decided to brave the great peril alone. She followed the safest path she knew, but when she was almost through the forest, the wicked sorcerer spied her and caused her to be devoured by the fire-breathing dragon.[17]

1. Who is most responsible for the death of the beautiful princess?
2. Who is next most responsible?
3. How would your view change if the princess had been a prince?
4. What short- and long-range programs of change would you initiate to keep the fate of the princess from happening to other princesses in the kingdom?

## Notes

1. Christopher Hodgkinson,"A New Taxonomy of Administrative Process," *The Journal of Educational Administration* 19 (1981): 142.

2. Thomas J. Sergiovanni, "Organizations or Communities? Changing the Metaphor Changes the Theory," *Educational Administration Quarterly* 30 (1994), p. 214.

3. Donald Willower,"Whither Educational Administration? The Post Postpositivist Era," *The Journal of Educational Administration and Foundations* 8 (1993), p. 26.

4. Lee Iacocca, *Iacocca* (New York: Bantam, 1984), p. 23.

5. Karl Weick, *The Social Psychology of Organizing,* 2nd ed. (Reading, MA: Addison-Wesley, 1979).

6. Linda S. Lotto,"Believing is Seeing," in *Alternative Perspectives for Viewing Educational Organizations,* D. L. Clark S. McKibbin, and M. Malkas, eds. (San Francisco: Far West Laboratory for Educational Research and Development, 1981), pp. 6–26.

7. Daniel Griffiths,*Administration Theory* (New York:Appleton-Century-Crofts, 1959),pp. 74–75.

8. Ibid., p. 76.

9. For a useful discussion of why social science research tends not to have a discernible influence on administrative practice see: Ronald G. Corwin and Karen Seashore Louis,"Organizational Barriers to the Utilization of Research," *Administrative Science Quarterly* 27 (1982): 623–640.

10. F. J. Roethlisberger and W. J. Dickson, *Management and the Worker* (Cambridge, MA: Harvard University Press, 1939).

11. W. Richard Scott, *Organizations: Rational, Natural and Open Systems* (Englewood Cliffs, NJ: Prentice-Hall, 1981).

12. From *John Brown's Body* by Stephen Vincent Benét. Holt, Rinehart & Winston, Inc. Copyright 1927, 1928 by Stephen Vincent Benét. Copyright renewed 1955, 1956 by Rosemary Carr Benét. Reprinted by permission of Brandt & Brandt.

13. Ronald G. Corwin, "Models of Educational Organizations," in *Review of Research in Education,* vol. 2, Fred Kerlinger, ed. (Itasca, IL: F. E. Peacock, 1974), p. 255.

14. Daniel Katz and Robert Kahn,*The Social Psychology of Organizations* (New York:John Wiley & Sons, 1966).

15. Rodney Ogawa, Betty Malen, and Patricia McLeese,"The Integration of Rational, Organizational and Political Perspectives in an Information Processing Framework: A Working Paper," prepared for presentation at the American Educational Research Association, San Francisco, 1986.

16. James G. March and Herbert A. Simon,*Organizations,* p. 139. Copyright © 1958 by John Wiley & Sons, Inc. Reprinted by permission of John Wiley & Sons, Inc.

17. J. B. Ritchie and Paul Thompson, *Organization and People: Readings, Cases and Exercises in Organizational Behavior,* 4th ed., pp. 68–69. Copyright © 1988 by West Publishing Company. All rights reserved. Reprinted with permission.

# Chapter 2

# The School as a Bureaucratic Organization

During the election campaign of 1960, a young and enthusiastic John F. Kennedy promised the people of America that if he were elected president his first 100 days in office would be an uncompromising period of productive change. On April 20, 1961, the ninetieth day after his inauguration, President Kennedy sat in his office in utter despair. He had just presided over one of the worst political blunders ever committed by the United States government. "How could I have been so stupid?" he asked himself as he considered the tragedy of the Bay of Pigs.

How did it happen? President Kennedy (not to mention the 1,400 members of the Cuban Brigade) was a victim of an organizational bureaucracy that had bit by bit shaped his thinking, pulled him along as if by political suction, and finally made him a prisoner of events.[1] While many intelligent men of goodwill were involved, the structure of decision making created conditions that produced miscalculations, wrong assumptions, vested interests, and bad information.

Initial preparation for the Cuban invasion began during the latter stages of the Eisenhower administration. Several hundred exiles had already been assembled by the Central Intelligence Agency (CIA) and were in training when President-elect Kennedy received his first briefing on the subject by then CIA Director Allen Dulles on November 29, 1960.

As events began to take shape, initial CIA planning was based on several assumptions.

1. The involvement of the United States could be kept secret.
2. An uprising would take place in Cuba with armed civilians and soldiers defecting to join the invaders.
3. The Cuban Air Force was estimated to be disorganized, mostly obsolete, and

not combat efficient. In any case, preemptive air strikes using B-26 bombers taking off from Nicaragua would destroy the Cuban planes on the ground.

4. If the invaders could not get inland, they could retreat to the mountains and carry out guerrilla activities.

At the time of the invasion, the Cuban Brigade members were still being told by CIA operatives that if things went badly on the beaches, the U.S. military would intervene. They were never told that President Kennedy had strictly forbidden U.S. involvement beyond transporting troops and supplies.

Fearing a leak, Cuban sympathizers were not notified in advance of the invasion. The critical, promised uprising behind the lines thus had no chance to develop. In addition, none of the Washington planners realized that their alternate plan, in case of failure, was unfeasible: The escape route to the Escambray Mountains lay across a hopeless jungle of swamps some 80 miles away. Besides, most of the brigade had not been trained in guerrilla warfare.

On the way to the beaches, many of the small boats struck and foundered on coral reefs no one had been told about. Castro's small T-33 training planes, discounted by the American generals, strafed the men and destroyed equipment on the beach with devastating effect. They also shot down four B-26 bombers. A Sea Fury (an airplane) sank the ship carrying most of the brigade's ammunition as well as most of its communication equipment. In short, the battle was over almost before it began.

Arthur Schlesinger argues that the battle was really lost in the bureaucracy of Washington rather than on the beaches of Cuba. The Plans Division of the CIA, popularly known as "Dirty Tricks," was responsible for planning and carrying out the operation. By the time Kennedy even knew about the project, many people had committed major portions of their time and energy to the planning.

A "need-to-know" cloak of secrecy was invoked so even the Intelligence Branch of the CIA and the Cuban desk at the State Department were frozen out. Thus, the two units with the best information and expertise about Cuba were not consulted even at a time when numerous alert newspaper reporters were printing stories involving the preparations.

The "need-to-know" security classification meant that the unit that was preparing the invasion plans was also the unit evaluating those plans. The project had gained powerful momentum, and CIA leadership was emotionally committed—it wanted to see the project go. An objective assessment on its part was no longer possible.

When Kennedy asked probing questions about the stragegy, Allen Dulles, then director of the CIA, turned to what he called the "disposal problem." That is, what would be done with the hundreds of men who had been in Guatemalan training camps for months. They were not likely to disperse and keep silent about the affair. The president was sensitive to this argument because during the presidential campaign, Nixon had referred to him as being soft on communism. Aborting a move against Castro that Washington insiders considered certain victory against communism would not enhance his political status among members of the voting public.

A telling point was also made that the Soviets were about to deliver MIG fighters to the Cuban Air Force. Time was therefore limited. If action were not taken soon, it would be too late.

Periodically, the secretaries of State and Defense, the director of the CIA, the joint chiefs of staff, the president, and several key aides from various units would meet to discuss the project. William Foote Whyte, an organizational sociologist, writes that "like any good organization man, each of these executives had to be concerned also with his relations with members of his own bureaucracy and with interagency relations."[2] To challenge another agency's plan would possibly be seen as an act of political jealousy or a grab for power and would risk future interagency relationships.

No one in the room was directly representing the president's interests. The junior officials present were reluctant to speak their doubts because they could not break ranks with their immediate superiors. "Nothing had been more depressing in the whole series of meetings than to watch a collection of officials . . . prepared to sacrifice the world's growing faith in the new American President in order to defend interests and pursue objectives of their own."[3]

Senator Fulbright, chairman of the Foreign Relations Committee, was the only real outsider invited to attend the final climatic meetings.

> Fulbright, speaking in an emphatic and incredulous way, denounced the whole idea. The operation, he said, was wildly out of proportion to the threat. It would compromise our moral position in the world and make it impossible for us to protest treaty violations by the Communists. He gave a brave, old-fashioned American speech, honorable, sensible and strong; and he left everyone in the room, except me and perhaps the President, wholly unmoved.[4]

My intent here is not to suggest that the drama and sweep of events just depicted can in any way be compared with events in American public schools (although I have heard more than one superintendent refer to his personal Bay of Pigs). My point is that complex organizational bureaucracies, while obviously not living creatures, can and do take on a life of their own—even in schools and school districts. Emotional commitment to projects, fear of what others may think, guarding scarce resources, hidden agendas, loyalty to friends, protecting one's own rear extremity, attacks by ideological warriors and the badly informed, and many other organizational characteristics can capture the moment and shake a system out of its sensibilities. Any senior school administrator can attest to this. The very notion of bureaucracy, however, was intended to prevent these unfortunate circumstances from happening.

In a Weberian sense, the term *bureaucracy* refers to an authority structure based on rational behavior. Rational authority is projected throughout the organization in such a way as to directly control human activity to the points of high predictability and maximum efficiency. "Bureaucratic administration," Weber wrote, "means fundamentally the exercise of control on the basis of knowledge." Knowledge endows authority with rationality.[5] Weber argued that the bureaucratic form of administration is the most efficient organizational form that can be utilized in modern, complex organizations.

A good friend of mine is an international pilot for American Airlines, and his answer to a question illustrates what a contemporary picture of Weber's form of bureaucracy might look like. I asked him if he always knew and had worked with the other members of the cockpit crew who flew with him. His reply was that frequently he had never before met the copilot and flight engineer who sat down with him to help fly the plane.

However, they quickly and smoothly work through their highly technical tasks in a coordinated and efficient manner without any of the emotional baggage, struggles for power, or conflict often associated with group behavior. They all know their jobs, who the boss is, and how to communicate with precision. In a sense these flight officers become interchangeable parts on the types of aircraft for which they are trained.

## Bureaucratic Administration

Weber defined a set of *principles of organization,* which were thought to be universal in their application. These principles should lead an organization toward higher levels of maximum efficiency.

1. *Hierarchical Structure:* Authority in an organization is distributed in a pyramidal configuration; each official is responsible for his or her subordinates' actions and decisions.
2. *Division of Labor:* Because the varied tasks to be performed in an organization are too complex for everyone to learn with equal competence, greater efficiency results when tasks are divided into specialty areas and individuals are assigned to tasks according to their training, skill, and experience.
3. *Control by Rules:* Official decisions and actions are directed by codified rules, thus assuring uniformity, predictability, and stability.
4. *Impersonal Relationships:* Control over people and activities in an organization can be established more efficiently if purely personal, emotional, and irrational elements are eliminated. The members of the organization are subject to strict and systematic discipline in the conduct and control of their offices.
5. *Career Orientation:* Employment is based on expertise, promotion is given according to seniority and/or merit, salary is tied to rank in the hierarchy, the individual is always free to resign, and retirement provisions exist. All of these elements contribute to the formation of career employees.[6]

According to Robert Merton,

The chief merit of bureaucracy is its technical efficiency, with a premium placed on precision, speed, expert control, continuity, discretion, and optimal returns on input. The structure is one which approaches the complete elimination of personalized relationships and nonrational considerations (hostility, anxiety, affectual involvement, etc.).[7]

Bureaucratic structure and administration are designed to *routinize* problem solving—to treat incoming questions and issues in a programmed, systematic way that will draw upon a minimum of human and material resources. If each issue or personal problem an organization confronted were treated as unique (e.g., enrolling students, waxing the floors, preparing examinations), then the problems of planning, coordinating, and controlling would require massive amounts of time and resources. By routinizing the processes of the organization, the myriad competing demands on the system can be dispatched quickly and efficiently through established standing operating procedures. Hence, the multitude of round holes are created into which pegs of all sizes and shapes must fit.

## Weber's Ideal-Type Bureaucracy

The principles of organization form the basis of what Weber calls the *ideal-type* bureaucracy. For Weber the ideal type acts as a conceptual tool that helps the administrator identify and understand more clearly areas and degrees of inefficiency within the organization. This is done by analyzing the discrepancy between the ideal type and the concrete realities of the system. In other words, a comparison is made between how the organization *should* function and how it *does* function.

Unfortunately, many have been confused about the intent of Weber's ideal type. Generations of administrators have been frustrated by failing to achieve the expectations of the ideal type, ascribing the reasons for the shortcomings of their organizations to their own leadership and administrative incapacities. As later sections of this book will illustrate, Weber did not understand many characteristics of organizational life. Attempts to create such an ideal system are self-defeating.

Accordingly, as the bureaucratic model is praised and revered by many for its attributes of efficiency, it is simultaneously feared and berated by others as a system that enslaves its workers—a kind of efficiently operated mental jail. Both strands of thought are preoccupied with the way processes of control are exercised within an organization.

Douglas McGregor has written, "If there is a single assumption which pervades conventional organizational theory it is that authority is the central indispensable means of managerial control."[8] Weber defined authority as the probability that a command with a specific content will be obeyed by a given group of persons.[9] This brings us to a key question: Why do people obey?

## Why People Obey

The question of why people obey relates to the legitimization of authority for the workers. Max Weber defined three "pure" types of authority. The first was legitimated by the sanctity of tradition, which defined issues of social direction as well as right and wrong. The acceptance of the divine right of kings is a historical example of traditional authority. An example in the contemporary world is the unshakable certitude of the Christian right in its efforts to save the schools from what it views as godless liberals and the odious National Education Association.[10]

The second type of authority was legitimated by the charismatic character of the leader, exemplified by the person who inspires great loyalty and confidence among his or her followers. The third type, according to Weber, is legal-rational—authority based on a belief in the supremacy of the law.[11]

In organizations based on legal-rational authority, the organization's charter and formally established policies vest the authority of command in specific offices to be used by the people who occupy those offices. The legitimacy of the controlling influence of the supervisor over the subordinate is a matter of organization law. Those who accept the terms of employment, in effect, accept a legal constraint on their behavior and consider it their duty to obey orders. In this context, when teachers choose to sign a contract with a school system, they are prepared and willing to be bound to the decisions of their superiors in all aspects of school tasks.

## The Gospel of Scientific Management

Basically three strands of organizational thought have intertwined into what we now think of as classical organization theory: (1) Max Weber's sociological description of bureaucratic structure,[12] (2) the scientific management approach of Frederick Taylor,[13] and (3) the public administration account of scientific management by Gulick and Urwick.[14] Max Weber's theory of bureaucracy was published posthumously in German in 1921 and was not generally known to organizational theorists until the 1940s, when Talcott Parsons demonstrated to the academic and practitioner communities the useful conceptual tool Weber had developed.

In the United States, therefore, the mantle of prime mover probably should rest on the shoulders of Frederick Taylor who defined principles and practices of scientific management that sent shock waves through all sectors of corporate life. Taylor was an industrial engineer at the Midvale Steel Company and a member of the American Society of Mechanical Engineers (ASME, founded in 1880). The ASME played a strategic role in developing and disseminating new scientific management ideas through its early publications and papers read at meetings. Their ideas applied engineering principles to management tasks.

In the scientific management context, an organization was viewed as a mechanical device built according to given specifications drawn from a blueprint. The organization was designed to achieve a given purpose. The workers on the floor of the shop were Taylor's unit of analysis and the workers were thought of as mere extensions of their machines.

### Natural Laws of Work

Taylor believed that there were natural laws of work just as there are natural laws of the physical sciences. By scientifically studying a task, the one best way of performing that task could be ascertained. Hence, the experimental, empirical approach to management was born. Mouzelis writes:

> According to Taylor, a standard method and time for a task established by the time study cannot be applied unless the other factors entering the working situation are standardized as well (machine speeds, tools, supply of raw materials, etc.). The analysis of the management engineer shifts from the individual worker to wider organizational problems: relations between the various workplaces, rational regulation of the workflow, "routing," storing, and accounting techniques, methods of supervision, functional foremanship and so on. Thus by the logic of the situation, the effort towards rationalization

cannot be limited to the individual worker; it spreads outwards and upwards, until ultimately, it covers and controls the whole organization.[15]

Taylor, the father of scientific management, was a true believer in the Golden Rule
"He who has the gold makes the rules." Almost all aspects of worker activity were controlled by rules.

To insure that the worker is prepared to accept a new, scientific system of work,
Taylor argued for the adoption of a reward system that would motivate workers to
achieve higher levels of productivity. While he strongly advocated "a fair day's work for
a fair day's pay," he had some rather intriguing ideas on calculating worker pay.

> It is the writer's judgment . . . that for their own good it is as important that workmen
> should not be very much overpaid, as it is that they should not be underpaid. If over-
> paid, many will work irregularly and tend to become more or less shiftless, extravagant,
> and dissipated. It does not do for most men to get rich too fast. The writer's observa-
> tion, however, would lead him to the conclusion that most men tend to become more
> instead of less thrifty when they receive the proper increase for any extra hard day's
> work. . . . They live rather better, begin to save money, become more sober, and work
> more steadily. And this certainly forms one of the strongest reasons for advocating this
> type of management.[16]

Frederick Taylor practiced what he preached. The messiah of scientific management, for example, was an avid golfer who, like most mortals, had problems of distance
and direction on the course. However, unlike most mortals, he designed a system of
straps and slings which, when affixed to his body, would structure a maximally efficient golf swing. Unfortunately, he was ruled off the course when he tried to enter formal competition.

Taylor also had the impression that dreaming was inefficient because it forced tensions and movement in the body during sleep when the body should be rejuvenating
itself. Thus, he designed a special hammock and fixed himself into it at night in a way
that he felt would eliminate the evils of dreaming.

Another influential contributor to scientific management was a leading French
industrialist, Henri Fayol (1841–1925), who published his noted work *Administration
Industrielle et Générale* in 1916 at the age of 75. Fayol's unit of analysis differed from
Taylor's in that Fayol concentrated on increasing efficiency at the upper levels of the
organizational hierarchy while Taylor gave his attention to the lower levels.

Fayol gave definition to *the administrative process,* which has since played an
important role in management thinking. Organizational efficiency, according to Fayol,
would result if management would order its efforts in the following sequence: planning, organizing, commanding, coordinating, and controlling.[17] Fayol also defined a set
of principles, which he called *precepts.* For example:

> The manager who has to command should—
> 1. Have a thorough knowledge of his personnel.
> 2. Eliminate the incompetent.
> 3. Be well versed in the agreements binding the business and its employees.

4. Set a good example.
5. Conduct periodic audits of the organization and use summarized charts to further this.
6. Bring together his chief assistants by means of conferences at which units of direction and focusing of effort are provided for.
7. Not become engrossed in detail.
8. Aim at making unity, energy, initiative, and loyalty prevail among the personnel.[18]

The scientific management orientation quickly began to spill over into the public domain through the advocacy of men like Luther Gulick and Lyndall Urwick. Gulick developed his famous "POSDCoRB" formula for efficient administration in the public sector: planning, organizing, staffing, directing, coordinating, reporting, and budgeting.[19] Urwick popularized such principles as the need for unity of command; the use of special and general staffs; departmentalization by purpose, process, persons, and place; delegation of authority; the balance between authority and responsibility; and the definition of span of control.

## *Basic Assumptions of Scientific Management*

The underpinnings of classical theory are rooted in a number of basic assumptions about the nature of work, organizations, and individuals. (Later it will be pointed out that the basic assumptions implicit in the classical model differ considerably from those associated with the social system and open system models.) Joseph Massie distilled the following assumptions from the multitude of principles of organization that were popular during the scientific management era.

1. Efficiency of an undertaking is measured solely in terms of productivity. Efficiency relates to a mechanical process and the economic utilization of resources without consideration of human factors.
2. Human beings can be assumed to act rationally. The important considerations in management are only those which involve individuals and groups of individuals heading logically toward their goals.
3. Members in a cooperative endeavor are unable to work out the relationships of their positions without detailed guidance from their superiors.
4. Unless clear limits to jobs are defined and enforced, members will tend to be confused and to trespass on the domains of others.
5. Human beings prefer the security of a definite task and do not value the freedom of determining their own approaches to problems; they prefer to be directed and will not cooperate unless a pattern is planned formally for them.
6. It is possible to predict and establish clear-cut patterns of future activities and the relationships among activities. The total groups of tasks can be outlined in advance of execution.
7. Management involves primarily the formal and official activities of individuals.
8. The activities of a group should be viewed on an objective and impersonal basis without regard to personal problems and characteristics.
9. Workers are motivated by economic needs, and, therefore, incentives should be in terms of monetary systems.

10. People do not like to work, and, therefore, close supervision and accountability should be emphasized. Management must lead people fairly and firmly in ways that are not part of their inherent nature.
11. Coordination will not be achieved unless it is planned and directed from above.
12. Authority has its source at the top of a hierarchy and is delegated downward.
13. Simple tasks are easier to master and thus lead toward higher productivity by concentrating on a narrow scope of activity.
14. Managerial functions in varied types of activities have universal characteristics and can be performed in a given manner, regardless of the environment and qualities of the personnel involved.[20]

In short, a new wave of management thought had begun to wash throughout the public and private sectors propelled by missionaries and disciples of scientific management who preached and practiced the gospel with unrelenting faith.

## Scientific Management and the School

### The School as a Factory

Almost immediately after the nation became acquainted with the principles of scientific management, pressures from all sectors of society forced this management orientation into the schools. In his seminal study of the times, Callahan observes that a "cult of efficiency" emerged as a management ideology.[21] For example, James L. McConaughy of Dartmouth University wrote in 1918, "This is an age of efficiency. In the eyes of the public no indictment of a school can be more severe than to say it is inefficient."[22] Bobbitt advised educators to do as industry does and provide teachers with "detailed instructions as to the work to be done, the standards to be reached, the methods to be employed, and the appliances to be used."[23]

One of America's most influential educators of the time, Ellwood P. Cubberley, characterized the school as a factory processing raw materials for social consumption.

> Our schools are, in a sense, factories in which the raw products (children) are to be shaped and fashioned into products to meet the various demands of life. The specifications for manufacturing come from the demands of twentieth-century civilization, and it is the business of the school to build its pupils according to the specifications laid down. This demands good tools, specialized machinery, continuous measurement of production to see if it is according to specifications, the elimination of waste in manufacture, and a large variety in the output.[24]

Cost-accounting procedures borrowed from business became important tools for cutting costs and demonstrating efficiency. At times, however, the penchant for cost efficiency was carried to its extreme, as Callahan pointed out.[25] Witness the calculations of Robert Harris who argued the use of "cost per year-minute" as a more refined measure of pupil expenditures. The procedure was to divide the cost per pupil by the year-minutes (minutes in a given class per academic year) of teachers. Based on this procedure, Harris made a recommendation for economizing in a high school foreign language program, which he said was costing 329 percent above average.

Suppose the salary remains the same, $1,460. Let the teacher have five periods per day instead of 3.5. Let the size of the class be 25 instead of 12.8. Let the term be 40 weeks instead of 34. Then we shall have: salary, $1,460; number of pupils per teacher, 125; teaching time of teacher, 200 year-minutes. From these figures the cost-per-year-minute is 5.84 cents, as compared with 27.31 cents in the present case. The average for all the schools in Foreign Language is 6.36.[26]

Along with generally unsubstantiated views on who made the best teachers, principals, and superintendents came pronouncements on the best school board members. Cubberley stated the best to be "men who are successful in the handling of large business undertakings—manufacturers, merchants, bankers, contractors, and professional men of large practice—would come first." The worst were "inexperienced young men, unsuccessful men, old men who have retired from business, politicians, saloon-keepers, uneducated or relatively ignorant men, men in minor business positions, and women."[27]

Emerging out of the scramble to adopt practices of scientific management were a few voices of dissent that tried to point out the dangers of listening too intently to the Siren's song. The journal *American Teacher,* which became the voice of the American Federation of Teachers, had this to say as early as 1912:

> The organization and the methods of the schools have taken on the form of those commercial enterprises that distinguish our economic life. We have yielded to the arrogance of "big business men" and have accepted their criteria of efficiency at their own valuation, without question. We have consented to measure the results of educational efforts in terms of price and product—the terms that prevail in the factory and the department store. But education, since it deals in the first place with organisms, and in the second place with individualities, is not analogous to a standardizable manufacturing process. Education must not measure its efficiency in terms of so many promotions per dollar of expenditure, nor even in terms of so many student-hours per dollar of salary; it must measure its efficiency in terms of increased humanism, increased power to do, increased capacity to appreciate.[28]

The ideology and technology of scientific management moved forward on a wave of popularity until the 1930s when scientific management began to lose its luster. The depths of a worldwide depression began to draw out new-felt needs among managers and workers alike. A reaffirmation of faith in the democratic philosophy arose out of those bitter times. Coupled with research such as the Hawthorne studies, a new wave of management philosophy began to spread through the land, advocating human relations and democratic administration. (Chapter Three discusses this new theory in detail.)

## Classical Theory Applied to Schools

Even though classical organizational theory lost considerable luster in its ideological appeal, it still shapes the form and function of much found in organizational life today. For example, if you ask almost anyone today how some system is organized and administered, the response will probably be in terms of the aspects of formal organization: hierarchy, goals, job descriptions, lines of authority, and the like.

Table 2.1 illustrates the important role classical theory plays in the organization and administration of contemporary education. The left-hand column lists key principles of scientific management, and the right-hand column gives an example of their adaptation to the school.

As the next section will point out, bureaucracy has withstood the test of time.

TABLE 2.1    Scientific Management Principles Applied to Schools

| *Scientific Management Principles* | *Adaptation to Education* |
| --- | --- |
| Formation of a hierarchy with graded levels of authority | Levels of control: superintendent to assistant superintendent to principals to vice principals to teachers to students. |
| Scientific measurement of tasks and levels of performance | Students thoroughly tested in subject areas, aptitude, and achievement and classified by levels of learning. |
| Shape unity of ends (of managers and workers) | Conventional wisdom in schools dictates that teachers and administrators have the same objective: doing what is best for kids. |
| Define a scientific order of work | Third-grade knowledge is differentiated and preparatory to fourth-grade knowledge, which is differentiated and preparatory to fifth-grade knowledge, and so on. |
| Establish a division of labor | English teachers, history teachers, coaches, teacher aides, janitors, administrators, and so on. |
| Determine appropriate span of control | Thirty elementary students per teacher, 20 high school students per teacher, four vice principals per principal. |
| Adhere to the chain of command | Teachers must first talk with the principal before going to see the superintendent. |
| Define rules of behavior | Teachers' handbook: "All teachers will be in their rooms by 8:00 a.m. and are obligated to remain on the school premises until 3:30 p.m. Teachers will stand outside their rooms and monitor the passing of students between periods. A copy of all messages being sent by teachers to parents must be on file at the principal's office." |
| Establish discipline among the employees | Students will abide by the rules of the school and the norms of good conduct. Teachers will adhere to the policies of the district and the norms of the teaching profession. |
| Recruitment based on ability and technical knowledge | Teaching and/or administrative credentials required for certification to enter the field. |
| Define the one best way of performing a task | Schools continually search for the best way of teaching reading, mathematics, history, and the like. |

## The Bureaucratization of Education in America

The process of bureaucratization involves the formalization, standardization, and rationalization of rules and roles around the mission of the organization. With increasing size comes the homogenization of the subunits and an expansion in the number of levels of authority.[29]

During this century, American schools have undergone a dramatic process of bureaucratization. The bureaucratization is illustrated by the data in Table 2.2, which

TABLE 2.2     Indicators of Public School Bureaucratization

|  | 1940 | 1950 | 1960 | 1970 | 1980 | 1990 | 1992 |
|---|---|---|---|---|---|---|---|
| No. of public school districts | 117,108 | 83,719 | 40,520 | 17,995 | 15,912 | 15,358 | 15,173 |
| Elementary and secondary public school students (in millions) | 25.4 | 25.1 | 35.1 | 45.9 | 40.9 | 41.2 | 42.4* |
| Elementary and secondary public school teachers (in millions) | — | — | 1.40 | 2.05 | 2.18 | 2.36 | 2.45 |
| Elementary public schools (in thousands) | 183.1 59%=1-T | 128.2 47%=1-T | 91.9 22%=1-T | 65.8 3%=1-T | 61.1 2.4%=1-T | 61.3 1%=1-T | 61.7 — |
| Elementary and secondary expenditures as % of GDP | — | — | 3.4% | 4.5% | 4.1% | 4.5% | 4.7% |
| Elementary and secondary per-pupil expenditures (constant 1992–93 dollars) | $898 | $1,266 | $1,820 | $3,079 | $4,170 | $5,570 | $ 5,721 |
| Elementary and secondary public schools funding sources | | | | | | | |
| federal | 1.8% | 2.9% | 4.4% | 8.0% | 9.8% | 6.1% | 6.2% |
| state | 30.2% | 39.8% | 39.3% | 39.9% | 46.8% | 47.3% | 47.3% |
| local | 68.0% | 57.3% | 56.3% | 52.1% | 43.4% | 46.6% | 46.5% |

National Center for Educational Statistics, *Digest of Educational Statistics: 1993* (Washington, DC: U.S. Government Printing Office, 1993), pp. 13, 14, 96, 151, 164.

\* = estimate or projection
T = the number of schools with one teacher
GDP = Gross Domestic Product
— = no data for category

show the rapidly expanding resource base as well as student and teacher populations in an ever-declining number of schools and school districts.[30]

How is our educational bureaucracy doing compared to other nations' educational systems? In 1991 the Educational Testing Service (ETS) conducted an international assessment of mathematics and science with 13-year-olds in public and private schools in 13 industrialized nations and Jordan. The average test scores for the U.S. students were significantly higher than only those from Jordan, were statistically equal to those of Slovenia and Spain, and lower than those of 10 other nations.

In science, the U.S. students did better. The Americans were statistically higher than Ireland and Jordan, equal to five countries, and below six others.

The U.S. students, however, did finish next to the top in one category; that is, the percent of students who watch TV five or more hours daily. In that category, Scotland took the prize with 24 percent, followed by the U.S. students with 20 percent.[31]

It is somewhat ironic that during this century the United States has served as the standard against which other industrialized nations compare themselves. Interestingly enough, for different reasons today, that is also the case in education.

Classical thought does not emphasize uniformity of procedure and routinization of process to the exclusion of all diversity in the organization. Indeed, the possibility of flexibility is provided for in the process of centralization and decentralization.

## Centralization and Decentralization

Although most people think they know exactly what *centralization* and *decentralization* mean, confusion still surrounds these concepts. There are actually three forms of decentralization that exist on a continuum of the decision-making process: deconcentration, delegation, and devolution.[32] *Deconcentration* involves the transfer of tasks and workload to subunits of the system. For example, a district office may establish a policy requiring all schools to introduce individualized instruction into the teaching-learning process. The tasks of developing the instructional packets are left to the individual schools.

*Delegation* is the transfer of decision-making authority from higher to lower hierarchical levels. Delegated authority must be exercised within a policy framework established at or near the top. Ultimate authority cannot be delegated since the chief executive officers are, in the final analysis, supposed to be responsible for the actions of their subordinates. Classical theory teaches this to be true. However, in practice there is an escape clause. Chief executive officers may accept responsibility for a screw-up in the ranks, but delegating blame and all that goes with it is a skill often developed to an art form.

*Devolution* is a form of decentralization involving the shifting of authority to an autonomous unit that can act independently. While devolution of authority is not all that common in education, the creation of new school districts and the formation of teachers' unions are illustrations.

*Privatization* is a form of devolution when control over certain units or tasks are transferred from public school control to the private sector. For example, in recent years janitorial services, security arrangements, the management of schools, and the formation of some types of charter schools represent devolution to the private sector.

Centralization of authority also occurs within the context of the three concepts. Centralization takes place when the work of a unit or its delegated authority is transferred to higher levels in the organization. The unification of small school districts into larger ones is an illustration of devolution in reverse. Morphet et al. respond to the issue of why certain decisions should be decentralized or centralized.

1. Those things should be done (or decisions made) centrally that do not require or involve local initiative and responsibility and can be done more efficiently and economically on a centralized basis.
2. Those things should be decentralized and carried out on a local level which require decisions relating particularly to local needs and which, if done centrally, would prevent or limit desirable initiative and handicap the development of effective local leadership and responsibility.[33]

Decentralization expands the processes of participation in decision making as well as draws in the observations of those who are closest to the problems at hand.

Decentralization is not an all-or-nothing concept; it usually occurs in measured doses. The following statements illustrate the differing gradations of decision-making authority, from highly centralized to highly decentralized. In these illustrations, we will assume that a school superintendent is talking with a high school principal.

1. "I am studying the problem here and will soon have a decision for you."
2. "You look into the problem and get me the facts. I will then decide what to do."
3. "Study the problem and send me your recommendations, pros and cons with each recommendation, and your preferred recommendation. I will then decide what to do."
4. "Study the problem and advise me on what you intend to do. Hold off until I give you my approval."
5. "Study the problem and advise me on what you intend to do. Go ahead and take action unless I tell you to hold."
6. "Take action on your own initiative, but tell me later what you did."
7. "Take the action you feel is necessary."

It is common to hear educators say, "Our district is decentralized" or "Our district is centralized." This use of the term is rarely, if ever, correct. What does happen in a school district or a school is that *certain decisions* are decentralized (delegated) to subordinates, and others are centralized (retained) in the hands of superordinates. In fact, some decisions cannot be decentralized from the district office to the school level. For example, central office personnel must maintain control over the district budget. If each school principal were delegated the authority to hire the number of teachers he or she wanted in the classroom or were delegated the authority to purchase any equipment desired, the result would be fiscal anarchy and administrative chaos.

Certainly the particular people who are hired can be decided at the individual school level, but the number of people to be hired at each school must be determined by and controlled from the central office level. The same is true for virtually all decisions requiring dollar costs to the district.

## Contrasting Ideals with Reality

Generations of school administrators and teachers have been taught to accept classical management theory as the given condition of organizational life and to attempt to achieve its rationalistic demands. In reality, the application of scientific management can be enormously inefficient and ineffective under given conditions in given organizations. Stress on achieving the ideal type of organization in the management of a school can lead to high levels of anxiety when the system does not function according to the conditions of the model. The difference between the world of "should be" and the world of "is" at times is considerable and far beyond the control of any single administrator.

However, the point is not that classical theory has limited value—in effect, it has great value. Its value, however, can only be realized if the user weighs its application carefully and maintains the classical perspective in balance with other management orientations. The classical theory orientation, with its assumption of rationality, does not consider the ingredients of a nonrational world. Thus, the issue of limitations to rationality comes to the forefront.

## The Limits to Rationality

As decision-making instruments, organizations make decisions and initiate action within a limited perspective of reality. If an organization were to function in a truly rational fashion, it would have to consider all the possible alternatives of a decision and select the one that would maximize (over all other possible alternatives) the desired end. Such a procedure would require almost unlimited resources, intelligence, time, and the ability to read the future. Because the consequences of an action lie in the future, precise evaluation is limited.

Herbert Simon identifies three types of constraints to rationality.

1. The skills, habits, and reflexes that are more or less unconscious and that determine automatically an individual's performance
2. The motivations, values, loyalties, and vested interests of individuals in the organization
3. The amount of precise information available on the subject.[34]

The complexities and the unknowns facing executives are so extensive that they find themselves accepting, with or without that intent, a simplified view of reality. Thus, as March and Simon point out:

> Most human decision-making, whether individual or organizational, is concerned with the discovery and selection of satisfactory alternatives; only in exceptional cases is it

concerned with the discovery and selection of optimal alternatives. *To optimize requires processes several orders of magnitude more complex than those required to satisfice. An example is the difference between searching a haystack to find the sharpest needle in it and searching the haystack to find a needle sharp enough to sew with.*[35]

In examining the world of "is" as opposed to the world of "should be" as depicted by March and Simon, Katz and Kahn write:

> Executives deal with problems in piecemeal fashion; they tend to handle one thing at a time, and they tend to follow an established repertory of programs for dealing with immediate problems. They do not consider all possibilities of problem solution because it is of the very nature of organizations to set limits beyond which rational alternatives cannot go. The organization represents the walls of the maze and, by and large, organizational decisions have to do with solving problems, not reconstructing the maze walls.[36]

As a related issue, Simon distinguishes two types of premises upon which executive decisions can be based. The first is a *factual premise,* subject to empirical test. The second is a *value premise,* not subject to such testing.[37] Also included in a category not subject to testing are those decisions that have an impact in the distant future, an impact that cannot be measured, or an impact that cannot be compared with alternatives because the alternatives were never tried. Under these latter conditions, rational decision-making procedures are excluded because the best alternative cannot be known at the time of selection or even in the near future. For example, should a school invest an additional amount of its limited resources to expand the athletic program, the reading program, or the janitorial staff?

Under conditions of doubt such as these, Charles Lindblom points out that organizations frequently turn to committee (participative) decision making as a way of giving validity to selecting alternative A as opposed to alternatives B, C, or D. After all, the explanation then goes, alternative A must be the best because everyone on the committee says it is.[38] For the need to validate this doubt type of decision, executives often twist every arm available to obtain a consensus among the committee members.

Now that some of the conditions that place limits to rationality have been established, it is important to discuss the unintended consequences that can occur when attempts are made to implement the principles of organization that are rooted in classical rationalistic theory.

## *Unanticipated Consequences of the Bureaucratic Model*

Like the broom in the story of the sorcerer's apprentice, organizations occasionally get out of hand. In an organizational setting, a prescribed action may have unanticipated consequences because it evokes a larger or different set of consequences than those expected. Robert Merton was one of the first sociologists to point out that if bureaucratic administration brought reliability and predictability of human behavior, it also brought rigidity and the tendency to turn means into ends.[39]

Daniel Duke argues the importance of *reciprocal determinism,* which calls for mutually supportive adjustments in the relationship of the administrative and instructional systems. Both systems thus benefit. Supportive adjustments in the behaviors of teachers and principals would not be possible under conditions of structural rigidity.[40]

The loss of individual initiative is the price to be paid for the enforcing conformity through the strict observance of established procedures. In short, attempts to incorporate rational procedures in organizations such as schools can lead to unintended consequences that are inefficient and limit the system's overall operation.

No attempt is being made here to suggest that classical theory notions are not useful, because they are extremely useful. However, such principles must be applied with extreme care. The following sections illustrate the nature of the unintended consequences often associated with strict application of the principles of classical theory.

## Deterring the Process of Change

All formal organizations must have a hierarchy, but the presence of such a mechanism, with its assumptions of rationality, has numerous unintended consequences. As Max Abbott points out, the hierarchy can deter the process of change.[41] In a hierarchy with five levels, for example, there are at least four people who can veto a good idea coming from the lowest level (which, of course, is nearest to the problem at hand). Thus, as necessary as an organizational hierarchy is, it has a natural tendency to slow down the process of change.

Also, within the ethos of our capitalistic society there exists a notion that success and status in one's working life are achieved by rising the hierarchy. Pay schedules are structured to reflect the view that the higher one rises in the hierarchy, the more valuable one is to the organization and therefore the more money one should receive. The unfortunate situation frequently resulting from these conditions is that good teachers often leave the classroom for administrative positions in order to become a "success" in the profession. Unfortunately, the skills required to be a good teacher and those required to be a good administrator are completely different. As a result, good teachers often become poor administrators.

Interestingly, the military is one of the few public organizations to deal effectively with the problems resulting from associating salary with rank. The higher enlisted ranks, for example, receive more pay than the junior officer ranks.

The character of the organizational hierarchy also requires that subordinates show deference to their chiefs. For example, a principal can interrupt events by walking into a teacher's classroom anytime he or she chooses, but the teacher cannot do the same in the work space of the principal. The expectation of deference can also generate antipathy and hostility among subordinates, who see their skills as equal or even superior to the skills of their supervisors.

## Mock, Representative, and Punishment-Centered Rules

Unintended consequences also stem from the use of rules designed to prescribe behavior and thereby give a system predictability. Alvin Gouldner states that rules serve five functions in an organization.

1. Rules exist as the equivalent of direct, personal orders.
2. Rules provide a substitute for the personal repetition of orders by a supervisor.
3. Rules serve to define and limit a subordinate's area of decision-making discretion.
4. Rules facilitate the "remote control" capability for managers.
5. Rules serve as punishment-legitimating functions.[42]

Not all rules are applied with the same vigor. In schools, for example, teachers and administrators frequently report they are not even sure what many of the rules are. In this light, Gouldner argues that organizations have three types of rules: mock, representative, and punishment centered. *Mock rules* are neither enforced by management nor obeyed by workers. Usually they are imposed on the group by some outside agency or written by the group to please some outside agency. Neither superiors nor subordinates identify with the rules nor think the rules apply to them. For example, rules requiring teachers to sign in and out when they enter or leave the school grounds, rules requiring the strict use of behavioral objectives in the classroom, or rules of behavior written in proposals to obtain federal grants often fall within the definition of mock rules.

*Representative rules* are enforced by management and obeyed by workers. Management and workers can legitimate the rules in terms of their own core values. For example, teachers and administrators fully support the rules governing the security of the children while on the grounds of the school and the rules requiring parents to check in at the principal's office before proceeding to the classroom to talk with the teacher. The principal often can cool off an angry parent.

A *punishment-centered rule* arises "in response to the pressure of either workers or management, but is not jointly initiated by them. The group which does not initiate the rule views it as imposed by the other." Enforcement of these rules violates the values of only one group and "entails relatively great tension and conflict."[43] These rules are enforced by punishment. An example of a punishment-centered rule is one forbidding public employees to strike. Teachers tend to view this rule as a tool of management and with increasing frequency directly defy it by walking out and creating storms of conflict.

## Anticipating the Unexpected

Unintended consequences develop due to the differing responses to different types of rules. For example, if someone tries to enforce a mock rule, both supervisors and subordinates may be outraged and try to subvert its intent.

Another unintended consequence of control by rules is that they are such impersonal instruments that they fail to anticipate and provide for the unexpected. The unexpected poses an especially difficult problem in organizations with complicated hierarchies in which little authority is vested in lower-level officials. State departments of education and large urban school districts are structured in this way. A rather dramatic example of an unintended consequence of a rule occurred when the energy crisis forced the entire nation to advance the clock by one hour. It was quickly realized that children were endangered when they had to walk to school or wait for the bus in the dark. A tragic delay set in as school officials tried to sort out and change a tangled web of rules governing bus schedules, teacher contracts, beginning and ending school times, and legal obligations.

Most instances of the unexpected are not so dramatic but nonetheless aggravating, such as two groups arriving to use the gym at the same time, parents angered because of a particular material being used in the classroom, or a pipe breaking in the washroom. If a local official such as a principal or vice-principal has decision-making discretion, the unexpected usually can be treated by his or her personal intervention. However, if permission to act must first be sought from higher authorities for unexpected events not covered by the rules, the trauma of delay sets in.

## Minimum Performance Levels

Another unanticipated consequence of rule making is that rules provide cues for organizational members about minimum levels of acceptable performance.[44] This type of knowledge can direct the work force of an organization to program its efforts to the minimum acceptable level. Also, the use of rules can produce a type of apathy toward creative efforts *not* recognized by rules.

## Goal Displacement

The personalities of individuals who constantly work within the problem solving framework of defined roles and prescribed rules tend to be affected. In time, Merton argues, many of these individuals cling to the security of the established problem-solving routines and thus are unable to adjust to the exigencies of new conditions.[45] They begin to suffer from bureaucratic diseases such as "trained incapacity," "occupational psychosis," and "professional deformation." Witness the teacher who rabidly clings to the teacher-centered classroom as the school turns to student-centered processes, or administrators who refuse to seek the counsel of their teachers in the face of continuous community agitation. Merton states:

> The conformance with regulations in all types of situations results in the . . . displacement of the original goals, develops into rigidities and an inability to adjust readily. Formalism, even ritualism, ensues with an unchallenged insistence upon punctilious adherence to formalized procedures. This may be exaggerated to the point where primary concern with conformity to the rules interferes with the achievement of the purposes of the organization, in which case we have the familiar phenomenon of the technicism or red tape of the official.[46]

The very nature of our lives in organizations brings us into contact with rigidities, rituals, and formalized procedures we would love to live without;[47] for example, attending a required weekly meeting that only rubber-stamps decisions made elsewhere, getting a ticket for parking in an empty parking lot, having to return the next day after waiting 30 minutes because "we can't accept any more green forms after 4 P.M.," or running up against a minor official who refuses to make a minor modification to a minor rule because the boss isn't around to approve it.

In the face of our protests the official does a "Pontius Pilate act" and claims the rule meets the tests of legality (the law requires it), precedent (it is honored by time), uniformity (it applies to all), and due process (proper and tried procedures have removed all reasonable doubt). The missing tests tend to be those of social service and common sense.

The preceding examples certainly are not events of staggering import; they are mundane and routine affairs with mildly disturbing consequences. However, when hundreds of such routine situations unfold in the administrative process, the result can be an organization that sits relatively dead in the water. Interestingly, the handling of these rather routine events determines the organization's capacity to act as a problem-solving instrument. Bold decision making has little import if these decisions are not carried forward similarly by the multitude of subordinates who work at obscure, routine tasks, which collectively are necessary for making the major decisions effective.

## *Rule Interpretation*

Complicating the issue of using rules to structure behavior is the problem of distributing and interpreting rules. In the classical theorist's world of "should be," the assumption exists that everyone is cognizant of a rule and shares a similar interpretation. Under real-world conditions it is rare for everyone to be aware of (or even care about) all the rules, and even rarer for everyone to share the same interpretation. In schools the problem is compounded because the educational institution has a relatively undefined technology that almost defies a precise and uniform definition among educators. The board of education, the superintendent, or the principal may make rules about "the application of firm procedures of discipline," or the "utilization of team teaching in the classroom," or the "participation of teachers in all major decisions concerning the school." A precise meaning of these regulations, however, is by no means self-evident. Hence, when different people interpret and implement the same rule, the possibility of different courses of action being taken is very real.

In discussing another of Weber's assumptions,[48] Blau and Scott point to a significant unintended consequence that can result from the interaction of two major principles (disciplined behavior and professional judgment) of classical theory.

> An implicit assumption of bureaucratic theory which we have had repeated occasion to question is that hierarchical authority and discipline are compatible with decisions based on expert judgments made in accordance with professional standards. It seems, on the contrary, that there is a conflict between these two conditions. Rigid discipline stifles professional judgments. Conversely, hierarchical authority is weakened by increasing technological complexity in an organization with its resulting emphasis on technical expertness for all personnel, including those on the lowest operating levels.[49]

The potential dangers of strife between the need for disciplined behavior and the need for inspired professional judgment are all too real in an organization like the school.

The outcome of such conflicting pressures can significantly impair the school's mission. The communication process, however, is intended to reduce this possibility.

## Coordination Collapse

Classical theory also argues that the hierarchy is the means through which problems of coordination are resolved in an organization. This model implies that supervisors discharge their tasks of coordination by serving as vertical communication channels. Thus, when a problem exists *between* departments, a decision is delayed until sufficient information on the issue can be passed up the hierarchy to enable a higher-level resolution.

Going beyond the context of classical theory, Mintzberg suggests five mechanisms that coordinate work in complex organizations: (1) mutual adjustment, specialists using informal communication to adapt to each other along ill-defined routes; (2) direct supervision; (3) standardization of the work process; (4) standardization of work outputs; and (5) standardization of skills.[50]

Thinking of the coordination task in the context of vertical communication processes can result in significant unintended consequences, since certain types of work flows can be more efficiently and effectively coordinated through extensive horizontal communication. Blau and Scott distinguish between two forms of departmental specialization that create differing problems of coordination. These forms of departmental specialization are called *parallel* and *interdependent*.[51]

Parallel departments need little or no coordination with other specialized departments; for example, the shoe department and the perfume department of the same retail store require little if any integration. Interdependent departments, on the other hand, need extensive coordination because they both contribute to the same flow of work. For example, the sales department and the purchasing department of a store are interdependent because of their important contribution to the movement of the same goods through the establishment. A lack of coordination here could result in huge inventories of out-of-demand goods or in empty shelves of hot items.

Turning to the school, lack of coordination in solving problems in the academic process can lead to serious, unintended consequences. The educational situation is also complex because specialized departments in schools tend to have both parallel and interdependent types of work flows. For example, specialized departments (e.g., history, science, auto mechanics) at the higher grade levels tend to need little coordination between them because it is generally assumed that students do not need to know much about physics before they study history. On the other hand, it is important to be competent in English before studying history or physics.

The point where the work flow in schools is truly interdependent, but receives parallel department treatment, is the movement of students between grades (e.g., seventh grade to eighth to ninth, etc.). Although tenth-grade chemistry classes, for example, may exist at a parallel level of specialization with tenth-grade Spanish classes, they are interdependent with the ninth-grade chemistry classes. Close coordination of subject content and student competency between grades in the same subject area often is negligible. This lack of coordination becomes especially noticeable as students move from the elementary to the secondary grades. A number of factors contribute to the lack of coordination between grades, such as the professional norms of teacher autonomy and the assumption that the students or the textbooks will do the coordinating.

Max Abbott argues that in human-service organizations, such as schools, the coordination process is considerably more complex than in private sector organizations that process symbols rather than people. Abbott points out that many of our traditional assumptions about coordination in educational organizations are wrong. We are now only beginning to understand how such coordination takes place.[52]

## *Hyperrationality*

Because most people tend to accept the rational model as the basic framework of schools, attempts at change tend to come by tightening up this procedure or adding that set of objectives—in other words, manipulating characteristics of the formal organization to bring about improved results. Arthur Wise argues that because of this strategy of change, educational institutions recently have been forced from being rational to hyperrational systems.[53]

Traditionally, policymakers focused their efforts to rationalize the system by prescribing *inputs,* such as specifying budget ceilings, minimum employment qualifications, the number of required school days per year, and so forth. In recent years, the policymakers turned to prescribing *throughputs,* such as requiring individualized instruction, behavioral objectives, and mastery learning. Lately, the policymakers have turned to prescribing *outputs,* such as minimum reading and computational skills required for graduation.

Intentions to increase efficiency, effectiveness, and accountability are often imposed on schools without changing existing procedures. Such prescriptions to further rationalize the system come from state legislatures, courts, the federal government, educational districts, and schools. The results are often logical and practical inconsistencies. For example, more rigorous teacher certification requirements are stipulated without increasing the salary structure, with the intent of bringing higher qualified college graduates into the system; or a state legislature mandates a curricular change when no teachers are available to teach the new subjects. In other words, different policymaking entities attempt to further rationalize the system, but do so in an independent, uncoordinated fashion.

Arthur Wise suggests the need to distinguish between *proper* and *excessive* rationalization in education. He poses the following questions. If they are answered affirmatively, a condition of hyperrationalization may exist.

1. Does the policy introduce new procedures without altering or deleting old procedures?
2. Does the policy prescribe output without taking cognizance of existing input and process prescriptions?
3. Does the policy imply that a structural problem can be solved by the education of an individual?
4. Is the policy to be implemented without considering organizational and group dynamics?

5. Are tentative research findings being used to define the policy?
6. Are solutions being proposed on the basis of superficial, incomplete, or incorrect analyses of the problem?
7. Are uniform solutions being proposed for nonuniform situations?[54]

Wise makes an important concluding statement:"The failure of schools to conform to the rational model may be seen in the failure thus far to create models which help explain the process of schooling empirically."

The preceding discussion of the unintended consequences associated with applying the principles of classical organization theory to the school is not inclusive. The list could go on as long as paper and ink could be found. An important point to be reiterated is that, when applied to schools, the notions of classical theory can have considerable value. However, when they are applied artlessly, they can leave considerable wreckage lying around the system.

## Do Organization and Administration Make a Difference?

Are student outcomes affected one way or the other by differing characteristics of the educational bureaucracy, such as: large schools versus small, tall structures versus flat, close supervision versus loose, centralization versus decentralization, departmentalization versus nondepartmentalization, extensive rule formalization versus limited formalization, tightly coupled systems versus loosely coupled, or differentiated staffing versus conventional staffing?

The research literature isn't even close to a consensus on this question. Indeed, the interplay between organizational structures, management processes, instructional activities, and enhanced student achievement is complex. In recent years, however, the *effective-schools literature* has increasingly taken the position that some organization and management activities do make a difference.

The effective-schools literature consistently reports, for example, that learning outcomes improve when there is schoolwide emphasis on improving instructional skills, the climate supports the learning process, the teaching-learning process is closely monitored, school personnel set high standards, student discipline is maintained, and a safe working environment is provided.[55]

Effective principals in effective schools are those found to exhibit the following characteristics: They provide strong instructional leadership, support improved academic programs, establish sound working relationships with the local community, shape clear instructional goals, develop performance standards for students, and emphasize shared role expectations, attitudes, and values.[56]

Examining the field, Deal states that the structural view of the effective school focuses primarily on productivity, "as enhanced by articulating clear goals, encouraging specialization, specifying roles so tasks can be approached with certainty, and controlling the technical core of activities through the exercise of authority, clear policies and procedures, and adequate measures of quality control. The key focus is on the relationship between the structure of schools and the technology of teaching." Deal says that management approaches establish processes to link behavior to precisely defined objectives, to evaluate the quality of personnel performance, "and to reorganize the structure to improve productivity."[57]

A strong current in the literature also reflects the opposite viewpoint, which is represented by the distinguished organization theorist James G. March. He writes that "any effort to improve American education by changing its organization or administration must begin with skepticism. Changing education by changing educational administration is like changing the course of the Mississippi by spitting into the Allegheny."[58]

In reality, administrative careers are relatively short, educational goals are ill defined, instructional technology is poorly understood, hierarchical controls are constrained by professionalism in the ranks, and classroom activities are semiautonomous. Given the diffuseness of the educational system, this argument goes, direct administrative leverage over educational outcomes is minimal at best.[59] "Students who do well in one school system will also do well in another; students who do poorly in one will also do poorly in another."[60]

Some critics argue that from the beginning, the effective-schools literature has emphasized cultural variables—including high expectations, shared values and norms, and emphasis on intrinsic motivation—rather than the more traditional structural and other multidimensional constructs that school professionals use when they refer to good schools.[61]

Bossert points out that the effective-schools literature appears quite comfortable in arguing both sides of seemingly contradictory positions, such as the need for strong instructional leadership, close supervision, and frequent evaluation of instructional activities as well as increased teacher professionalism and classroom autonomy.[62]

Barr and Dreeben argue that the structure of a school is really like a railroad switching yard "where children within a given age range and from a designated geographical area are assigned to teachers who bring them into contact with approved learning materials, specified as being appropriate to age or ability, during certain allotted periods of time."[63] The task of the principal is to assure that there is a plan and that established structures function to make "switching cars" effective and efficient.

The structure of the school, in terms of its organization and management, will indeed make a difference in student achievement *up to the point* where time and materials, teachers and students, facilities, and security can be brought together at the right time and place and in the appropriate quantities. If, on the other hand, the system malfunctions or gets screwed up, and the football coaches are assigned to teach advanced calculus, the books for first semester World Civilization arrive during the second semester, and the heating unit breaks down six times during the coldest month in the century, it is bound to compromise student achievement.[64]

In short, up to the point of making the school "switching yard" work effectively and efficiently, organization and management can, and no doubt do, make important contributions to school outcomes. Beyond that, as Wayne Hoy writes, "the link between the school properties and student outcomes has been elusive."[65]

Chapter Four will argue that the special situational characteristics of local schools will be the determining factor. That is, if your school has an active, well-trained and motivated math department, it is best for the principal to give the teachers all the autonomy they desire. If, on the other hand, the math teachers are tired, unenthusiastic, and hanging on until retirement, then close supervision and invigorated instructional leadership are called for. This management strategy fits into a conceptual framework called *contingency theory.*

## Conclusion

An old story is told about the Englishman visiting Rome for the first time, who, as he strolled through the ancient boulevards of that eternal city, came upon three workmen laboring over a patch of stone and concrete. With his curiosity aroused, the foreigner approached the first worker and asked him what he was doing. "I'm breaking my back for a lousy 475 lira an hour." Undaunted, the Englishman turned to the second worker and asked the same question. "I'm putting up bricks for a big wall." When the question was posed to the final worker, he looked up for a moment before replying and said, "I'm building a cathedral." Each workman's efforts were probably influenced by his perspective on the task at hand.

Perspective is an important issue for educators, who must try to give structure to human and material resources so the outcome will be goals achieved at minimum cost. Classical theory has given the school manager and researcher a model of organization and administration with a rather compelling logic behind it. The model is based on a set of assumptions about the nature of work, the motivations of the worker, the characteristics of the manager, the processes of control, the structure of authority, and the application of expertise.

Through extensive lists of administrative principles, the model provides prescriptive answers to problems of how a rational organization *should* function. Because in the real world there are limits to rationality, many of the basic assumptions of the classical model have been seriously challenged. Attempts to design and operate a school in the real world using a classical management orientation can result in serious unintended consequences, which can generate inefficient rather than efficient activity if care is not taken.

Although classical thought continues to play a major role in the contemporary practice of school governance and decision making, another orientation toward the issues of management emerged during the depression of the 1930s. This orientation conceives of the organization as a complex of social systems (or groups). Within this context, the management problem differs considerably from the one conceived of by classical theorists. The school as a complex organization made up of interacting social groups will be the subject of the next chapter.

## The New Principal

Dr. Eniwald Toledo, superintendent of Williard Unified School District, felt warm inside as he gazed at the model of the soon-to-be-completed Stonehenge High School. It was his pride and joy. Long after his retirement, Stonehenge would stand as a symbol of his educational leadership in the community he had served faithfully for 14 years.

The superintendent shifted the focus of his concentration from the model on his desk to the two folders laying beside it. The search for a principal for Stonehenge had been narrowed down by a review committee to two candidates. In three days he would have to recommend one of the candidates to the board of education.

Dr. Toledo knew both candidates well since they were principals of smaller high schools in nearby districts. The choice would not be easy. He respected both candidates, but for very different reasons.

In making a choice, the school's attendance area would have to be considered. About 70 percent of the students would come from blue-collar families working in industrial sectors of town. The rest would be from upper-middle-class, executive-type families living on the east side of town. Many parents from that area traditionally sent their children to private schools, and Dr. Toledo hoped the new public school would attract that group.

The superintendent had no illusions about the school being easy to manage. A lot of the students were from rough neighborhoods where self-discipline was uncommon. A few of them thought that having any front teeth was a sign of being a coward.

About 80 percent of the teachers were to come from a smaller school in the district that was being retired from long years of service. Dr. Toledo secretly thought that about half the teachers ought to be retired along with it.

One of the candidates was Thomas Rangoon, a former army major who ran a tight ship and went by the book. The kids called him "Bullhorn." Every day he walked around his school directing student traffic by shouting through a voice amplifier. He was strong on discipline, pushed the sports program, and left the teachers alone.

As far as the superintendent could recall, no one had ever accused Mr. Rangoon of being very bright or of trying to develop a strong academic program, a job he felt belonged to the teachers. On the other hand, nobody had ever accused him of not being in control of his school.

The second candidate for the principalship was a different type of individual altogether. Barbara Floorshift was an intellectual of the first order who gave top priority to upgrading her school's academic program. Unfortunately, her scholarly enthusiasm tended to upset a lot of teachers who either felt comfortable with what they were currently doing or believed the principal had no business involving herself in classroom affairs. Miss Floorshift's school tended to be constantly inflicted with teacher-administrator tensions. However, the academic program and student test scores were better than one would anticipate for that attendance area.

Unfortunately, Miss Floorshift sometimes neglected to be ever-watchful of school discipline matters, and more than a few parent complaints had been recorded. Her priorities didn't seem to be well balanced. In fact, she didn't even attend her school's football games.

Superintendent Toledo stared at the two folders as if the answer to his dilemma would leap out at him. He wasn't sure which way to go.

## Notes

1. The Bay of Pigs material is based on the account of Arthur Schlesinger, Jr., *A Thousand Days* (Boston: Houghton Mifflin, 1965).

2. William Foote Whyte, *Organizational Behavior: Theory and Application* (Homewood, IL: Irwin, 1969), p. 689.

3. Schlesinger, p. 255.

4. Ibid., p. 252.

5. Max Weber, *The Theory of Social and Economic Organization,* Talcott Parsons, ed., A. M. Henderson and Talcott Parsons, trans. (New York: The Free Press, 1964), p. 339.

6. Ibid., pp. 333-334.

7. Robert Merton, *Social Theory and Social Structure* (New York: The Free Press, 1957), p. 196.

8. Douglas McGregor, *The Human Side of Enterprise* (New York: McGraw-Hill, 1960), p. 18.

9. Weber, *The Theory of Social and Economic Organization,* p. 324.

10. George R. Kaplan, "Shotgun Wedding: Notes on Public Education's Encounter With the New Christian Right," *Phi Delta Kappan* (1994), pp. 1-12.

11. Weber, p. 328.

12. Ibid.

13. Frederick W. Taylor, *The Principles of Scientific Management* (New York: Harper and Bros., 1923). Reprinted by W. W. Norton, 1967.

14. Luther Gulick and Lyndall Urwick, eds., *Papers on the Science of Administration* (New York: Columbia University Press, 1937).

15. Nicos P. Mouzelis, *Organisation and Bureaucracy* (Chicago: Aldine Publishing Co., 1967), p. 82.

16. Frederick W. Taylor, *Shop Management* (New York: Harper and Bros., 1911), p. 27.

17. Henri Fayol, *General and Industrial Management* (London: Sir Isaac Pitman, 1949), pp. 5-6.

18. Ibid., pp. 97-98.

19. Gulick and Urwick, *Papers on the Science of Administration,* p. 13.

20. Joseph L. Massie, "Management Theory," in *Handbook of Organizations,* James G. March, ed. (Chicago: Rand McNally, 1965), p. 405.

21. Raymond E. Callahan, *Education and the Cult of Efficiency* (Chicago: University of Chicago Press, 1962).

22. James L. McConaughy, "The Worship of the Yardstick," *Educational Review* 55 (1918): 191-192.

23. John F. Bobbitt, *The Supervision of City Schools* (Chicago: University of Chicago Press, 1913), p. 89.

24. Ellwood P. Cubberley, *Public School Administration* (Boston: Houghton Mifflin, 1916), p. 325.

25. Callahan, *Education and the Cult of Efficiency,* p. 160.

26. Robert C. Harris, "Comparative Costs of Instruction in High Schools," *School Review* 22 (1914): 377-378.

27. Cubberley, *Public School Administration,* pp. 124-125; reported in Callahan, *Education and the Cult of Efficiency,* p. 151.

28. Benjamin C. Gruenberg, "Some Economic Obstacles to Educational Progress," *American Teacher* 1 (1912): 90.

29. John Meyer et al., "Bureaucracy without Centralization: Changes in the Organizational System of U.S. Public Education, 1940-80," in *Institutional Patterns and Organizations: Culture and Environment,* Lynne Gray, ed. (Cambridge, MA: Ballinger, 1988), pp. 139-167.

30. National Center for Educational Statistics, *Digest of Educational Statistics: 1993* (Washington, D.C.: U.S. Government Printing Office, 1993), pp. 13, 14, 96, 151, 164.

31. Ibid., pp. 414, 417.

32. Dennis A. Rondinelli, "Government Decentralization in Comparative Perspective: Theory and Practice in Developing Countries," *International Review of Administrative Science* 47 (1981): 133–145.

33. E. Morphet, R. Johns, and T. Reller, *Educational Organization and Administration: Concepts, Practices and Issues* (Englewood Cliffs, NJ: Prentice-Hall, 1967), p. 27.

34. Herbert A. Simon, *Administrative Behavior* (New York: Macmillan, 1957), p. 40.

35. James G. March and Herbert Simon, *Organizations,* pp. 140–141. Copyright © 1958 by John Wiley & Sons, Inc. Reprinted by permission of John Wiley & Sons, Inc.

36. Daniel Katz and Robert Kahn, *The Social Psychology of Organizations,* p. 283. Copyright © 1966, John Wiley & Sons, Inc. Reprinted by permission of John Wiley & Sons, Inc.

37. Simon, *Administrative Behavior,* p. 273.

38. Charles E. Lindblom, "The Science of Muddling Through," *Public Administrative Review* 19 (1959), pp. 79–88.

39. Merton, *Social Theory and Social Structure,* p. 199.

40. Daniel Duke, "What Can Principals Do? Leadership Functions and Instructional Effectiveness," *NASSP Bulletin* (October 1982): 1–12.

41. Max Abbott, "Hierarchical Impediments to Innovation in Educational Organizations," in *Organizations and Human Behavior: Focus on Schools,* Fred Carver and Thomas Sergiovanni, eds. (New York: McGraw-Hill, 1969).

42. Alvin W. Gouldner, *Patterns of Industrial Bureaucracy* (New York: The Free Press, 1954).

43. Ibid., p. 216.

44. Ibid.

45. Robert Merton, "Bureaucratic Structure and Personality," *Social Forces* 18 (1940), pp. 560–568.

46. Merton, *Social Theory and Social Structure,* p. 199.

47. Peter Blau, *The Dynamics of Bureaucracy* (Chicago: The University of Chicago Press, 1963), p. 233.

48. Weber, *The Theory of Social and Economic Organization.*

49. Peter Blau and Richard Scott, *Formal Organizations* (San Francisco, CA: Chandler Publishing, 1962), p. 185.

50. Henry Mintzberg, *The Structuring of Organizations* (Englewood Cliffs, NJ: Prentice-Hall, 1979), pp. 3–6.

51. Blau and Scott, *Formal Organizations,* pp. 183–185.

52. Max G. Abbott, "Coordination: A Neglected Variable in the Study of Schools" (University of Oregon, working draft, 1983): 1–14.

53. Arthur Wise, "Why Educational Policies Often Fail: The Hyperrationalization Hypothesis," in *The Dynamics of Organizational Change in Education,* J. Victor Baldridge and Terrence Deal, eds. (Berkeley, CA: McCutchon, 1983).

54. Ibid., p. 104.

55. David Clark, Linda Lotto, and Terry Astuto, "Effective Schools and School Improvement: A Comparative Analysis of Two Lines of Inquiry," *Educational Administration Quarterly* 20 (1984): 41–68; Luz Gonzales, Rosemary Papalewis, and Rick Brown, "Effective Schooling and Student Achievement: A Longitudinal Study," *National Forum of Educational Administration and Supervision Journal* 5 (1988–89): 60–68; T. Good and J. Brophy, "School Effects," in *Handbook of Research on Teaching,* 3rd ed., C. Whitrock, ed. (New York: Macmillan, 1985).

56. Max Abbott and Francisco Caracheo, "Power, Authority, and Bureaucracy," in *Handbook*

*Research on Education,* Norman Boyan, ed. (New York: Longman, 1988), pp. 239–257; Arthur Blumberg and William Greenfield, *The Effective Principal: Perspectives on School Leadership* (Boston: Allyn and Bacon, 1986).

57. Terrence Deal, "Effective School Principals: Counselors, Engineers, Power-brokers, Poets . . . or Instructional Leaders?" in *Instructional Leadership,* William Greenfield ed., (Boston: Allyn and Bacon, 1986), p. 235.

58. James G. March, "American Public School Administration: A Short Analysis," *School Review* 86 (1978): 219.

59. Abbott and Caracheo, p. 255; Paul Hechinger, "Does School Structure Matter?" *Educational Researcher,* 17 (1988): 10-13.

60. March, p. 221.

61. Sara Lightfoot, "On Goodness in Schools: Themes of Empowerment," *Peabody Journal of Eduction* 63 (1986): 12; Robert Owens and Carl Steinhoff, "Toward a Theory of Organizational Culture" (Paper presented at the American Educational Research Association, New Orleans, LA, 1988), p. 2.

62. Steven Bossert, "School Effects," in *Handbook of Research on Educational Administration,* Norman Boyan, ed. (New York: Longman, 1988), p. 346.

63. Rebecca Barr and Robert Dreeben, *How Schools Work* (Chicago: University of Chicago Press, 1983), p. 6.

64. Bossert, p. 348.

65. Wayne Hoy, "Foundations of Educational Administration: Traditional and Emerging Perspectives," *Educational Administration Quarterly* 30 (1994): 195.

# Chapter 3

# *Schools as Sociopolitical Systems*

The preceding chapter shaped a management orientation as seen through the conceptual eyeglasses of classical organization theory. Organizations were viewed as hierarchical structures controlled from the top by rational procedures, oriented toward precise goals, bound together by a network of comprehensive rules, with everything focused on achieving maximum efficiency. In this sense, the process of organizational governance is like a chess game. The person at the top is singularly in control of his or her strategy and rationally moves the organization's components in a way that maximizes benefit over cost.

All of us know that organizations do not operate that way. In the real world, they appear to function as unequal parts of democracy, bureaucracy, and autocracy. Theodore White relates a story about the degree of organizational control the most powerful man in the world exercised.

> The most startling thing a new President discovers is that his world is not monolithic. In the world of the Presidency, giving an order does not end the matter. You can pound your fist on the table or you can get mad or you can blow it all and go out to the golf course. But nothing gets done except by endless follow-up, endless kissing and coaxing, endless threatening and compelling. There are all those thousands of people in Washington working for you in the government—and everyone is watching you, waiting, trying to guess what you mean, trying to get your number. Can they fool you? Can they outwait you? Will you be mad when you hear it isn't done yet?[1]

As a counterpoint to classical theory, the perspective of an organization as a collection of social systems (sometimes referred to as sociopolitical systems or groups) has evolved. This perspective holds that people share power and differ in their views of what must be done. "This milieu necessitates that policy be resolved by politics."[2] In this instance, one person is formally in charge of the chess game, but in reality he or she is surrounded by groups of associates who have their hands on various pieces and move them around the board with considerable discretion. Frequently, different groups (on the same side) begin pulling in different directions and wind up with a final outcome no one planned, controlled, contemplated, or even wanted.

Graham Allison describes the decision-making process as it takes place within a pressure-packed, sociopolitical system at the highest levels of government. Individuals, small groups, and shifting coalitions of groups engage the full fury of their intellects, power bases, senses of value, vested interests, and visions of the future (their own and the organization's) to influence the ultimate policy choice. Allison also views this kind of decisional activity as one might a game of chess. Each game has its own environment, pace, structure, set of rules, and rewards.

> Note the *environment* in which the game is played: inordinate uncertainty about what must be done, the necessity that something be done and crucial consequences of whatever is done. These features force responsible men to become active players. The *pace of the game*—hundreds of issues, numerous games, and multiple channels—compels players to fight to "get others' attention," to make them "see the facts," to assure that they "take the time to think seriously about the broader issue." The *structure of the game*—power shared by individuals with separate responsibilities—validates each feeling that "others don't see my problem," and "others must be persuaded to look at the issue from a less parochial perspective." The *rules of the game*—he who hesitates loses his chance to play at that point, and he who is uncertain about his recommendation is overpowered by others who are sure—pressures players to come down on one side of a 51–49 issue and play. The *rewards of the game*—effectiveness, i.e., impact on outcomes, as the immediate measure of performance—encourages hard play. Thus, most players come to fight to "make the government do what is right."[3]

Allison's chess-game analogy is an extreme example of high-risk decision making in which reputations, careers, billions of dollars, and sometimes lives are at stake. No argument is made here that the intensity of the game Allison describes has arrived at the level of the educational organization, although in the last decade there has been accelerating movement in that direction (e.g., teacher strikes, taxpayer revolts, minority-group demands). The argument is made that understanding the processes of governance and decision making as they take place within a sociopolitical system framework (as opposed to a classical hierarchical framework) is a meaningful perspective for those seeking clearer insight into the operation of schools.

A sociopolitical system finds its conceptual roots in the makeup of a social system. In essence, a *social system* consists of a defined set of actors whose patterned interactions are intended to lead toward some more or less defined goal. The political context suggests the *application of strategies* by one or more members of the social system to influence the decision-making process toward a preferred choice.

The intention of this chapter is to identify and analyze the set of significant forces that influence decision-making processes within the framework of a social system. The

first step in this direction began with the so-called Hawthorne Studies, which resulted in a body of findings that virtually redirected the study of life in organizations.

## Informal Groups in Organizations

### The Hawthorne Studies

Until the late 1930s, the basic assumption was that the chief factors behind employee motivation and morale were wages and physical working conditions. However, a theoretical avalanche swept over these traditional beliefs when the findings of the
Hawthorne Studies (carried out from 1927 through 1932) entered the intellectual
mainstream of management thought.[4] The experiments were conducted near Chicago at the Western Electric Company's Hawthorne Works under the guiding hand of
Elton Mayo, a professor of industrial research at the Harvard School of Business.

The initial objective of the research at the Hawthorne Works was to test the effect
of illumination on worker productivity. To the great surprise of the experimenters, the
results showed that production rose and fell without direct relation to the intensity
of illumination at the work bench. Thus, with scientific caution and controls, the
researchers set out to find the locus of the intervening variables that were interacting
among the physical environment, the profit motive, and the worker.

Among the multitude of findings stemming from the Hawthorne Studies, the most
significant were associated with the discovery that workers tend not to act or react
as individuals but as members of informal groups. The informal group is defined in this
text as a "system of interpersonal relations which forms within an organization to affect
decisions of the formal organization, and this system is omitted from the formal scheme
or is in opposition to it."[5]

A precise example of the powerful influence the group on production was revealed
by the research that took place in the Bank Wiring Room. Thinking along traditional lines,
management had introduced a complex formula of wage incentives with the expectation that they would stimulate higher productivity. However, the workers demonstrated they had their own ideas about what was a fair day's work—the wiring of two switch-
board units. Having this target in mind, each worker would speed up or slow down
production according to how close he or she was to the goal (defined by the group) of
wiring two units. The researchers found no relationship between productivity and such
factors as intelligence or finger dexterity. What they did find was that the workers were
controlling their own productivity because they feared that management would change
the piece-work rate if they consistently produced at higher levels. Roethlisberger and
Dickson identified the situation at the Hawthorne Works as follows.

> They (the employees) went on at great length explaining that adjustments were almost
> impossible in many cases because of variations in the quality and quantity of piece
> parts available, until I wondered how they were able to accomplish anything. I also
> noticed a general dissatisfaction or unrest. In some, this was expressed by demands for
> advancement or transfers; in others, by a complaint about their lot in being kept on
> the job.

These serious continuous defects, about which they talked a great deal, were not reflected by variations in their output curves. In other words, it looked as if they were limiting their outputs to a figure just below the bogey; and evidently this output could be accomplished even though machines were running poorly.[6]

The discovery that informal groups of subordinates could take control of the production process, independent of the formal rules and regulations of management, of centralized power, and of established communication channels, shattered many of the pillars of classical thought. Etzioni identifies the social-psychological ingredients that bind the members of an informal group into a semiindependent instrument of control: social norms, noneconomic rewards and punishments, and the role of informal leadership.[7]

Mayo wrote of norms as "non-logical social codes which regulate the relations between persons and their attitudes to one another."[8] If management interferes with the social code by insisting upon a merely economic logic of production, the social code may assert a restriction of output. The most important norms that guided behavior in the Bank Wiring Room were:

1. Don't be a rate-buster (you should not produce at too high a level).
2. Don't be a chiseller (you should not turn out too little work).
3. Don't be a squealer (you should not report your associates).
4. Don't act officiously (you should act like a regular guy).
5. Don't be noisy, self-assertive, and anxious for leadership.[9]

Don Willower points out that schools also have social codes intended to informally control behavior, such as the norm among teachers "don't criticize a colleague in front of students," and the student norm against being a "stool pigeon." Basic norms like these exist in all organizations and serve as defense mechanisms to protect the workers from both within and without.[10]

Porter et al. suggest there are four ways a group can influence a member's work performance. First, the group members can provide knowledge and skills that upgrade member performance. This method, however, is weakest of all because the employer can provide assistance faster and more efficiently than can the work group. Second, the group can influence substantially the psychological arousal of a member because of the identity bonds between the members. The arousal can be either uplifting or depressing.

A worker's decisions about his or her level of effort depend to a great extent on the expectations of the group and the degree to which the individual desires membership. For example, if a group of history teachers decides to use a new instructional method, any holdout would feel less a part of group activities.

Reflecting on the last two controlling forces, the authors write that the impact of the group "is realized both directly (i.e., by enforcement of group norms) and indirectly (i.e., by affecting the beliefs and values of the members). When the direct and indirect influences of a group are congruent—which is often the case—the potency of the group's effects on its members can be quite strong."[11]

In his analysis of the Hawthorne Works Bank Wiring Room data, Homans argues that high informal status among the workers goes with normal productivity, not with superior productivity. Only if the expert exercise of skill is a dominant value of the group does high status become associated with superior performance.[12]

Besides noting the existence of norms that act as standards of behavior, the researchers observed that the group members had devised subtle means of controlling the behavior of those who deviated from the norms. For example, at times workers affixed caustic nicknames to deviant workers, or gave minor physical blows to their upper arms (referred to as "binging"). However, the withdrawal of affection and respect of coworkers was more effective. As numerous researchers have discovered, social isolation can be a devastating experience for someone accustomed to amiable friendship patterns.[13] The need for social contact, acceptance, and friendship is indeed strong, and the manipulation of this need has proved to be an effective tool of behavioral control.

The informal leadership of the worker group accrued to those who were skilled in resolving problems within and outside the group, problems that threatened the normative patterns of the group. Roethlisberger and Dickson wrote of two such informal leaders.

> I then noticed that two of the workers in particular held rather privileged positions in the group and were looked up to by the rest of the members. On these two the group seemed to place considerable responsibility. Of A they said: "He can handle the engineers, inspectors, and the supervisors. They have to come to him if they want to know anything." In speaking of B they expressed admiration for his work habits and capacities. The common remarks about him were: "He taught me my job"; "when he adjusts a machine, he never raises his eyes until it works."[14]

In contrast, the formal leader of the group, the supervisor, exerted very little influence over the behavior of the workers, and he was under considerable pressure to conform also to the norms of the group he was supposed to be directing.

## The Human Relations Movement

As a consequence of discoveries pinpointing the importance of the social-psychological needs of the worker and his or her group, a new management ideology called *human relations* began to sweep the country in the public, business, and educational sectors of organizational life. The human relations approach to management maintained that

> employees should have a feeling that the company's goal is worth their effort; they should feel themselves part of the company and take pride in their contributions to its goal. This means that the company's objectives must be such as to inspire confidence in the intentions of management and belief that each will get rewards and satisfactions by working for these objectives.[15]

The human relations ideology promoted the view that the most satisfying organization would be the most efficient. Instead of attempting to quash the informal groups, their basic needs are recognized and brought into harmony with the goals of the organization. This task is performed by supervisors who are skilled in human relations practices. The human relations methodology emphasizes that by practicing democratic principles of management and advocating employee participation in structuring the work environment and in establishing open channels of communication, management and workers could resolve their differences in a spirit of goodwill and cooperation.

A study of great influence on the human-relations management perspective was conducted in 1938 at the Iowa Child Welfare Station.[16] The investigators of the welfare station, while examining the responses of groups of 11-year-old children to differing leadership patterns, identified the concepts of democratic, authoritarian, and laissez-faire leadership styles. Although it was not a conclusion of the original study, the notion that a democratic style is "good" and an autocratic style is "bad" in promoting effective work habits became ingrained in management ideology and has retained its position of general acceptance. Chapter Seven will discuss a serious challenge to this long-held assumption.

Following World War II, the human-relations ideology lost considerable appeal because of charges that it was nothing more than another tool managers used to manipulate workers. Also, the human-relations approach to the complex problems of management was overly simplistic, as Etzioni points out:

> By providing an unrealistic "happy" picture, by viewing the factory as a family rather than as a power struggle among groups with some conflicting values and interests as well as some shared ones, and by seeing it as a major source of human satisfaction rather than alienation, Human Relations comes to gloss over the realities of work life. Worker dissatisfaction is viewed as indicative of lack of understanding of the situation rather than as symptomatic of any underlying real conflict of interests.[17]

Although the human-relations ideology has been severely attacked by its critics, the movement survives. Every year millions of dollars are spent for human-relations training programs for managers in the educational, business, and public sectors. Tricks of the trade, such as the controlled use of nonverbal cues, meeting with teachers in the classroom instead of the principal's office, or greeting a visitor at the door instead of from behind the desk, can be very helpful in establishing a climate of mutual respect. On a day-to-day basis, this type of climate is usually healthy and appreciated. However, when the demands of vested interests, such as increased salaries or reduced instructional loads, pull the teachers and administrators into opposite corners, human-relations practices alone tend to be a rather ineffective tool in resolving the issues. As more and more educator groups at all levels argue, "Human relations are nice, but power wins."

In short, by discovering the role the informal group plays, the Hawthorne Studies resulted in a new perspective on the organization and administration of systems such as the school. Attention was diverted from studying the organization as a rational model that emphasized the way a system *ought to* function. The new social-systems perspective concentrated on the view of organizations as *natural* systems, emphasizing the way organizations *do* function.

Gouldner points out that the natural-system model focuses on the unplanned and spontaneous, therefore informal, patterns of belief and behavior that develop within rationally planned organizations.[18] Scott writes that in the natural-system context, "organizations are viewed as coalitions of participants who lack consensus on goals, sharing only a common interest in the survival of the organization. Organically emerging informal structures supplement or subdue mechanically designed rational frameworks as the basis for organizational behaviors and beliefs."[19]

An awareness of the importance of informal organization emerged during the Hawthorne Studies and has played a key role in the study of natural systems ever since.

## Informal Organization

Drawing from their experiences in the Hawthorne Studies, Roethlisberger and Dickson wrote:

> Many of the actually existing patterns of human interaction have no representation in the formal organization at all, and others are inadequately represented by the formal organization. . . . Too often it is assumed that the organization of a company corresponds to a blueprint plan or organization chart. Actually, it never does.[20]

Informal organization can be viewed as those processes and behaviors in an organization that are not formally planned but emerge spontaneously from the members' needs. As Scott points out, "Individual participants are not merely 'hired hands' but bring along their heads and hearts; they enter into the organization with individually shaped ideas, expectations, and agendas, and they bring with them differing values, interests, and abilities."[21]

Figure 3.1 illustrates that the informal characteristics of organizations are both extensive and influential. They represent the great hidden portion of the iceberg—out of sight but ever present.

Informal activities emerge when the formal organization is not fulfilling some particular need. As a general rule, the intensity of activity of the informal organization varies with the degree to which its needs are not met.

The unfulfilled needs that give rise to informal systems can be in opposition or in support of the formal organization's activities. Illustrations of the former type are: a group of teachers trying to change the discipline policy by not enforcing it, a group of administrators trying to alter the superintendent's budget by using the "grapevine" to pass messages to school board members, and a group of secretaries trying to get additional help by slowing down the paper-flow.

At times the real or perceived gap between the formal and informal organization becomes so great that a siege in the classic manner develops: a powerful invading force applies pressure to a resolute defensive body. Under conditions such as these, there is no joy in Mudville.

The informal organization can also support the formal organization. For example, groups of teachers can form softball teams or plan holiday parties to uplift school morale. Administrators sometimes attempt to resolve certain types of personnel problems out of channels when formal procedures seem overly harsh.

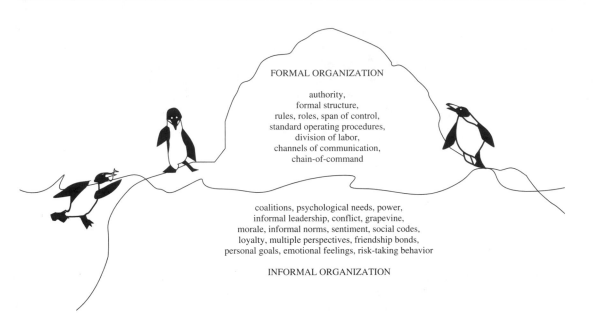

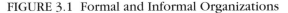

FIGURE 3.1  Formal and Informal Organizations

In short, one cannot say the informal organization is good or bad, for it can be either or both depending on the circumstances. School managers who do not understand how the informal organization operates in their schools or districts are in real trouble. Attempting to manage an educational system solely by using the rationalistic machinery of the formal organization is a sure ticket on the Titanic. Although good administrators may tell you they go by the book, they don't.

## The Social System

Natural systems are usually identified as social systems. The school, like other types of organizations, is composed of a multitude of social systems, some of which are formal, such as the tenth-grade English department, and others of which are informal, such as the lunchroom clique. Social systems are contrived and imperfect vehicles through which the labors, desperations, and delights of the day are carried out. They can come apart at the seams overnight or they can outlast the lifespan of their original creators. The cement that holds them together is social-psychological rather than biological and is rooted in such elements as beliefs, expectations of others, norms, motivations, and attitudes.[22]

The minimum components necessary for a social system are two or more interacting people whose behavior has become patterned over time toward similar goals. The key characteristics are (1) a plurality of actors, (2) interaction, (3) a goal, (4) patterned behavior, and (5) a duration or time dimension. With these characteristics in mind, would eight people waiting at the street corner for the light to turn green comprise a social system? Probably not, because they lack the necessary interaction and the time dimension. They are merely a collection of people; therefore their behavior does not become bonded together by a social unity. The 12 children riding in a bus on the first day of school do not form a social system either, but after they have made the trip a number of times, friendship patterns will spring up and the bonds of a social system (or several distinct systems) will probably evolve.

The terms *social group* and *social system* often are used interchangeably in sociological analysis, but there is a distinction at the abstract level. Bredemeier and Stephenson discuss the difference by pointing out that members of a social group cannot be changed without changing the character of the group, while a social system remains the same whether the individual people acting in it change or not.[23] In this text, however, the two terms will be used interchangeably.

As Figure 3.2 illustrates, an organization like a school system is made up of a multitude of interrelated subsystems. Each subsystem is a part of a greater subsystem, which is part of an even greater system. For example, the two Spanish teachers form a subsystem of the language department, which is a subsystem of the humanities division, which is a subsystem of the high school, which is a subsystem of the school district, which is a subsystem of the state legislature. The action patterns of any one of these subsystems cannot be fully understood independent of its immediately linking subsystems. For instance, the actions of the history department cannot be understood independent of the constraints and demands placed upon it by the policy of the high school or by the expectations and needs of various groups of teachers.

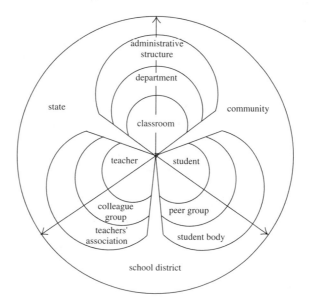

FIGURE 3.2  Educational Subsystems

McLaughlin and Talbert refer to these and other subsystems (e.g., academic societies, teacher education programs) as professional communities. The interactions of these professional communities are extremely important, they argue, because they mediate the contexts of teaching. "We encountered professional communities that enforced traditional standards and so fostered burnout or cynicism among teachers and failure among today's students; communities that supported lower standards for many students and so engendered disengagement among teachers and students alike; and professional communities that enabled teachers to learn new practices that engaged today's students in learning consistent with the nation's education goals of excellence for all."[24]

## Social System Elements

Vital to understanding the actions of peer groups, colleague groups, formal departmental groups, and the like is understanding the variables and processes that make up a social system. Research on this subject has gone considerably beyond that reported in the Hawthorne Studies of the 1930s. One of the best discussions of the subject can be found in Charles P. Loomis's book *Social Systems*.[25] Loomis's social system model is made up of what he calls *elements* and *master processes*. A conceptual model is defined as an "image of reality as seen by a scientist." The model is the scientists' way of organizing the phenomena they wish to study as they search for clearer understanding of the inventions of people and nature. Loomis observed:

> The elements that stand in a given relation to each other at a given moment do not remain in that relation (except by abstraction) for any length of time. The processes mesh, stabilize, and alter the relations between the elements through time; they are the tools through which the social system may be understood as a dynamic functioning continuity—a "going concern."[26]

Loomis argues that the elements in the following discussion can be found in any social system, whether it be a kindergarten class, a basketball team, or the board of directors of General Motors.

*Belief (Knowledge)*    Beliefs furnish a cognitive basis for social action. The membership of a group tends to share patterns of belief important to their own universe, such as that teachers' unions are healthy for education, students are lazy, or a college education leads to financial success. Whether the belief is true is of little importance; what is important is that the belief serves as a guide to action within the social system.

*Sentiment*    Sentiments relate to what the members feel about the world around them as well as about one another. Loyalty because of friendship is an expression of sentiment.

*End, Goal, or Objective*    The purpose the members set out to accomplish defines this element. The purpose, for example, may be to bring about change, to preserve the status quo, or to acquire social or intellectual satisfaction.

*Norms*    Norms are written or unwritten rules of the game. They refer to all criteria for judging the character or conduct of both individual and group actions in any social system. They constitute the standards determining what is right and wrong, appropriate and inappropriate, just and unjust, good and bad in social relationships."[27] Many of the standards of conduct found among workers in the Hawthorne Studies can be found in student subcultures, norms such as don't be a rate-buster, chiseller, or squealer, or act officiously. Teacher subgroups also develop norms regarding such things as what to do about problem students, volunteering for committee service, use of planning time, how to handle the principal, and about every other subject that is likely to come up.

*Status (Position) and Role*    A *status* may be defined as a position in a social system independent of specific actors; a status or position is occupied by different actors at different times. All social systems maintain different status positions, such as teacher, student, and department chairperson. *Roles* are the patterns of behavior expected of those who hold particular status positions. Teacher, administrator, and student, for example, are three different statuses, and teaching, directing, and studying are their commensurate roles.

An individual comes to occupy a status position in two distinct ways. *Ascribed statuses,* such as social class, sex, and race, are acquired by virtue of circumstance at birth. *Achieved statuses* are earned by some form of competition calling for significant effort, such as the status positions of doctor, lawyer, and professional football player.

*Power*    Power is the capacity to control or influence the behavior of others. If the capacity is high, power is the exercise of control. If it is low, power is the exercise of influence. The degree of control or influence can be judged by the number of people or the extent of the decisions and policies involved. The so-called power game is endemic to almost any level in an educational system, from the members of the board of education to the students in the classroom. French and Raven have identified five different types of power: legitimate power (often called formal authority), reward power, coercive power, expert power, and referent power (influence based on liking or identifying with another person).[28]

Possessing various types of power can be seen as holding chips in the game. Trying to win the pot requires alternate strategies of being bold, cunning, and cautious. Using the wrong chips at the wrong time can be disastrous. As Captain Queeg in *The Caine Mutiny* put it, "There are four ways of doing a job: the right way, the wrong way, the Navy way, and my way." His application of power resulted in a mutiny, a court martial, and a permanent place on the beach for himself.

*Rank*    Rank is a function of how important a member is to the system. Although prestige and social standing may be indicative of rank, they are not the equivalent. An administrator has considerable rank, but so might a janitor, cook, teacher, or even a student who can successfully call on people to disrupt established procedures (e.g., through a strike) or who must be consulted before new events are initiated.

*Sanction*    Sanctions are rewards and penalties members of a system employ to insure that behavior follows established norms. A family may reward a child with money or special privileges for receiving good grades or penalize the child for poor grades. The potential for crisis is always present when a student, teacher, or administrator is a member of two social systems and is rewarded by one and penalized by the other for the same set of behaviors; for example, the student who is rewarded by his or her parents for receiving good grades and criticized by the coach for not practicing enough.

*Facility*    A facility is any means used to attain a desired end. It can be either physical in nature, such as a telephone, a building, or a computer, or social, such as a smile, an ideal, or a strategy of work.

*Stress-Strain*    Stress-strain as an element is inherent and inevitable in all social systems. Because members can never be equally socialized, goals can never be completely clear, and status roles can never be completely specific, the system is always subject to stress. Strain is a behavioral manifestation of conditions under stress. Teachers or administrators who seek transfers, for example, often do so because they feel that expectations and tasks placed upon them are unprofessional, unfair, or even improper. (Alvin Bertrand added this element to the Loomis model.)[29]

## Comprehensive or Master Social System Processes

The comprehensive or master processes of the social system are those through which the elements relate to one another and the whole. These processes involve more than one of the elements of the social system at a time.

*Communication*    "Communication is the process by which information, decisions, and directives are transmitted among actors and the ways in which knowledge, opinions, and attitudes are formed or modified by interaction."[30]

*Boundary Maintenance*    A boundary determines who is and who is not a member of a specific social system. Boundaries may be physical, such as the walls of a school; political, such as membership in a political party; or social, such as the life-style of a social class. Boundary maintenance refers to the preservation of the social system against encroachment by outside factors. A boundary can be high, such as that set to obtain enrollment in an elite private school, or low, such as that set to obtain membership in the Democratic party.

*Systemic Linkage*    The process of establishing temporary alliances among independent social systems for the purpose of achieving a common objective results in a systemic linkage. For example, when the PTA, the Administrators' Association, and the Teachers' Union join forces to pass a school bond issue, systemic linkages have been formed.

*Social Control*    The process of social control implies placing constraints on nonconforming or deviant behavior. The elements of norms, sanctions, and power are closely associated with this master process.

*Institutionalization*    When specific patterns of behavior become legitimized, that is, accepted as right and proper, they are said to be institutionalized. Ideas that once were not accepted generally but have been institutionalized are universal education for children, tenure for qualified teachers, and the need for state certification of teachers and administrators. Ideas that are on their way to being institutionalized, although on a rough road, are school desegregation and the right of teachers to strike.

Not surprisingly, a school is filled with a multitude of informal (as well as formal) social systems at the student, teacher, and administrator levels. An informal social system tends to be organized around a dominant element without which the system might cease to exist. If people could not enhance their prestige by joining an exclusive country club, for example, they probably would not join and possibly cause the club to disband. The dominant element often is easily recognizable, such as that in student peer groups known as the bad guys, the jocks, the brains, the acid heads, the artsy-craftsy bunch, and the cheerleaders. Among the teachers, there is the old guard, the young, and the community activists. The boundaries of these social systems can be established from sources outside or inside the system, such as social class, ethnicity, religion, time spent in the system, and prior training or experience.

The elements that make up a social system are not discrete items isolated from one another like tree stumps in a forest. Their interdependence can be seen in virtually every act within the social system. For example, when a student is kept on detention after school, the event can be seen as an exercise of sanction and power due to a violation of norms. Beliefs, goals, norms, sanctions, and so on are so interdependent they cannot be understood apart from one another.

The elements of the social system have proved to be powerful diagnostic tools. Conceptual frameworks are constructed from the elements through which behavior can be analyzed. As an illustration, in a case study I was recently involved in, the research team became intrigued by the high level of stress between the home economics teachers and the cooks at a large urgan high school. In complaining to the principal, the home economics teachers were very condescending about the cooks and called them lazy and incompetent. The cooks, on the other hand, said the teachers were sloppy in their work and thought that the entire school was devoted to teaching nothing but home economics. The problem centered on the shared use of the large school kitchen, which the teachers used as a training area for institutional cooking classes and the cooks used for preparing noon meals for students and teachers. On the surface, the kitchen sharing plan looked simple enough. Why did it break down in practice?

In studying the case, the researchers discovered that because the teachers and the cooks did not share the same *goals* and *norms,* they did not share the facilities efficiently. The teachers believed in a goal they called a "quality educational experience for the students." Among the multitude of norms supporting the goal were the guidelines that

1. the teachers should make maximum use of facilities available in the district;
2. the teachers are professionals and it is not their job to clean the kitchen;
3. the students are learning to be cooks and not dishwashers, so they should not be required to clean the kitchen; and
4. the learning experience should be carried out each day to its natural conclusion, and if that meant encroaching into the cook's time, it had to be done for the good of the academic program.

On the other hand, the cooks had the goal of "quality food prepared on time." Norms governing their behavior included the need for a clean and sanitary environment in which to work and enough devotion to the task to make the product appealing to the eye as well as the palate. The cooks objected vehemently when the mess from the home economics classes was left for them to clean up before they could even begin their own work.

In appealing to the principal, the teachers pointed out the centrality of their status role to the mission of the school. The principal used his legitimate power to order the cooks, who were of lower rank, to clean up the mess left by the teachers. However, students soon started arriving late to class after lunch because the food was late in being prepared. The cooks pointed out that having to clean up after the teachers did not allow them enough time to do their own job within the specified periods allotted to them. At this point conditions looked bleak for the cooks: The principal placed increasing degrees of pressure on them, threatening punishment and even applying it at times.

Surprisingly, the cooks won the ensuing struggle. Strange events began to occur in the school, such as people arriving for meetings and finding the doors locked, power failures in the school at inappropriate times, and a mysterious breakdown of equipment. The cooks had developed a multitude of systemic linkages among noncertified personnel. Through the subtle application of coercive power, the cooks and their allies were able to disrupt school events to the extent that the principal had to reverse his position on the cooks having to clean up after the teachers. In this instance, a conceptual framework built around divergent goals, incompatible norms, systemic linkages, and the application of illegitimate power was helpful in delineating the cause-and-effect characteristics of the case under study.

Loomis argues that the elements are meshed in a social system like the many strands of a spider's web. This feature has important consequences for the process of change. Pulling (manipulating) one strand has varying effects on all the rest. These side effects must be anticipated and planned for if directed change is to take place.

An understanding of these elements and their relationship to the operation of a social system gives an educator numerous options for bringing about change in the school or classroom. Many educators limit themselves to manipulating the power variable (e.g., "Do your homework or you will get a low grade") in one form or another in bringing about change. This emphasis is probably common because classical theory stresses the power variable as a central key to managing organizational behavior. However, for an educator who knows the various elements and processes in a social system, the alternatives for bringing about change are expanded to include a manipulation of any one of a number or even a combination of elements.

## Social Exchange and the "Economics" of Group Behavior

Without a degree of cohesiveness between participants, a social system could not exist. *Cohesiveness* refers to the degree of reinforcement members find in the activities of the group. The concept of reinforcement involves reciprocation. In other words, if one is to receive, one must also give. In a friendship group, for example, both parties must share their trust, loyalties, and concerns. The moment one party declines to do so, the group dissolves.

George Homans draws a close parallel between the exchange process that makes up the substance of social systems and the exchange process that makes up the more familiar economic systems.[31] Social behavior in groups involves the exchange of goods, but in this instance nonmaterial goods. Nonmaterial goods can be in the form of granting or receiving such things as prestige, symbols of approval, expert information, deference, or loyalty.[32]

Peter Blau writes about the economics of social exchange:

> If a person supplies important services to another, the second becomes dependent on and obligated to the first. If the second can reciprocate by rendering important services to the first, he has discharged his obligations and balanced his dependence by making the other also dependent on him. But, if the second cannot reciprocate in this manner, his dependence remains one-sided, and he must discharge his obligations by deferring to the other's wishes in order to continue to receive the benefits on which he has become dependent, which means that the first person has acquired power over the second.[33]

If the social system is to stabilize over time, an equilibrium must evolve in which there is a balance of exchanges. Different members can make their contributions by different means acceptable to the group, but if they are to continue to receive, they must contribute. For example, some may contribute by their skill at handling the principal, others may contribute expertise or comic relief, while others serve by being scapegoats.[34]

In his analysis of the behavior of 16 agents in a federal law enforcement agency, Blau found the exchange process generated constraints on the agents' feeling of freedom to solicit the advice and help of superiors, as well as colleagues.[35] Agents felt that if they went to their superior too often for advice or help, the superior would begin to think them incompetent and reflect that impression in their evaluations.

The agents were also reluctant to consult freely with colleagues because not only would consultation draw the colleagues away from their work but it would also serve to build up "debts" for the agents in need. As these debts began to build up, they served as the basis of informally generated status differences in the group.

In essence, in the process of social exchange, each member seems to have a limited amount of "currency" to spend. If members spend all their currency and it cannot be replenished, their status falls and they may be rejected by the system. For example, a teacher can send students to the principal's office just so many times before the teacher begins to get the reputation that he or she can't handle the kids. At some point, the principal may simply start returning them to the classroom. However, if the principal finds a student has been sent to his or her office by a teacher who rarely takes that action, that student will no doubt receive the utmost attention. In a similar vein, teachers or administrators who constantly lean on colleagues for help in gathering data or in covering special duties, or principals who continually appeal for help from the superintendent, may soon find they have run out of currency and their status and influence has diminished considerably.

In short, the concept of social exchange provides the educator with a significant diagnostic tool. Following a proper analysis, the teacher or administrator can intervene in the exchange process of student or educator groups, in order to enhance the benefits and diminish the costs accruing to the members of the organization. At times, the bonds of social exchange become key ingredients in the brew that forms the culture of the school.

## Organizational Culture

### What Is an Organizational Culture?

I have visited schools where the principals argue that the only things that tie their systems together are central heating and a common concern for parking. In truth, this is not the case. The school's culture is the tie that binds.

To an anthropologist, an organization's culture isn't something that it *has* but rather something that it *is*. When we become part of an organization, Fombrun writes, "we become something different, something new."[36] The organization's culture shapes our view of the world. The head of the American Federation of Teachers, Albert Shanker, identifies the power the culture of schools has over its members.

> Ten thousand new teachers each year enter the New York City school system as a result of retirement, death, job turnover, and attrition. These new teachers come from all over the country. They represent all religions, races, political persuasions, and educational institutions. But the amazing thing is that after three weeks in the classroom you can't tell them apart from the teachers they replaced.[37]

Organizational culture is composed of the shared beliefs, expectations, and values and norms of conduct of members.[38] In any organization, the informal culture interacts with the formal organizational structure and control system to produce a generally clear understanding of "the way things are done around here."[39] Even more than the forces of bureaucracy, the organization's culture is the glue that binds people together. It is through this culture that our images of reality are shaped, often unconsciously. In making a point about how various interpretive schemes are shaped by differing cultural images, Gareth Morgan tells the tale of a man whose wife's portrait Picasso was painting:

> One day the man called at the artist's studio. "What do you think?" asked Picasso, indicating the nearly finished picture. "Well . . ." said the husband, trying to be polite, "it isn't how she really looks." "Oh," said the artist, "and how does she really look?" The husband decided not to be intimidated. "Like this!" said he, producing a photograph from his wallet. Picasso studied the photograph. "Mmm . . ." he said, "small, isn't she?"[40]

In schools, as in other organizations, participants are caught in a web of significance spun by themselves—often a web they cannot see or even understand. The firmness of the web can usually be attested to by any new teacher or administrator who attempts to change things.

### Why Do Organizational Cultures Emerge?

Educational systems, like other organizations, must operate under the impact of powerful external, political, economic, demographic, and legislative forces.[41] Forces creating degrees of uncertainty also operate from within a school system. These internal forces are intense because "there is no well-established or generally-accepted body of pedagogical knowledge that says how teachers should perform in any given situation."[42] Teachers and students who possess the complete range of interests and abilities, are guided by abstract goals, and utilize an uncertain technology of instruction need something to tie together the flotsam and jetsam of school activities. That something usually is the school's culture.

Edgar Schein argues that an organizational culture comes into being as follows:

1. a body of solutions to external and internal problems that has worked consistently for a group and that is therefore taught to new members as the correct way to perceive, think about, and feel in relation to those problems;
2. which eventually come to be assumptions about the nature of reality, truth, time, space, human nature, human activity, and human relationships;
3. so that these assumptions come, over time, to be taken for granted and finally drop out of awareness. Indeed, the power of culture lies in the fact that it operates as a set of unconscious, unexamined, assumptions that are taken for granted.[43]

The unconscious assumptions about "the way we do things around here" form a specific challenge to leadership. "The bottom line," Schein writes, "is that if they do not become conscious of the cultures in which they are embedded, those cultures will manage them."[44] If a school's organizational culture become dysfunctional, such as being slowly submerged in the status quo or perfecting the practice of shirking after-school responsibilities, the leaders must understand what is going on and manage the culture in a direction that supports constructive rather than detrimental forms of behavior.

## What Are the Tangible and Intangible Aspects of School Culture?

Even though culture often operates at an unconscious level, its artifacts are usually quite visible.

Anyone who has visited many schools develops a sense of their different personalities—a concept frequently used to describe an organization's particular culture. Walking through a school, an observer can see physical manifestations of an underlying set of values: perhaps a huge trophy case immediately facing the visitors entrance, classroom desks bolted to the floor, a clean campus, football and basketball programs that overshadow math and science programs (or vice versa), faculty and staff constantly patrolling the halls, and so forth.

The intangible aspects of a school's culture can and often do parallel those values cited by Peters and Waterman in their influential book *In Search of Excellence.* In America's most successful companies, they found a number of consistent values held, such as: There is no substitute for superior quality and service; be the best; pay attention to detail; stay close to the client; do what you do best; work through people (not around or over them); facilitate innovation; and be tolerant of failed attempts.[45]

Schools attempting to develop shared values often have signs around their buildings: "Knowledge is power"; "Wildcat Pride"; "Education Is about Alternatives"; "Just Say No"; and "No Knives or Guns in the Building."

A school's organizational culture does not necessarily mean that everyone will be treated the same. In fact, an organization's culture can easily incorporate social class values that seemingly legitimize better treatment for some than for others. Arnold Danzig argues that social class tends to provide unequal treatment as the school is willing to listen to some parents more than others on such things as class assignments, complaints and teacher preferences. The result is a customized education for some students at a school and a generic education for others.[46]

Deal stresses that the particular culture of a school becomes visible in its heroes, rituals, ceremonies, and stories about celebrated people, places, and events. Also, an informal network of cultural players watches over the culture to keep it alive and consequently act as a barrier to change.[47]

Studies of school cultures often try to capture the central zone of shared values through the use of metaphors. For example, Steinhoff and Owens interviewed teachers in eight schools and classified them through the use of four metaphors:

1. the *family,* often referred to as home, womb, team, and the principal as parent;
2. the *machine,* described as well-oiled, gears turning, beehive, and the principal as workaholic and a slug;
3. the *cabaret,* described as a circus or a Broadway show with the principal as the master of ceremonies; and
4. the *little shop of horrors,* referred to as unpredictable, nightmare driven, reminiscent of the French Revolution, and the principal as a self-cleaning statue.[48]

Deal and Wise use other metaphors to describe schools as factories, jungles, or temples, with the principals described as chief executive officers, lion tamers, and gurus.[49]

The culture of a school is never homogeneous. The existence of special interests, a hierarchy, ethnic identities, socioeconomic backgrounds, and skill differences guarantees the emergence of subcultures at professional and student levels. Each subculture often has its own set of symbols in its language, dress, and norms of conduct that serve to set it apart and protect its interests.[50]

Teachers also break into subcultures organized around personal issues (smoking or nonsmoking in the teachers' lounge) or work-related issues (use or nonuse of calculators in math classes). Willower and Smith point out that the stronger the subcultures become, the more fragmented and weak the overall organizational culture becomes. Consequently, the leadership tasks of coordinating and focusing the energies of these disparate subcultures become considerably more complicated as well as essential.[51]

## How Can Organizational Cultures Influence School Actions?

In an anthropologist's view, Charles Fombrun argues that the stability and continuity an organization's culture provides are outcomes of three essential characteristics: reproduction, institutionalization, and legitimization.[52]

The *reproduction* aspect of a school system can be seen in the process of executive succession, which functions as lineage does in some societies. In education, after the formal requirements of holding a teaching credential, completing specified years of classroom experience, and obtaining an administrative credential have been accomplished, the local cultural requirements kick in.

Local requirements usually include such informal requirements as senior mentor sponsorship, membership to an in-group, loyalty to superiors, and pledged support to existing programs. Unfortunately, women and minorities historically have been victims of cultural barriers in the executive succession process. A male sponsor who provides support and guidance for a woman to gain access to the traditionally male-dominated in-group of senior administrators must often violate the cultural norms of that male group to do so.[53]

The *institutionalization* of cultural characteristics provides for the introduction and stability of norms that lead to organizational stability. By paying attention to such institutionalization, it may become possible to "de-emphasize bureaucratic controls in favor of shared normative commitments."[54] Effective principals are often those noted for their skill at aligning the norms and goals of teachers and students around satisfaction achieved through the learning process.[55]

The *legitimization* function of school culture permits the organization to carry out its mission even in times of crisis because those concerned recognize that the system is doing what it should be doing. When, for example, ideological challenges are mounted to purge school libraries of specific books or objections arise over teaching sex education, schools with strong academic cultures normally triumph, because they believe their missions are to educate young minds to the real world, not shelter them.

## Do Strong Cultures Make Effective Schools?

Certainly, a strong culture can be a barrier to change and undercut effectiveness. A former vice president at AT&T writes:

> A few years ago, a colleague of mine at AT&T analyzing our situation remarked that "a locomotive has no steering wheel because it's on tracks, and the tracks guide it to its destination." His point was that AT&T had been on a set of tracks for 70 years, a set of regulatory, strategic, organizational and cultural tracks. Meanwhile, the competition had come in through interstate highways, with speedy cars that could turn on a dime. [What we had to do] was not just a change or transformation; it was more like trying to make six killer submarines out of a battleship within a year or two.[56]

Principal characteristics of organizational culture are stability and consistency; therefore, attempts to significantly modify the outcomes to higher levels of effectiveness are inherently difficult.

The links between school culture and effectiveness are relatively ambiguous argue Rossman, Corbett, and Firestone, partly because definitions of effectiveness are also culture bound. Definitions depend on the definers' beliefs about what is important; for example, job satisfaction, attendance, turnover, and student achievement often are introduced as criteria of effectiveness.[57]

In many ways, the link between an organization's culture and effectiveness functions the same way as an organization's structure and effectiveness. They both can undercut outcomes by stagnating or disrupting the system through, for example, rigidities, conflict, time loss, and hidden agendas. It is not difficult to imagine that a school's culture captured in the metaphor "the little shop of horrors" would detract from positive educational outcomes.

Indeed, structure and culture also can provide conditions that support improved outcomes when they align with the educational mission of the school, such as high expectations for student achievement, a climate with an incentive for learning, minimal discipline problems, and so forth.[58] Whether the presence of these supportive structural and cultural conditions will directly translate into increased levels of student learning remains an open question.

As Bossert points out, research advances into the subject still have not disentangled the multilevel variables internal and external to the school that shape "the nature of the instructional activities in which teachers and students engage."[59] Continued exploration into the complexities of this milieu of factors influencing student achievement will no doubt chart the future of school-effectiveness research.

## Governance and Decision Making

Decision making is a much discussed subject. A considerable amount of that discussion focuses on how decisions *should be* made.[60] With minor adaptations to the idiosyncracies of specific writers, most works on decision making summarize the process as follows:

1. Recognize, define, and limit the problem in the light of system goals.
2. Analyze and evaluate the problem.
3. Establish criteria and standards by which a solution will be evaluated or judged as acceptable and adequate to the need.
4. Define the alternatives.
5. Collect data on each alternative.
6. Apply evaluative criteria to each alternative.
7. Select the preferred alternative.
8. Implement the choice.
9. Evaluate the results.

The decision-making process as described here is derived from classical theory. It emphasizes that rational thought should be applied under ideal conditions in a stable environment. All alternatives are considered in terms of an empirical analysis of the costs and benefits associated with each. Ends are selected before means. The participants in the decision-making process must define and agree upon the values associated with the ends and means. A basic assumption is that a person or a few persons at the top of the pyramid are in direct control of the process, complete data are available, and the end result of selecting one or the other of the alternatives can be known. Governance is defined here as control over the decision-making process.

The process of making rational decisions depends on linking directly related activities to the organization's goals and policy. This requirement specifies that the goals must be precise enough to give definite direction to organizational events.

## Formal and Informal Goals

In setting the direction of schools, and especially trying to change them, "Goals are ideals," Mike Milstein writes. They must be clear, attractive and challenging to participants, and be sufficiently measurable to test what has been achieved.[61] However, as soon as we attempt to establish meaningful, direction-setting goals for education, we are in trouble, because goals are a derivative of values. Glasman reminds us that values are not constant in time, place, or people. Particular points of view reflecting particular ideological orientations come and go. At times, values become politicized and cause a different type of problem.[62]

In our schools, we have trained the whole child, established priorities for intellectual achievement, preserved the cultural heritage, fostered cultural pluralism, pushed individualized instruction, gone back to the basics, stressed self-discipline, enforced corporal punishment, established permissive environments, segregated, desegregated, emphasized classroom tracking, deemphasized classroom tracking, centralized decision making, decentralized decision making, and so on. Reflecting on the complexities of goal setting in school governance, Rodney Muth concludes:

> Simply put, schools are torn by competing ideologies and interests, exemplified in one way by the struggle between bureaucracy and professionalism and in another way by that between labor and management. At the heart of these struggles is the issue of power: who decides which values prevail? Whose sense of order determines priorities?[63]

Attempting to understand the actions of an organization in terms of its formal goals can be a misleading, if not fruitless, endeavor. As Katz and Kahn point out:

> We can easily be misled by teleological fictions presented by organizational spokesmen. The organization is a social system and the consciously expressed intent of some of its members is not to be confused with the functioning of the system. Hence, when officials announce a change in policy to embrace new objectives, we should look at the actual systemic changes taking place rather than accepting the statement at face value. We should follow such a procedure not because there may be insincerity in official pronouncements, but because the functioning of a system is not necessarily given in the statements of its leaders, no matter how sincere they may be.[64]

Organizational goals are related to the entire planning and evaluation sequences. The formal goals of the educational organization are usually grouped under six broad headings:

1. Intellectual discipline
2. Citizenship and civic responsibility
3. Economic independence and vocational opportunity

4. Social development and human relationships
5. Moral and ethical character
6. Self-realization

Formal goals such as these sound heartwarming and desirable, but they have created a very weighty problem for the schools. March and Simon point out, "When a means of testing actions is perceived to relate a particular goal or criterion with possible courses of action, the criterion will be called *operational.*"[65] Educational goals tend to be *nonoperational* because no measuring rods are available to determine the relationship between a specific educational experience and, for example, good citizenship or moral character. The Joint Committee on Educational Goals and Evaluation for the State of California put it bluntly: "The relationship of instructional technique, school organization, and pupil performance to educational goals is unknown."[66]

Thus, the school can proclaim success with relative impunity because of the difficulty of measuring the achievement of nonoperational goals. Furthermore, nonoperational goals inhibit the school from evaluating and selecting the most appropriate and effective instructional techniques, classroom organization, and school lessons because comparative measures cannot be evaluated against goals. A heavy damper, therefore, is also placed on the change dynamic of the school because of the difficulty of comparing the results of existing practices with alternatives.

In reality, an organization is a basketful of disorganized informal and formal goals that frequently represent conflicting demands and jumbled priorities.[67] Each member of the organization has his or her own informal goals. These goals are derived from differing career expectations, academic ideologies, classroom curricular priorities, reference groups, vested interests, levels of idealism, and impulses for change. The school is able to function and still retain a multitude of cross-purpose goals, because only a limited number of the informal goals are pressed forward at any particular time.

Thus, the school administrators, teachers, students, and parents can simultaneously hold a belief in social-adjustment education, powerful athletic teams, strong vocational programs, academic emphasis on the classics, a sound three R's approach, neighborhood schools, desegregation, classroom tracking, individualized instruction, and the like. Under conditions such as these, the administrator's task is to neutralize as many of the conflicting goals as possible so that at a given time the school can proceed with a somewhat coordinated plan with minimal distractions from conflicting demands.

"It is doubtful," Herbert Simon writes, "that decisions are generally directed towards achieving *a* goal. It is easier, and clearer, to view decisions as being concerned with discovering courses of action that satisfy a whole set of constraints."[68] As an organization solves problems, it must continually traverse a set of differing and formidable constraints by bargaining, blocking, compromising, and conceding. Under such conditions, the imminent possibility of organizational drift always exists.

*Organizational drift* refers to the discrepancy between the organization's formally stated goals and the day-to-day events. Under pressure to find acceptable solutions to short-range problems, the organization often loses sight of its long-range goals. Any given decision, such as to give way to a group of parents demanding the abolishment of sex education courses, may not have a noticeable impact on the system's direction.

However, at some point, the school officials may realize they have lost basic control of the instructional process to vocal parent or teacher groups. This may come about because in order to stay in business, educators have to compromise continually. As Katz and Kahn point out, day-to-day decisions, often made on an ad hoc basis, are frequently made by lower-level subordinates, and their cumulative effect is as powerful as though a new policy had been articulated by the formal leadership.[69] These are conditions that invite emergence of a political environment.

## Schools as Political Systems

Schools are politically vulnerable from sources inside and outside their systems. Vulnerability comes not only because both their means and ends are ambiguous, and therefore invite challenge at any crisis point, but because of their stewardship over the young and impressionable.[70] The decision-making process energizes the actions of an organization; therefore, it is the target of the political environment. Morgan writes:

> Organizational politics arise when people think differently and want to act differently. This diversity creates a tension that must be resolved through political means. As we have already seen, there are many ways in which this can be done: autocratically ("We'll do it this way"); bureaucratically ("We're supposed to do it this way"); or democratically ("How shall we do it?"). In each case the choice between alternative paths of action usually hinges on the power relations between the actors involved.[71]

Power struggles are as natural to educational systems as they are to any other form of organization. They are especially acute when there is no clearly defined hierarchical relationship or the power inherent in the formal roles is weak, as is the case in education. Sometimes subordinates have their own outside constituencies, as do winning coaches and band directors, and can therefore play a winning hand.

The objective in using power is to gain control over the system's resources and direction. At some point in every system power struggles become visible, perhaps between members of the board, between the superintendent (expert power) and the board (constituency power), and between the state legislature (formal authority) and the state department of education (bureaucratic power).[72]

A particularly aggressive player in the power game of the 1990s has been the Christian Right which has transformed school districts throughout the country into ideological battlegrounds. The New Right, which unabashedly links public policy, education and spirituality, has become tireless, skillful and relentless in its efforts to capture power in school boards as well as the souls of children in the classroom. As George Kaplan observes, adherents are unshakably convinced of the correctness of their views; "Issues become right-or-wrong, life-or-death choices between God's will and the misguided incompetence of the tenured functionaries who are running our schools into the ground."[73]

Sometimes the agendas of specific groups are overtly debated as expressions of the will of the people. However, agendas are increasingly being hidden from public view only to be sprung on an unsuspecting public *after* school board elections have been held. This typically results in a situation where everyone, especially the students, lose something of value.

## Hidden Agendas

"What do clowns, the CIA, actors, business people and court room defendants all have in common?" Greiner and Schein ask. "All use some form of deception, at times to achieve their objectives."[74] That is, through deception they attempt to create a false sense of reality. In 1976, the U.S. Department of Defense organized a conference, bringing together various members of these groups and the equipment of their trades in an attempt to better understand the art of deception.

Creating illusion is often part of power strategies applied in education. Will the teachers really go on strike, as they say they will, unless they get a contract including a new dental plan?

Not all applications of power are directed at getting the work done more effectively and efficiently. Often personal or group goals involving promotion, status, job survival, and so forth are the real objectives beneath deceptive arguments stressing a more acceptable, greater good. When hidden agendas are involved, dialogue becomes difficult because the issue on the agenda is not the real issue at all.

## The School as a Collection of Coalitions

The thesis of this chapter is that an organization such as a school or a school district is not governed by a monolithic power structure but by a multitude of semiautonomous power centers that contribute significantly to the direction or directions the system takes. As the case study in Chapter 4 will illustrate, these centers, in turn, have their own power bases and have devised sophisticated means of protecting and preserving their own interests. Centers of power within an organization tend to form or break out of coalitions, depending on the particular issue confronting the organization.

Distinct centers of power, whether part of informal groups or formal departments, can cause serious management headaches. Leonard Sayles relates the following story form the *New York Times:*

> After assuming office, Carter detected mice in the Oval Office; the very focal point of the Presidency. He called the General Services Administration who then came and handled the matter. Shortly after Carter continued to hear mice; but worse, one died in the wall and the stench was quite noticeable during formal meetings. However, when he again called the G.S.A. he was told that they had carefully exterminated all the mice; therefore any new mice must be "exterior" mice, and exterior work is apparently the province of the Interior Department. They at first demurred but eventually a "joint task force" was mounted to deal with the problem.[75]

Coalitions are collections of individuals and groups united by common interests. As Bacharach and Lawler point out, coalitions are strategic devices to improve their bargaining leverage against others in the struggle to protect or enlarge control over domains, policies, or resources.[76] Thus, coalitions are not ends in themselves but means to ends.

Coalitions form the power centers around which *intra*organizational politics take place. They are not necessarily made up of the formal units of an organization but of socially constructed groupings "that are important because they can undermine, modify, or buttress the power relations formally established by the hierarchy of authority."[77] However, coalitions are not enduring. Like shifting dunes of sand, they rise and fall as conditions change.

The formation of coalitions is limited by constraints inherent in the school and the community. Constraints such as size (large or small), wealth (rich or poor), ideology (conservative or liberal), structure (bureaucratic or nonbureaucratic), and location (urban or rural) are only a few of the various forces that will influence coalition formation. The *dominant coalition* is usually the one that controls the authority structure and the resources.[78]

If an administrator views the organization as a collection of coalitions, his or her management task becomes one of forging a network of coalitions that will work in semicoordinated fashion to achieve a level of stability or a program of change. The school district surrounds and is surrounded by one of the most complex mixes of coalitions found in modern organizations. This feature exists because, among other things, the school cannot conceal vital information as so many other organizations can. The business of the school is not only public business, it is *local* public business. Data on district operations, albeit sometimes embarrassing, are available to a host of vested interest groups, which are ready to join forces when the occasion presents itself. Perhaps the most common example of coalition formation occurs when major changes are proposed (e.g., bond issues, curricular reforms). This sets off a scramble of supporting and opposing parties seeking allies.

Coalition formation *within* the school district is also common. When school districts across the country in the 1970s and 1980s moved toward adopting such changes as using behavioral objectives in the classroom, team teaching, merit pay, and teacher competency testing, almost visceral responses in opposition and support developed among groups allied in common causes. The issue is further complicated by the fact that teachers are semiautonomous in their professional activities, and most of them have security of employment through tenure. These features, not present in most organizations, compound the problems of governance in schools.

As managers struggle to maintain some semblance of control over their organizations, they must contend with formal or informal coalitions that are busy trying to build their own resources, personnel, autonomy, and power.[79] When these subgroups compete with each other for funds from a fixed budget, the inevitable result is tension, if not conflict. When the football coaches, for example, want new helmets for the players as well as more seats in the stadium, they are not going to sympathize with the geography teachers who want the same money for maps, globes, and a jeep for field trips.

In short, the school can be characterized as a collection of coalitions with differing degrees of stability, depending on the issues confronting the system. Even though the members and their coalitions support a variety of formal and informal goals, the

From *Dollars and Sense,* September 1976. Used with permission.

divergent goals generally are not all put forward at the same time. Management also seeks ways to neutralize the conflicting goals.

As the next section will point out, in the long run the school is characterized by two natural coalitions: teachers and administrators. Formally, the administrators are characterized as superiors and the teachers as subordinates, but informally the subordinates obtain considerable control over the governing process.

## Governing from the Lowerarchy

Like other formal organizations, the school must deal with the tasks of structuring, managing, and giving direction to a complex mix of human and material resources. Unlike most other formal organizations, the school has a human output that gives rise to a unique problem of managerial control. Managerial control of schools is subject to divergent thrusts.[80] On the one hand, requirements of learning suggest an unencumbered, nonprescriptive environment. On the other, requirements of efficiency and predictability in human and material resource management suggest a rational, programmed environment. Put another way, "The one demands personalistic, idiosyncratic and flexible behavior; the other requires impersonal, universalistic and consistent behavior."[81] Charles Bidwell sheds further light on this organizational tension:

> The looseness of system structures and the nature of the teaching task seem to press for a professional mode of school system organization, while demands for uniformity of product and the long time span over which cohorts of students are trained press for rationalization of activities and thus for a bureaucratic base of organization.[82]

Thus arises the spectre of two very different sources of organizational control in schools: one rooted in the classical bureaucratic tradition of formal centralized authority and the other based on the informal prerogatives and professionalism of the teacher. To be sure, the power in the lowerarchy is a power to be reckoned with. (The lowerarchy refers to those employees (subordinates) who hold positions in the middle and bottom levels of the organizational pyramid.)

"The leader," says Homans, "cannot bring his group from one state to another unless his orders are, to some extent, obeyed."[83] As early as 1938, Chester Barnard argued that the actual locus of authority in organizations was at the middle and lower levels of the hierarchy rather than at the top, as most people assumed. He also argued that authority is delegated from lower levels to higher levels rather than vice versa.[84] Homans speaks of Barnard's thesis:

> *If an order given by a leader to a member of his group is accepted by the member and controls his activity in the group, then the order is said to carry authority.* This definition implies that the authority of an order always rests on the willingness of the person to whom it is addressed to obey it . . . we talk as if authority were something inherent in leaders and flowing from them. Our definition reminds us that the power of the leader always depends on his being able, by whatever methods, to carry his group with him.[85]

Subordinates decide, personally or collectively, whether to obey or disobey a directive from superordinates. When they decide to obey a directive, they imply that, on a particular issue, they are willing to be governed from above. By doing so, they in effect delegate authority to those above them in the hierarchy.

The very nature of the learning process, as currently conceived, argues for discretion and latitude of behavior in the hands of teachers at the lower end of the hierarchy. By its very nature, the job of teaching argues for resistance against intrusions of formal authority that restrict the subordinates' exercise of judgment and flexibility. The proper performance of the teaching task, with its requirements of personalistic, idiosyncratic, and flexible behavior, entails that teachers' compliance with authority be restricted to areas that do not bear directly on their primary responsibility of instruction. From the perspective of managerial control, then, the unique quality of teaching organizations is that the core activity, the teaching-learning process, requires and justifies control by teachers, who are subordinates in the educational hierarchy. Whereas in other organizations refusal to comply might result in severance, the teacher's refusal frequently is legitimated by an understanding of the unusual needs of classroom instruction.

Beyond the nature of the teaching task, a number of other features of the teaching profession and certain organizational characteristics of schools provide teachers with the opportunity to govern from below and to reinforce the justification for such governance. Among the most important are the looseness of system structures mentioned earlier by Bidwell; traditions of autonomy and professionalism; collegiality; a low level of visibility in the classroom; and the claim of teaching expertise.

In addition to those needs already mentioned, teachers have a special need to control the learning process, and it is related to incentive systems. Blau and Scott point out two types of incentive systems, those that reward results and those that reward conformity to established procedure.[86] Because the educational process is a cumulative experience for the student, enduring over many years and involving many teachers, and because the influence of factors external to schools in inscrutable, it is not possible to determine the efficacy of individual teachers. Therefore, the rewards of teachers are closely bound to the procedures associated with their work rather than to the results.[87] This being the case, teachers have a vested interest in controlling those procedures.

The superintendent's relationship to his or her board of education also reflects a position of control from a lowerarchy. Legal charters as well as conventional wisdom hold that boards of education make policy and superintendents carry it out. On the contrary, Ziegler et al. write, "Our overall conclusion is that boards are likely to become spokesmen *for* the superintendent *to* the community; their representational roles are reversed and the superintendent becomes the dominant policymaker."[88]

In their study of two new superintendents, Hall and Hall argue that the superintendent's dominance over the board is not as automatic or predetermined as Ziegler et al. suggest. Much depends on the conditions under which the old superintendent left and the context of the situation confronting the new leader on arrival.

The authors stress that to achieve dominance the new superintendent must build a *base of power* through the acquisition of resources. Power and dependence center on the concept of resource. "Whether it was information, experience, loyalty or commitment, credibility, legitimacy, support, trust, or autonomy, they would have to find ways to increase their resources, decrease counter claims to the same resources, and increase their control over the resources. They, more or less, developed explicit plans and programs to achieve those ends."[89]

Thus, new superintendents seeking to dominate the policy-making process must set out to do so by neutralizing, overcoming, and transcending internal and external constraints. Only the acquisition of resources (e.g., loyalty, information, credibility) will allow them to acquire dominance.

## A Contrast of Basic Assumptions

Chapter One pointed out that different people using distinct conceptual lenses tend to view the causes and consequences of organizational events diversely. A person's idea of how an organization works acts as an organizing instrument for the data that person observes. Behavior that does not fit into the mental model can easily be cast off as deviant and therefore not representative.

School administrators, for example, sometimes talk about certain acts of teachers as unprofessional. Teachers also at times talk about irrational and undisciplined student behavior. However, as viewed through another organizational perspective, these behaviors may be seen as extremely rational, disciplined, and, in the case of teachers, professional. The difference is that a finite social system and not the organization as a whole is the motivator of these "deviant" behaviors. Not understanding the multitude of organizational forces deriving from different sources in the school can lead to considerable frustration, and may result in applying the wrong solution to the wrong problem.

The basic assumptions underpinning the major conceptual models presented thus far differ on many key issues. A few of the major differences are illustrated in Table 3.1.

Both the formal characteristics of classical theory and the informal characteristics of social system theory play an important role in the life of a school system. A body of research literature has emerged in recent years that depicts an organization as a system that shifts its emphasis between formal and informal structures and processes according to external or internal decisions and pressures that it faces at any given time. In other words, certain types of pressures or decisional requirements result in a response by the formal system and others result in a response by the informal system. Yet a third set of pressures or decisional requirements result in formal and informal system responses, which often place the two in conflict. The diagnostic task is to define and predict which conditions internal and external to the organization call out which type of response. The emerging body of literature associated with this problem is called *contingency theory*, which will receive a much closer examination in Chapter Six.

TABLE 3.1    A Comparison of the Assumptions of Classical Theory and Social System Theory

| *Classical Theory* | *Social System Theory* |
| --- | --- |
| 1. An organization is characterized as a hierarchical order of roles and responsibilities. | 1. An organization is characterized as a coalition of sociopolitical groups frequently working outside the formal system. |
| 2. Power is centralized in the role of the chief officer. | 2. Power is diffused into groups or coalitions of groups. |
| 3. Formal goals give specific direction to events. | 3. Formal and informal goals often conflict, with the latter leading in a multitude of directions. |
| 4. Communication follows established channels. | 4. Communication follows the vested interests of the groups involved. |
| 5. Control over production (teaching/learning) is established by the rules of the organization. | 5. Control over production (teaching/learning) is established by the informal norms of groups. |
| 6. Superiors manage subordinates. | 6. Subordinates frequently manage superiors. |
| 7. Conflict is dysfunctional and should be eliminated. | 7. Conflict is frequently very functional (constructive) and is inevitable. |
| 8. Subordinates are motivated by economic needs. | 8. Subordinates have motivational needs that extend far beyond economic issues. |
| 9. People do not like to work; therefore, close supervision is necessary. | 9. If *some* people do not like to work, that behavior is learned and not inherent in their character. |
| 10. Human beings are interchangeable on the job as long as they have the requisite skill. | 10. Each human being brings unique social and psychological characteristics to the job that influence the productivity of the role he or she occupies. |

## Conclusion

An associate of mine likes to draw an analogy between managing a complex organization such as a school system and driving a multihorse stagecoach lacking traces between the beasts. The horses are all shapes and sizes; some are tired and want to lie down, others are full of energy and want to charge the road, a few want to turn around and return to the barn, and a couple want no more out of life than to throw the driver off his perch. Somehow the driver must get them going in the same general direction at the same general speed at more or less the same time, or no one goes anywhere.

The existence of informal goals, power centers in the lowerarchy, multiple communication channels, shifting coalitions, and differing need structures makes the life of a school administrator somewhat like that stagecoach driver. However, knowing these conditions exist and the reasons why they exist permits a planning effort that takes them into account as much as possible.

## *The Superintendent's on My Back*

A troubled Stanley Moose, principal of Valley Springs Elementary School, walked to his car following a principals' meeting with Superintendent Brigade. Stan's boss had just declared war on the district's reading problem and had ordered all elementary schools to adopt a new Whiz-Bang reading program that had been talked about so much at a recent AASA meeting. When pressed, the superintendent had been unable to provide hard evidence that the program really worked—only a few glowing testimonials from some midwestern superintendents.

"One good thing about the Whiz-Bang method," Dr. Brigade said, "is that it won't cost the district any additional money." True, Stanley thought, but it will cost the teachers a lot of additional hours in preparing materials and grading papers. They won't be thrilled about that.

The superintendent's parting words to the elementary school principals a few minutes ago were, "The board of education is on my back about the reading scores in this district. So I'm going to be on your backs. I want it done, and I want it done yesterday!"

The principal of Valley Springs was genuinely troubled about the probable reaction of the teachers to this second change in the reading program in three years. Besides, at Valley Springs there was a long tradition of teacher participation in major decisions. Now they would be told the decision had already been made.

While the district office had mandated the existing reading program in a much similar way, several teachers had objected at first but then closed their doors and ignored the directive. Thinking about it, those teachers seemed to be surprisingly organized in defiance of that district and school policy.

The principal wasn't sure how to handle the present situation. Should he try to reason with the superintendent in order to buy time for genuine planning? Maybe he should delay things on his own in order to mount a realistic program with the teachers. Both approaches were risky as either could earn him the reputation of being a weak leader.

What would happen if he dropped the new program directly on the teachers as the superintendent had suggested? Probably a repeat of the first time that happened. That whole experience had cost him a lot of respect among many of the teachers. He didn't want to walk that rocky road again.

"So where do I go from here?" Stan Moose mumbled under his breath as he started the engine of his car.

## *Notes*

1.  Theodore White, *The Making of the President,* 1960 (New York: Atheneum, 1965), pp. 366–367.

2.  Graham T. Allison, "Conceptual Models and the Cuban Missile Crisis," *The American Political Science Review* 63 (1969): 707.

3.  Ibid., p. 710. By permission of the American Political Science Association and the author.

4.  Elton Mayo, *The Human Problems of an Industrial Civilization* (New York: Macmillan, 1933).

5.  Daniel E. Griffiths, "Toward a Theory of Administrative Behavior," in *Administrative Behavior in Education,* Roald Campbell and Russell Gregg, eds. (New York: Harper & Row, 1957), p. 384.

6.  F. J. Roethlisberger and W. J. Dickson, *Management and the Worker* (Cambridge, MA: Harvard University Press, 1939), p. 383.

7.  Amitai Etzioni, *Modern Organizations* (Englewood Cliffs, NJ: Prentice-Hall, 1964), pp. 34–38.

8.  Mayo, *Human Problems,* pp. 120–121.

9.  Roethlisberger and Dickson, *Management and the Worker,* p. 522.

10.  Donald Willower, "Micropolitics and the Sociology of School Organizations," *Education and Urban Society,* 23 (1991): 444.

11.  Lyman Porter, Edward Lawler III, and J. Richard Hackman, "Ways Groups Influence Individual Work," in *Motivation and Work Behavior,* 3rd ed., Richard M. Steers and Lyman Porter, eds. (New York: McGraw-Hill, 1983), p. 395.

12.  George C. Homans, *The Human Group* (New York: Harcourt, Brace and World, 1950), pp. 140–144.

13.  Donald F. Roy, "Banna Time: Job Satisfaction and Informal Interaction," *Human Organization* 18 (1960): 158–168.

14.  Roethlisberger and Dickson, *Management and the Worker,* p. 383.

15.  Burleigh B. Gardner, *Human Relations in Industry* (Chicago: Irwin, 1945), p. 283.

16.  For an account of this research see: Ralph White and Ronald Lippitt, *Autocracy and Democracy: An Experimental Inquiry* (New York: Harper & Row, 1960).

17.  Etzioni, *Modern Organizations,* p. 42.

18.  Alvin W. Gouldner, "Organizational Tension," in *Sociology Today,* Robert Merton et al., eds. (New York: Basic Books, 1959), p. 407.

19.  W. Richard Scott, "Developments in Organization Theory, 1960–1980," *American Behavioral Scientist* 24 (1981): 408.

20.  Roethlisberger and Dickson, *Management and the Worker,* p. 559.

21.  W. Richard Scott, *Organizations: Rational, Natural and Open Systems* (Englewood Cliffs, NJ: Prentice-Hall, 1981), p. 83.

22.  Talcott Parsons and Edward Shils, "The Social System," in *Toward a General Theory of Action,* T. Parsons and E. Shils, eds. (New York: Harper & Row, 1951), chapter 4.

23. Harry Bredemeier and Richard Stephenson, *The Analysis of Social Systems* (New York: Holt, Rinehart and Winston, 1962), pp. 34–35.

24. Milbrey McLaughlin and Joan Talbert, *Contexts that Matter for Teaching and Learning* (Stanford, CA: Center for Research on the Context of Secondary School Teaching, Stanford University, 1993), p. 8.

25. Charles P. Loomis, *Social Systems* (Princeton, NJ: D. Van Nostrand, 1960).

26. Ibid., p. 6.

27. Ibid., p. 17.

28. J. R. P. French, Jr. and B. H. Raven, "The Bases of Social Power," in *Studies in Social Power,* D. Cartwright, ed. (Ann Arbor: University of Michigan Press, 1959).

29. Alvin L. Bertrand, "The Stress-Strain Element of Social Systems: A Micro Theory of Conflict and Change," *Social Forces* 42 (1963).

30. Loomis, *Social Systems,* p. 30.

31. George C. Homans, "Social Behavior as Exchange," *American Journal of Sociology* 62 (1958): 597–606.

32. Dan C. Lortie, *School Teacher* (Chicago: The University of Chicago Press, 1975), chapter 8.

33. Peter Blau, *The Dynamics of Bureaucracy* (Chicago: The University of Chicago Press, 1963), p. 141.

34. Ellen Goldring, "Principals, Parents and Administrative Superiors," *Educational Administration Quarterly* 29 (1993): 95.

35. Blau, chapter 7.

36. Charles Fombrun, "Of Tribes and Witch Doctors: The Anthropologist's View," in *Corporate Culture and Change,* Melissa Berman, ed. (New York: The Conference Board, 1986), p. 7.

37. As reported in Terrence E. Deal, "The Culture of Schools," in *Leadership: Examining the Elusive,* L. Sheive and M. Schoenheit, eds., (Washington, DC: 1987 Yearbook of the ASCD, 1987), pp. 3–15.

38. Terrence Deal and A. A. Kennedy, *Corporate Cultures: The Rights and Rituals of Corporate Life* (Reading, MA: Addison-Wesley, 1982); Thomas Peters and Robert Waterman, Jr., *In Search of Excellence* (New York: Warner Books, 1982).

39. Terrence Deal, "The Symbolism of Effective Schools," *The Elementary School Journal* 85 (1985): 605; Marsha Levine, "Excellence in Education: Lessons from America's Best Run Companies and Schools," *Peabody Journal of Education* 63 (1986): 152.

40. Gareth Morgan, *Images of Organization* (Beverly Hills, CA: Sage, 1986), pp. 130–131.

41. William Tierney, "Organizational Culture in Higher Education," *Journal of Higher Education* 59 (1988): 3.

42. Samuel Bacharach and Joseph Shedd, "Power and Empowerment: The Constraining Myths and Emerging Structures of Teacher Unionism in an Age of Reform," in *Politics of Education Yearbook,* Robert Crowson and Jane Hannaway, eds. (London: Falmer Press, 1989), p. 14.

43. Edgar Schein, "How Culture Forms, Develops and Changes," in *Gaining Control of the Organizational Culture,* Ralph Kilman et al., eds. (San Francisco: Jossey-Bass, 1985), pp. 19–20.

44. Edgar H. Schein, *Organizational Culture and Leadership,* 2nd ed. (San Francisco: Jossey-Bass, 1992), p. 15.

45. Peters and Waterman.

46. Arnold Danzig, "Parents Versus Professionals: Social Class and Services to Children and Families," *People and Education* 3 (1994).

47. Terrence Deal,"The Symbolism of Effective Schools," *The Elementary School Journal* 85 (1985): 605–607.

48. Carl Steinhoff and Robert Owens,"The Organizational Culture Assessment Inventory: A Metaphorical Analysis of Organizational in Culture Educational Settings" (Paper presented at the American Educational Research Association, New Orleans, LA, 1988).

49. Terrence Deal and Martha Wise,"Planning, Plotting, and Playing in Education's Era of Decline," in *The Dynamics of Educational Change,* Victor Baldridge and Terrence Deal, eds. (San Francisco: McCutcheon, 1983).

50. Donald Willower,"Organization Theory and the Management of Schools," in *World Yearbook of Education, 1986: The Management of Schools,* Eric Hoyle and Agnes McMahon, eds. (London: Kogan Page, 1986), pp. 4–5.

51. Donald Willower and Jonathan Smith,"Organizational Culture in Schools: Myth and Creation" (Paper presented at the American Educational Research Association, San Francisco, 1986).

52. Fombrun, p. 8.

53. Catherine Marshall, "Analyzing the Culture of School Leadership," *Education and Urban Society* 20 (1988); Flora Ida Ortiz, *Career Patterns in Education: Women, Men and Minorities in Public School Administration* (New York: Praeger, 1987).

54. Willower and Smith, p. 1.

55. Arthur Blumberg and William Greenfield, *The Effective Principal: Perspectives in School Leadership,* 2nd ed. (Boston: Allyn and Bacon, 1986); Marsha Levine, "Excellence in Education: Lessons from America's Best Run Companies and Schools," *Peabody Journal of Education* 63 (1986): 150–186.

56. W. Brooke Tunstall,"Disconnecting the Bell System: An Insider's View," in *Corporate Culture and Change,* Melissa Berman, ed. (New York: The Conference Board, 1986), p. 36.

57. Gretchen Rossman, H. Dickson Corbett, and William Firestone, *Change and Effectiveness in Schools: A Cultural Perspective* (New York: SUNY Press, 1988), p. 133–141.

58. Stephen Bossert,"School Effects," in *Handbook of Research on Educational Administration,* Norman Boyan, ed. (New York: Longman, 1988).

59. Ibid., p. 351.

60. Daniel E. Griffiths, *Administrative Theory* (New York: Appleton-Century-Crofts, 1959), p. 94.

61. Mike Milstein, *Restructuring Schools: Doing It Right* (Newbury Park, CA: Corwin Press, 1993), p. 11.

62. Naftaly S. Glasman,"The Effects of Government Evaluation Mandates," *Administrator's Notebook* 23 (1978–1979): 1.

63. Rodney Muth,"Power, Conflict, Consensus, and Organizational Effectiveness" (Paper presented at the annual meeting of the American Educational Research Association, April 1983), p. 1.

64. Daniel Katz and Robert Kahn, *The Social Psychology of Organizations,* p. 94. Copyright © 1966 by John Wiley & Sons, Inc. Reprinted by permission of John Wiley & Sons, Inc.

65. James G. March and Herbert A. Simon, *Organizations,* p. 155. Copyright © 1958, John Wiley & Sons, Inc. Reprinted by permission of John Wiley & Sons, Inc.

66. Joint Committee on Educational Goals and Evaluation, *The Way to Relevance and Accountability in Education* (Sacramento: State of California Legislature, 1970).

67. Richard Cyert and James G. March, *A Behavioral Theory of the Firm* (Englewood Cliffs, NJ: Prentice-Hall, 1963), chapter 3.

68. Herbert Simon, "On the Concept of Organizational Goal," *Administrative Science Quarterly* 9 (1964): 20.

69.  Katz and Kahn, *The Social Psychology of Organizations,* p. 262.

70.  Donald Willower, "School Principals, School Culture and School Improvement," *Educational Horizons* 63 (1984): 35–38.

71.  Morgan, p. 148.

72.  Samuel Bacharach and Stephen Mitchell, "The Generation of Practical Theory: Schools as Political Organizations," in *Handbook of Organizational Behavior,* Jay Lorsh, ed. (Englewood Cliffs, NJ: Prentice-Hall, 1987), p. 410.

73.  George R. Kaplan, "Shotgun Wedding: Notes on Public Education's Encounter With the New Christian Right," *Phi Delta Kappan* 75 (1994): 5.

74.  Larry Greiner and Virginia Schein, *Power and Organization Development: Mobilizing Power to Implement Change* (Reading, MA: Addison-Wesley, (1988), p. 58.

75.  Leonard R. Sayles, *Leadership* (New York: McGraw-Hill, 1979), p. 3. The story was printed in *New York Times Magazine,* January 8, 1978, p. 29.

76.  Samuel B. Bacharach and Edward J. Lawler, *Power and Politics in Organizations* (San Francisco: Jossey-Bass, 1980), p. 106.

77.  Ibid., p. 214.

78.  Bacharach and Mitchell, p. 411.

79.  Katz and Kahn, *The Social Psychology of Organizations,* p. 99.

80.  Robert Dreeben, "The School as a Workplace," in *Second Handbook of Research on Teaching,* Robert Travers, ed. (Chicago: Rand McNally, 1973), p. 458.

81.  Laurence Iannaccone, *Problems of Financing Inner City Schools* (Columbus: The Ohio State University Research Foundation, 1971), p. 14.

82.  Charles Bidwell, "The School as a Formal Organization," in *Handbook of Organizations,* James G. March, ed. (Chicago: Rand McNally, 1965), pp. 976–977.

83.  Homans, *The Human Group,* p. 417.

84.  Chester Barnard, *The Functions of the Executive* (Cambridge, MA: Harvard University Press, 1938), chapter 12.

85.  Homans, *The Human Group,* pp. 418–419.

86.  Peter M. Blau and W. Richard Scott, *Formal Organizations* (San Francisco: Chandler Publishing Co., 1962), p. 166.

87.  James G. Anderson, "The Authority Structure of the School: System of Social Exchange" in *Educational Administration: Selected Readings,* Walter Hack, et al., eds (Boston: Allyn and Bacon, 1971), p. 250.

88.  L. Harmon Ziegler and M. Kent Jennings with G. Wayne Peak, *Governing American Schools* (North Scituate, MA: Duxbury, 1974), p. 250.

89.  Peter M. Hall and Ann Spencer Hall, "The Creation of Power: How Two New Superintendents Achieve Dominance Over the Boards of Education" (University of Missouri-Colombia and Central Missouri State University, working paper, 1982), p. 10.

# Chapter 4

# The Professional-
# Bureaucratic Interface

## A Case Study

Both classical theory, as depicted in Chapter Two, and social system theory, depicted in Chapter Three, have something valuable to say about the organization and administration of educational systems. However, the school administrator who vigorously sets out to tackle the daily problems of running an educational system by employing one of the frameworks to the exclusion of the other probably will not be very successful.

This chapter is based on a study designed to draw into a single model the strong points of classical theory with those of social system theory. Using the findings of the research, this chapter will wed theory with practice and it is hoped will depict a school-specific framework that describes the way in which schools are governed more accurately than those paradigms that are predominately used in education but actually are designed for business or industrial organizations.

The conventional wisdom of most researchers and writers suggests that the school is best described and analyzed within the classical bureaucratic framework.[1] Clearly, the public school has many characteristics that suggest it is managed according to derivatives of classical bureaucratic theory. For example, the school maintains a well-defined hierarchy of authority (teacher to principal to superintendent); power is centralized in the superintendent; rules stipulate expected and prohibited behavior (education code, district policy, school handbook); a specific division of labor exists (English teachers, history teachers, counselors, aides); positions require university diplomas and state certificates; and a precisely defined work flow is established (first to second to third grade).

However, as Talcott Parsons and Alvin Gouldner have stressed, the classical approach of Weber to the study of organization and administration fails to recognize the effects of professionalism on the process of governance.[2] In recent years a literature has been developing that defines more adequate conceptual models through which the process of school decision making can be understood.[3] Lortie points out:

> The bureaucratic model, in emphasizing the formal distribution of authority, does not prepare us for many of the events that actually occur in public schools. Teachers, for example, lay claim to and get, informally, certain types of authority despite lack of formal support for it in either law or school system constitutions.[4]

In his analysis of the school as a formal organization, Charles Bidwell stresses that we have limited knowledge about the "interplay of bureaucratization and professionalism is schools" and the function this relationship plays in decision making.[5] How does this interplay influence governance and decision making in the school system?[6]

## The Interacting Spheres Model

The fundamental outcome of the study reported in this chapter is the delineation of a model referred to as the Interacting Spheres Model (ISM), as seen in Figure 4.1, which treats ramifications of governance and decision making derived from the professional-bureaucratic interface. *Decision making* is defined here as the process of making choices in organizations.[7] *Governance* is defined as control over the decision-making process.

The ISM model illustrates the simultaneous existence and interaction of two dissimilar decisional environments—rational and programmed *versus* unencumbered and nonprescriptive. Each supports differing organizational requirements essential to the school's purpose. The rational and programmed environment for decision making represents classical hierarchical theory, and the nonprescriptive environment reflects social system theory.

The ISM model suggests the presence of the following organizational characteristics that shape the processes of school governance and decision making:

- Problems emerge and decisions must follow as the organizational environment shifts from a placid to a turbulent condition.
- Problems must be resolved in a milieu of multiple interacting spheres of influence.
- Each sphere of influence is shaped by the needs of a specific decision-making environment.
- The dominant spheres of influence are those that surround the task needs of the professionals (teachers) and the bureaucrats (administrators), although the noncertified personnel, parent groups, and so on also have their own spheres of influence.
- Specific decisions are formally or informally zoned to different spheres of influence.
- Each sphere of influence has a measure of decision-making autonomy (discretion) as well as identifiable constraints on that autonomy.

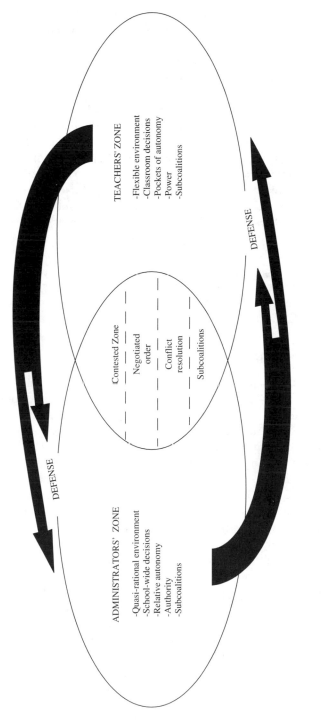

FIGURE 4.1 Interacting Spheres Model

From *Organizational Behavior in Schools and School Districts*, edited by Samuel B. Bacharach. Copyright © 1981 Praeger Publishers. Reprinted and abridged by permission of Praeger Publishers.

- Formal and informal coalitions form and break apart within and between spheres depending on the character of the particular emergent decision to be made.
- Each sphere has a source of power enabling it to take action.
- Specific decisions that fall within more than one sphere of influence are in a contested zone.
- Decisions made regarding problems within a contested zone are the products of informal or formal negotiation, and a negotiated order emerges.
- The multiple spheres of influence that are linked together by the negotiated order form the basis of a loosely coupled system.
- Administrators have developed tactics to attempt informal interventions into the teachers' sphere of influence, and the teachers have developed defensive strategies to defend their sphere against such outside interventions.
- Teachers have developed tactics to attempt informal interventions into the administrators' sphere of influence, and the administrators have developed defensive strategies to defend their sphere against such outside interventions.

Of specific interest to this study are those aspects of governance and decision making that are tied directly to the bureaucratic-professional interaction (or semiprofessional, as Lortie applies the term).[8]

## Design and Method

The research data were drawn from studies of two elementary schools, one middle school, and two high schools found in what will be called the Silverwood School District, located in a city of approximately 150,000 people. The city, which has a mixed light industrial and agricultural economic base, is located on the fringe of a large metropolitan area in the western part of the United States. The Silverwood School District consists of four high schools, three middle schools, and 28 elementary schools. It has a reputation for being well supported by the community, relatively free of disruptive tensions (e.g., student/teacher/administrator), near the state norm in the quality of its academic programs, and continually close to the bone in its budget.

The data were gathered using a participant-observer technique or, as Richard Scott would say, studying "people on the hoof."[9] This approach, as described in the literature and practiced in the field, establishes the researchers in the role of legitimized investigators who, after establishing bonds of confidence with inside members, were allowed sufficient group membership to view natural situations in the schools.[10] In this context the researchers spent approximately six months gathering data at each of the three levels of schooling, covering a total time of approximately two years.

The data-gathering process included intensive interviews (30 to 60 minutes each), direct observation (faculty cafeteria, classrooms, school meetings, etc.), and document analysis (minutes of meetings, correspondence, policy handbooks, etc.). As the researchers recorded the descriptive data of what was happening, categories began to form that eventually emerged as patterns of behavior. This approach led from *description* to *analysis* to *explanation;* in other words, from *what* is happening to *why* and finally to *what consequence* for the system.

Limitations to the research existed. The teacher-administrator interaction was of primary importance; therefore, the roles of the central office officials, students, and non-certificated personnel were recognized but given limited attention. Also, detailed attention will not be given here to discussing differences between elementary or secondary levels; only formal and informal organizational processes common to schools of both levels will be treated.[11] This is because in many ways doing research is like building a multistage rocket; the first stage is built and tested before the additional stages are added on.

## Spheres of Influence

The first few weeks of observation in each school typically unfolded as a confusing buzz of events, like static on a wireless. At any given moment in a high school, for example, we could find one administrator reviewing personnel files in a quiet office, a second being verbally abused by an angry parent, and a third chairing a crisis meeting of department heads, exhorting them to get out the behavioral objectives because of an upcoming accreditation visit.

Some of the teachers were found lecturing to their students in highly structured settings, while others sat under trees discussing the subject of the day. Students were found studying in the library, smoking clandestinely behind the cars in the parking lot, listening attentively in the classroom, or just standing around looking bored.

Some specific organizational patterns were immediately visible, such as buses coming and going, bells ringing on the hour, football players turning out for practice, lunches being served, meetings being called, roll being taken, and examinations being given. Other patterns took weeks to sort out, such as the struggle by teachers to gain extensive participation in the selection of new administrators, the drive to improve the testing program, or the attempt to obtain greater support and resources for specific academic programs.

We often saw teachers and administrators working together in a somewhat collaborative fashion toward a more or less defined goal. However, we also saw these same groups at times taking their own leads and working in opposition to one another and often in defiance of established school policy and rules (e.g., the rejection of team teaching through thinly disguised noncompliance).

In short, rather than finding a rationally planned and logically executed process of organization and administration controlled from the top of the hierarchy, we found a mixed bag of structured and unstructured activities, formal and informal procedures, and controlled and autonomous behaviors. One of the first major research questions to be treated was: How is it possible that a school can function with such a set of seemingly coordinated as well as random activities and behaviors going on all at once? Or, as one teacher so poignantly phrased the issue, "Is there really a method behind all this madness?"

Our data suggested that there was a method, and on reflection it appears quite reasonable and understandable. In all of the schools studied, the researchers discovered *spheres of influence,* or what might be called *domains* or *decisional zones* (hereafter used interchangeably). Although among the many schools we studied the spheres differed in kind and content, they did exist. Visible spheres of influence were maintained by noncertificated personnel (e.g., secretaries, janitors, cooks), school administrators, guidance personnel, teachers, students, parent groups, and central office officials. Each sphere maintained relative degrees of power, autonomy, decision-making discretion, legitimacy, and their own ill-defined tasks and objectives. The two dominant spheres of influence were maintained by the local school administrators and by teachers, and these two domains will be the central focus of this chapter.

The development of two dominant spheres of influence seems to be an organizational response to a fundamental decision-making problem in schools. Cast in the form of a question, this issue becomes: How does the school simultaneously provide for at least two necessary and distinct decisional environments, one of which supports a rational, programmed, and consistent environment, while the other supports a personalistic, unencumbered, and flexible environment? On the face of it, two such unlikely decision-making environments, one responsive to bureaucratic needs and the other to professional needs, could not live together under one roof without continually creating insurmountable problems for one another.

In response to the question, our data fell into a pattern that supports a process identified by Dan Lortie as decisional "zoning."[12] Roughly speaking, each sphere of influence was built around and rooted in a decisional zone where, by either formal delegation, informal assumption, or traditional dominion, a specific group tends to control the choices that take place in that zone. The administrators' primary concerns revolve around schoolwide issues, while the teachers tended to devote their energies to the classroom.[13] Charles Bidwell writes, "The looseness of system structures and the nature of the teaching task seem to press for a professional mode of school system organization, while demands for uniformity of product and the long time span over which cohorts of students are trained press for rationalization of activities and thus for a bureaucratic base of organization."[14]

Even though the theory of shared teacher/administrator decision making often officially is promoted as a means of improving the quality of decisions involving schools, the eventual outcome often returns to reinforcing the spheres of influence. Weiss, Cambone and Wyeth write that shared decision making "calls on teachers to undertake a variety of tasks that they have not previously been responsible for. It makes very heavy demands on their time. It asks them to become familiar with issues, like safety codes and district regulations, that they used to happily leave to the concern of administrators."[15] Especially, when the decision-making process drags out and a teacher consensus is nowhere on the horizon (not an unknown condition in American education), some benefit is seen in the presence of an administrator who will earn his or her pay by making decisions.

## Structural and Cultural Linkages

At a time when schools are heavily burdened with economic, social, and instructional problems, extensive structural looseness could create massive problems of coordination, collaboration, and information access at a time when cohesive problem-solving efforts are essential.[16]

Firestone and Wilson identify the bureaucratic structure of the school and its culture as two natural links between the two spheres of influence. The bureaucratic links establish a prescribed framework that limits freedom of action of administrators and teachers. Structural characteristics of particular importance are

1. the *schedules of events,* which establish time, activity, and location constraints
2. the *budget,* which defines the distribution of resources
3. the *instructional program,* which must be articulated across grades
4. the *vertical information system,* which shapes the flow of information
5. the *hierarchical supervision process,* which legitimizes external critiques.

Cultural links also establish a measure of stability between zones of authority. Shared values, norms, and expectations within a school's culture can help define commitment to mission and level of energy and loyalty teachers and administrators willingly invest.[17] However, a school's structure and culture often are counterbalanced, and sometimes overwhelmed, by the requirements of teacher autonomy.

## *Autonomy*

The concept of autonomy became a key to understanding the special characteristics of the spheres of influence at the Silverwood schools. According to Katz, *autonomy* "refers to the independence of subunits of an organization from control by other parts of the organization or even by the whole organization."[18]

The presence of the teachers' autonomy in the instructional process revealed itself in four ways, as illustrated by the following examples that are representative of patterns. First, the teachers tended to feel they were the ultimate authorities in the teaching-learning process because of their expertise in specialized fields. The teachers were asked who their supervisor was in the instructional process. "Because of my philosophy of education," came one typical response, "I turn to other science teachers in the district who are kind of attuned to the way I am. I don't consider that I have a supervisor in my subject matter in this building."

Second, the teachers generally felt they had the right to organize the learning process as they chose. An administrator commented:

> Each teacher has the right to develop the content and thus the class as he or she feels most comfortable and most successful. I think they are left pretty much on their own as long as there are favorable results. If suddenly the structure or students break down, then it is time for [administrators] to work with them.

Third, the instructional process was relatively unencumbered by a network of school rules defining how the teaching-learning events were to be shaped. The rational network of impersonal school rules tended to stop at the classroom door. At that point, the teachers began formulating their own personalized, flexible rules to aid them in the instructional process.

Fourth, there were occasions when a teacher would not respond in accordance with stated district policy or the instructions of the school principal. Would it be possible, a principal was asked, for a teacher to say no to an administrative directive? "Yes," he replied, "and it is done. In a sense this is what many are saying—'I don't have to.' But if you have a teacher who is making legitimate headway and is humanistic in approach, I believe it would be very difficult for me and the district to say 'You must change.' "

The teachers were asked what gave them the right to say no to the formal authority structure of the school district. "It's just the functioning of the system that allows the teacher to do that," was a common response. "It's kind of an abstract thing; nothing you can pin down—a teacher is put in that position. To a degree it is probably tenure, but it certainly is more than that." Later it will be argued that the illusive concept this teacher was struggling for is part of the attitude of the professional employee in the bureaucratic organization.

A number of teachers as well as administrators articulated the notion of "separateness" by using words such as *our domain, our world, our sphere,* or *an invisible line between us.* In response to a question on what administrators do in school, one teacher said:

> *A:* Frankly, I am so busy in the classroom and having 140 "vibes" bouncing off me every day that I'm not always aware or concerned about what is going on at the administrative level. I sometimes feel, and this is very subjective, that there are two worlds. There is ours; we teachers have our concerns and our oneness, and the administrators have their concerns and their oneness. Sometimes the twain do not meet.
>
> *Q:* Do teachers try to directly preserve their oneness?
>
> *A:* No, it is a very random thing, we don't have meetings or gripe sessions. It's a very informal thing. You just see a friend you trust and you discuss some things that may be worrying you.

The teachers and administrators seemed to be conscious of crossing from one sphere to another. Perceptions on the dimensions and scope of the spheres differed between individuals and schools, but an awareness of the spheres was usually in evidence.

As stated earlier, autonomy "refers to the independence of subunits of an organization from control by other parts of the organization or even by the whole organization."[19] Power, on the other hand, is the ability of one unit to influence or impose its will on another unit.[20] To say that teachers have autonomy in the classroom, or at least a certain measure thereof, is not to say they have power. Corwin is quick to point out "autonomy and control represent independent dimensions; the two terms do not refer to opposite ends of a single continuum. The absence of external control, for example, doesn't necessarily imply that teachers themselves have internal control."[21] Autonomy, however, usually is a necessary but not sufficient condition for power.

As several writers have pointed out, teachers possess few of the sources of power found in other professions.[22] For example, teachers generally do not have control over those who are admitted to the profession, do not hold powers of sanction over those in the profession, do not control communication processes, are not indispensable, and cannot develop strong bases of independent support outside the school (with the possible exception of coaches).

As found in this study, teachers' sources of power appear to be a mix of academic expertise, the ideology of the teaching mission that suggests the teacher is the guardian of the classroom, and at times the support of colleagues. Corwin writes in this vein:

> The professional employee . . . denies the principle that his work always must be supervised by administrators and controlled by laymen. Because of his training, pressures from his colleagues, and his dedication to clients, the professionally oriented person considers himself competent enough to control his own work. Hence, he sometimes must be disobedient toward his supervisors precisely in order to improve his proficiency and to maintain standards of client welfare—especially if there are practices that jeopardize the best interests of students.[23]

The Silverwood study illustrates that the teachers have a degree of autonomy in classroom affairs, although their autonomy has well-defined parameters. Their formal power to act represents a low level of power that is drawn from their position in the hierarchy, is limited, and is directed primarily at students. The administrators also tend to act to establish, preserve, and protect the autonomy and power of teachers because the activities of the teachers are viewed as being in the best interests of the school and the administrative leadership.

Interestingly enough, teachers, as well as police officers, welfare workers, legal-assistance lawyers, health workers, and other public employees have many of the characteristics of what Lipsky calls "street-level bureaucrats." These individuals normally are at the lower levels of the hierarchy and in direct contact with clients or the public. Typically they are overworked, underpaid, assigned responsibilities that affect the lives of those with whom they deal, and provided inadequate resources for their jobs.

Street-level bureaucrats have something else in common, and that is decision-making discretion, because "the nature of the service provision calls for human judgment that cannot be programmed and for which machines cannot substitute."[24] Because street-level bureaucrats must process large amounts of work with limited resource support, they must develop shortcuts and alternate procedures to cope with the press of responsibilities. Managers, trying to insure standardized results, attempt to resist worker discretion, but the workers often see these efforts as illegitimate. For example, police officers often individually or collectively decide not to arrest derelicts. Teachers often have students grade homework rather than grading it themselves.

Floden argues that the "welter of conflicting mandates has the ironic effect of promoting teacher autonomy."[25] Because they are asked to follow so many directives, some conflicting, teachers are forced to pick and choose.

The relative discretion and autonomy of street-level bureaucrats result in their actually making policy for their organizations. This is the case because the workers must decide which of the organization's policies to carry out and how they will do so. When managers set a new policy, they never know how it will function in practice until the street-level bureaucrats interpret it and put it into practice. "Then, when taken in concert, their individual actions add up to agency behavior."[26]

Autonomy does not mean power, nor does it mean license. In the Silverwood schools, the teachers and administrators were quite clear and articulate about those decisions upon which they felt they could act independently and those about which they felt they needed to consult others or share the act of choice. Rather than blanket and uniform autonomy within the separate domains of teachers and administrators, it is more appropriate to speak of pockets of autonomy, each differing in membership (e.g., history teachers or football coaches), in freedom from outside intervention, and in levels and limits of discretion (e.g., coaches have more discretion on the football field than history teachers have in the classroom).

The researchers found the degrees of autonomy within each sphere of influence in general, and within each pocket of autonomy specifically, were constrained by limits imposed, for example, by the state legislature (e.g., books must be selected from an approved list), the court system (e.g., no prayer in the classroom), the school board (e.g., individualized instruction is the only acceptable teaching mode), and the principal (e.g., all teachers must be in the classroom by 8 A.M.). In some instances the limits to autonomy were fixed and inflexible, such as the requirement that teachers take the roll in each class, while at other times flexible and subject to interpretation, such as the degree to which behavioral objectives were actually used to guide classroom instruction.

School administrators also reported on a network of constraints that limited their own decisional domains. These constraints ranged from legal to psychological. They spoke of limits imposed by state laws, accreditation teams, budgets, district policy, community expectations, teacher creative needs, federal grant requirements, health and safety codes, court decisions, and the like.

The researchers ultimately concluded that a principal consequence of the zoning process was to lay the foundation for a measure of *predictability* between the teachers and the administrators. Although in each school the inclusive character of the spheres of influence differed to some extent, generally all parties (teachers, administrators, students, janitors, etc.) understood "the way we do things around here." New arrivals to any one school were quickly socialized through faculty meetings, teachers' handbooks, conversations with "old hands," and so on. Most school personnel admitted to the researchers that "after a few weeks around here, there are few surprises." Hence, the predictability derived from the existence of spheres of influence serves as a tension-reducing mechanism that permits the tasks of schooling to be carried out more smoothly.

In short, as Figure 4.1 illustrated, the schools were characterized by a well-orchestrated mix of centralized decision making, with the reins of control in the hands of the principals, and pockets of decisional autonomy, with the teachers using their own descretion in decision making. The bureaucratic model, with its emphasis on centralized decision making and rationally defined structures, is correct when applied to schools, but only to a point. Elements alien to the classical model are present in the school's governance process because of the presence of employees who have a professional orientation. The instructional mission of the school becomes the organizing force of the teachers' professionalism. The need for efficient resource allocation and rational planning procedures becomes the organizing force for the administrators. A picture of two different sources of organizational control in the school then emerges. One source of control is rooted in the classical bureaucratic tradition of formal centralized authority, and the other in the professionalism of the teacher, which operates more informally.

Given the existence of spheres of influence, the next research question becomes: What are the types of decisions made by the bureaucrats and the professionals in their own domains?

## Decision-Making Categories

The researchers identified five categories of decisions being made in the Silverwood schools.

1. *Allocation decisions:* the distribution of human and material resources in the school
2. *Security decisions:* the preservation of physical and psychological safety of faculty and students
3. *Boundary decisions:* the determination of who controls the passage of materials, information, and people from one domain to another within the school or between the school and the community
4. *Evaluation decisions:* the passing of judgment on the quality of performance (teacher or student)
5. *Instructional decisions:* the determination of classroom teaching-learning processes and content

A close inspection of each category in the Silverwood schools revealed that some decisions within a given category fell within the administrators' sphere of influence, others fell within the teachers' sphere, and others fell within the overlap area we called the "contested zone" (as illustrated in Figure 4.1). The material dealing with decisional categories reported in this section was drawn principally from the high schools, although the same categories were also found in the lower grades. Examples of the five categories, some of which had subcategories, are presented in Table 4.1. No attempt is made here to identify all the decisions found in each sphere; only a single example is presented as an illustration.[27]

Having examined categories of decisions, the research question becomes: Do the teachers or administrators act in concert on decisions falling within their own sphere of influence?

## Subcoalitions within Spheres of Influence

As depicted thus far, a school is made up of differing spheres of influence. However, even within their own domains, the teachers or administrators in the Silverwood

TABLE 4.1    Decision-Making Categories

| *Administrators' Sphere* | *Contested Sphere* | *Teachers' Sphere* |
| --- | --- | --- |
| *Allocation Decisions*<br>Budgeting:<br>Schoolwide budget responsibility | Special project money utilization (for example, stoves versus football equipment) | Specific department spending (for example, books, fieldtrips) |
| Scheduling:<br>Use of school facilities | Master schedule preparation | Student placement in honors classes |
| Personnel:<br>Classified or administrative employment | Certificated employment | Selection of department heads |
| *Security Decisions*<br>Protection:<br>Use of police on campus | Campus supervision | In-class safety |
| Attendance:<br>Legal attendance policies | Campus attendance control | In-class attendance procedures |
| Discipline:<br>Campus discipline | Referred discipline problem cases | In-class discipline measures |
| *Boundary Decisions*<br>Represent school in community activities | Dealing with parents on campus | Teacher ties with union activities |
| *Evaluation Decisions*<br>Probationary teacher performance | Tenured teacher performance | Student performance |
| *Instructional Decisions*<br>Teaching-learning:<br>Emergent crisis over controversial subjects | Large-scale innovation | Classroom instruction |
| Curricular decisions:<br>Mandated subjects | Special programs (for example, bilingual, accelerated) | Course content |

From *Organizational Behavior in Schools and School Districts*, edited by Samuel B. Bacharach. Copyright © 1981 Praeger Publishers. Reprinted and abridged by permission of Praeger Publishers.

schools typically were not observed acting in concert. Instead, they could be seen acting in small groups (sometimes merging into larger groups) that would struggle to achieve some objective (e.g., "We must improve our relations with parents," or "We need more bilingual teachers").

Providing insight into this perspective, Cyert and March write, "Let us view the organization as a coalition. It is a coalition of individuals, some of them organized into subcoalitions."[28] The subcoalition members usually can be identified over a specified, relatively brief period of time or for a particular decision. Over a more extended time, Cyert and March argue, we can usually identify certain classes of decisions that are treated by ongoing subcoalitions.

These subcoalitions share with one another only those ambiguous goals that act as public flags with great symbolic value. Goals such as "to develop an awareness of the values inherent in our democratic society and loyalty to its underlying principles" serve as symbolic cement that holds the school together. In an informal sense, however, the researchers observed the subcoalition members (e.g., client, community, teacher, school, etc.) establishing their own priorities based on their own interpretations of dominant needs. In any given school, the researchers might observe, for example, one group of teachers trying to change the reading program, a second concerned with improving working conditions, and a third trying to block changes in the testing program. The impact on school policy and procedures by the different subcoalitions differed because of a number of variables, such as the alliances any given subcoalition could form, the extent of outside pressure in support of or opposition to the goal of the subcoalition, the visibility of the issue, and the relative power of the subcoalition.

After identifying various subcoalitions in the Silverwood Schools, the researchers set out to understand how they were organized the role they play in the decision-making process.

## Formally Organized Subcoalitions

At the elementary and secondary school levels, the researchers found formal and informal subcoalitions that were organized around longstanding "durable interests" ("We are always looking for ways to build strong community relations") or episodic troublesome issues ("It hit the fan last week regarding a reading assignment"). We found the subcoalitions generally had focus, task direction, and identifiable membership (although some members were rather fluid in participation), a rough but generally understood set of norms and expectations, a sense of legitimacy, sources of power, and a set of constraints limiting the arena of action.

At the elementary level, for example, typically they found three types of formally organized subcoalitions: *the lower-grade teachers,* who were concerned primarily with the formation of student-role norms and social values; *the upper-grade teachers,* who were primarily concerned with the formation of basic skills; and the *standing committees,* such as the guidance committee and the student activities committee. At the elementary level usually there weren't enough administrators to form formally organized subcoalitions, but such groups could be found at the high school level. These formally organized subcoalitions played active roles in the life of their schools, meeting more or less on a regular basis and making choices on issues that involve their specified decision-making domains.

## Informally Organized Subcoalitions

Gross and Trask have pointed out:

> Important value issues arise over such questions as the respective responsibilities of the home and the school, the definition of a "good education," the teaching of moral values, the school's obligations to typical and atypical children, and the questioning of the status

quo. On each of these and other value questions, there may be contradictory points of view among school personnel and between school personnel and the community.[29]

In the Silverwood schools, informal subcoalitions could be seen forming around these "contradictory points of view." Unlike the formal subcoalitions, the informal systems had an ebb and flow quality. For a time, an informal subcoalition was highly visible, influential, and active; then it would drop from sight only to return again at a later date. Informal subcoalitions seemed to emerge where formal subcoalitions were unwilling, unprepared, unstructured, or unauthorized to serve as the advocate or problem-solving vehicle for a troublesome issue.

The researchers often observed teachers banding together in a small alliance to fight for or against such things as the implementation of a central-office-mandated instructional program, or an attempt by an outside teacher association to influence decision making at the school sites. At times, subcoalitions would form and clash with one another on opposite sides of an issue.[30]

The types of informally organized subcoalitions that played an active part in shaping processes of school governance and decision making are briefly discussed here.

*Mini-teams:* These teams, usually composed of an informal alliance of two or three teachers, typically formed to treat a specific emergent problem or task and dissolved when it had been resolved or the participants tired of the effort. Mini-teams often were observed doing such things as developing new curricular units, writing behavioral objectives, or pressuring the principal for more resources.

*Administrative-oriented alliances:* Frequently, issues surfaced that placed in direct confrontation a position held by the majority of teachers and one held by administrators, such as a problem dealing with the appropriate use of teacher planning time, the unionization of teachers, or the need for increased communication between academic programs. On those issues where administrators were taking a strong position, an alliance of administrators and those teachers who aspired to become administrators often formed a temporary subcoalition.

*Equal education opportunity subcoalitions:* Each school had an informal subcoalition organized around an identification with special concerns about the ethnic minority communities. The subcoalitions became active when such issues arose as the need for subject materials treating black or Chicano history, the consequences of student tracking, or the importance of hiring more minority teachers.

*Outer-directed teacher subcoalitions:* A subcoalition of teachers often emerged and become active when outside (e.g., central office, districtwide, teachers' union) issues emerged, such as salaries and benefits, teacher selection, teacher evaluation, or additional time demands on after-school activities.

*Teacher-pedagogical alliances:* Most schools had informal teacher alliances based on shared beliefs about teaching. These subcoalitions were organized around a philosophical-pedagogical orientation to what should be taught in schools and how it should be taught. Specifically, the researchers frequently encountered conservative-essentialist teachers banding together and arguing about such things as declining academic standards, the need for more basic education, and a stricter approach to student discipline. The liberal-progressive teacher coalition, on the other hand, pressed concerns about the negative effects of classifying students through test scores, the need for relevant and meaningful educational experiences, and the importance of building a sense of self-discipline within the students (as opposed to externally enforced discipline). *Administrator-specialist-teacher alliances:* Temporary alliances of specific teachers, administrators, and specialists sometimes emerged. These alliances were typically formed as a base from which to influence the central office on problems affecting the whole school, such as a pending program funding cut, or the need to obtain additional specialized teachers.

The list of formal and informal subcoalitions identified here is not all-inclusive nor were these same subcoalitions found in every school. The significant point is that specific, identifiable subcoalitions representing specific interests were found in *all* schools. Some of these subcoalitions were relatively enduring while others formed and broke apart with the rise and decline of specific issues. Also, interestingly enough, specific administrators and teachers at times formed informal alliances that would bridge their own spheres of influence to tackle an emergent schoolwide problem.[31]

It is important to note the leadership roles of the principals, who typically played important parts in establishing the levels of coordination and collaboration achieved in schools. The researchers concluded that those school administrators who were most knowledgeable about the informal coalitions and could work *through* them instead of *against* them had the most success in implementing new academic programs. These administrators were able to build a large coalition out of several smaller subcoalitions.

The impact on the broader teacher or administrator sphere of influence was significant. The individual subcoalitions and alliances of subcoalitions gave the broader spheres of influence a direction through a cohesiveness on priorities, or a lack of direction through fragmentation and infighting over specific issues. In attempting to manage events in the schools, it became quite clear that the formal powers the principals exhibited were quite limited.

## Weak Power of the Principalship

A school does not have the command structure that is present in the industrial model. School principals do not have the formal authority to command the obedience of teachers in the classroom, nor do they have control over other influential means of controlling behavior.[32] In their study of schools in five states, Floden et al., for example, found that "few districts tended to use appeals to power. Teachers do not generally believe that they will be either rewarded for teaching the content indicated by district policies or punished for failing to teach that content."[33]

The principalship lacks most of the bases of power found in industrial models. The salary reward structure of teachers, for example, is set primarily by seniority. Routine classroom supervision can be escaped by just closing the classroom door. Personnel costs consume most of the budget, which leaves little discretionary money to play with. Subjects, amounts of time, methods, and focus of instruction tend to be set by state and district policy, textbook publishers, and university admissions requirements.

For personal satisfaction as well as professional advancement in their careers, principals need to get along with their teachers. "As a result," Lortie writes, "many principals take few risks with new programs and seek to build strong personal relations with teachers."[34]

Principals typically are not inclined to intrude in the world behind the classroom door because close supervision practices or attempts to revise the instructional program can endanger close and comfortable working relationships with the teachers. Informal noninterference pacts or "treaties" that provide for peaceful coexistence between teachers and administrators often emerge as part of the culture of the organization.[35]

Firestone and Wilson found a certain ambivalence governing the teacher-principal relationship.

> Teachers look to their principal for certain kinds of support. They want to know that the principal will maintain an orderly climate in the school and back them when they have discipline problems. Too, they want protection from parents and community groups who challenge their decisions. Finally, they look to the principal for moral support, for a word of praise after spending almost all their working day with no adult contact. At the same time, they want autonomy to teach the way they want and often what they want.[36]

The pacts negotiated at the Silverwood schools were almost always respected except in those few cases when a major problem arose in one of the classrooms. Under those conditions, the principal intervened under the umbrella of instructional supervision and leadership to help resolve the issue.

A popular rhetoric stresses the importance of school administrators concentrating their time and energy on the tasks of instructional leadership. Do we practice what we preach? Unfortunately, we don't now and never have.

Larry Cuban assembled 15 studies, conducted from 1911 to 1981, that reflect on how principals spend their time in schools. In all 15 cases, the principals spent most of their time on administrative tasks. In the four studies reported since 1975, involvement in instructional activities (as reported through structured observation techniques) for the three studies of elementary schools were 17 percent, 5 percent, and 27 percent, respectively. The high school instructional supervision time was 17 percent.[37]

Certainly, we may quarrel over research issues as sampling and data-gathering techniques used in these fifteen studies. Nevertheless, the sum of the evidence is quite clear, as Boyd and Crowson point out: School administrators give most of their attention to managing the school and pupil control.[38] Responding to the challenge of engaging a majority of time and energy in the practice of direct instructional leadership still remains ahead of us.

However, as Sister Kleine-Kracht observes, even though teachers are not always receptive to principals face-to-face initiatives, the importance of *indirect* actions of instructional leadership should not be discounted. Principals' efforts to shape a supportive instructional environment within the school (e.g., high achievement expectations, participating parents, quality teacher selection, teacher empowerment) can have an important influence on the teaching-learning process.[39]

In sum, the existence of norms of teacher autonomy and the lack of significant administrator control over formal reward structures (e.g., budget, salary levels, and increases) tend to reinforce the presence of separate bureaucratic and professional spheres of influence. Thus, the question becomes: How are decisions made when these two spheres of influence overlap?

## The Negotiated Order

The spheres of influence do not, of course, come as neatly separate entities. As Figure 4.1 illustrated, a considerable amount of overlap exists between the spheres; this area is referred to as the *contested zone*. Table 4.1 illustrated the type of decisions that fall in the contested zone, ranging from setting the master schedule to campus supervision.

Key issues within the contested zone revolve around such issues as how decisions are made, how collaborative actions are structured, and how problems are solved. A process must be worked out that insures that all parties clearly understand what must be done, who is to do it, and when. The process must insure minimum levels of conflict and thus secure sufficient order to get the job done.

Hospital literature also is useful in providing insight into this important issue because hospitals too have a contested zone between professionals and bureaucrats. In a case study by Strauss et al., the authors write that in the contested zone, "professionals and nonprofessionals are implicated together in a great web of negotiation." Thus, when a problem flares up, "a complicated process of negotiation, of bargaining, of give-and-take necessarily begins," and the authors refer to the outcome as the "negotiated order."[40]

The negotiations in schools are informal rather than formal and virtually everyone participates when their interests are involved. When a troublesome situation arises for an individual or group, it seeks to spin a network of negotiation around it. Teachers negotiate with administrators for a different approach to handling tough discipline cases, administrators negotiate with teachers for more parent contact, students negotiate with teachers for less homework, teachers negotiate with janitors for replacing a burnt-out light-bulb now instead of tomorrow, department chairpersons negotiate with office secretaries for typing a specific letter ahead of all the others on the pile, and so on.

The agreements made in the contested zone are usually temporary and fragile, subject to renegotiation the next time the same issue surfaces. Because of the constant flow of small and large tasks that emerge in the contested zone, the teachers and administrators constantly shift their energies and efforts to new problems and negotiations that enable them to get through each day. The end product of the ongoing negotiation process is to bring an acceptable degree of order and stability to a zone of potential disruption and discord.

### Loosely Coupled Systems

An additional concept that provides insight into the negotiated order is Karl Weick's notion of "loosely coupled systems." Weick writes that the concept intends to convey the image that coupled events are responsive, but that each event also preserves its own identity and some evidence of its physical or logical separateness. Thus, in the case of an educational organization, it may be the case that the counselor's office is loosely coupled to the principal's office. The image is that the principal and the counselor are somehow attached, but that each retains some identity and separateness and that their attachment may be circumscribed, infrequent, weak in its mutual effects, unimportant, and/or slow to respond.[41]

As pointed out earlier in this chapter, the separate spheres of influence maintain degrees of autonomy and decisional discretion. Thus, at times the spheres have loose coupling, which suggests they are tied together weakly with a qualified interdependence.

The Silverwood researchers observed that a large measure of the coupling took place in the contested zone of the school and concluded the firmer (clearly established and agreed upon) the negotiated order the tighter the coupling, and vice versa. The researchers found the tightness in the intersphere coupling between the teachers and the administrators varied with the situation confronted, and frequently the membership of these two bodies acted in concert where they might normally act with relative autonomy.

The researchers identified five primary situations signaling a tightening of the intersphere coupling:

1.  Responses to legal decisions, such as modifications in the language programs in accord with new state laws
2.  Conditions of crisis, such as the time the new sex education program in a secondary school came under fire from an active group of parents
3.  Situations where outside evaluation was imminent, such as the pending arrival of an accreditation team
4.  The potential for a negative community reaction existed, such as in the selection of instructional materials that would not offend any ethnic population
5.  Time was extremely limited, such as when a federal grant application deadline approached

Given the lack of a command structure bridging the professional-bureaucratic interface, the next research question becomes: Are the teachers and administrators willing to give one another complete discretion of action in their own sphere of influence?

## Behavioral Management Across Spheres

"Because subordinates are personally affected by their superiors' decisions, they seek to influence them."[42] In the Silverwood schools teachers employed some subtle and some less subtle practices of behavioral management when trying to manage events taking place in the administrators' sphere of influence, and administrators tried to manage events taking place within the teachers' sphere. These tactics frequently were quite creative and at times unrecognized by the other parties. Direct intervention usually was avoided whenever possible.

## How Administrators Manage Teacher Behavior

The basic strategies administrators used involved manipulating the teachers' intrinsic reward structure and manipulating the normative sense of being a professional inherent in most teachers. (Manipulation is used here in a sociological sense and has no negative connotation attached.) For example, a principal responded to the following question:

*Q:* Do you have strategies you employ to get teachers to adopt new activities?

*A:* Yes, probably the most successful is positive reinforcement. In other words, we get one teacher started who really believes in it and makes it a success. By praising this teacher in a staff meeting, I make her feel good and successful. Everyone wants to feel like this, so soon other teachers start coming to my office and say, "Come and see such and such," and I find they have copied what the other teacher has done. This is the way to get my attention and they know that.

Manipulating the teacher's normative sense of being a professional is used frequently to give the administrator leverage. An official in the district observed:

I hear over and over in the school, "We are professionals." You hear it in about every sentence. Those words imply there are certain things we don't do. There is a certain code of behavior to which we adhere. And who defines what is professional or unprofessional? The administrator does.

A variation of the "We are professionals; therefore, we will do this and not that" theme surrounded the teacher-student relationship. In the Silverwood schools, it was common to hear administrators telling teachers (and teachers telling teachers), "We must do this because it is best for the kids." Administrators could be referring to almost anything that reflected current district policy: team teaching, individual instruction, cross-age teaching, or the whiz-bang reading method. No hard data were presented to support the administrator's contention, because clear and convincing evidence was rarely available to support one method over another. The conviction, based more or less on face validity, was, "This is best for kids, and for you (the teacher) to do less is not fulfilling your professional responsibility."

Direct appeals to the moral conviction of teachers who want to fulfill their professional responsibility and do what is best for their students can move large numbers of teachers to extraordinary efforts. In the Silverwood schools, teachers expended vast sums of energy and devoted enormous blocks of their own time to fulfilling their professional responsibilities.

These behavioral management practices are social mechanisms of control that take the place of a command structure often found in bureaucratic organizations that do not have professional employees.

## How Teachers Manage Administrator Behavior

Teachers in the Silverwood schools were also observed using informal tactics for managing administrator behavior. At times it would be undramatic, such as a single teacher asking the principal for additional resources for a specific class. At other times, however, it could get very dramatic, such as when a group of teachers marched into a principal's office, demanded a greater voice in the selection of new personnel, and threatened to march down to the central office and see the superintendent if they did not get their way.

A common occurrence was for teachers to form coalitions among subgroups and then take collective stands on an issue at faculty meetings. The sense of unanimity among teachers often made a convincing impression on the administrators. Bridges has captured the essence of the tactics of informal management in his discussion of the administrator as a pawn of subordinates. He describes three such conditions: pawn without the administrator's knowledge, pawn against the administrator's will, and pawn by choice.[43]

All three situations Bridges defined existed in varying degrees in the Silverwood schools. Significantly, principals considered the third condition, "pawn by choice," the ideal role—even beyond some form of unilateral control.

However, attempts at informal management between spheres of influence were not always well received, and frequently the members of each sphere found themselves actively protecting their domain from outside intrusion.

## Defending the Spheres

In the day-to-day conduct of affairs, the teachers and administrators in the Silverwood schools went about their jobs in predictable, systematic ways, following established patterns. The school district, however, had a history of adopting innovative practices that might be passed down to teachers as mandates or as increasingly intensified pressure for change. In any case, superordinates launched an attempt at direct intervention.

### Teachers Defending Their Domain

Teachers respond in differing ways when they feel their domain is being challenged. Many teachers adjust their thinking and practices as quickly as possible from the conviction that this is the proper response of a professional. Other teachers dig in their heels and hold the line against what they see as bandwagon fads that roll through this nation's educational system like ocean waves. After all, no hard data illustrate convincingly that a current fad is any better than the last one. The more traditional teachers also view themselves as guardians of the classrooms, interpreting their professional duty as preserving the "tried and true" in the students' best interests.

Both types of teachers respond to what they consider the best interests of the profession; therefore, both see their actions as legitimate. When assuming a defensive posture, teachers in the Silverwood schools who did not support a proposed change argued, "We are not given extra time, equipment, or resources to perform this new activity," or "If we do this we will be lowering our standards." A classic defensive response was, "I've been teaching for 35 years, and I've been successful with 90 percent of my kids." Because pedagogical issues are still relatively judgmental, it is difficult for anyone, including administrators, to put forth an objective (as opposed to subjective) argument to this position. After all, who is to say these teachers and all others like them might not be right in their self-evaluations?

The following comment by a teacher is interesting because it describes the defensive position and suggests that the professional responsibility of teachers is to stand firm against intrusions into their affairs.

> The district is going to milk you for everything they can. If they can get you to handle a classroom of 40 kids without an aide or 200 learning packets a night—if you are dumb enough to do it—they are going to let you keep doing it. My thought is, *what will happen to the kids if I don't keep holding out?* [emphasis added]

Teachers in the Silverwood schools appeared to possess what might be called a "pocket veto" over administrative attempts to intervene in instructional events in the classroom. The concept of a pocket veto is used because its power is exerted through *inaction;* in other words, the teachers simply did not respond to requests or mandates for change. Witness the comments of one teacher.

> When I came here the big thrust then was—and I believe we have a new education game we play every year—the big thrust then was teaming. Two teachers were to develop a program and instruct together. In some cases it just didn't work out. In our case we could see that day by day we were falling away from the work we had set up originally, and we couldn't make it work for us. We didn't tell the principal about it and just got busy with new ideas because a new wave came in about that time called individualized learning. I'm sure the principal was finally aware of it, but he didn't say anything about it; and we haven't said anything to him.

The principal of a school is usually the one who directly encounters the teachers' defensive stands. In describing the strategies she has encountered, one principal observed:

> A few teachers feel comfortable enough to come to me and talk over their disagreement with district policy and openly say "I don't agree, and this is what I am doing." I have others who will wait until they have an audience, like at a staff meeting, and a few will band together and argue against it, trying to get others to go along. Others say, "Okay, I'll try it," but they are playing a game because after a month they will say, "See, it didn't work." Actually, they weren't going to let it work. We would go into their classrooms and find that they were only doing pieces of it. And it was a deliberate . . . plot to prove that the method they have been using for years and years is better than this new method.

Many teachers were magnificent actors who made it appear as though they were in complete support of an administrator's formal or informal intervention while all the time they ignored its intent. It is important to note these teachers typically were not lazy or incompetent; they genuinely saw themselves as the guardians of the classroom and had to hold the line against what they considered fads and classroom gimmicks that enjoy a short burst of popularity across the country and then fade away.

However, as the next section points out, administrators also know something about taking defensive stands.

## Administrators Defending Their Domain

The researchers found that different school administrators used different protective tactics to defend their domain, but all did in fact employ some tactics. Administrators had one advantage over teachers since administrators could directly say no to the teachers' requests. The formal hierarchical roles of administrators permitted that type of response. However, administrators avoided direct negative responses to the teachers' requests because whenever possible administrators usually wanted to appear supportive of the teacher role.

The administrators' tactics of defending their domain against a perceived outside intrusion attempt (e.g., proposals, demands) fell into the following patterns: *ignore it* (decide not to decide and hope the proposal dies a natural death); *delay it* (leave the proposal off the agenda of the faculty meeting); *study it* (form a committee and pack it with sympathetic members); *buck it* (pass the buck upward and claim the superintendent won't support such a proposal); or *publicly support it* (privately use a pocket veto).

As was the case with the teachers, in taking these actions the administrators generally did not scc themselves or the researchers as unmotivated or self-seeking. They typically had in mind what they considered the best interests of the school.

A field study such as this usually attempts to move from a system of description to a system of explanation and finally to a set of generalizations, propositions, or hypotheses that are derived from the data. Propositions drawn from the data are presented in the next section.

# Propositions

The propositions presented here represent the central characteristics of the Interacting Spheres Model that the researchers believe will be found in other settings. Testing for them using other methodologies is an important next step.

1. *Major proposition:* As the organizational environment of a school shifts from a placid to a turbulent condition, problems emerge that must be resolved with a milieu of multiple interacting spheres of influence.

2. *Major proposition:* The administrators' sphere of influence is organized around the rationalistic decisional requirements of a consistent and predictable environment, whereas the teachers' sphere is organized around the personalistic decisional requirements of an unencumbered and flexible environment.

 2.1 *Minor proposition:* Each sphere of influence has a measure of decision-making autonomy and power, with visible limits to both.

 2.2 *Minor proposition:* The understanding and acceptance of existing spheres of influence lend predictability and stability to the school's activities.

2.3 *Minor proposition:* Within the differing spheres of influence, formal and informal subcoalitions of members form to address and influence special interest issues.

3. *Major proposition:* Specific decisions that fall within more than one sphere of influence are resolved in a temporary way through informal negotiations.

3.1 *Minor proposition:* The spheres of influence that are linked together by the negotiated order form the basis of loosely coupled systems.

3.2 *Minor proposition:* The degree of looseness that characterizes the coupling between spheres of influence varies with the degree of perceived outside threat to the established activity of the school.

4. *Major proposition:* Administrators develop tactics to attempt informal interventions into the teachers' sphere of influence, and the teachers develop defensive strategies to defend their sphere against such outside interventions.

5. *Major proposition:* Teachers develop tactics to attempt informal interventions into the administrators' sphere of influence, and the administrators develop defensive strategies to defend their sphere against such outside interventions.

## Conclusion

With respect to contemporary issues of school governance, Corwin has observed:

> Most administrators were trained in an era when the problems of classroom teaching could be reduced (so it was thought) to the psychology of individual learners and when the central administrative problems seemed to revolve around efficient internal management. The current generation of teachers, by contrast, has been reared in a sociological era characterized by rapid social change and group conflict. Administration has become largely a matter of managing an increasingly complex balance of forces from outside as well as from within the schools. Many school administrators still in positions of authority today are not trained to cope with these problems.[44]

Corwin's view adds to the argument that our conceptual frameworks are proving less than satisfactory in useful description, analysis, and prediction of behavior and events in educational organizations.

As the introduction to this chapter points out, there is a need to develop a school-specific organizational model that can treat the features that make the school a unique organization. Toward that end, the research reported here resulted in the construction of a model that draws useful concepts and ideas from the conventional frameworks of classical hierarchical theory and social system theory. The principal area of interest is the interaction of the administrators (bureaucrats) and teachers (professionals).

The Interacting Spheres Model depicted in Figure 4.1 suggests that school governance and decision making take place within the context of multiple spheres of influence. Teachers and administrators maintain the dominant spheres at the school level.

Hence, school governance, defined as the control over the decision-making process, certainly is not the product of a hierarchy. Rather, school governance has coalescent and disjunctive qualities at its extremes. At times, control over decision making is dominated by administrators or teachers or both (within their domains) or shared (in the contested zone). In this sense, governance is coalescent—the work gets done, differentiation and integration exist between subcoalitions, and there are few surprises. At other times, however, struggles between spheres and/or within spheres develop, coordination and integration of subcoalitions are negligible, and limited unity, thus predictability, surrounds the decision-making process. In this context, school governance is relatively disjunctive and consequently is unable to respond effectively to the community's changing demands.[45]

Certainly the complexities of school governance are enormous and extend far beyond the range of this chapter. However, trying to understand issues of governance and decision making as processes taking place within interacting spheres of influence is an encouraging approach to a complex problem.

## Notes

1.  Cf. Max Abbott, "Hierarchical Impediments to Innovation in Educational Organizations," in *Organizations and Human Behavior: Focus on Schools,* F. Carver and T. Sergiovanni, eds. (New York: McGraw-Hill, 1969); J. G. Anderson, *Bureaucracy in Education* (Baltimore: Johns Hopkins University Press, 1968); and D. Rogers, *110 Livingston Street* (New York: Random House, 1968).

2.  Talcott Parsons in Introduction to Max Weber, *The Theory of Social and Economic Organization,* Talcott Parsons, ed., A. M. Henderson and T. Parsons, trans. (New York: Free Press, 1964), pp. 58–60; and Alvin Gouldner, *Patterns of Industrial Bureaucracy* (Glencoe, IL: The Free Press, 1954), pp. 22–24.

3.  Dan Lortie, "The Balance of Control and Autonomy in Elementary School Teaching," in *The Semi-Professions and Their Organizations,* Amitai Etzioni, ed. (New York: The Free Press, 1969); Edwin Bridges, "Administrative Man: Origin or Pawn in Decision-Making?" *Educational Administration Quarterly* 6 (1970); and Mark Hanson, "The Emerging Control Structure of Schools," *Administrator's Notebook* 21 (1973).

4.  Dan Lortie, "The Teacher and Team Teaching: Suggestions for Long-Range Research," in *Team Teaching,* J. T. Shapin and H. F. Olds, Jr., eds. (New York: Harper & Row, 1964), p. 273.

5.  Charles Bidwell, "The School as a Formal Organization," in *Handbook of Organizations,* J. G. March, ed. (Chicago: Rand McNally, 1965), p. 992.

6.  For a discussion of the special features of organizations incorporating a cadre of professionals see: Amitai Etzioni, "Administrative and Professional Authority," *Modern Organizations* (Englewood Cliffs, NJ: Prentice-Hall, 1964), ch. 8; and Henry Mintzberg, "The Professional Bureaucracy," *The Structuring of Organizations* (Englewood Cliffs, NJ: Prentice Hall, 1979), ch. 19.

7.  Herbert A. Simon, *Administrative Behavior* (New York: Macmillan, 1957), p. 4.

8.  For a discussion of the concept of the teacher as a semiprofessional see: Lortie, "The Balance of Control and Autonomy."

9.  W. Richard Scott, "Field Methods in the Study of Organizations," in *Handbook of Organizations,* James G. March, ed. (Chicago: Rand McNally, 1965), p. 262.

10.  Methodological aspects of the field study approach employed in this research can be found in the following: Harry Wolcott, "Criteria for an Ethnographic Approach to Research in Schools," *Human Organization* 34 (Summer 1975); Frank Lutz and Laurence Iannaccone,

*Understanding Educational Organizations: A Field Study Approach* (Columbus, OH: Charles E. Merrill, 1969); Stephen Wilson, "The Use of Ethnographic Techniques in Educational Research," *Review of Educational Research* 47 (1977); and Marion Lundy Dobbert, *Ethnographic Research:Theory and Application for Modern Schools and Societies* (New York: Praeger, 1982).

11. This paper represents a synthesis of studies conducted on selected schools of a single school district. Individual component parts of the research are reported elsewhere. Because of space limitations, the "raw data" cannot be reported here but can be found in the originals of the following: E. Mark Hanson, "Beyond the Bureaucratic Model: A Study of Power and Autonomy in Educational Decision-Making," *Interchange* 7 (1976); E. Mark Hanson, "The Professional/Bureaucratic Interface: A Case Study," *Urban Education* 11 (October 1976); Michael E. Brown, "A Contingency Approach to Educational Decision Making: A Case Study of Governance in the High School," Ph.D. dissertation, University of California, Riverside, 1976; and Edith B. McKenzie, "Multiple Interacting Spheres of Influence: A Contingency Model of School Governance," Ph.D. dissertation, University of California, Riverside, 1977.

12. Lortie, "The Balance of Control and Autonomy," pp. 35–36.

13. Several studies have focused on this issue; for example, see: Dan C. Lortie, *School Teacher* (Chicago: The University of Chicago Press, 1975); and Daniel L. Duke, Beverly K. Showers, and Michael Imber, "Teachers and Shared Decision Making: The Costs and Benefits of Involvement," *Educational Administration Quarterly* 16 (1980): 93–106.

14. Bidwell, "The School as a Formal Organization," pp. 976–977.

15. Carol Weiss, Joseph Cambone, Alexander Wyeth, "Trouble in Paradise: Teacher Conflicts in Shared Decision Making," *Educational Administration Quarterly,* 28 (1992): 351.

16. Samuel Bacharach and Joseph Shedd, "Power and Empowerment: The Constraining Myths and Emerging Structures of Teacher Unionism in an Age of Reform," in *Politics of Education Yearbook,* Robert Crowson and Jane Hannaway, eds. (London: Falmer Press, 1989).

17. William Firestone and Bruce Wilson, "Using Bureaucratic and Cultural Linkages to Improve Instruction: The Principal's Contribution," *Educational Administration Quarterly* 21 (1985): 13.

18. Fred E. Katz, *Autonomy and Organization: The Limits of Social Control* (New York: Random House, 1968), p. 18.

19. Ibid.

20. A. Kaplan, "Power in Perspective," in *Power and Conflict in Organizations,* R. Kahn and E. Boulding, eds. (New York: Basic Books, 1964), pp. 13–14.

21. Ronald G. Corwin, "Models of Educational Organizations," in *Review of Research in Education,* Vol. 2, F. Kerlinger, ed. (Itaska, IL: F. E. Peacock, 1974), p. 257.

22. Cf. Myron Lieberman, *Education as a Profession* (Englewood Cliffs, NJ: Prentice-Hall, 1956); and Lortie, "The Teacher and Team Teaching."

23. Ronald G. Corwin, "The School as an Organization," in *The School in Society,* S. Sieber and D. Wilder, eds. (New York: The Free Press, 1973), p. 165.

24. Michael Lipsky, *Street-Level Bureaucracy: Dilemmas of the Individual in Public Services* (New York: Russell Sage Foundation, 1980), p. 151.

25. Robert Floden et al., "Instructional Leadership at the District Level: A Closer Look at Autonomy and Control," *Educational Administration Quarterly* 24 (1988): 99.

26. Lipsky, p. 13.

27. For a complete presentation of decisions in all categories see: Brown, "A Contingency Approach to Educational Decision Making."

28. R. M. Cyert and James G. March, *A Behavioral Theory of the Firm* (Englewood Cliffs, NJ: Prentice-Hall, 1963).

29.  Neal Gross and Anne Trask, "Some Organizational Forces Influencing the Role of the Teacher," *Educational Horizons* 38 (1960): 173–174.

30.  For a detailed analysis of formally and informally organized subcoalitions see: McKenzie, "Multiple Interacting Spheres of Influence," ch. 4.

31.  For a discussion of coalitions as political bargaining units see: Samuel B. Bacharach and Edward J. Lawler, *Power and Politics in Organizations* (San Francisco: Jossey-Bass, 1980).

32.  J.M.B. Fraatz, "Political Principals: Efficiency, Effectiveness, and the Political Dynamics of School Administration." *Qualitative Studies in Education* 2 (1989), p. 22.

33.  Floden, p. 108.

34.  Dan Lortie, *Education News* (1988): 10.

35.  William Boyd and William Hartman, "The Politics of Educational Productivity," in *Micro-Level School Finance,* D. H. Monk and J. Underwood, eds. (Cambridge, MA: Ballinger, forthcoming).

36.  Firestone and Wilson, p. 20.

37.  Larry Cuban, *The Managerial Imperative: The Practice of Leadership in Schools* (New York: SUNY Press, 1988), p. 62.

38.  William Boyd and Robert Crowson, "The Changing Conception and Practice of Public School Administration," in *Review of Research in Education,* vol. 9, David Berliner, ed. (Washington, DC: AERA, 1981), pp. 357–358.

39.  Sister Paula Kleine-Kracht, "Indirect Instructional Leadership: An Administrator's Choice," *Educational Administration Quarterly* 29 (1993), pp. 197–212.

40.  Anselm Strauss, et al., "The Hospital and Its Negotiated Order," in *The Hospital in Modern Society,* Eliot Freidson, cd. (New York: The Free Press of Glencoe, 1963). For a discussion of this concept in education see: Peter M. Hall and Dee Ann Spencer-Hall, "The Social Condition of the Negotiated Order," *Urban Life* 11 (1982): 328–349.

41.  Karl E. Weick, "Educational Organizations as Loosely Coupled Systems," *Administrative Science Quarterly* 21 (1976): 3.

42.  Willard Lane, Ronald Corwin, and William Monahan, *Foundations of Educational Administration: A Behavioral Analysis* (New York: Macmillan, 1966), p. 135.

43.  Bridges, "Administrative Man," p. 12.

44.  Ronald G. Corwin, *Education in Crisis: A Sociological Analysis of Schools and Universities in Transition* (New York: John Wiley and Sons, 1974), pp. 238–239.

45.  Joan Talbert and Milbrey McLaughlin, "Teacher Professionalism in Local School Contexts," *American Journal of Education* 102 (1994): 123–153.

*C h a p t e r* **5**

# *Open System Theory and Schools*

Off the coastal waters of North Korea on January 23, 1968, the USS *Pueblo* was captured under a hail of gunfire by North Korean naval vessels. Thus began a drama that was to hold the attention of the world press for almost two years. The *Pueblo* was a World War II auxiliary supply vessel resurrected from a mothball fleet and fitted out as a spy vessel acting as an oceanographic research ship. Placed under the command of Lloyd M. Bucher, the *Pueblo's* Operational Orders leading her into that fateful mission read in part:

DETERMINE KORCOM AND SOVIET REACTION RESPECTIVELY TO AN OVERT INTELLIGENCE COLLECTOR OPERATING NEAR KORCOM PERIPHERY AND ACTIVELY CONDUCTING SURVEILLANCE OF U.S.S.R. NAVAL UNITS.

ESTIMATE OF RISK: MINIMAL, SINCE PUEBLO WILL BE OPERATING IN INTERNATIONAL WATERS FOR ENTIRE DEPLOYMENT: [KORCOM is navalese for Korean Communist.][1]

On January 23, the *Pueblo* was unexpectedly surrounded and fired upon by five gunboats using 57-mm cannons and machine guns. One of the *Pueblo* crewmen was killed outright and several more were wounded, including Commander Bucher, who was struck by several pieces of shrapnel. During the attack, the crew of the *Pueblo* worked feverishly to destroy their classified documents and equipment. An armed boarding party finally forced a halt to all activity on the *Pueblo,* thus leaving undestroyed an extensive amount of highly classified material in the hands of an old enemy.

The reaction by many of the Navy's top brass was furious and visceral. " 'It's a goddamn disgrace,' one admiral said. 'I'll tell you what I would have done. I would have headed zero-nine-zero [due east] as fast as I could and opened up on the first patrol boat and put it out of action. I would have gone down fighting.' "[2] Another admiral exclaimed," 'I just can't believe that this man Bucher would not have tried to fight—no matter what his orders were. . . . I'd have scuttled the ship if I couldn't do anything else. A Navy ship just shouldn't have to go down in defeat that way. I'd rather see it sunk.' " However, Commander Bucher's perspective of the situation differed considerably from those presented above, as he would later recount. "You can liken *Pueblo's* position on the day of her capture to that of a man with a holstered .22 pistol standing in the middle of an open field surrounded by forty men with guns drawn and aimed at him from a distance of twenty yards. Not much chance for him to escape or offer meaningful resistance, is there?"[3]

The USS *Pueblo* incident is important to those interested in behavior in organizations, because it is a good example of two different perspectives being used to analyze the same episode, resulting in two different conclusions being drawn from the same phenomena. In this instance, the military applied the precepts of classical organization theory, and Commander Bucher examined the events through an open system perspective.

After 11 months of incarceration in a North Korean compound, the officers and crew of the *Pueblo* returned home. On January 30, 1969, a court of inquiry was convened in which five admirals met for over 200 hours to hear testimony from 104 witnesses who provided 3,392 single-spaced, legal-sized pages of testimony. After many weeks of testimony and deliberation, the members of the court of inquiry reported the following:

> The Court recommends that Commander Bucher be tried by General Court-Martial and charged with the following alleged offenses under the Uniform Code of Military Justice:
> 1. Permitting his ship to be searched while he had power to resist.
> 2. Failing to take immediate and aggressive protective measures when his ship was attacked by North Korean forces.
> 3. Complying with the orders of the North Korean forces to follow them into port.
> 4. Negligently failing to completely destroy all classified material aboard the USS Pueblo and permitting such material to go into the hands of the North Koreans.
> 5. Negligently failing to insure before departure for sea that his officers and crew were properly organized, stationed, and trained for emergency destruction of classified material.[4]

In gathering evidence leading up to these charges, the court tended to focus its attention on *events immediately relating to the seizure of the Pueblo*. Was the captain aware of his ultimate responsibility for his ship? Why didn't the captain try to shoot his way out? Were the crew members familiar with the Military Code of Conduct? Why did the captain keep the two machine guns covered? Were small arms broken out? Did the captain try to set fire to the ship or scuttle it? When the captain made his decision to surrender, did he make that decision without the counsel of his other officers? When the North Koreans set foot on the ship, did the captain have the power to resist? Was it not true that the captain was ultimately responsible for all classified material on the ship?

In his defense, Commander Bucher tried to turn the attention of the court to the network of support systems (1) within the ship and (2) between the ship and the outside world, which were supposed to function and protect the USS *Pueblo* but did not. Bucher tried to point out that most of these support systems were completely *outside* his control and that he therefore was virtually a helpless victim rather than a causal agent.

Bucher identified a number of support systems that broke down. The Navy assigned a Minimum Risk evaluation to the operation. The National Security Agency, however, issued a warning message dealing with the Minimum Risk designation of the *Pueblo's* mission. This warning message failed to reach Bucher's superior, the operational commander in charge of the mission, even though it had been seconded through the chain of command all the way to and including the joint chiefs of staff.

Two days prior to the capture of the *Pueblo,* a group of 30 North Korean infiltrators had crossed into South Korea in an attempt to assassinate President Park. The infiltrators were caught and killed before completing their mission, and the event made headlines around the world. Commander Bucher, however, was not informed of the situation, which had increased tensions in the area to the highest level seen for a long time.

The two U.S. Marine Corps interpreters assigned to the *Pueblo* did not possess a proficiency level in the Korean language that would enable them to discharge their duties. This deficiency became extremely critical at the time leading up to and during the attack. The interpreters heard but were unable to understand the orders flashing back and forth between the North Korean ships and the shore command posts as plans for the attack were mounted, and so they could not advise Bucher of the hostile intentions. Commander Bucher had not been informed of the interpreters' lack of proficiency in the language. At the time of assignment, however, the two Marine interpreters had informed their superiors of their lack of skill, but their warnings had gone unheeded.

Bucher had been briefed that contingency plans existed to bring U.S. aircraft into action to protect the *Pueblo* if she got into trouble. As the top priority messages flashed from the *Pueblo* advising her superiors of the desperate situation, U.S. Naval authorities attempted to locate aircraft to send in support. The U.S. Air Force had seven F-4s at bases in South Korea, but their racks were configured to carry nuclear weapons and not conventional bombs. Racks for the conventional bombs were stored in Japan. The other planes, including those belonging to the South Korean Air Force, had no air-to-ground capability and were no match for the North Korean MIGS. The United States had only 24 attack aircraft in Japan and none were combat ready.[5] However, the USS *Enterprise,* which had been sailing within 510 miles of the scene, had an attack capability. The aircraft carrier intercepted the *Pueblo's* messages, which had not been addressed to her, but she received no instructions from the command structure to go to the aid of the *Pueblo.* Hesitation, equivocation, and debate had set in throughout the command structure of the U.S. military. The *Pueblo* was tied up at a North Korean dock long before the Americans could prepare the response that Bucher had been promised.

Many of the internal systems within the *Pueblo* also contributed to her fate and were also outside the control of her captain. For example, a few days prior to sailing someone in the command structure decided that the *Pueblo* should be armed. Two 50-caliber machine guns were installed on deck, but no one who had been trained to use them was assigned to the ship. Bucher's commander also advised him to keep the guns covered, because the only real protection the *Pueblo* had against a potentially hostile gunship was the sanctity of freedom of the sea. Under attack by five gunships using 57-mm cannons and machine guns, Bucher did not uncover his two 50-calibers because he judged this would initiate the total destruction of his ship and crew.

For purposes of destroying many tons of classified documents and equipment, the crew possessed only a small incinerator, some sledge hammers, and axes. Onboard equipment included no capability for scuttling the ship. Prior to sailing, Bucher made numerous requests to superiors for sophisticated destruction devices as well as the necessary explosives to provide a capability to scuttle the ship in case of military necessity. Bucher's requests were not acted upon by his superiors. The captain of the *Pueblo* even tried to scrounge some TNT canisters from his old submarine friends, but that too proved to be impossible. Later at the court of inquiry, a headquarters intelligence officer testified that it would have taken one hour to destroy the classified material on the ship. Bucher vehemently disputed this, saying that from eight to nine hours would have been necessary. The captain of a sister spy ship *did* destroy such material when hearing of the *Pueblo's* fate, and it required 24 hours to do so.

Also, the *Pueblo's* intelligence-gathering mission was a separate detachment and not under the command of Commander Bucher, thus setting up a "ship-within-a-ship" arrangement. Therefore, Bucher was not in control of much that went on within his ship, and he was not even aware of how much classified written material and equipment were on board. Nor could he control much of the communication that flowed by radio from the intelligence-gathering section of the ship. Before sailing Bucher objected strongly to this unusual command arrangement within the *Pueblo*, but his concerns were ignored.

As Commander Bucher tried to prepare effective and efficient external (macro) and internal (micro) systems for his ship, he continually ran into a stagnant mentality and a code of regulations that were based on the assumptions that for 161 years U.S. Navy ships had been safe in peacetime in international waters; that nothing had happened to the *Pueblo's* sister spy ships on similar missions; and that nothing was going to happen to the *Pueblo*. As Armbrister writes, "No one has ever imagined that such a thing could happen. And this is the most disturbing aspect of the entire affair. . . . So in a sense *Pueblo* was a doomed ship, her fate sealed in advance, not so much by the North Koreans as by the Americans themselves"[6]

Several months after the court of inquiry recommended a court martial for Commander Bucher, one of the officers who sat on the court of inquiry, Admiral Bowen, made an observation that places in clear relief the classical theory perspective.

> That man could have been the greatest hero in the history of the U.S. Navy, but he let government property get away. When the captain fails, the system fails [emphasis added]. It opens up seams all the way to the top. For a commanding officer to do anything other

than guard his ship with his life is indefensible. I'll admit it takes guts; that's what you gotta have. The thought of saving his crew is interesting, humane, but it had nothing at all to do with the job he was assigned to do. Tradition? Yes. The reason it's tradition is that most people have done it.[7]

The contrary point of view would hold that *when the system fails, the captain fails.* The captain as leader is only a person at the interface of the macro and micro systems. If these macro and micro systems have major flaws built into their structures that are beyond the control of the leader, there is little that a leader can do to save the situation. It wasn't until May 1990, 21 years after the *Pueblo's* officers and crew were released, that the Navy finally awarded Bucher and his men the medal extended to all American prisoners of war.

The objective of this chapter is to introduce the third major conceptual lens that facilitates our understanding of issues of organization and management in education. *Open system theory* concentrates on the dependency relationships and exchanges between the organization and its external environment. An organization such as a school is a creature of its environment because it is supported by and in turn supports the social, political, and cultural offerings and demands of society.

In the late 1980s, the RAND Corporation studied six large, central-city school systems in an attempt to understand the processes by which educational improvement was begun and sustained. In a concluding statement, the RAND authors illustrate that their methodological approach to the research included an open system perspective.

> Communitywide educational improvement strategies have two strands: an outside strand that gathers broad community support and resources and an inside strand that changes the ways schools are run and instruction is delivered. In many cities, the outside strand is the more fully developed of the two. The prospects for real and sustained improvements in the schools are greatest where the inside and outside strands are both well developed and closely articulated.[8]

This chapter will discuss the special characteristics of the relationship of the school with its environment. The conceptual framework of a management information system will also be discussed as the mechanism that links the school system with the constantly shifting environment. The chapter concludes with an identification of the basic assumptions underlying open system theory as contrasted with those underlying classical organization theory.

The next section of this chapter will examine the special characteristics of an organization when it is conceptualized as a system.

## *The Concept of System*

Following World War II, the depth and scope of the various fields of science expanded at a near-explosive rate. Greater levels of knowledge, however, did not bring about closer collaboration between the scientific disciplines. The founder of general systems theory, Ludwig von Bertalanffy, wrote, "The physicist, the biologist, the psychologist and

the social scientist are, so to speak, encapsulated in a private universe, and it is difficult to get word from one cocoon to another.[9]

Regarding the special characteristics of a system, Parsons and Shils write:

> The most general and fundamental property of a system is the interdependence of
> parts or variables. Interdependence consists of the existence of determinate relation-
> ships among the parts or variables as contrasted with randomness of variability. In other
> words, interdependence is order in the relationship among the components which
> enter into a system.[10]

The elements of a system can be *symbols,* such as a language. They can also be
*objects,* such as desks, books, and light fixtures in a classroom. The elements of a system can be *subjects,* such as the teachers in a high school. Hence, a system is made
up of an aggregation of the living and nonliving entities of symbols, objects, and subjects that contribute to the character of the patterns of behavior existing in the system.

Like Chinese boxes, systems contain wholes within wholes, just as human organs
are made up of cells that are made up of molecules. Similarly, organizations are made
up of groups that are composed of individuals.[11]

Systems can be understood in terms of varying levels of complexity. Kenneth
Boulding identifies several levels of system complexity, four of which are important to
this chapter.

1. *Frameworks:* This is the most basic level of system complexity in which there
   is a static or fixed relationship of the parts to a whole. A chair or the anatomy
   of an animal are examples.
2. *Clockworks:* This is a simple dynamic system that permits movement within
   highly defined parameters. A watch or solar system are examples.
3. *Cybernetic system:* This system is capable of a limited amount of self-regulation, such as a thermostat.
4. *Open system:* This is a self-maintaining system that regulates its existence by
   importing from and exporting to its environment.[12]

Adopting an open system perspective does more than simply bring the external
environment into the picture. It shifts attention from organization to organizing, from
structure to process.[13]

## Open System Theory

The notion of open system theory is often used rather imprecisely. When speaking of
open system theory, it is wise to emphasize the words of Katz and Kahn.

> In some respects open-system theory is not a theory at all; it does not pretend to the
> specific sequences of cause and effect, the specific hypotheses and tests of hypotheses
> which are basic elements of theory. Open-system theory is rather a framework, a meta-
> theory, a model in the broadest sense of that overused term. Open-system theory is an

approach and a conceptual language for understanding and describing many kinds and levels of phenomena.[14]

Although the evolution of organizational thought had been significantly advanced through the articulation of classical theory and sociopolitical group theory, as pointed out in Chapter Two and Three, a major conceptual link was missing until the 1950s (see Figure 1.1). That link is the one that ties an organization into a dependency relationship with its surrounding environment. Without that link, an organization is viewed as a closed system that somehow stands alone, isolated and unaffected by its own environment. A conceptual model that considered the interactive nature of the organization and its environment was necessary.

Although social scientists and practitioners were working with conceptual models that forced a closed system perspective (e.g., the hierarchical model of classical theory), the organizations were in reality open systems interacting with and being influenced by their surrounding environments. Educators just did not understand them as such on an intellectual level. Talbert, Mclaughlin and Rowan point out that

> it is not surprising that social science and policy research in education has paid little attention to the relations between classroom processes and factors in the immediate and distant environment of schooling. The fact that school teaching occurs within the confines of classrooms, where teachers are insulated from colleagues' and administrators' scrutiny and support, gives the impression that teaching is buffered against influences beyond the classroom. Indeed, "behind the classroom door" became the catch-phrase explanation of variability in teachers' practices and the problematic relationship between policy and practice.[15]

Thus, organizations such as open systems have not changed through time; social scientists have just developed a more sophisticated understanding of how organizations have always worked. The clearer perspective on the functioning of organizations such as schools give social scientists better tools with which to analyze and predict human behavior. The practitioner also gains greater insight into managing system operations more effectively and efficiently. Applying an open system perspective to the events surrounding the seizure of the USS *Pueblo* sheds much more light on the factors contributing to this tragedy than the sole application of classical theory ever could.

## Cycles of Events

In classical theory an *organizational structure* is thought of as "the relationship of roles" within a hierarchy. This perspective of an organization shapes a *static* as opposed to a *dynamic* state. A static state can be conceptualized as a still photograph in which the properties present are fixed (stable) in their relationships. A dynamic state, on the other hand, can be conceptualized as a motion picture in which the properties engage in constant action over time. Allport shifted the perspective of an organization from a static to a dynamic state when he conceptualized organizational structure as *recurring cycles of events.*[16]

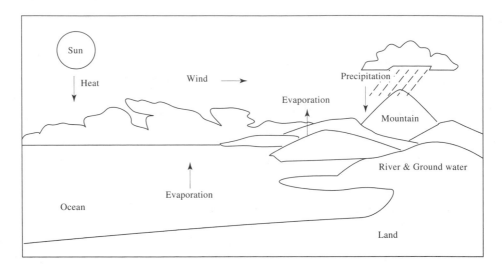

FIGURE 5.1  The Fresh Water Cycle

Figure 5.1 represents a cycle of events that results in an ongoing system. The various events in the water cycle must occur over and over again in a more or less patterned fashion or the cycle will break down. The sun must come up to generate heat, which initiates evaporation, which is picked up as moisture by the wind and blown toward land surfaces, and so on. If one event in the cycle ceases to occur, the cycle breaks down; in this case, a desert would result. Someone trying to understand the phenomenon of rainfall without understanding the various events that contribute to the fresh water cycle would attribute the phenomenon to nothing short of magic.

Two points should be emphasized here. First, the cycle must be self-reinforcing or it will run down and die; that is, it will disintegrate through what is called the *entropic process*.[17] In a condition of negative entropy, the system receives and stores more energy than it expends. Therefore, it can survive and perhaps even flourish. Second, the cycle must continue over time if a system can be said to exist. If the sequence of events takes place only once or just a few times, only a sequence of actions has taken place and no real system exists. Our next step is to turn to the school and examine it as a complex of self-reinforcing cycles of events.

## Cycles of Events in the School

An organization is structured by what might be thought of as an entire network of major and minor cycles that are interdependent, reinforcing and together make up the whole system. In the school, for example, a major cycle can be seen in the patterned events of an academic year. Students enroll at the beginning of the year, the teacher-learning process is engaged, examinations are given, grades are noted, credits are accumulated, and at the end of the year students are promoted or they graduate. Then the cycle begins anew with the next year. At the high school level, four yearly cycles make up the complete academic program for the students.

The yearly cycles can be broken down into numerous minor cycles for each department, informal group, program, classroom, teacher, or student. Within time frames of hourly, daily, weekly, monthly, or yearly patterns, cycles of events for each element in the system can be identified. The Monday cycle of a teacher, for example, might be to get out of bed, eat breakfast, drive to school, teach five hourly classes, counsel students during the sixth period, attend a meeting, go home, grade student homework, and drop into bed exhausted. The Tuesday cycle of events probably is very similar to the Monday cycle, as are those for the rest of the work week. Each person in the school also has a complete set of minor cycles; together, they interlace into major cycles, which link together to make up the entire structure of the organization. If an event happens only once, such as a group of teachers marching down to the central office to complain about a principal's decision, the situation is considered to be no more than a singular episode and does not lay a role in the ongoing life of the school.

At this point a significant question arises. In the context of open system theory and contingency theory, what happens to the elements that are so important to classical and social systems theories, such as rules, job descriptions, informal norms, hierarchy, and the like? Do concepts such as these exist in open system theory? Indeed, they do exist and do play important roles. The organizational elements mentioned above (and others as well) serve to pattern and give direction to the cycles of events that make up the school system. For example, as a school teacher proceeds through his or her cycle of the day or week, the rules, informal norms, and roles structure and pattern the sequence of events of his or her day. The teacher arrives at a specified time, instructs in a prescribed sequence of classes, works with an established lesson plan, attends a meeting called by the department chairperson, eats lunch at a scheduled time with friends, and so on through the day. Although such a sequence of events that forms the cycle is not rigid, the rules, expectations, and norms do play significant roles in shaping its content and direction. The same is true for the other individuals and groups operating throughout the school.

The patterns of events that make up the cycles tend to be reasonably stable over time, but when a shift develops in them, change is said to have occurred. In other words, bringing about change in the school means modifying the events in the cycles. Change is reflected only when a new pattern of events is repeated systematically. If two teachers, for example, collaborate in teaching a subject for only a couple of weeks, no change has actually taken place because the pattern of events returns to its original condition rather quickly. However, if these two teachers collaborate in teaching a class as part of their regular instructional methodology, change has taken place, because a new pattern of events has been built into the cycle.

## Input, Throughput, and Output Events

The input, throughput, and output of an organization are all stages in the system's cycle of events. In diagnosing the operations of an organization, Katz and Kahn argue that it is much better to begin with the input, throughput, and output characteristics than with the organization's formal goals or with the rational purposes of its founders or leaders.[18] Although the organization's goals and purposes are well meaning and rational, there is little reason to suggest that it will function according to its goals and purposes. In other words, formal goals and rational purposes stipulate how an organization *should* function, whereas open system theory concentrates on how an organization *actually functions.*

As Figure 5.2 points out, an organization imports various forms of energy from the environment, transforms that energy into some other form in the production process, and exports the output (with value added) into the environment. It then becomes an input for another system.[19] Finally, a return comes to the organization in the form of *payment,* which renews the cycle and begins the process once again. The payment to the school, of course, is not the dividend of a sale to the environment, as is the case

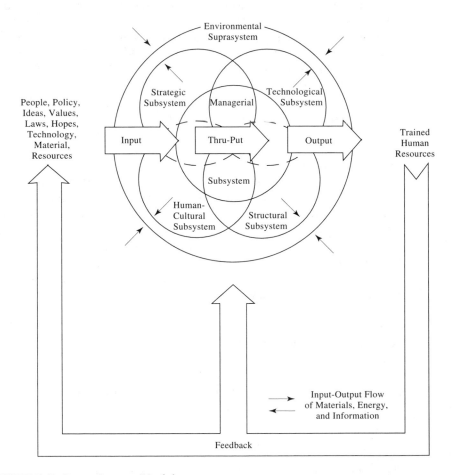

FIGURE 5.2  Open System Model
Adapted from *Contingency View of Organization and Management,* from Fremont E. Kast and James E. Rosenzweig, Science Research Associates, Inc., 1973. Reprinted by permission of the authors.

in the private sector. It is the continued funding by society, which is the beneficiary of a valued service.

The vital components in the life of a school clearly fit into the open system perspective. The environment, for example, is made up of numerous social, economic, and political institutions. Inputs can be categorized under (1) *human inputs,* such as teachers, students, administrators, cafeteria workers, janitors, and bus drivers; (2) *material inputs,* such as buildings, desks, pencils, books, transportation equipment, and footballs; and (3) *constraints,* such as expectations of parents, requirements of law and policy, values, and social norms.

The throughput process is made up of subsystems that interact to convert inputs into outputs. Using the Kast and Rosenzweig model as an illustration, (a) the *structural subsystem* formalizes procedures through roles, rules, and authority relationships; (b) the *human-cultural subsystem* introduces informal expectations and norms into the mix; (c) the *strategic subsystem* generates information on the opportunities and problems in the near and distant futures; and (d) the *technological subsystem* focuses on all aspects of the teaching-learning process. Tying these core subsystems together and giving them direction is the managerial subsystem.[20]

The throughput process (the conversion of energy) mainly involves the teaching-learning process; all other activities, such as faculty meetings and disciplinary procedures, are viewed as supportive of that act. Involved in the throughput process are such categories as (1) instructional technology (e.g., database, learning theory, teaching tactics); (2) formal and informal subsystem roles (e.g., teacher, student, administrator); (3) decision-making strategies (e.g., centralized or decentralized); (4) reward systems (e.g., intrinsic or extrinsic); (5) evaluative strategies (e.g., collegial, supervisory); and a host of other categories, as illustrated in Figure 5–3.[21]

The output process includes such elements as learning gain, attitudinal change, skill preparation, custodial control, critical thinking, behavioral changes, and romantic attachments. Finally, the information and economic returns to the school, which permit a rejuvenation of the cycle, are society's continued contribution to a valuable service.

## A Balance-of-Systems Concept

Within the context of open system theory, organizations are linked into a *balance-of-systems web.*[22] As Figure 5.4 illustrates, each organization imports resources from a variety of organizations in the web and exports a product to other organizations. In an ideal sense, the balance-of-systems process suggests that the organizations in a web reinforce each other through a well-planned and coordinated exchange of inputs and outputs. In practice, of course, frequently that is not the case. Just as one organization is made up of recurring cycles of events, so is the entire web of interlocking organizations.

In principle, the organizational balance of systems is closely modeled on that of nature. However, theory is not practice, and somehow our balance of systems, lacking the majestic precision of natural systems, often is thrown seriously out of alignment. We find ourselves with serious shortages, excesses, or residuals in organizational networks, as illustrated by famine in time of plenty, inner-city decay, dirty air, and unemployed

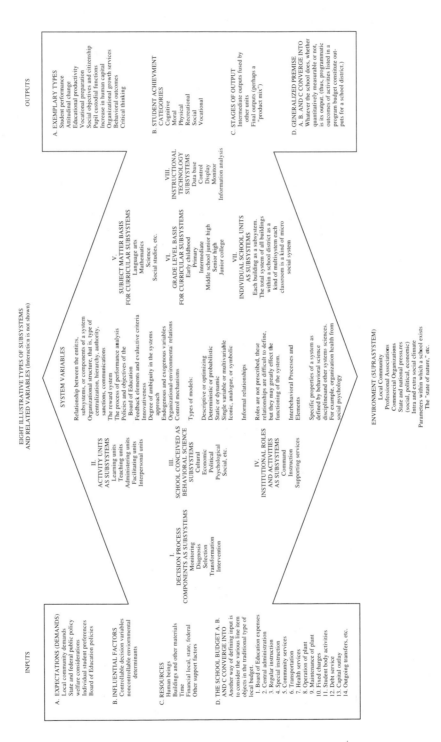

FIGURE 5.3  General Properties of an Educational System.
From Harry J. Hartley, *Educational Planning-Programming-Budgeting: A Systems Approach*, © 1968, p. 72. Reprinted by permission of Prentice-Hall, Inc., Englewood Cliffs, New Jersey.

114

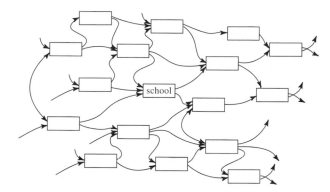

FIGURE 5.4  Balance of Systems Web

college graduates. The issue of reestablishing a balance between organizations has never been as prominent in our national priorities as it is today. The relationship of the school to its marketplace is no exception.

School systems are linked into a web of many types of organizations, such as university teacher-training centers, accreditation boards, building contractors, federal-funding agencies, textbook publishers, city governments, state legislatures, and so forth. Typically, these organizations in the environment of the school system are outside its control. The school system very often is at the mercy of these external organizations; for example, the school cannot accredit teachers, give preservice training, switch city or state governments if the existing ones do not please them, selectively choose which laws to obey and which ones to ignore, or establish their own priorities and guidelines on proposals for federal funding. Hence, the input-output cycle of the school system is inextricably linked with other organizations. At times these linkages can be liberating and supportive, but at other times they can be confining and nonsupportive.

Just as Commander Bucher was not really in control of the support systems that led to the seizure of the USS *Pueblo,* school administrators are not in control of the external systems that play major roles in the conduct of affairs in their organizations. School administrators rarely write their conclusions and make their decisions on a clean slate. The choices open to them are all too confined by decisions made by unseen managers, judges, or bureaucrats in other places who are applying other priorities.

Next we will look at the special characteristics of the organizational environment. Organizational environments have all the gradations of the climatic conditions we see when we look out our kitchen windows. Sometimes the sky appears bright, warm, and clear, whereas at other times it looks blustery, cold, and swept by thunderstorms.

With respect to organizations, Emery and Trist identify the polar environmental conditions as *placid* at one extreme and *turbulent* at the other. The gradations between these two extremes are generated by changes in technology, shifts in market demand, governmental action, increased competition, shifts in values, levels of economic prosperity, and changes in demographic characteristics.[23]

## Environmental Fragmentation

Democracy and our federal system of government create the conditions that produce what Meyer, Scott, and Strang call "environmental fragmentation."[24] Public schools by their very nature are open to the public policy demands imposed by diverse constituency groups, court systems, and legislative bodies at the local, state, and national levels. "It is no accident," Chubb and Moe write, "that public schools are lacking in autonomy, that principals have difficulty leading, and that school goals are heterogeneous, unclear, and undemanding."[25]

A fragmented environment is a complex and heterogenous environment. According to Cohen and Spillane, the high degree of federal, state and local fragmentation have produced a clutter of programs and policies that lay strewn around the national educational landscape. Because Americans have always been much better at adding than subtracting, ". . . efforts to reduce fragmentation would only add several new and unrelated layers of educational requirements and instructional refinements on top of many old and inconsistent layers."[26]

The degree of fragmentation reflects the number, distribution, and power of those organizations on which a given organization depends.[27] In their study on the impact of the external environment on the administrative complexity of school districts, Meyer, Scott, and Strong found that administrative systems expand as the requirements of the external environment become more complex and demanding.

Until mid-twentieth century, the governance and funding of public schools remained a local responsibility, with policy being made by schools boards, and resources predominantly based on property taxes. In the 1920s, 83.2 percent of the funding for public elementary and secondary schools came from local sources. By the 1950s, local funding provided slightly over 57 percent and by 1992, it was down to 46.5 percent.[28]

Even though the sources of funding have gradually shifted upward from the school district level, the tasks of running a school system remain extremely complex. "Multiple, urgent, and shifting pressures are placed on school systems, making demands on board members, principals, and teachers, but not of a type to foster much administrative expansion."[29]

State policy involvement generally was associated with the unification of the many small school districts into larger, more economical districts, as pointed out earlier in Table 2.2. Even though states have increasingly assumed the burden of financing public schools, from 16.5 percent in 1920 to 47.3 percent in 1992,[30] the increased role in funding has not necessarily brought increased fragmentation to the educational environment.

Historically, the role of the states has been to consolidate and standardize school districts for consistency and uniformity. "From early on the state departments of education may have had the net effect of undercutting the complexities of local political pressures on schooling and providing for a simpler environment for local administration."[31]

The U.S. Constitution gave the federal government no formal role in the governance and financing of education; therefore, it did not add substantially to the fragmentation of the environment. However, reform efforts during the 1960s and 1970s directed at specific populations of students with special needs (e.g., rural, inner-city, handicapped, minority, migrant, undernourished) considered unmet at local and state levels became the target of federally funded special-purpose programs.

Federal funding of public elementary and secondary education across the decades ranged from 1.8 percent of the total in 1940 to a high of 9.8 percent in 1980. By 1992, federal support had declined to 6.2 percent.[32]

Scott and Meyer write that "most observers agree that the use of categorical funding targeted to the support of particular groups and programs allowed the federal government to exercise disproportionate influence on education."[33] By 1992, 27.9 billion dollars of federal money was supporting special public elementary and secondary school programs. Eleven different government, cabinet-level departments, with their own maze of subunits, manage an immense spectrum of special programs, such as impact aid; Indian, adult, and vocational education; junior ROTC; energy conservation for school buildings; job training; prison inmate training; milk distribution; and so forth.[34]

The environment of a school district is fragmented out of proportion to the level of federal funding. It is thus more likely to expand the administrative infrastructure at the local level, because the multitude of federal agencies typically require that their programs and funds be kept separate organizationally and use distinct accounting procedures. In addition, reports on implementation, progress, and evaluations must be filed very frequently. Some districts find themselves filing reports every year numbering into the hundreds.[35]

The educational environment has been complicated by the continued growth of local, state, and federal influence on the public school affairs without a decrease at any of the three levels (not to mention the courts). Scott and Meyer write:

> One set of authorities has been layered over another, with each claiming legitimacy to make some types of educational decisions—the federal agencies basing their claims on overriding "national interests," the states standing on their constitutional grounds, and the communities affirming continuing faith in the "religion of localism," a dogma with many adherents in the realm of education.[36]

Even though all three levels contribute to the extensive fragmentation found in the environment of the public schools, the Meyer, Scott, and Strang study concludes that federal funding requires higher levels of administrative expansion at the school level than do state and local activities. This is partly the case because, unlike local and state governments, federal involvement lacks the direct authority over school systems to provide an integrated and simplified approach to specialized problem solving.[37]

The school environment is composed of many converging forces; for example, groups and institutions, such as local, state, and federal governments and courts; political persuasions and constituencies, such as liberals, conservatives, and radicals; ethnography, such as race, religion, and national heritage; and social problems, such as alienation, drug abuse, racism, ethics, crime, and physical violence. Fortunately for educators, all of the systems in the environment are not turbulent at the same time. Some just sit out there like sleeping volcanos that give an occasional rumble to let you know they are still around. Others are more or less continually active, changing back and forth from placid to turbulent, such as the taxpayers' association, the teachers' union, and the minority-group advisory council.

Charles Lindblom, in his provocative article "Success Through Inattention" argues that all these converging forces in and around the schools should be viewed as an asset that permits a market system based on mutual adaptations to organize the course of events rather than enforced coordination from the top. "Mutual adjustment," he writes, "is . . . a method of decision making or social organization that thrives not on sharing of values, an excess of which implies conformity in thought, but on diversity of thought. Rather than stifle, it liberates the mind. Where hierarchy says, 'Don't think; conform!', mutual adaptation says, 'Don't conform, but do think.' "[38]

## The Management Information System

The management information system (MIS) is a tool that provides various forms of information that facilitate adjusting to the changing demands of one's environment. For a school to be changed, information must be available about what is happening inside as well as outside the system.

In the educational sector, many pressures are at work to force change in the practices and policies of the school district; for example, new laws mandated by state legislatures, teacher militancy, student pressures for increased participation in decision making, increased or decreased material wealth of schools, technological innovations, and so forth. These and other uncoordinated forces tend to buffet the school and drive it in an irregular, unsystematic, and unplanned direction. In short, if the school system is a creation of its environment, in many respects it is also a victim of its environment.

However, within the boundaries of most organizational types, including the school district, there is a mechanism at work designed to provide specific, planned direction to the process of change. This mechanism is referred to as management information system (MIS), which operates like a navigation system. For example, an airplane flying across country depends on the outboard altimeter and forward radars to gauge oncoming environmental events, such as mountains and storms, and on inboard instruments to detail the performance of the craft, such as gas consumption, air pressure, and cabin temperature. Thus, a combination of the outboard and inboard feedback enables the crew to make the necessary decisions to navigate safely and efficiently from one point to another.

In a like manner, if the MIS of an organization functions correctly, it will feed external environmental and internal performance information to the decision makers. This information enables the decision makers to change the character of the output so that it matches the society's shifting demands. Without an operational MIS, the school would be forced to adopt a decision-making pattern guided by tradition, conventional wisdom, and incrementalism, which is central to what Lindblom calls "the science of muddling through."[39] Flying by the seat of one's pants and crisis decision making are standard operating procedures in school systems that do not have management information systems to monitor what is going on inside and outside the organization.

Unfortunately, most writing that deals with MIS focuses on issues of technology and hardware (e.g., computer processing, data banks, distribution networks, information-retrieval procedures, etc.). Although the issues of technology and hardware are important, they serve only as tools to facilitate the manipulation, storage, and distribution of information. But how does the MIS function as a management tool to establish a close, continuing relationship between the organization and its environment?[40]

## Characteristics of the Management Information System

Virtually any organization that has an output (automobiles, radios, or high school graduates) and that must compete in the marketplace needs an MIS to facilitate a continuing, close relationship between the organization and the changing needs of society. Figure 5.5 gives a simplified picture of a generic organizational model containing the basic information loops central to a MIS.

The MIS is defined as "a communication process in which information (input) is recorded, stored and retrieved (processed) for decisions (output) on planning, operating, and controlling."[41]

A MIS comprises five systematic information loops that feed information to a decision-making (control) mechanism. These loops are (1) an internal feedback, quality control loop, (2) an external feedback loop, (3) a pending resources loop, (4) an internal feedback, personnel support loop, and (5) a market futures loop. Based on the systematic information received from the five loops, the decision-making control mechanism can carry out an ongoing process of change to direct a school toward a patterned equilibrium with its environment. The terms *information loop* and *information cycle* will be used interchangeably in this chapter.

The special characteristics of the information loops and the decision-making control mechanism making up the MIS are described in the following sections.

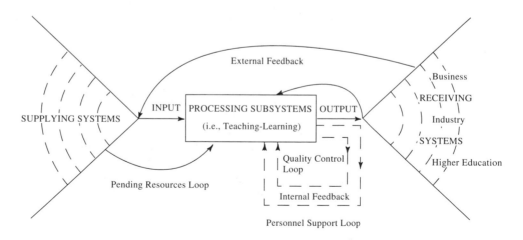

FIGURE 5.5  The Generic Organizational Model
From E. Mark Hanson, "The Management Information System as an Instrument of Planned Change," *Educational Technology* 16 (1976): 53. Used with permission.

*The Market Futures Loop*    This information cycle closely monitors the changing needs of the marketplaces (which receive graduates) by accumulating information such as specific workforce projections, new work technologies, changing college admissions requirements, and needed job skills. Because the loop draws in this information on the local, regional, and national scenes at projected time intervals (e.g., two, six, ten, fifteen years hence), the school is capable of changing its academic program at the appropriate points in time. Students then arrive at the marketplace with the knowledge and skills that are in demand when they graduate.

*The Internal Feedback, Quality Control Loop*    This information cycle provides data about the effectiveness of the teaching-learning process; data are derived from comparing test scores with predetermined objectives. The tests usually are standardized or teacher-made tests. Measures of the teaching-learning process are important because they inform teachers and administrators about how well students are learning what is being taught in the classroom. However, the measures do not tell educators if they are teaching the right things. For example, the quality control loop may provide data that say students are performing within the upper 10 percent of all students studying Latin, ancient Estonian history, and pyramid construction. But should these subjects be taught in the classroom? The market futures loop should be depended upon to provide a response to the issues of program content.

*The External Feedback Loop*    This information cycle informs the decision-making control mechanism about the level of success of the output in the marketplace. Almost all organizations that generate a product for a market go to extremes to obtain external feedback, to guide the process of change. If an automobile company, for example, has difficulty selling its automobiles or if its product receives bad marks from the consumer, the producer needs this information so it can review and modify the character of the output.

The school needs similar information on the success of its output (graduates) in the marketplace (on the job or in the university). This type of feedback can be obtained, for example, through follow-up studies, telephone calls and letters exchanged between educators and employers, discussions with graduates (and dropouts) who return to school for a visit, and by educators visiting institutions that receive graduates.

*The Pending Resources Loop*    This information cycle provides the control mechanism with a picture of the human and material resources the school will receive over the short and long run. Data obtained from this information cycle set parameters for what is economically feasible in the way of change-oriented projects for the students entering the educational system. For example, a program change to computer-assisted instruction makes no sense if financial resources are not available and will not become available to support such an effort.

*The Internal Feedback, Personnel Support Loop*    For a program of planned change to be successful, it needs support from people directly involved, such as parents, teachers, and students.[42] The personnel support information cycle provides data about the amount of support or resistance key parties will lend to specific programs of change.

Programs that seem desirable and feasible—as determined by information assembled through the other information loops—may fail completely if these is not sufficient backing from parents and teachers.

*The Decision-Making, Control Mechanism*    The control mechanism of the school receives the data derived from the five systematic information cycles already defined: information on the changing nature of the marketplace, information comparing internal measures of student performance against predetermined objectives, information on what happens to the output once it arrives on the marketplace, information on the availability of resources to support specific programs of change, and information on the levels of support and resistance among the personnel who will be directly involved or affected by the change effort.

Based on the accrued information, the educational leadership determines where and how the educational process ought to be steered in a direction of change. At least this is what the theory of the MIS suggests should happen. As Murdick and Ross warn, however, the concept of control extends beyond the framework of the management information system. External factors, such as custom, the competitive environment, and governmental regulations,[43] enter in. Nevertheless, the MIS should play a critical role in directing the change process and leading the organization toward a closer relationship with its surrounding environment. If information flows were to cease, the organization would have no systematic way of establishing a direction of change and would therefore have to grope blindly for direction, or depend on tradition, instinct, and conventional wisdom. Unfortunately, groping blindly is a condition of management not altogether unfamiliar to the educational institution.

The presence of turbulence in the environment of a school, however, does not mean that the educational organization will necessarily feel its impact. As the next section will illustrate, organizations can function as relatively closed systems and thus are able to screen out such turbulence.

## Open and Closed Systems

Organizations are neither open nor closed systems in an absolute sense. A fully closed system would obtain no human or material resources for its production system nor distribute a finished product into the environment, and therefore could not exist. A completely open system, on the other hand, would practice no selection or screening procedures, thus swamping the operation with superfluous data and unnecessary raw materials. In effect, it is more appropriate to think of organizations as maintaining degrees of openness and closedness with respect to *specific* decisions, pressures, or materials facing the system at any given time. For example, a school may find it is quite open to advice from parents on pending curricular changes, but quite closed to advice on the proper procedures for disciplining students.[44]

Hence, across the school's entire decisional spectrum there are differing degrees of openness and closedness. However, in a comparative sense, certain types of organizations lean toward one side or the other of the open-closed continuum. Carlson identifies two different classes of organizations that maintain significantly different types of relationships with their environments. The first class he refers to as the "domesticated" organizations, and it includes the public school. They are not compelled to attend to all of an organization's ordinary and usual needs. For example, they do not compete with other organizations for clients; in fact, a steady flow of clients is assured. There is no struggle for survival for this type of organization—existence is guaranteed. Though it does compete in a restricted area for funds, funds are not closely tied to quality of performance. These organizations are domesticated in the sense that they are protected by the society they serve.[45]

Carlson also identifies a type of organization he calls "wild" in character. These organizations must struggle for survival, their existence is not guaranteed, support is closely related to the quality of their output, they select their clients, they compete with one another for resources and markets, and at times they cease to exist.

In recent years Darwin's theory of evolution, based on the ability to adapt to the demands of the environment and the survival of the fittest, has come to play an important conceptual role in organization theory. In this context, based on their ability to compete, some organizations are selected by their environments to survive and others are not.[46] So-called "wild" organizations are not protected at vulnerable points as are domesticated organizations. They also are quicker to adapt to the changing demands of their environments because of their more precarious survival needs. Most private organizations are classified as wild, such as businesses, private schools, and private hospitals.

In a wild organization such as a business, the amount of return it receives as profit (input) depends the quality and quantity of its output. If the business does not capture and hold a share of the marketplace by producing a quality product in an appropriate volume, the return in profits will diminish and competitors will drive it out of business. Hence, the business organization must be continually prepared to change the character of its production processes so that it can continue to hold a sufficient share of the market and maintain competitive advantages. Also, the business organization has a measure of its success in the profits it extracts from the marketplace.

The "domesticated" organization, on the other hand, exists as a local monopoly. Public institutions such as city governments, school districts, police departments, public health agencies, and the like have a *guaranteed input,* which continues from year to year and is not dependent on the quality or volume of their output. If a city council or a state legislature, for example, is extremely inactive and ineffective, it still receives the same financial support as it would if it were highly effective and active. A disenchanted populace cannot turn to another city government or legislature because there are no competitors. The same is true for a public school system. Because they are cut off from their environments, the natural selection process cannot function and weak institutions can continue on indefinitely.

The resource input (e.g., number of students or financial support) of a school system is *not tied to the quality of its output.* The school will receive more or less the same inputs from year to year, whether or not its graduates go to Harvard University or end up walking the streets unemployed. A sound argument could be made that there is an inverse relationship between the ability of a school system to obtain additional financial support and the quality of its output. In recent years, school systems that have successfully argued that their graduates are highly *deficient* in specific skills have been the most successful in obtaining additional resources from local school communities and from state and federal agencies. Rarely does one hear of a school district that passes a bond issue based on a boast that a quality education program exists that can be improved even more. Bond issues usually are passed when the quality of a program is declining rapidly. Often the threat of having to abandon highly visible and attractive activities such as football and band will gain approval for additional funds.

A contributing factor to the domestication of the school system is that the quality of the output is not easily measured. No real agreement exists on the purpose of the school and its many programs, so limited attention is given to the system's output aspect. The business organization of course can count its profits and therefore know exactly where it stands with respect to its purpose.

The voucher system frequently is proposed as a mechanism to place public schools in a competitive situation where environmental selection, by means of parents selecting schools for their children, will weed out the weak schools and reinforce the strong. A true experiment to determine the intended and unintended outcomes of such an approach will be interesting and perhaps even inevitable one day soon.

In short, because the public school system is basically a local monopoly and has a guaranteed input regardless of the character and quality of its output, there are pressures, opportunities, and incentives at work in the organization to adopt a relatively closed system. Such an orientation can screen out much of the turbulence in the environment that could serve as a guide to educational change.

This closed system orientation is reminiscent of the position the U.S. Navy took as it judged that fateful mission, that nothing would happen to the USS *Pueblo*. The Navy therefore made no meaningful provisions to protect her in case of trouble. In that instance the sleeping volcano sprang to life and the U.S. Navy could do little more than blame the ship's captain for the ensuing events.

The U.S. Navy sent the USS *Pueblo* into its espionage mission with the necessary support systems (e.g., defense, communication, internal security, destruct mechanisms, etc.) to function effectively and efficiently. However, the support the Navy provided assumed that on the high seas the established equilibrium with the North Koreans would prevail. When the equilibrium was disrupted, the *Pueblo* was incapable of handling the new situation. The next section responds to the question, What constitutes an organizational equilibrium?

## Organizational Equilibrium

An open system interacts with its environment by exchanging inputs and outputs in a patterned, cyclical fashion. The cycles of events that occur within the organization gravitate toward relatively constant input-output ratios, establishing a steady state, or equilibrium. The open system tends to be self-regulating in the sense that when a disruption occurs in an event cycle, energy and resources are introduced at that point in order to reestablish the equilibrium. If the equilibrium cannot be reestablished, organizational change sets in and a new equilibrium is formed.

The patterns of equilibrium between the school and its environment can be seen in such things as enrollment patterns, graduation rates, teacher-student ratios, dropout rates, and financial-support indices. All of these ratios usually fluctuate only a few percentage points a year. If major swings in these equilibrium patterns were present—for example, if a school had no clear idea of the amount of financial support it would receive or the number of students and faculty it could support from year to year—it would be impossible to develop planned educational programs.

The concept of organizational equilibrium does not suggest a static or stationary system. As Scott and Mitchell point out, an equilibrium is a dynamic entity that changes as the organization seeks to survive in a changing environment.[47] If a lag sets in between the environmental and organizational exchanges, a type of chain reaction is set off through the entire web of linked organizations. As an illustration, when high schools begin to graduate fewer students, enrollment begins to drop in colleges; when schools find their budgets progressively reduced, they purchase fewer goods from local commercial enterprises.

In short, the perception of a school in an open system context forces attention away from the static properties of roles, rules, formal goals, and rigid structures toward the dynamic qualities of cycles of behavioral events, intricate relationships within a network of interdependent organizations, and lags that frequently disrupt the flow through the balance of systems. Accordingly, the differing degrees of turbulence in an organization's environment have an impact on its ability to function and therefore on the system's stability.

An organization, as well as the web of organizations surrounding and interlocking with it, must therefore acquire enough stability to promote an equilibrium that in turn permits planned and predictable patterns and exchanges to take place. However, if the equilibrium becomes rigid and fixed in its patterns and predictability, any predilections toward change will be quashed. Conditions such as these are symptoms of an unhealthy situation and are often preconditions of a stormy future.

## The Problem-Solving Cycle

As already pointed out, the beauty of open system theory is that it nicely incorporates the sound and valuable characteristics of bureaucratic theory and social system theory, but avoids the natural tendencies of these two theories toward a closed system bias and static properties. Viewing schools as a network of interlocking cycles of events that incorporates characteristics of the bureaucratic and social system models enables us to more effectively conceptualize a decision-making process within a problem-solving cycle.

This section presents the findings of a study that helped shape a problem solving perspective by placing the interacting spheres model (ISM) identified in Chapter 4 within an open system framework.[48] In broad terms, the research identifies seven key stages in the problem-solving cycle (see Figure 5.6).

1. Problem-recognition stage
2. Problem-screening stage
3. Problem-distribution stage
4. Decision-making stage

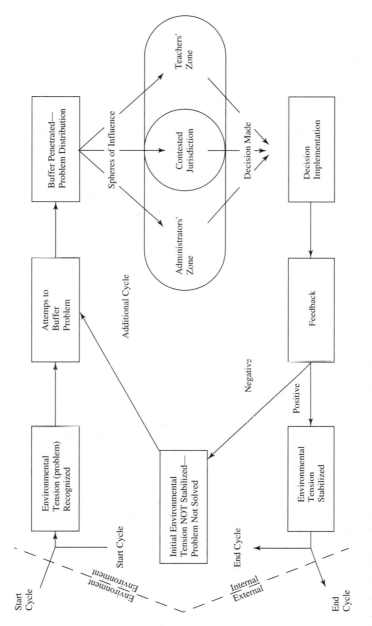

FIGURE 5.6 The Problem-Solving Process as a Cycle of Events

125

5. Decision-implementation stage
6. Feedback stage
7. Problem-resolution or renewal stage

## *Problem Identification*

Within the context of a tension management model, an issue becomes a problem to be treated when it surpasses some vaguely defined tolerance level built into the organization—like the point at which an individual chooses to take an aspirin to treat a growing headache. Educators usually find themselves at the beginning stages of the problem-solving process when they encounter an *expectation* (from weak to strong) that something in the school needs to be changed (dropped, added, modified). Thus, the *problem-recognition stage* has been reached.

The expectations can come from inside the school, such as an abnormal number of teachers requesting transfers, or an increasing number of discipline problems; or from outside the school, such as parents demanding that the biology program drop teaching Darwinism or that more money be spent on the basketball program. As any experienced educator can attest, the problems range from good ideas that are impossible to implement, to complete no-brainers.

An educational system does not take on every problem that knocks on the door demanding attention. To do so would choke the school with an overload of petty, impractical, at times improper or illegal, and frequently impossible petitions for change. Thus, how does a school screen out problems it does not care to treat?

## *The Organizational Buffer*

The problem-screening stage functions in the context of different types of buffers that are placed between the problem presented and the school. The buffering is not accidental or haphazard. It is a conscious effort by administrators and teachers to weigh, measure, and select the problems they choose to address. The study found many types of buffers, most of which fell within four basic categories.

*Buffer 1: No Jurisdiction*    The administrator's disclaimer that he had no ability to act was a very important buffer. For example, a parent called complaining about students smoking pot in a house across from the school. "That's a police matter," came the reply. A teacher worried about a student having problems with his family. "That's out of my realm of authority," the principal stated. A parent complained to a teacher about old textbooks used in the classroom. "You need to talk with the principal," the parent was told.

*Buffer 2: Strategic Catharsis*    This strategy allows the complainants to "talk it out." If they are given an opportunity to "let off steam," their problem often seems less critical to them.

*Buffer 3: Strategic Stalling*    A third strategy results from consciously or unconsciously assigning such a low priority to the problem, or sending it "out to committee for study," that it dies a natural death. Another approach is to tie more apparently unbreakable strings to the problem than the Lilliputians ever used to shackle Gulliver. Frequently used stalling tactics emphasize the points that besides being unprofessional (and maybe even illegal), attempts to solve that particular problem would require an extensive (perhaps humongous) amount of additional but unavailable resources and an impossible degree of parent support.

*Buffer 4: Mutual Reinforcement*     Coalitions often form around high principles or strong vested interests that serve as protective shields to thwart challenges. For example, administrators are expected to back up their teachers on issues of instruction and student discipline. Teachers rarely openly criticize the professional performance of colleagues. Union leaders operate to obtain more benefits during contract negotiations as teachers parade together out on the bricks.

In short, buffering is a combination of techniques teachers and administrators use to serve a gatekeeping function in the problem-solving process. From an organizational point of view, initiating some form of screening process is necessary.

## Penetrating the Buffer

The study identified five patterns of activity which resulted in penetrations of the buffer.

*Intermittent Renewal Pattern*     Sometimes the tension surrounding an issue refused to die and repeatedly reappeared, seeking yet another hearing. For example, the way the budget was allocated, class size, and parents wanting to choose their student's teachers were problem issues the study identified that wouldn't go away.

*Crisis Management*     Problems in the form of a crisis easily penetrated the buffer, such as racial conflict on a school campus or a group of influential parents petitioning the school board.

*Central Office Directives*     Although the school personnel frequently screened out suggestions central office personnel made, when directives arrived the issues were addressed.

*Identifying the Soft Spot*     The buffer surrounding the schools is not impermeable at all points. Enterprising students, teachers or parents often found an influential insider or prestigious group to sponsor their request. This type of sponsorship often makes an important difference in the outcome.

*Voluntary Removal of the Buffer*     The teachers and administrators often voluntarily decide to take on and solve a problem because it appears to be in the best interests of the school. This is a healthy response of a school prepared to make changes when they are called for.

Following the penetration of the buffer, the complex process of making a decision begins. How is the problem-solving process managed in the power environment of the school?

## Spheres of Influence

After the buffer is penetrated and the school begins to search for a problem solution, the problem typically goes into the *distribution stage*. At this stage the problem is taken up by one of the semiautonomous spheres of influence (or zones) identified earlier in the Interacting Spheres Model (see Figure 4.1).

After decision-making responsibility is distributed to a center of power, the *decision-making and implementation stages* of the cycle are initiated in sequence. Once the decision is made and implementation begins, the *feedback stage* begins. If the feedback is positive, or there is no feedback at all, the tension initiating the cycle has been neutralized and the problem resolved. However, a *problem-resolution stage* begins if the feedback is not positive and a significant level of tension continues. Under these conditions, a second cycle is initiated, and then later possibly a third as the search for a solution is sought out.

The problem-solving process addressed in Figure 5.6 has suggested a movement to link certain strengths of the open system model, the bureaucratic model, and the social system model into one conceptual framework. Studying certain educational-system processes within the context of this conceptual open system framework could contribute to our understanding of how schools function. These processes might include conflict-management procedures, system-planning activities, resource-allocation techniques, curriculum-development initiatives, and teaching-learning methods.

## A Contrast of Basic Assumptions

As stated before, different people using different conceptual lenses tend to view the causes and consequences of events differently. The basic assumptions underlying conceptual models differ significantly on many key points for the same reason. A few of the major conceptual differences between classical theory and open system theory are listed in Table 5.1.

## Conclusion

One Christmas Eve, a Washington, D.C., radio station called the British ambassador and asked, "What would you like for Christmas?" The ambassador thought for a while and gave his answer. The next day he heard the announcer tell what foreign ambassadors wanted for Christmas: "The French ambassador, said, 'I earnestly desire that next year should be a year of peace.' The Soviet ambassador hopes for a year of justice for all men. The German ambassador wants to see a great sharing of wealth in the world. And the British ambassador said, 'I would like a box of candied fruit.' " The British ambassador obviously forgot to ask the name of the game and therefore made the wrong assumption about what was being asked. The purpose of including the story here is to underscore the point that assumptions are important in directing behavior.

The basic assumptions and therefore the conceptual perspective underlying open system theory differ from those underlying classical theory and social system theory.

TABLE 5.1    A Comparison of the Assumption of Classical Theory and of Open System Theory

| *Classical Theory* | *Open System Theory* |
|---|---|
| 1. An organization is characterized as a hierarchical order of roles and responsibilities. | 1. An organization is characterized by interlocking cycles of events within and between subsystems. |
| 2. Power is centralized in the role of the chief officer. | 2. Power is diffused into the subsystems, which must differentiate and integrate their activities. |
| 3. Formal goals give specific direction to events. | 3. The demands and needs of the environment give direction to events. |
| 4. Communication follows established channels. | 4. Communication follows a systemwide information network designed to integrate the activities of subsystems and to establish linkages with the environment. |
| 5. Control over production is established by the rules of the organization. | 5. Control over production is established by the effectiveness of the linkages between the internal subsystems and the external environment. |
| 6. Superiors manage subordinates. | 6. The managerial subsystem must function in support of the needs of other subsystems. |
| 7. Conflict is dysfunctional and should be eliminated. | 7. Conflict is inevitable and can lead to positive change through creative management. |
| 8. There is one best way of performing a task. | 8. There are many ways of performing a task that are equally satisfactory. |
| 9. Focus on the way an organization *should* function. | 9. Focus on the way an organization *does* function. |
| 10. Closed to the environment. | 10. Open to the environment through input-output exchanges. |
| 11. Static relationships. | 11. Dynamic relationships. |
| 12. Chief officer holds ultimate authority and responsibility. | 12. Chief officers are often subject to events that are not their making and beyond their control. |
| 13. Rules and roles give order to an organization. | 13. Equilibrium in environmental-organizational exchanges gives order to an organization. |

When trying to deal with school problems such as the revelation of declining achievement scores, some officials are quick to put on their classical lenses and blame the principal and the teachers for low-quality performance. Other officials take a more expansive look at the nature of the problem. They explore the various forces supporting or detracting from the quality of the academic program, such as the priority held for resource allocation, the funds available to the curricular program, the community tax structure and its financial support of the school, demographic shifts in the community, the community's socioeconomic background, the availability of research literature in the school, the level of teacher turnover, degrees of horizontal and vertical conflict, levels of parent participation in the classroom and in the community advisory committee, degree of parent involvement in home study programs, existence of specialized study programs for children with specific learning problems, and so forth. In short, the teachers and local administrators may well be the cause of the problem, but on the other hand, they may be victims of their organization and its environment, just as students may be. The multidimensional characteristics of the situation leading up to the seizure of the USS *Pueblo* illustrate this point.

## Notes

1. Lloyd M. Bucher with Mark Rascovich, *Bucher: My Story* (Garden City, NY: Doubleday, 1970), p. 418.

2. Trevor Armbrister, *A Matter of Accountability: The True Story of the Pueblo Affair* (New York: Coward-McCann, 1970), p. 247.

3. Bucher, *Bucher: My Story,* p. 407.

4. Ibid., p. 393.

5. Armbrister, *A Matter of Accountability,* p. 212.

6. Ibid., preface.

7. Ibid., p. 385.

8. Paul Hill, Arthur Wise, and Leslie Shapiro, *Educational Progress: Cities Mobilize to Improve Their Schools* (Santa Monica, CA: RAND, 1989), p. v.

9. Ludwig von Bertalanffy, "General Systems Theory," in *General Systems: Yearbook of the Society for the Advancement of General Systems Theory,* volume 1, Ludwig von Bertalanffy and Anatol Rapoport, eds. (1956): 8.

10. Talcott Parsons and Edward Shils, "Categories of the Orientation and Organization of Action," in *Toward a General Theory of Action,* T. Parsons and E. Shils, eds. (New York: Harper and Row, 1962), p. 107.

11. Gareth Morgan, *Images of Organization* (Beverly Hills CA: Sage, 1986), p. 45.

12. Kenneth Boulding, "General Systems Theory: The Skeleton of Science," *Management Science* 2 (1956): 200–208.

13. W. Richard Scott, *Organizations: Rational, Natural and Open Systems* (Englewood Cliffs, NJ: Prentice-Hall, 1981), p. 119.

14. Daniel Katz and Robert Kahn, *The Social Psychology of Organizations,* p. 452. Copyright © 1966 by John Wiley & Sons, Inc. Reprinted by permission of John Wiley & Sons, Inc.

15. Joan Talbert, Milbrey McLaughlin and Brian Rowan, "Understanding Context Effects on Secondary School Teaching," *Teachers College Record* 95 (1993): 45.

16. F. H. Allport, "A Structuronomic Conception of Behavior: Individual and Collective," *Journal of Abnormal and Social Psychology* 64 (1962).

17. For a discusson of the entropic process, see: Katz and Kahn. *The Social Psychology of Organizations,* p. 21.

18. Ibid., p. 16.

19. Talcott Parsons, "Suggestions for a Sociological Approach to the Theory of Organizations," in *Complex Organizations,* Amitai Etzioni, ed. (New York: Holt, Rinehart and Winston, 1961), p. 33.

20. Fremont Kast and James Rosenzweig, eds. *Contingency Views of Organization and Management* (Chicago: Science Research Associates, 1973).

21. Harry Hartley, *Educational Planning, Programming, Budgeting:A Systems Approach* (Englewood Cliffs, NJ: Prentice-Hall, 1968), p. 72.

22. Peter Blau and Richard Scott, *Formal Organizations* (San Francisco: Chandler, 1962), p. 195.

23. F. E. Emery and E. L. Trist, "The Causal Texture of Organizational Environments," *Human Relations* 18 (1965): 21-32.

24. John Meyer, W. Richard Scott, and David Strang, "Centralization, Fragmentation, and School District Complexity," *Administrative Science Quarterly,* 32 (1987): 186-201.

25. John Chubb and Terry Moe, "Politics, Markets and the Organization of Schools" (Paper presented at the American Political Science Association 1987), p. 29.

26. David Cohen and James Spillane, "Policy and Practice: The Relations Between Governance and Instruction," in *Review of Research in Education,* ed. Gerald Grant (Washington, D.C.: American Educational Research Association, 1992), p. 41.

27. Meyer, Scott, and Strang, p. 187.

28. National Center for Educational Statistics, *Digest of Educational Statistics:* 1993 (Washington, DC: U.S. Government Printing Office, 1993), p. 152.

29. Meyer, Scott, and Strang, p. 189.

30. National Center for Educational Statistics, p. 152.

31. Meyer, Scott, and Strang, p. 200.

32. National Center for Educational Statistics, p. 124 152.

33. W. Richard Scott and John Meyer, "Environmental Linkages and Organizational Complexity: Public and Private Schools," in *Comparing Public and Private Schools,* vol. 1, Thomas James and Henry Levin, eds. (New York: Falmer, 1987), pp. 130-131.

34. National Center for Educational Statistics, p. 365.

35. Meyer, Scott, and Strang, p. 192.

36. Scott and Meyer, p. 132.

37. Meyer, Scott, and Strang, p. 200.

38. Charles Lindblom, "Success Through Inattention in School Administration and Elsewhere," *Educational Administration Quarterly* 30 (1994), p. 212.

39. Charles Lindblom, "The Science of Muddling Through," *Public Administration Review* 19 (1959).

40. The material for this section was drawn from: E. Mark Hanson and Flora Ida Ortiz, "The Management Information System and the Control of Educational Change: A Field Study," *Sociology of Education* 48 (1975).

41. Robert Murdick and Joel Ross, *Information Systems for Modern Management* (Englewood Cliffs, NJ: Prentice-Hall, 1971), p. 292.

42. E. Mark Hanson, "The Emerging Control Structure of Schools," *Administrator's Notebook* 21 (1973).

43. Murdick and Ross, *Information Systems for Modern Management,* pp. 300-301.

44. Benjamin Levin, "School Response to a Changing Environment," *Journal of Educational Administration* 31 (1993): pp. 4-21.

45. Richard Carlson, "Barriers to Change in Public Schools," in *Change Processes in the Public Schools,* Richard Carlson et al., eds. (Eugene, OR: Center for the Advanced Study of Educational Administration, University of Oregon, 1965), p. 6.

46. Morgan, p. 66.

47. William Scott and Terence Mitchell, *Organizational Theory:A Structural and Behavioral Analysis* (Homewood, IL: Richard D. Irwin, 1976), p. 238.

48.  E. Mark Hanson, "The Professional/Bureaucratic Interface: A Case Study," *Urban Education* 11 (1976): 313–332; E. Mark Hanson and Michael E. Brown, "A Contingency View of Problem Solving in Schools: A Case Analysis," *Educational Administration Quarterly,* 13 (1977): 71–91.

# Chapter 6

# Contingency Theory

Like the business of building better mousetraps, this century has seen the continuous scholarly pursuit of a clearer picture of how organizations work, and thus how they can be made to work even better. A variety of useful management orientations have emerged from this pursuit (e.g., scientific management, social system theory, open system theory), each with conceptual linchpins rooted in differing basic assumptions about the nature of work, motivation, rationality, efficiency, governance, and the like.

These management orientations have something in common. Each functions like the Old Woman's shoe, encompassing every member of the family of organizations. In recent years, however, a view more appropriate to Cinderella's slipper has emerged, which treats each organization as relatively unique. For centuries this orientation has been at the core of practitioner behavior but has been seen as an anomaly, reflective of inefficiency or unpreparedness, and thus has been overlooked by management scientists. Currently, the changing situational character of management is now coming to be understood as a key to the management process itself. A clear illustration of *contingency theory,* as this orientation is called, is presented by Leo Tolstoy in his classic *War and Peace.* Following a major battle near Moscow between the armies of Napoleon and the Russian General Kutuzov, Tolstoy discusses a problem with which every manager who makes critical decisions can identify.

> A commander-in-chief never finds himself at the beginning of an event—the position from which we always contemplate it. The general is always in the midst of a series of

A portion of Chapter 6 was drawn from E. Mark Hanson, "School Management and Contingency Theory: An Emerging Perspective," *Educational Administration Quarterly,* Vol. 15, No. 2 (spring 1979), © The University Council for Educational Administration.

shifting events and so he can never at any point deliberate on the whole import of what is going on. Imperceptibly, moment by moment, an event takes shape in all its bearings, and at every instant of this uninterrupted, consecutive shaping of events the commander-in-chief is at the heart of a most complex play of intrigues, cares, contingencies, authorities, projects, counsels, threats and deceits, and is continually obliged to reply to innumerable, often mutually contradictory questions.[1]

Many management scholars and practitioners would now agree with the observation that "at the moment, contingency theory is perhaps the most powerful current sweeping over organizations. The history of many fields shows a movement from universalistic principles to *situational* relationships and principles. The current prominence of contingency theory suggests that organization theory is entering a period of scientific maturity."[2]

At this stage in its development, however, contingency theory is not really a theory at all. Rather, it is a conceptual tool that facilitates our understanding of the situational flow of events and alternate organizational and individual responses to that flow. Thus, as a conceptual tool, contingency theory does not possess the wholistic character of the three major models discussed in previous chapters. In many ways contingency theory can be thought of as a subset of open system theory because it is through open system theory that we come to understand the dynamic flows of events, personnel, and resources that take place in organizations.

With the intent of gaining insight into the situational character of organizations, the objectives of this chapter are:

1. to examine the basic assumptions and conceptual foundations of contingency theory
2. to portray the contingency theory of management as a technique of flexible response to conditions of uncertainty in organization settings
3. to identify three contingency theory frameworks that have important implications for education: (a) organizational structure and the environment, (b) problem solving in organized anarchies, and (c) managerial work behavior
4. to conclude with a series of questions intended to establish lines of inquiry regarding contingency theory in education

## Under Conditions of Uncertainty

Almost any experienced manager can testify to the pendulumlike shifts in the nature of the job. One moment the organization can be in the heady pursuit of supreme success and the next it is fighting for its life.

The complex organization's core problem is *uncertainty,* and "coping with uncertainty,"Thompson observes, is "the essence of the administrative process."[3] Under conditions of uncertainty the decision makers cannot assign precise probabilities of success to a specific intiative. Hence, the element of risk enters in the decision-making formula.[4] Organizations, including school systems, have tended to respond to this issue by what Cyert and March refer to as "uncertainty avoidance."[5] For example, managers might divert the energy and resources necessary for long-term planning to the short-term need of putting out fires, imposing standard operating procedures, attempting to influence the passage of favorable state legislation, or writing uncertainty-absorbing contracts. "In short," Cyert and March conclude, "they achieve a reasonably manageable decision situation by avoiding planning where plans depend on predictions of uncertain future events and by emphasizing planning where the plans can be made self-confirming through some control device."[6]

In contrast, the emergence of continency theory represents an orientation that enables us to conceive of an organization as an open system composed of complex interacting subunits faced with uncertainty. By adapting organization structure, planning strategies, and leader behavior, acceptable levels of certainty can be achieved—or at least the risks can be reduced.

## The Context of Contingency Theory

Imagine a situation in which an ominous demand is placed on a school or school district. As usual, sufficient information is not available to understand the consequences of either fulfilling or ignoring the demand. Unknowns dominate the thought process. How much will it cost? Do we have the resources available? Will heads roll if we ignore it? Is it political? Is this a short- or a long-range problem? Can we bargain? Is this only a bluff or are we genuinely threatened? The goal is for the organization to land firmly on its feet after all is said and done.

An alert school district will not sit on its duff waiting until the last minute for complete information and a fully accurate picture to come into focus. By then it's usually too late to help shape events or even prepare for their arrival. Crisis decision making becomes the principal course of action. An alert district would have formed contingency plans.

Contingency plans are alternate responses formulated to influence the relationship between situations (that ominous demand) and outcomes (landing on its feet). Stated another way:

A = a situation (threat or problem)

B = contingency plans (e.g., "If it's a mouse we stand; if it's a dragon we run.")

C = outcomes (safety and security)

The relationship between A and C is moderated by B. Management strategies require information as it becomes available in order to assess and eliminate proposed alternatives.

Contingency theory stresses that variability in environmental needs and demands requires variability in organizational responses. Standard operating procedures are not appropriate in the face of all types of demands. For example, when an armed terrorist leaps to his feet on a routine commercial flight and demands that the craft be flown to Lower Slobovia, the pilot and crew must shift their thoughts into one of several contingency plans available. For example, (1) they can ignore the gunman entirely and proceed toward their established destination, (2) they can attempt to overpower the terrorist during an unguarded moment, (3) they can try to talk the gunman out of his intentions, (4) they can feign mechanical problems and descend toward the nearest airport, or (5) they can argue that they have neither the fuel nor the maps for such a trip and that the craft must land to acquire the necessary provisions.

The flight crew must examine its available information and seek additional information that will help evaluate the relative risks of each of the continency plans. The crew will examine, for example, the amount of fuel remaining in the tanks, the relative calm of the terrorist and passengers, the availability of maps, the type of navigation system in the aircraft, the type of weapons the terrorist possesses, and so on. Once on the ground, the crew hopes that those individuals who are monitoring events from below will have contingency plans of their own to manage the situation safely and successfully.

The concepts of *force, target,* and *source* are important in diagnosing the special characteristics of environmental demands. In an educational setting, *force* implies the intensity of the turbulence confronting a school or a school district: "Did six letters of protest about the district busing program arrive or did 600 angry parents surround the bus parking lot and forbid the vehicles to leave?" The *target* of the turbulence relates to that part of the school system that is the focus of discontent: "Is the disturbance over the new grading policy or over the changes in the athletic program?" The *source* of the turbulence is also important because the response of the school district will no doubt differ if the source is, for example, a state accreditation board as opposed to a group of disenchanted extremist parents.

## Basic Assumptions

Contingency theory is rooted in a number of basic assumptions about organizations and individuals. A few key assumptions are as follows.

1. *Middle ground:* Contingency theory stresses the views that (a) there is some middle ground between the existence of universal principles of management that fit all organizational types, and (b) each organization is unique and therefore must be studied as unique.
2. *Goals:* Although an organization may have a basic overarching goal (e.g., to educate children, to make sick people well, to win the war), a maze of formal and informal goals, often overlapping, uncoordinated, and contradictory, govern the development of events.[7]
3. *Open systems:* All organizations are open systems.[8]
4. *Performance:* The level of performance is determined by the match between external requirements and internal states and processes.[9]
5. *Basic function:* "The basic function of administration appears to be co-alignment, not merely of people (in coalitions) but of institutionalized action—of technology and task environment into a viable domain, and of organizational design and structure appropriate to it."[10]
6. *Best way:* There is no one best way of organization and administration.

7. *Approaches:* "Different [management] approaches may be appropriate in subparts of the same organization. Managing the campus police is not the same as managing the history department."[11]
8. *Leadership style:* Different leadership styles are appropriate for different problematic situations.
9. *Initiation:* Managers rarely have the opportunity to take on a problem at its beginnings, which are usually numerous and stem from many sources (e.g., courts, parental expectations, etc.).[12]
10. *Information:* Managers never know all that is going on around them.

As discussed in the following section, another basic assumption is that all educational organizations are loosely coupled systems.

## *Loosely Coupled Systems*

When examining contingency theory in the context of organizational structure and technology, organizational problem solving, and managerial work behavior, all three have at least one conceptual common denominator—that of loose coupling.[13] Contingency theory, with its focus on adaptive responses to shifting situations, does not suggest that the entire school system be modified to meet the demands placed on only one or a select few of its components. Such rigidity of structure and process would make change virtually impossible.

Rather, the loose coupling imagery holds that the various subunits of a school (e.g., academic departments, guidance office, principal's office) have their own identity, functions, and boundaries. These units are interdependent, though tied together weakly or infrequently. Karl Weick writes that loose coupling "tends to convey the image that coupled events are responsive, *but* that each event also preserves its own identity and some evidence of its physical or logical separateness."[14]

Loose coupling permits an educational organization to make adaptive movements in several different directions by focusing on various problems at the same time. Thus, the football team trying to develop a passing game can adjust almost independently of the English department trying to develop student awareness of Shakespeare.

Under conditions of loose coupling, parts of the system may be quite innovative and other parts highly traditional, even archaic. Change does not move through the system smoothly and systematically, but by fits and starts as the loosely coupled, semi-independent subunits each must be dealt with on a different basis. On the other hand, a breakdown in one unit can be sealed off and kept from spreading to other units. Given the complexities of loosely coupled systems, "holistic change" is extremely difficult to carry out.[15]

Interestingly enough, the literature on loose coupling and the literature on effective schools create an educational dilemma. While the effective-schools literature stresses the importance of administrators exerting strong instructional leadership and classroom supervision, the loose-coupling and teacher-autonomy literature suggest that exerting such leadership is not easy or perhaps not even desirable.[16]

Mintzberg has identified ways organizations attempt to bridge gaps and tighten the coupling: (1) *mutual adjustment,* informal coordination of work; (2) *direct supervision,* one person taking responsibility for the work of others; (3) *standardization of work,* programming content and work procedures; (4) *standardization of outputs,* quality control through standardized testing; and (5) *enculturation,* informal socialization and professional training emphasizing organizational norms.[17]

The next section deals with the first of three organizational components that have received extensive treatment in contingency theory literature.

## Organizational Structure and the Environment

Zoologists have long been interested in the way animals have evolved in order to survive and prosper in their environments. Giraffes, for example, developed long legs and tall necks to enable them to feed on greens high in the air, and monkeys developed prehensile tails to facilitate movement between and among trees. In a similar manner, the so-called contingency theorists, following the tradition of the structural-functionalists[18] but with a greater emphasis on changing situations, have a special interest in the adaptation of organizations to their environments. The reward of successful adaptation is survival and perhaps even prosperity.

The pioneer contingency theorists who laid the conceptual foundation in organization structure are Woodward, Burns and Stalker, Thompson, and Lawrence and Lorsch.[19] Woodward, in her study of 100 English manufacturing companies, set out to find if generally acknowledged traditional principles of formal organization were in operation.[20] After finding that the principles of organization were widely ignored, she traced the patterns of general uniformity of structure found in different types of organizations to the type of technology those organizations employed. For example, technology calling for continuous-process production and technology calling for custom manufacturing resulted in different organizational structures. Successful firms with similar production technologies tended to display similar organizational structure. Hence, the technology of an organization became a key situational variable in determining the character of its structure.

Burns and Stalker studied 20 British firms in the electronics industry.[21] They identified two polar types of management styles, referred to as *mechanistic* and *organic,* found at the ends of a continuum. The organizations studied were found at various points on the continuum, and they were capable of moving back and forth, depending on the pressures for stability or change. "Both forms represent a 'rational' form of organization," Burns and Stalker concluded, "in that they both, in our experience, [are] explicitly and deliberately created and maintained to exploit the human resources of a concern in the most efficient manner feasible in the circumstances of the concern."[22]

In some respects, a *mechanistic* organization has many characteristics that can be compared to those of Weber's bureaucratic organization.[23] For example, both rely on the hierarchy for communication, coordination, task definition, and role expectations as well as centralized decision making and a highly defined network of rules and procedures. The mechanistic form of organization and administration was most efficient in those organizations in basically stable situations with predictable conditions prevailing.

The *organic* organizational form is the most effective in organizations faced with changing conditions. A continuous reassessment of tasks and assignments is conducted with a specialized knowledge and experience that can contribute to real problem solving. Centers of communication and decision making often shift to those individuals and points in the system that are best able to handle them in a given situation rather than to standing operating procedures and hierarchical rigidities. Thus, the stability of conditions, as contrasted with their instability, become key situational variables in determining the most efficient and effective style (mechanistic or organic) of organization and administration.

Lawrence and Lorsch probably are the prime movers behind contingency theory as a field of study.[24] Based on their empirical study of 10 organizations with varying levels of economic performance in three different industrial environments (plastics, consumer foods, and standardized containers), they argue that different types of organizations face different types of environments, such as uncertain to certain, homogeneous to diverse. The differing characteristics of the environment result in different types of structures and processes emerging within corresponding organizations.

Organizations with an uncertain and diverse environment, for purposes of obtaining high levels of efficiency, tended to be composed of *differentiated* and *integrated* subsystems. The organization needs differentiated subunits because each subunit confronts a different task posed by the organization's diverse environment. Within these various subunits, differentiation occurs in terms of distinct objectives, time requirements, interpersonal orientation, delegation of decision making, and formality of structure. In a school, for example, subsystems of teachers, vice principals, and maintenance personnel have different objectives, degrees of authority, time frames, and academic skills.

Within a differentiated organization, the integration of subunits is critical. Integration refers to the quality of the state of collaboration essential for achieving a unity of effort. This collaboration comes in the form of flexibility of procedures, open communication, shared information, and the presence of special integrating personnel. In contrast, those organizations operating in certain and homogeneous environments tend to operate mechanistically. Hence, the *certainty* or *uncertainty* of the environment and its *diversity* or *homogeneity* became key situational variables in determining the most effective and efficient form (degree of differentiation and integration) of organization and administration.

In short, issues of organization and administration cannot be understood in isolation of the situational character of the environment. Kast and Rosenzweig stress the following.

1. The closed/stable/mechanistic organizational form is more appropriate for routine activities where productivity is a major objective, and/or technology is relatively uniform and stable; where decision-making is programmable; and where environmental forces are relatively stable and certain.

2. The open/adaptive/organic [differentiated and integrated] organizational form is more appropriate for nonroutine activities where creativity and innovation are important; where heuristic decision-making processes are necessary; and where the environment is relatively uncertain and turbulent.[25]

In the educational setting, Gabarro, in his study of two small urban school systems, supported the arguments of Lawrence and Lorsch.[26] He found that the school system that was more adaptive according to several performance indicators (achievement scores, quality of placement, dropout rates, attendance, and incidence of violence) had attained higher states of differentiation and integration than the less adaptive system. Baldridge also supported the arguments in his analysis of two research studies of organizational change in schools.[27] He found that schools with differentiated subsystems operating in heterogeneous environments are more likely to be innovative than less differentiated schools operating in relatively stable homogeneous environments.

Hanson and Brown found that problems emerging from a school's turbulent environment must proceed through a series of stages and that these problems can be deflected in any number of directions, depending on the set of contingencies surrounding each stage.[28] Similar types of problems (e.g., discipline, academic weaknesses, or resource shortages) tend to generate similar types of contingencies; therefore, some degree of predictability emerges once the type of problem and the nature of the contingencies facing it are identified.

At this point it is useful to construct a conceptual framework that incorporates the major contingency theory ingredients discussed thus far. Figure 6.1 is cast in an educational setting to illustrate the core elements of the emerging perspective.

Traditional views of organizational structure concentrate on such elements as the hierarchical relationship of roles, centralized authority, rules and regulations, and span of control.[29] System theorists, however, tend to view structure more in terms of the interdependence of subunits among each other and of each to the whole.[30] The school, for example, is made up of academic departments that in turn are made up of specific classes. Central to understanding the actions of the system as a whole is an understanding of what each subsystem is doing and the functional (or dysfunctional) contribution each is making to the whole.

Leavitt has categorized the key ingredients of a subsystem as the interactions of (1) tasks, (2) structure, (3) technology, and (4) people.[31] Additionally, the various subsystems maintain degrees of differentiation and integration. The differentiation and integration establish the condition for a loosely coupled system, with the subunits maintaining various degrees of autonomy and decisional discretion. A school system maintains many such subsystems: guidance, maintenance, personnel, evaluation, learning and instruction, information management, food service, and athletics. As Figure 6.1 shows, these various subsystems interact with one another and are linked through a leadership, or management control, subsystem to make up the whole.

Contingency theory suggests that as some aspect of the environment becomes turbulent (e.g., parental complaints over course content or an increase in school accidents), the appropriate subsystem is in place and can emerge to treat the issue. Thus, time and energy from the *entire* organization do not have to be diverted from various priority projects.

In short, as an outgrowth of the open system framework, this view of contingency theory gives special emphasis to the relationship between the organization of internal subsystem processes and the demands of the external environment. The effectiveness and efficiency (and ultimately, the survival) of an organization depend on its

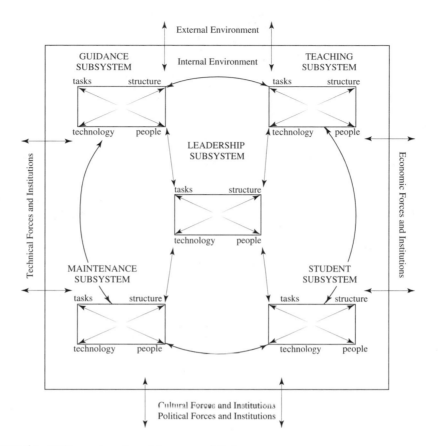

**FIGURE 6.1  Differentiated and Integrated Subsystems**
From E. Mark Hanson, "School Management and Contingency Theory: An Emerging Perspective," *Educational Administrative Quarterly*, Vol. 15, No. 2 (Spring 1979), p. 107. Copyright © 1979 by The University Council for Educational Administration.

capacity to change its internal operations (input, throughput, output) in the face of a changing environment. However, the same effect can be had by finding a means to *control or manipulate directly the levels of environmental turbulence* so that turbulence is reduced without having to change the organization at all. How is this feat accomplished? There are legitimate, illegitimate, and "gray-area" means. A noted illustration of an illegal attempt to control the external environment is recorded by Robbins.

> According to the U.S. Department of Justice, on or about February 1, 1982, the president of American Airlines, Robert L. Crandall, had a telephone conversation with Howard D. Putnam, who was chairman of Braniff International. Part of the conversation dealt with the competitive battle between American and Braniff on routes served out of the Dallas-Fort Worth airport. The following represents a segment of that telephone conversation, with the expletives deleted:

> Crandall: I think it's dumb as hell for *** sake, all right, to sit here and pound the *** out of each other and neither of us making a *** dime.
>
> Palmer: But . . . I can't just sit here and allow you to bury us without giving our best effort. . . . Do you have a suggestion for me?
>
> Crandall: Yes, I have a suggestion for you. Raise your *** fares 20 percent. I'll raise mine the next morning. . . . You'll make more money, and I will, too.
>
> Putnam: We can't talk about pricing.
>
> Crandall: Oh ***, Howard. We can talk about any *** thing we want to talk about.[32]

While avoiding illegitimate methods, school districts are by no means passive in their attempts to shape their environments. Using Robbins's categories, a few illustrations follow.[33]

1. *Advertising:* The PTA spreads the word about the benefits of the new approach to teaching math.
2. *Contracting:* The school busing program is contracted out to ensure steady, safe service.
3. *Coalescing:* A district joins forces with local community groups to pass a bond issue.
4. *Lobbying:* School districts hire a legislative advocate to lobby their causes in the state houses of government.
5. *Boundary spanning:* A district hires a Hispanic professional to communicate with the migrant community on issues of school enrollment and academic programs.

## Problem Solving in Organized Anarchies

No doubt most educators have sensed at one time or another that they are working in an organized anarchy. However, it was not until 1972 that an argument surfaced in the research literature suggesting that schools and public organizations might authentically be conceptualized as organized anarchies—at least in the way problems are solved. This *organized anarchy* perspective represented a reaction to most existing theories that assumed problem solving took place in the context of organizations with well-defined goals and technologies and benefited substantially from extensive participant involvement.[34]

Cohen, March, and Olsen argued that educational organizations can best be understood as organized anarchies because of three special properties. First, the *goals are ambiguous* and frequently inconsistent. The age-old question is: What are the goals of education? In reality, everybody and his or her brother—teachers, administrators, football coaches, PTA president, janitors—have thoughts on goals for any given school. The goals frequently run at cross-purposes when the social, political, economic, and academic content are analyzed. As Cohen and associates write, the organization "can best be defined better as a loose collection of ideas than as a coherent structure; it discovers preferences through action more than it acts on the basis of preferences."[35]

Second, the *technology of action is unclear* even to the participants. Trial-and-error procedures tend to be used with an emphasis on learning by accident and from past experience. Certainly, in education the technology is unclear. How does learning take place in a classroom? Why does a particular instructional method seem to work with one teacher but not another? In schools we are under constant pressure to change from one unclear instructional or management technology to another without really under-standing or evaluating either method.

The third major characteristic of an organized anarchy is the *fluid participation of members:* Participants vary in the amount of time, involvement, and energy they are willing to expend on any given issue. Teachers have norms of autonomy and pro-fessionalism that give them some discretion on what and how much they will do on given issues. They also have union contracts.

So how do problems get solved in an organized anarchy? Cohen, March, and Olsen, along with a growing number of other scholars, have depicted the process in what has become known as the *Garbage Can Model.*

## The Garbage Can Model of Problem Solving

Cohen and associates argue that a decision in an organized anarchy is ultimately the product of three relatively independent streams that intermingle in a choice oppor-tunity that arises in an organization. The first is a constant stream of *problems* intro-duced by both insiders and outsiders to the system. There is never a scarcity of prob-lems in schools, and the flow seems endless: reading scores are too low, the football team needs new helmets, the parking lot is overcrowded, the buses are late, the Span-ish teacher can't speak Spanish, the mayor's son got busted for selling drugs on cam-pus, and so on.

The second stream is a constant flow of *solutions.* Everyone has a solution for his or her pet problem. It could be to close the bar three blocks from the school, or to require mandatory suspension for certain student behaviors, or to introduce the Whiz-Bang reading method. However, the right moment has to present itself for the holders to press their solution forward. One just doesn't send a solution through the mail or nail it on the principal's door in the tradition of Martin Luther.

The third stream is the *fluid participation* of participants as they choose to engage or withhold the limited amount of time and energy they can devote to a particular prob-lem. The more discretion an individual has, the more unstructured the participation.

The garbage cans are referred to as *choice opportunities,* or those occasions when the organization is expected to produce a problem-solving decision. Choice opportu-nities arise when an attention-getting event takes place; for example, new teachers or administrators are hired, the budget is formulated, an accident occurs in the play-ground, math scores are published in the newspaper, or a group of parents complains about reading assignments in the history program. Such an event focuses attention and presents an opportunity to change something.

Cohen and associates use the imagery of a gargage can to describe a choice opportunity. Into the can (let us say one created by a discipline event) participants dump a load of problems, such as the impact on the athletic program if students are barred from playing football, legal questions of due process, staff resources for monitoring detention classes, the image presented to parents, and so forth. A load of solutions is dumped in also, such as automatic suspension, continuation schools, positive reinforcement, behavioral modification, self-pride exercises, corporal punishment, and so on.

Christensen argues that choice opportunities tend to arise in one of three ways. First, there are *institutionalized* choice opportunities where routinely held events, such as staff meetings, provide a regular forum for dumping in garbage. Second, they are triggered unexpectedly by *external effects,* such as a firing or resignation. Third, they are created by a *social process* that results from a growing awareness that something should be done about a particular problem.[36]

There are always numerous garbage cans (choice opportunities) present at any one time. The mixture of the garbage in any given can depends on the number of cans available and the labels on them, the speed at which the garbage is being produced, and how frequently the garbage is collected and removed (a decision made). "From this point of view, an organization is a collection of choices looking for problems, issues and feelings looking for decision situations in which they might be aired, solutions looking for issues to which they might be the answer, and decision makers looking for work."[37]

Along with the host of problems and solutions swirling around in the can are the participants. As already noted, participant involvement is fluid. That is, participants have considerable discretion to move in and out of the can to participate, based on their available time, interest, sense of obligation, and so forth.

A decision gets made because a particular solution and a particular problem floating around in the can find a sponsor. That is, a participant, or a coalition of participants, decides to use extensive time and energy to promote a particular solution to a specific problem. That participant or coalition may prevail because other participants sponsoring other problems and solutions reduce their participation or drop out from involvement altogether.

Stephen Weiner points out that the imposition of a deadline has a dramatic impact on what goes on in the garbage can. To be effective a deadline must attract attention by being fixed as well as coercive. That is, meeting the deadline involves rewards, and failing to do so involves punishments. Placing a deadline on a garbage can that is overloaded with problems and solutions changes it from a reception mode to an ejection mode. Problems and solutions without sponsors get set "adrift either to be considered elsewhere in the organization or to flow out of the organization entirely."[38] Ejecting some garbage from the can has the effect of focusing attention on the problems and solutions that remain.

An illustration of what unintended consequences a deadline can have can be seen in Weiner's study of the San Francisco desegregation effort. The presiding judge required a plan by a specific date. "The deadline led to the domination of the decision-making process by middle- and upper-class white women, who had available time during the day because they were not employed and could arrange care for their children."[39]

During that period the professional educators were caught up in responding to "a veritable nightmare of other crises and catastrophes" and could not participate extensively. Weiner argues that a key to understanding the planning and choice processes under conditions of a deadline becomes an understanding of who will devote time and energy to a particular choice opportunity. Estler makes the important point that the Garbage Can Model is an attempt to formulate a "rational (logical, deductive) model to explain nonrational events."[40] It identifies *patterns* of events that in themselves are situational. An interesting illustration of the flow of situational events is provided by Professor Daniel Duke as he reflects on his return to an elementary school classroom as a teacher's aide.

> Frequently the integrity of the day was disturbed by special assemblies, expected and unexpected visitors, teacher absences, testing, and field trips. Several teachers openly questioned the value of planning in a situation characterized by many interruptions and last-minute changes.
>
> Besides being unable to count on having particular students in class or carrying out a planned activity on schedule, teachers lived with the uncertainty of never knowing when certain troubled students would have a "bad day." Anticipation of such incidents probably was as enervating and frustrating as the actual occurrence. One teacher likened the experience to waiting for a hidden time bomb to explode.[41]

McDaniel-Hine and Willower in their structured observation research involving five elementary school teachers over five consecutive workdays recorded 2,042 observed teacher activities that were interrupted. Students were responsible for 67.6 percent of all interruptions and the teachers themselves accounted for 28.7 percent.[42]

The point is that out in the trenches where teachers are trying to deal with kids that only their mothers and Freud could love, interruptions seem to appear almost at random. However, taking a step backward, an observer can see that while the teachers are struggling with the specific situations of students—say, enrolling in the middle of a term, losing their books, or getting into fights in the playground—all these incidents come in patterns. One can actually count on students enrolling in the middle of terms, losing their books, and getting into fights. In fact, with a little recordkeeping, one can actually predict how often these, as well as many other aggravating incidents, will occur in a given school.

In sum, as Estler observes, the Garbage Can Model enables us to picture not just chaos, but the process of chaos. "It suggests an order to things but an order that is situational."[43] Weiner offers some tactical advice for those managers who view problem solving in terms of the Garbage Can Model.

1. Distract the opposition by assigning opponents to issues that will absorb much of their time. If no competing issues are attractive to capturing attention, create some.
2. Recognize your own limits of time and energy and be selective in the number of decisions you seek to mold.
3. Impose deadlines with care because they may work for or against you. If you

can't impose a deadline yourself, try to obtain the assistance of the press, the courts, or pressure groups.

4. Use outside friends to assist you. They may have experience, prestige, and expertise that can help.[44]

In sum, the conceptual perspective of the school as an organized anarchy (ambiguous goals, unclear technology, and fluid participation) leads to the image of a situational problem-solving process that fits the contingency theory framework. The situational character of that process is determined by interested individuals who choose to devote an amount of their limited time and energy in sponsoring a solution to a problem (among many solutions to many problems) that happens to be around when a choice opportunity arises.

The next section switches focus from the situational nature of the setting where problem solving takes place, to situational behavior of the problem solver.

## Managerial Work Behavior

Henry Mintzberg began an important line of thought and inquiry when he asked the question, What do managers do?—not What should they do? or What do they say they do? but What do they *really* do?[45] Through most of this century, generations of managers have been taught that they practiced the preachings of Henry Fayol's famous administrative process of planning, organizing, commanding, coordinating, and controlling.[46] Mitzberg had his doubts.

Starting in the mid-1960s, Mintzberg used a method called "structured observation," in observing five chief executives of five medium-to-large organizations for a period of one week each. One of the chief executives was a school superintendent. He collected data in three records: a *chronology record* of activity patterns throughout the work day; a *mail record* involving format, sender, attention it received, and the action it stimulated; and a *contact record* for each of the interpersonal interactions in terms of purpose, medium (scheduled meeting, telephone call), location, and participants.

Mintzberg drew two sets of conclusions. The first deals with characteristics of managerial work, which includes a numerical analysis of how, with whom, and under what conditions managers spend their time. The second set of conclusions identifies the content of managerial work in terms of ten distinct roles utilized to perform that work.

Several Mintzberg-type studies have been conducted in the field of education in recent years. This line of research in education has supported Mintzberg's original conclusions on the characteristics and content of managerial work.[47] His conclusions on the special characteristics of managerial work, along with some supporting research, are as follows.

> *Characteristic 1: Managers perform a great quantity of work at an unrelenting pace.*
> In their study of five high school principals, Martin and Willower found that the principals averaged 42.2 hours of work during the week and 11.0 more at night. An average of 149.2 separate tasks were performed daily.[48] There tends to be no real break in the pace and almost no time for leisurely reflection about the job during office hours.

*Characteristic 2: Managerial activity is characterized by variety, fragmentation, and brevity.* In a study of eight superintendents, Friesen and Duignan found the these chief executives to be given to short encounters (65 percent of all activities lasting less than 10 minutes), verbal contacts (70 percent of total time was spent in verbal contacts), and devoted to a multitude of separate purposes.[49] Indeed, systematic, patterned behavior was not a part of the normal work day.

*Characteristic 3: Managers prefer issues that are current, specific, and ad hoc.* Consistent with Mintzberg's observations, Martin and Willower concluded that school principals prefer the action components of their roles, trying for quick closure whenever possible. They concentrated their energy in the most current and demanding situations and invested little time in reflective thought and planning.[50]

*Characteristic 4: Managers sit between their organization and a network of contacts.* Managers are at the center of a diverse and complex web of contacts that provide them with necessary information to run the organization. The network includes formal linkages with superordinates and subordinates as well as informal linkages with associates, friends, state officials, former college professors, textbook publishers, and so forth. "Figuratively, the manager appears as the neck of an hour-glass, sifting information into his own organization from its environment."[51]

*Characteristic 5: Managers demonstrate a strong preference for the verbal media.* Managers have five information media associated with their work: mail, telephone, unscheduled meetings, scheduled meetings, and published documents. Information transfers involving verbal exchanges were preferred over written or visual modes, no matter what the setting.

*Characteristic 6: Despite the preponderance of obligations, managers appear to be able to control their own affairs.* At first glance managers appear to be puppets jerked around by the capricious demands of large and small events. Such seems not to be the case. Mintzberg found that managers can *use* the turbulent flow of events, as they are being used by it, to motivate subordinates, provide leadership, impose their system of values, and use crisis opportunities to innovate. In the turbulence, the managers kept sight of their long-range commitments.

## The Manager's Work Roles

Mintzberg defines a role as "organized sets of behaviors belonging to identifiable offices or positions."[52] He found 10 roles in his research that could be classified as part of one or more of three basic behaviors: interpersonal, informational, and decisional.

Interpersonal behavior focuses on interpersonal contact and can be found in the: (1) *figurehead role,* the manager as ceremonial head and visible symbol of the organization; (2) *leader role,* the driving force behind the work efforts of subordinates; and (3) *liaison role,* the channel of horizontal contact with other managers.

The second set of behaviors is categorized as informational and include the: (1) *nerve center role,* the manager is connected with every individual and every issue in the system and sends out those vital pulses that keep it unified and moving; (2) *disseminator role,* one of transmitting facts, values, and ideas within and between the organization and its environment, and (3) *spokesman role,* one of transmitting information to influential outside individuals and groups about the organization's performance policies and plans.

The third set of behaviors is categorized as decisional and include the: (1) *entre-preneur role,* which sets up the manager as designer and initiator of planned change efforts; (2) *disturbance handler role,* which places emphasis on striving for peace and stability; (3) *resource allocator role,* in which the manager decides who gets how much of what; and (4) negotiator role, of resource trading to bring about an accept-able solution to the needs of individuals and the requirements of the organization.

One role Mintzberg did not treat is the much heralded role of the principal referred to as *instructional leader.* In their study of five high school principals, Martin and Wil-lower found that only 17.4 percent of their time and 7.6 percent of their tasks involved the academic program.[53] In their study of five elementary school principals, Kmetz and Willower found that 29.1 percent of their time and 12.3 percent of their tasks involved the academic program.[54] One might conclude that in the allocation of a principal's time, instructional leadership is not as big a winner as people believe. In summing up managerial work behavior, Mintzberg writes:

> The quantity of work is great; the pace is unrelenting; there is great variety, fragmen-tation, and brevity in the work activities; the manager must concentrate on issues that are current, specific, and ad hoc, and to do so, he finds that he must rely on verbal forms of communications. Yet it is on this man that the burden lies for designing and oper-ating strategy-making and information-processing systems that are to solve his orga-nization's (and society's) problems.[55]

In short, viewing the nature of work through the conceptual lens cast by Mintzberg places great importance on the situational character of the management task. As conditions shift rapidly throughout the day, the manager must adapt his or her behavior just as quickly by responding in the appropriate role. The difficult task is rec-ognizing with clarity the substance of each ensuing problem and responding with the appropriate role.

An important feature of the growing volume of research that is providing new answers to such old questions as, What do managers do? is the methodology of inquiry employed. In recent years, ethnographic techniques, such as those employed in the seminal work of Harry Wolcott, have provided vivid new insight into the complex processes of educational administration.[56]

## Research Questions on Contingency Theory

At this time, no contingency theories specific to educational administration exist. A number of issues that might give an initial sense of direction to the development and application of the theory have been introduced. Cast as general research questions, these issues are as follows:

1. As the environment of a school becomes turbulent, is there a tendency for the internal subsystems to become more differentiated and integrated in order to respond to the turbulence—or do they become more mechanistic and stan-dardized to defend against the turbulence?

2. Do educational organizations develop different mechanistic or organic responses according to different types of environmental turbulence (e.g., cultural, political, economic, informational, technical, and physical)?

3. In what ways do the ill-defined, teaching-learning technology of educational organizations inhibit or facilitate a close match with the demands and constraints of the external environment?

4. What are the limits to the fluid participation of educators in school problem solving?

5. Do conditions of organized anarchy make parent involvement easier or more difficult?

6. What are the core uncertainties we must deal with in education?

7. What are the major choice opportunities in education?

8. What are the principal ways that educators select their problems and solutions from the garbage can?

9. What are the various roles that educators must play in schools?

10. What are the special characteristics of schools that tend to result in managerial behavior that is verbal, fragmented, and ad hoc?

11. As the external environment becomes more technologically complex, do the management systems of schools respond to pressures to make their planning methods more sophisticated?

Work toward understanding the situational character of schools and the resulting impact on managerial practice is now perhaps one of the most exciting and productive challenges in the field. Research in this area would be welcomed by academics and practitioners alike.[57]

## Conclusion

In ancient Persia there were once two cellmates condemned to death by the sultan. Knowing how much the sultan loved his great white stallion, one prisoner offered to teach the horse to fly within a year in exchange for his life. The sultan, fancying himself as the rider of the only flying horse in the world, agreed. The other prisoner looked on in disbelief. "You *know* horses don't fly. You're only postponing the inevitable."

"Not so," said the clever tactician. "I have actually given myself *four* chances for freedom. First, the sultan might die during the year. Second, I might die. Third, the horse might die. And fourth, you know, I might just teach that horse to fly." The clever prisoner is, of course, responding to his problematic situation with a contingency plan.

This chapter dealt principally with a discussion of three existing contingency theory orientations that focus on separate components of the organization. The points of focus are: (1) organizational structure and the environment, (2) problem solving in organized anarchies, and (3) managerial work behavior. The situational character of what happens to and within organizations is the common denominator of all three orientations.

In the first orientation, dealing with uncertainty in a way that reduces risks through intelligent forethought and preparation is at the core of contingency planning. Such efforts generally require a flexible response capability. The school system as a loosely coupled organization makes it possible for the various units to function with a measure of independence. Thus, as the school's environment shifts between placid and turbulent, the separate components of the system (e.g., guidance office, curriculum planning committee) can respond as the situation requires.

The Garbage Can Theory of problem solving in organized anarchies is not inconsistent with the view of organizations adjusting to shifting conditions in their environments. It is precisely because of these shifting environments that the streams of problems and solutions keep flowing into the cans (choice opportunities). When stability arrives at a particular arena of action, that garbage can is no longer necessary. Nauseating as the garbage can imagery is, it does provide food for thought.

Finally, Mintzberg's notions about managerial work behavior appear to be consistent with the first two focuses of contingency theory. A colleague of mine likes to think of managers not as garbage collectors who throw the whole lot out, but as rag-pickers who quickly rummage through the piles of solutions and problems trying to extract those that may have some value before the garbage truck (deadline) comes by.

While the analogies may be a bit overdrawn, the reality is that contingency theory is upon us. In its various forms, this situational view of our schools and the people who work in them appears to be very important in helping us obtain a clearer view of how educational systems function in the real world. It is important to note that the explorations of contingency theory and its applications to education are in their infancy.

## Notes

1. Leo Tolstoy, *War and Peace,* 2 vols., R. Edmonds, 2, trans. (Middlesex, England: Penguin, 1957), p. 979.

2. P. Khandwalla, *The Design of Organizations* (New York: Harcourt Brace Jovanovich, 1977), p. 248.

3. James D. Thompson, *Organizations in Action* (New York: McGraw-Hill, 1967), p. 159.

4. James G. March and H. A. Simon, *Organizations* (New York: Wiley, 1958), p. 137.

5. Richard Cyert and James G. March, *A Behavioral Theory of the Firm* (Englewood Cliffs, NJ: Prentice-Hall, 1963), p. 119.

6. Ibid.

7. Michael D. Cohen, James G. March, and J. P. Olsen, "A Garbage Can Model of Organizational Choice," *Administrative Science Quarterly* 17 (March 1972): 1–25.

8. Daniel Katz and Robert L. Kahn, *The Social Psychology of Organizations,* 2nd ed. (New York: Wiley, 1978), p. 2.

9. J. Lorsch and P. Lawrence, *Studies in Organizational Design* (Homewood, IL: Irwin and Dorsey, 1970), p. 1.

10. Thompson, *Organizations in Action,* p. 157.

11. F. Kast and J. Rosenzweig, eds., *Contingency Views of Organization and Management* (Chicago: Science Research Associates, 1973), p. x.

12. Henry Mintzberg, *The Structuring of Organizations* (Englewood Cliffs, NJ: Prentice-Hall, 1979).

13. For a discussion of the background of this concept see: Ronald Corwin, "Patterns of Organizational Control and Teacher Militancy:Theoretical Continuities in the Idea of 'Loose Coupling,' " in *Research in Sociology of Education and Socialization,* vol. 2, Alan C. Kerckhoff, ed. (Greenwich, CT: AJAI, 1981), pp. 261–291.

14. Kark E.Weick, "Educational Organization as Loosely Coupled Systems," *Administrative Science Quarterly* 21 (1976): 1–19.

15. For an excellent analysis of the "loose coupling" concept see: Donald J.Willower, "School Organizations: Perspective in Juxtaposition," *Educational Administration Quarterly* 18 (1982): 89–110.

16. William Firestone, "The Study of Loose Coupling: Problems, Progress, and Prospects," in *Research in Sociology of Education and Socialization* 5 (1985): 3–30; Frank Lutz, "Tightening Up Loose Coupling in Organizations of Higher Education," *Administrative Science Quarterly* 27 (1987): 653–669.

17. Henry Mintzberg, *Structures in Fives: Designing Effective Organizations* (Englewood Cliffs, NJ: Prentice-Hall, 1983).

18. Talcott Parsons, *The Social System* (New York: Free Press, 1951); and Talcott Parsons, *Structure and Process in Modern Societies* (New York: Free Press, 1960).

19. Joan Woodward, *Industrial Organization:Theory and Practice* (London: Oxford University Press, 1965);T. Burns and G. M. Stalker, *The Management of Innovation* (London: Tavistock, 1961);Thompson, *Organizations in Action;* and P. Lawrence and J. Lorsch, *Organizational Environment: Management Differentiation and Integration* (Boston: Harvard University Graduate School of Business Administration, 1967).

20. Woodward, *Industrial Organization.*

21. Burns and Stalker, *The Management of Innovation.*

22. Ibid., p. 119.

23. Max Weber, *The Theory of Social and Economic Organization,* A. M. Henderson and T. Parsons, trans. (New York: Oxford University Press, 1947; Free Press, 1964), pp. 333–334.

24. P. Lawrence and J. Lorsch, *Developing Organizations: Diagnosis and Action* (Reading, MA: Addison-Wesley, 1969); and Lawrence and Lorsch, *Organizational Environment.*

25. Kast and Rosenzweig, *Contingency Views,* p. 331.

26. John Gabarro, "School System Organization and Adaptation to a Changing Environment," Ph.D. dissertation, Harvard University Graduate School of Business, 1971.

27. J.Victor Baldrige, "Organizational Innovation: Individual, Structural, and Environmental Impacts," in *Managing Change in Educational Organizations,* J.V. Baldridge and T. Deal, eds. (Berkeley, CA: McCutchan, 1975).

28. E. Mark Hanson and Michael E. Brown, "A Contingency View of Problem Solving in Schools: A Case Analysis," *Educational Administration Quarterly* 13 (1977): 71–91.

29. Charles Perrow, "The Short and Glorious History of Organization Theory," *Organization Dynamics* 2 (Summer 1973): 2–15.

30. Parsons, *The Social System.*

31. H. J. Leavitt, "Applied Organizational Change in Industry: Structure,Technological, and Humanistic Approaches," in *Handbook of Organizations,* J. G. March, ed. (Chicago: Rand McNally, 1965).

32. Stephen Robbins, *Organizational Theory: Structure, Desgin, and Applications,* 2nd ed. (Englewood Cliffs, NJ: Prentice-Hall, 1987), p. 298.

33. Robbins, p. 289.

34. Cohen, March, and Olsen, "A Garbage Can Model," pp. 1–25.

35. Ibid., p. 1.

36. Soren Christensen, "Decision Making and Socialization," in *Ambiguity and Choice in Organizations,* James G. March and Johan Olsen, eds. (Bergen, Norway: Universitetsforlaget, 1976), p. 373.

37. Cohn, March, and Olsen, "A Garbage Can Model," p. 2.

38. Stephen Weiner, "Participation, Deadlines, and Choice, in *The Dynamics of Organizational Choice,* J. Victor Baldridge and Terrence Deal, eds. (Berkeley, CA: McCutchan, 1983), p. 302.

39. Weiner, "Participation," pp. 288–289.

40. Susanne Estler, "Decision Making" in *Handbook of Research on Educational Administration,* Norman Boyan, ed. (New York: Longman, 1988), pp. 313–314.

41. Daniel Duke, "Understanding What It Means to Be a Teacher," *Educational Leadership* (October 1986): 27.

42. Louise McDaniel-Hine and Donald Willower, "Elementary School Teachers' Work Behavior," *Journal of Educational Research* 81 (1988): 277.

43. Estler, p. 314.

44. Weiner, "Participation," pp. 303–304.

45. Henry Mintzberg, "Managerial Work: Analysis from Observation," in *Readings in Organizational Behavior and Performance,* Andrew D. Szilagyi, Jr. and Marc J. Wallace, Jr., eds. (Santa Monica, CA: Goodyear, 1980), pp. 158–174. For a more complete discussion see: Henry Mintzberg, *The Nature of Managerial Work* (Englewood Cliffs, NJ: Prentice-Hall, 1980).

46. Henri Fayol, *General and Industrial Management* (London: Sir Issac Pitman, 1949), pp. 5-6.

47. David Friesen and Patric Duignan, "How Superintendents Spend Their Working Time" *The Canadian Administrator* 19 (1980): 1-5; Nancy Pitner and Rodney Ogawa, "Organizational Leadership: The Case of the School Superintendent," *Educational Administration Quarterly* 17 (Spring 1981): 45-65; Thomas A. Ross and J. N. Adamson, "Profile of a Principal," *The Practicing Administrator* 3 (1981): 12-14; John Kmetz and Donald Willower, "Elementary School Principals' Work Behavior," *Educational Administration Quarterly* 18 (1982): 62-78; and William Martin and Donald Willower, "The Managerial Behavior of High School Principals," *Educational Administration Quarterly* 17 (1981): 69-90.

48. Martin and Willower, "The Managerial Behavior," p. 71.

49. Friesen and Duignan, "How Superintendents Spend," pp. 3-4.

50. Martin and Willower, "The Managerial Behavior," p. 80.

51. Mintzberg, "Managerial Work," p. 162.

52. Ibid., p. 165.

53. Martin and Willower, "The Managerial Behavior," p. 77.

54. Kmetz and Willower, "Elementary School Principals," p. 71.

55. Mintzberg, "Managerial Work," p. 172.

56. Harry Wolcott, *The Man in the Principal's Office* (New York: Holt, Rinehart and Winston, 1973).

57. For an interesting examination of "motivation" in a situational context see: Robert R. Newton, "Theory X? Theory Y? You May Be Theory N," *NASSP Bulletin* 64 (1980): 64-66.

Chapter $7$

# Organizational Leadership and the School Administrator

The exhortation to be a leader has always been a teaching point of American culture. From the awakening stages of youth, young men and women are counseled that special rewards await those who achieve the coveted skill of leadership. (As a counterpoint, in my own youth I had a philosophy professor who argued that what this world needs is fewer—not more—great leaders, because the great leaders are the ones who are always getting us into trouble.)

An examination of the mountain of literature on leadership has led numerous reviewers to suggest that there is less there than meets the eye. "Several thousand empirical studies," Yukl writes, "have been conducted on leader traits, behavior, power and situational variables as predictors of leadership effectiveness, but most of the results are contradictory and inconclusive."[1]

The concept is a many-faceted one, surrounded by a mass of myth, conventional wisdom, idealism, and illusion. Part of the reason for this confusion is that as a social science concept, as well as in popular usage, the idea of leadership evolves from the particular perspective one holds. James Lipham reminds us, "In much of the literature the myth is perpetuated that leadership is unitary in nature. Hence, one tries to identify it, describe it, capture it, exercise it, rate it, measure it, and above all, correlate and predict it. And all the while, the simple 'it' is a very complex 'them.' "[2]

The intent of this chapter is to sink a few critical shafts into the literature on leadership and organize it so we can see where the concept of leadership has been, where it stands now, and where it appears to be going. Like other social science concepts, the notion of leadership is continually evolving, often moving in numerous directions simultaneously. Ernest Dale points out, "While the power of good leadership to produce extraordinary results is a fact, it is difficult to produce facts about what it actually consists of."[3] Perhaps he should have added that it is difficult to produce facts that are generally accepted and hold over time.

The shifting character of leadership is captured in the exasperated voice of the colorful former baseball manager, Leo "The Lip" Durocher, commenting on the complexities of managing today. "Whatever happened to 'sit down, shut up and listen!' "

The concept of leadership will be developed as it is seen differently through the organizational perspectives of classical theory, social system theory, and open system theory. A brief overview of the three perspectives will be presented first, followed by a comprehensive discussion of each.

The *classical theory perspective* finds the leader in the upper reaches of the hierarchy and endowed with natural psychological traits that give him or her advantages over most mortals. Woven through this perspective is the notion that leaders are born and not made. As an illustration, within this context, Robinson Crusoe was a leader on the island even before he met Friday, his eventual companion.

The *social system* perspective involves a situational view of leadership. As the relationship among environment, organization, and workers changes, so must the leadership in response to the new situation. Leadership is not seen as fixed in some superior psychological traits but in the ability to recognize changing situations and respond to new needs with the appropriate set of behaviors. For example, Crusoe would be very directive with Friday in giving instructions about the construction of their stockade and defensive positions. However, when it came to catching fish or living off the land, Crusoe would recognize Friday's superior knowledge and experience and thus employ democratic leadership procedures.

*Open system theory* suggests that the leader works to establish an effective fit between the internal and external environments of the organization. In the open system context, Crusoe as leader would study the special characteristics of the external and internal environments and link them in such a way that resulting plans would provide for security, health, and feeding of himself and Friday. For example, he would study the weather cycle, especially the typhoon and rainy seasons, build shelters, and plant corn accordingly. Raiding trips by hostile natives from neighboring islands would be analyzed and attempts made to make peace treaties based on trade. Finally, Crusoe would teach Friday how to read, and both would learn the other's language so that human contact and more effective working relationships would be facilitated.

The next section will deal in detail with the context of classical organization theory.

## The Leadership Role

### Leaders and Managers

People who spend a lot of time in educational systems are frequently asked why schools are so different from each other. More often than not the answer is leadership. Harbison and Myers stress the point: "The tone of an organization is usually sounded by its top executive, and the success of the enterprise may well depend on whether he infuses the whole hierarchy with energy and vision or whether, through ineptness or neglect, he allows the organization to stagnate."[4] Napoleon Bonaparte had his own way of saying much the same thing: "There are no bad regiments, only bad colonels."

The organization's formal leader is in a unique position to set the tone in schools, or regiments, because of his or her broad mandate to carry out the unit's mission. "He is the only one," Mintzberg points out, "who can meddle at will."[5]

The terms *leader, manager,* and *administrator* tend to be used interchangeably (as they have been in this text and will continue to be so after this section). However, there are differences. *Manager* and *administrator* are practically synonymous, except that the former tends to be more contemporary and carries the implicit connotation of possessing some significant degree of decision-making authority. An administrator, on the other hand, may be little more than an organization functionary carrying out routine tasks.[6]

The concept of *leader* concentrates on two areas: the leader's strategic vision about the direction the organization should go, and the leader's noncoercive skill at drawing subordinates into the active pursuit of the strategic view.[7] The concept of *manager,* on the other hand, focuses on the nuts and bolts of making the organization work, such as hiring, evaluating, distributing resources, and enforcing rules. As a footnote to the irony of history, Richard Nixon points out that leaders "do the right thing" while managers "do things right."

Edgar Schein argues that a principal function of leadership, as distinguished from management and administration, is shaping and directing the organization's culture. "What the leader needs most is *insight into the ways in which culture can aid or hinder the fulfillment of the organization's mission* and the *intervention skills to make desired changes happen* [emphasis in original]."[8]

The terms *leader* and *manager* can be conceptualized as two lines with an intersecting axis. The polar positions of each of the lines are labeled *strong* and *weak.*

Considering the leader-manager axis, we have the potential of encountering strong leaders who are weak managers. In education we often see this individual generating grand ideas about sweeping reforms or innovative new programs. He or she effectively whips up enthusiastic support on all sides. Unfortunately, ideas and enthusiasm are not enough, and not long after execution of the changes is attempted, the vision begins to crumble. By that time the strong leader, more often than not, has a better job somewhere else and is creating a vision for another audience. Those who were left behind, like the unfortunate lemmings, are in deep water.

The strong manager who is a weak leader also exists in education. This is the person who keeps his or her nose to the grindstone, ear to the ground, foot on the throttle, and finger to the wind. Trying to make all subordinates emulate that posture earns such a manager the title of "the one you love to hate." This individual usually can get a job done, but has trouble sustaining quality performances over the long run.

Reflecting on the two concepts, Mintzberg writes, "It is in the *leader* role that managerial power most clearly manifests itself. Formal authority vests the manager with great potential power; leadership activity determines how much of it will be realized."[9] What we need, therefore, are strong leaders who are also strong managers. Unfortunately, such a combination, like the abominable snowman, is larger than life but rarely encountered. Having a competent leader *and* manager is the best most schools can hope for—and they'll be overjoyed if they get that!

## Leadership Definitions

Hunt and Osborn point out that most contemporary leadership theorists tend to treat leadership as an influence process directed at either an individual *or* a group. They argue that the leadership role requires attention to individuals *and* organizations. "Essentially, we see him [the leader] filling the gap between subordinate desires and abilities on one hand and organizational goals and requirements on the other. In essence, when the gap is filled, there should be satisfied subordinates in a high performance organization."[10]

Cribbin expands on this theme, differentiating between what he calls successful leadership and effective leadership. "Successful leadership is the ability to get others to behave as the manager intended. The job gets done and the manager's needs are satisfied, but those of the other people are ignored." Effective leadership, on the other hand, results in the manager's intentions being realized as well as the needs of the employees being satisfied.[11]

Definitions of leadership differ because writers' perspectives differ. As writers attempt to dissect the leadership phenomenon and articulate its essence, however, three basic elements seem to be emphasized either singly or in combination: people, processes, and systems. Each of these basic elements possesses important variations that define leadership, for example: (1) the presence of unique psychological traits or behavior characteristics (*people*); (2) the art of compelling compliance or inducing compliance (*processes*); (3) the presence of formal structure, informal structure, differential problem situations (e.g., task complexity, personnel competence), or the external organizational environment (*systems*).

Ralph Stogdill has observed that the vast multitude of definitions of leadership can be categorized under the headings listed below. A close examination of these categories reveals the presence of one or more of the three basic elements identified above.

1. Leadership as a focus of group processes
2. Leadership as a personality and its effects
3. Leadership as the art of inducing compliance
4. Leadership as the exercise of influence
5. Leadership as an act or behavior
6. Leadership as a form of persuasion
7. Leadership as an instrument of goal achievement
8. Leadership as an effect of interaction
9. Leadership as a differential role
10. Leadership as the initiation of structure[12]

All three of the organizational perspectives discussed in this chapter contain the three basic elements—people, processes, and systems; the difference is the degree of emphasis attached to each element. Classical theory definitions of leadership emphasize psychological traits (people), compelling compliance (processes), and formal structure (systems). Sociopolitical theory definitions of leadership emphasize behavior characteristics (people), inducing compliance (processes), and differential problem situations and formal and informal structure (systems). Open system theory definitions emphasize the characteristics of the other two models, but only as they relate to the demands of specific situations.

### The Leadership Environment: Classical Theory

Within the classical theory perspective, the leadership environment assumes rationality in people, processes, and structures. In an effort to understand the complexities of dynamic organizational processes, people simplify the world around them by interpreting events in understandable human terms. Events are seen as the rational acts of people rather than the consequence of uncontrollable social and economic forces.[13]

The leader holds a high position because he or she is an elitist of sorts—superior in mind, knowledge, and experience. The leader possesses, as Barnard observes, the ability "to bind the wills of men to the accomplishment of purposes beyond their immediate ends, beyond their times."[14] Therefore, no one else is more qualified to sort out the tangles of problem situations and set the organization back on the track of maximum efficiency. In pursuit of this task, the leader is supported by the full weight of the formal organization hierarchy and all the power, information, and resources that the hierarchy can bring into focus.

In much of the effective-schools literature, Burlingame points out, the principal is supremely and pragmatically rational, "and has the intellectual abilities to ascertain appropriate goals for the school, to review possible alternatives, to weight consequences, and to select appropriate solutions."[15] The leadership environment assumes predictability in people, events, and processes. In organizational decision making, sufficient data and time are always available, resources are adequate, people are motivated, and the logic is clear with respect to the best solution a leader should choose among all the available alternatives.

In pursuit of the best solution, the leader manipulates the formal organization by creating new structures, forming new policy, adding, eliminating, or merging departments, and so forth.[16] In the eyes of the leader these events take place within the limited confines of a closed system. If his or her psychological traits are the right ones, and if these traits are strong enough, the leader has the capacity to overcome the toughest organizational problems.

### Leadership and Psychological Traits

Early in this century Thomas Carlyle postulated the "great man theory" of leadership, which argued that world progress can be attributed to the individual achievements of great men.[17] Katz and Kahn write:

> The "great man" school views history as a study of biography. The Protestant reformation is the story of Luther, of Calvin, and of Zwingli; the French revolution, the story of Voltaire, Robespierre, Danton, and Napoleon; and our own period, the tale of Hitler, Roosevelt, Churchill, Stalin, Gandhi, Mao, DeGaulle and Tito. On the other hand, the cultural determinists see history in terms of social patterns relatively unaffected by the intervention of leaders.[18]

This great man notion has been a recurring theme in literature, often being cast into the question: Do great men cause great times or do great times cause great men? Shakespeare entered the debate when he wrote, "Some are born great, some achieve greatness, and some have greatness thrust upon them," to which Kelly adds, "[others] purchase it; some win it by strength, force, or nepotism; and not a few marry into it."[19]

During the decades prior to World War II, research on leadership was based on the assumption that a leader's skill can be explained by the identification of psychological (and at times even physiological) traits that manifest themselves in superior managerial abilities. Shortly after World War II, Stogdill published a bench-mark study in which he reviewed 124 studies of psychological traits as they related to leaders. The research question under investigation was: What are the discrete psychological traits that can be said to distinguish leaders from followers?

> The following conclusions are supported by uniformly positive evidence from 15 or more of the studies surveyed: The average person who occupies a position of leadership exceeds the average member of his group in the following respects: (1) intelligence, (2) scholarship, (3) dependability in exercising responsibilities, (4) activity and social participation, and (5) socio-economic status. The following conditions are supported by uniformly positive evidence from 10 or more of the studies surveyed: The average person who occupies a position of leadership exceeds the average member of his group to some degree in the following respects: (1) sociability, (2) initiative, (3) persistence, (4) knowing how to get things done, (5) self-confidence, (6) alertness to, and insight into, situations, (7) cooperativeness, (8) popularity, (9) adaptability, (10) verbal facility.[20]

Stogdill argued that traits considered as isolated entities hold little diagnostic or predictive significance. In clusters or combinations, however, they interact in a way advantageous to the individual seeking leadership responsibilities. He identified the clusters of traits as:

1. Capacity (intelligence, alertness, verbal facility, originality, judgment)
2. Achievement (scholarship, knowledge, athletic accomplishments)
3. Responsibility (dependability, initiative, persistence, aggressiveness, self-confidence, desire to excel)
4. Participation (activity, sociability, cooperation, adaptability, humor)
5. Status (socio-economic position, popularity)
6. Situation (mental level, status, skills, needs and interests of followers, objectives to be achieved, etc.)[21]

Number 6 in the list above makes it especially clear that leadership is actually a combination of specific personal attributes fulfilling leadership needs that arise in specific situations. As Stogdill wrote later:

> Strong evidence indicates that different leadership skills and traits are required in different situations. The behaviors and traits enabling a mobster to gain and maintain control over a criminal gang are not the same as those enabling a religious leader to gain and maintain a large following. Yet certain general qualities—such as courage, fortitude, and conviction—appear to characterize both.[22]

At midcentury a transition was under way.

## From Psychological Traits to Sociological Settings

Researchers prior to World War II tried to isolate psychological traits that could distinguish leaders from followers. However, reviews of the literature such as those by Jenkins[23] and Stogdill[24] revealed the futility of this effort. A number of difficulties are associated with the trait approach to leadership, such as:

1. As behaviors that appeared not to be related to existing traits were revealed in the data, new traits were postulated, "until it became apparent that that which included everything discriminated nothing. Traits became mere tautologies due to the fact that no independent measures of the traits were available."[25]
2. Because there were no finite and suitable psychological taxonomies, lists of leadership traits, as Lipham points out, "often included somewhat contradictory traits—kind but firm, pensive but active, steady but flexible, forceful but cooperative."[26]
3. Test scores identifying leadership traits were not predictive of later leader effectiveness in organizations.
4. The psychological trait approach ignored the important interaction between the individual and the group.

A number of distinguished researchers helped put the *coup de grâce* to the prolonged and unfulfilled quest for a taxonomy of psychological traits that would distinguish leaders from followers. On this issue Alvin Gouldner wrote, "At this time there is no reliable evidence concerning the existence of universal leadership traits."[27]

During the years following World War II, emphasis shifted from the study of psychological factors in individuals to the sociological factors of groups. James Lipham writes, "This shift in focus was rapid and drastic. Bearing some similarity to ancient nature-nurture, heredity-environment, and instinct-training controversies, a struggle ensued between the 'traitists' and the 'situationists,' the latter emerging victorious from the fray."[28]

The study of leadership in group settings will be the subject of the next section of this chapter.

# Leadership in Sociopolitical Groups

## Leadership Definitions

Perhaps no single definition of leadership will ever be found to be entirely satisfactory, but at least the various definitions in the literature serve to call attention to different orientations and degrees of emphasis in the leadership problem. Definitions in the sociopolitical group context also tend to include, but with differing degrees of emphasis, the *people, processes,* and *systems* ingredients of the leadership formula. For example:

1. Katz and Kahn consider the essence of leadership to be "the influential increment over and above mechanical compliance with the routine directives of

the organization."[29] The focus here is on the leader's ability to induce "extra effort" from the followers.

2. Lipham writes of the inherent contradiction in most definitions of *administrative leadership*. "The administrator is concerned primarily with maintaining, rather than changing, established structures, procedures, or goals. Thus, the administrator may be viewed as a stabilizing force. . . .We may define leadership as the initiation of a new structure or procedure for accomplishing [or changing] an organization's goals or objectives."[30]

3. Jacob Getzels argues that definitions describing the leader as one who initiates a *new structure* in social systems, as many definitions do, are inadequate. He contends, "The missing ingredient is recognition that leadership depends on *followership*, a function of cooperation or mutuality *with* the leader rather than forcible domination and coercion *by* the leader."[31]

4. Getzels et al. distinguish between superordination, where authority is granted to the individual by the institution, and leadership, where the authority is extended by the followers. The source of superordination lies in *vested authority*, whereas the source of leadership lies in *entrusted authority*.[32]

5. Kelly stresses that it is the group that attains goals and not the leader, and that "leadership is the performance of acts which assist the group in achieving certain ends."[33]

6. Boles and Davenport say that leadership is a process—not a category of behavior, a prerogative of position or personality, nor a collectivity of persons. "By our definition, leadership is a process in which an individual takes initiative to assist a group to move toward production goals that are acceptable, to maintain the group, and to dispose of these needs of individuals that impelled them to join it."[34]

Not only do the definitions of leadership associated with the sociopolitical group context differ from those associated with the classical theory context, but as can be expected, the organizational environment within which leadership takes place is seen as radically different.

## *The Leadership Environment*

The leadership environment as seen through the lens of classical theory emphasizes rationality, clarity, and precision. The same environment as seen through the lens of sociopolitical group theory emphasizes inconsistency, ambiguity, and compromise. Willar Lane et al. write that educational leadership cannot be understood apart from its *complex power environment.*

> For although leaders deal directly with individuals, ultimately it is organizations—that is, group traditions, established relationships, and vested interest groups—which are their main concern. Clearly, the problems, dilemmas, and inconsistencies of the organization and of the society are the problems of the leader. They constitute the leadership setting.[35]

Simply holding the formal leadership role is not enough to ensure that the collectivity of human involvement will be responsive to the initiatives of the leaders. They also must establish a base of power and trust that will ensure followership. George Homans thinks of this process as "the tactics of position maintenance." Among these tactics are: The leader lives up the the norms of his or her group; the leader originates interaction; and the leader does not give orders that he or she believes will not be obeyed.[36]

In addition, instead of being the person in direct control of the school or the school district, the leader is seen as the person in the middle who must somehow perform acts that satisfy a multitude of complex and often conflicting demands. These demands for action do not afford the luxury of surfacing one at a time; they often come like a cattle stampede at midnight and strike out in every direction.

The problem of leadership is further complicated by the presence of what Lane et al. call "tempos"—"the rise and decline of pressures generated by deadlines and by close supervision." Tempos often reflect the fact that the power of the leader is not constant in all situations. For example, "the school principal will sense that he has more authority, greater responsibility for the school, and more obedience from subordinates when the school is being 'inspected' by the superintendent or visited by State Department of Education representatives or by a parent group."[37]

Superintendents also are acutely aware of the ebb and flow of power between themselves and the boards of education. In some situations superintendents feel confident to use their discretion and in other situations the board of education takes the initiative away from the superintendent. Many conditions influence the organization's tempo and the ebb and flow of power in the leadership environment of a school district, for example: the superintendent's security of position, the solidarity of the school board on a specific issue, the size of the district, community contentment with student achievement, and levels of visible conflict.

The leadership task does not simply involve selecting the proper course of action by making the right decision for the school district. The task is to select among the *many* right demands; the nature of what is right lies in the eyes of many beholders. Thus, the leadership environment calls for compromising between differing demands of various pressure groups both inside and outside the school district. The end product of the compromise process often pleases no one, including the leader. As a decision-making process, however, the device of compromise is an essential management tool.

In order to work in this complex environment, Cribbin argues that the leader needs three guides to action: clue sense, cue sense, and negotiating sense. *Clue sense* is the ability to receive and understand subtle signals that come to the manager like pieces of a puzzle. An astute observer can find the patterns and "tune into behavior that is considered valued, rewarded, tolerated, ignored, unacceptable, or intolerable."

*Cue sense* involves the ability to pick up and interpret signals coming from significant individuals and groups inside or outside the organization. Because managers usually cannot act unilaterally, they must build a base of support. "Without the cooperation of superiors, peers, and key subordinates, managers will encounter more failure than success."

After reading the clues and judging the elements of individual and group support, a *negotiating sense* must come into play. A cohesive unit is important in any contemplated action. Thus, the leader must negotiate "to bring about win-win relationships with superiors, peers, and subordinates whenever possible."[38]

In their study of superintendents, Pitner and Ogawa found effective sensing behaviors to be crucial. "They monitor their environments to obtain readings of public opinion. Such readings identify issues to which schools must respond and detect conditions which will enable superintendents to move their organizations in directions of their own choosing."[39] In short, those individuals who believe in the importance of sensing behaviors, no doubt will agree with Peter Drucker's observation that "there is no substitute for the brewmaster's nose."

## Leadership and Gender

When it comes to acquiring positions in educational management, women have the deck stacked against them. Slightly over 72 percent of all teachers are women;[40] yet, approximately 10.5 percent are superintendents, 12 percent are secondary school principals, and 34 percent elementary school principals.[41]

In attempting to analyze the lack of success women have had entering educational administration, Charol Shakeshaft identifies three conceptual models often used to explain the phenomenon. The *Women's Place Model* assumes that women belong in the kitchen and not the boardroom. The *Discrimination Model* assumes that men conspire to keep women out of management positions. The *Meritocracy Model* assumes that only men have the unique blend of skills and competence needed to succeed in administration. In short, women have always had to face sex-role stereotyping that is defined by the male-dominated culture of our society.[42]

Catherine Marshall writes of the *culturally defined* women's role as conforming to a feminine identity of being attractive, passive, modest, and pleasant, as well as wife, mother, and woman of the community. In her study of 25 female educators, she found that the culturally defined norms of female identity clashed with the perceived demands of the administrative role.[43]

The women encountered barriers in organizational norms and structures that restrained their progress. They did not receive appointments to important committees that dealt with far-reaching issues of finance, law, conflict, and discipline. Even in those cases where the women felt they handled their tasks effectively in a style that differed from men's, all too often, their style and efforts were not recognized.[44]

Shakeshaft's review of the literature identifies employment barriers that resist the upward mobility of women. The basic discriminatory factor is that men make the appointment decisions, and men tend to devalue the management skills of women. The barriers are particularly noticeable in the hiring process. For example, male candidates are often particularly recruited for specific jobs; women are more often offered lower salaries on a nonnegotiable basis; women are more often held to non-performance criteria (e.g., minimum number of years in a specific position, completion of all the career ladder steps); the interviewers are commonly men; male activities such as military service often count but a woman's volunteer service does not; and women are more frequently asked family questions involving husbands and whether they expect to have children.[45]

An interesting development has taken place on the Davis campus of the University of California which may signal changes to come in educational personnel processes. After a study revealed that women professors were receiving lower salaries than men with the same length of employment, the chancellor ordered "gender equity raises" for those women whose personnel files seem to have been undervalued.[46]

Women, however, often create certain barriers for themselves. Shakeshaft writes that women tend to apply only for those jobs for which they feel highly qualified, and men make a considerably more liberal interpretation of their skills and apply for many more positions. Also, when a man is turned down for a position, he tends to deal with it by blaming outside forces. Women, on the other hand, "are more likely to believe that the reason they weren't hired was because they weren't good enough."[47] Internalizing a negative response to a job search can be very inhibiting the next time an interesting position comes on the market.

The lack of support systems developed by women for women is also a limiting factor in finding and securing jobs. Breaking through the glass ceiling is never easy for someone acting alone in a competitive job market. Collective action, networking and sponsorship tend to be keys to success, and women have as much right to those keys as men.[48]

Marilyn Loden writes that it is indeed possible for a woman to succeed in a male-dominated organization without being "one of the boys." Feminine leadership brings characteristics that are increasingly important in the complex, modern organization. Relative to a traditional male style, she argues, the female manager's operating style emphasizes cooperation (win-win) rather than competition (win-lose); participation and intuitive artistic decision-making rather than rationalistic, hierarchical control; and developing personal rapport through empathy and sensitivity rather than strict role relationships.[49]

Contrasting female and male leadership styles is often the subject of much commentary. With tongue partly in cheek, Gareth Morgan offers his comparisons in Figure 7.1.[50]

## Leadership Styles

### Initiating Structure-Consideration Leadership Styles

With the conviction that attempting to understand leadership as a profile of psychological traits was fruitless, the Personnel Research Board of the Ohio State University began a fresh approach in the early 1950s. The emphasis of study shifted from psychological *traits* to leadership *behavior.* In a few short years the orientation pioneered at Ohio State and the measurement instrument developed there was acclaimed as a breakthrough in the social sciences. The LBDQ (Leader Behavior Description Questionnaire) became almost synonymous with the concept of leadership itself. In one year

As one looks around the organizational world it is possible to identify different ways in which people manage gender relations. Here are a variety of poular strategies. Each can be successful or unsuccessful, according to the persons and situations involved.

**Some Female Strategies**

| | |
|---|---|
| Queen Elizabeth I | - Rule with a firm hand, surrounding oneself as far as possible by submissive men. Margaret Thatcher provides a modern example. |
| The First Lady | - Be content to exercise power behind the throne: a tactic adopted by many "corporate wives" such as executive secretaries and special assistants. |
| The Invisible Woman | - Adopt a low profile and try and blend with one's surroundings, exercising influence in whatever ways one can. |
| The Great Mother | - Consolidate power through caring and nurturing. |
| The Liberationist | - Play rough and give as good as you get; be outspoken and always make a stand in favor of the role of women. |
| The Amazon | - Be a leader of women. This style is especially successful when one can build a powerful coalition by placing like-minded women in influential positions. |
| Delilah | - Use the powers of seduction to win over key figures in male-dominated organizations. |
| Joan of Arc | - Use the power of a shared cause and mission to transcend the fact that you are a woman, and gain widespread male support. |
| The Daughter | - Find a "father figure" prepared to act as sponsor and mentor. |

FIGURE 7.1  Gender Leadership Styles
From Gareth Morgan, *Images of Organization* (Newbury Park, CA: Sage, 1986) pp. 182–183, by permission of author.

alone, in the field of education over thirty studies using the LBDO were recorded in *Dissertation Abstracts.*

In order to construct a measurement instrument, a group of social scientists contributed over 1,800 items that described a wide range of leadership behaviors. After sorting and eliminating duplicate behaviors, the items appeared to fall into 10 categories of leader behavior. At this stage Halpin and Winer examined the leadership behavior of Air Force commanders as seen by their crews.[51] Emerging from a factor analysis of these data were two major factors, labeled *initiating structure* and *consideration.*[52] Halpin defines the two factors as follows:

1. Initiating structure refers to the leader's behavior in delineating the relationship between himself and members of the workgroup, and in endeavoring to establish well-defined patterns of organization, channels of communication, and methods of procedure.
2. Consideration refers to behavior indicative of friendship, mutual trust, respect, and warmth in the relationship between the leader and the members of his staff.[53]

**Some Male Stategies**

| | |
|---|---|
| The Warrior | - Frequently adopted by busy executives caught up in fighting corporate battles. Often used to bind women into roles as committed supporters. |
| The Father | - Often used to win the support of younger women searching for a mentor. |
| King Henry VIII | - Use of absolute power to get what one wants, attracting and discarding female supporters according to their usefulness. |
| The Playboy | - Use of sex appeal (both real and imagined) to win support and favor from female colleagues. A role often adopted by executives lacking a more stable power base. |
| The Jock | - Based of various kinds of "display behavior" concerned to attract and convince women of one's corporate prowess. Often used to develop admiration and support from women in subordinate or lateral positions. |
| The Little Boy | - Often used to try and "get one's way" in difficult situations, especially in relation to female co-workers and subordinates. The role may take many forms, eg., the "angry little boy" who throws a temper tantrum to create a stir and force action; the "frustrated or whining little boy" who tries to cultivate sympathy; and the "cute little boy" who tries to curry favor, especially when he is in a jam. |
| The Good Friend | - Often used to develop partnerships with female colleagues, either as confidants or as key sources of information and advice. |
| The Chauvinist Pig | - Often used by men who feel threatened by the presence of women. Characterized by use of various "degradiation" rituals, which seek to undermine the status of women and their contributions. |

A manager scoring high on initiating structure and low on consideration would be Samuel Goldwyn, who reputedly said to his staff one day, "I want you all to tell me what's wrong with our operation—even if it means losing your job!" The opposite situation might be the manager who received an efficiency evaluation that read, "He serves with cooperative and willing incompetence."

Generalizations drawn from the mass of studies conducted with the LBDQ suggest that "both consideration and structure are positively related to various measures of group cohesiveness and harmony. Initiating structure is related to group unity. Consideration is related to low absenteeism, grievances, turnover, and bureaucracy."[54]

Halpin found that perceptions of leadership effectiveness depended on the role relationship the observer had with the leader. School board members (the observers), for example, indicated a preference for their superintendents to initiate structure; subordinates (the observers), on the other hand, indicated a preference for the superintendents to be high on consideration.[55] In his review of the literature, Hencley observed that incongruence in expectations of leader behavior as held by workers has an impact on confidence in leadership, satisfaction, effectiveness, and attitudes toward the work situation. Value differences and misperceptions of group members may seriously compromise the leader's effectiveness in interpersonal relations. Further complications are introduced when the leader's perception of his or her own behavior differs from other people's perceptions.[56]

Edwin Fleishman, one of the original social scientists who developed the LBDQ reviewed the 20-year history of the instrument and distilled a general conclusion out of the mass of findings. He wrote, "The preponderance of findings . . . seem to indicate that the high-structure-high-consideration pattern optimizes more different effectiveness criteria, whereas the low-consideration-low-structure pattern most often appears the least desirable."[57]

Through the years, a number of variables similar to initiating structure and consideration have been identified, although none have been so thoroughly tested. Although it is not possible to say that the researchers cited in the following list have isolated the same leadership variables, on the surface there seems to be a surprising similarity of variables.

| *Researcher* | *Behavioral Dimensions Identified* | |
|---|---|---|
| Barnard[58] | Effectiveness | Employee orientation |
| Argyris[59] | Formal behavior | Individual behavior |
| Likert[60] | Performance goals | Supportive relationships |
| Getzels et al.[61] | Nomothetic | Ideographic |
| Bass[62] | Task effectiveness | Interaction effectiveness |
| Brown[63] | System-oriented | Person-oriented |
| Fiedler[64] | Task-motivated | Relationship-motivated |

The presence of both dimensions can be important in the leadership role, as illustrated by the comments of Douglas McGregor as he departed from his position as a college president after six years.

> I believed . . . that a leader could operate successfully as a kind of advisor to his organization. I thought I could avoid being a "boss." Unconsciously, I suspect, I hoped to duck the unpleasant necessity of making difficult decisions, of taking the responsibility for one course of action among many uncertain alternatives, of making mistakes and taking the consequences. I thought that maybe I could operate so that everyone would like me—that "good human relations" would eliminate all discord and disagreement. I couldn't have been more wrong. It took a couple of years, but I finally began to realize that a leader cannot avoid the exercise of authority any more than he can avoid the responsibility for what happens to his organization.[65]

## A Note of Caution

Although the leadership factors of consideration and initiating structure have been important in the research literature on leadership and durable for an unusually long time, the LBDQ has not escaped scholarly criticism. Greenfield, for example, points out that the items on the LBDQ and the items on an interest inventory or a personality scale are similar. This leads him to speculate that the items measured might really be attributes the individual brings independently to the group and are therefore not shaped by the needs of the group.[66] Greenfield also points out that the LBDQ refers to leadership at a single point in time. The instrument does not treat changes or sequences in leadership patterns, the characteristics of the group in which the patterns are studied, or the relationship of the group to its surrounding environment.[67]

Korman suggests there is little evidence that LBDQ scores are predictive of *later* effectiveness of the leader or of later satisfaction of his or her subordinates.[68] Korman was also unable to find any studies in which the variables of consideration and initiating structure were experimentally manipulated in order to determine their impact on a criterion variable. He adds that the LBDQ researchers "have tended almost always to follow the two-variable design which consists simply of correlating the test variable with the criterion variable, with little appreciation of the possible situational variables that might be moderating these relationships."[69] Situational characteristics such as unit size, task, organizational technology, climate, and subordinate attitudes tend to not play a role in the research designs.

A strand of research on leadership, which does take into consideration situational variables in the organization, began to emerge in the 1970s. It is referred to as the contingency theory of leadership.

## Contingency Theory of Leadership

If research based on the LBDQ dominated the imaginations of investigators during the 1960s, then the contingency theory of leadership can be said to have captured the field in the 1970s. The propelling force in this transition to contingency theory has been Fred Fiedler.[70] Fiedler reports that over a 14-year period approximately 300 theoretical and empirical studies were stimulated by his contingency model. A true believer in his own work, he also reports that "most competent studies have supported the theory."[71]

### The Fiedler Version of Contingency Theory

Looking back over the sum of the LBDQ research, Fiedler,[72] citing Korman's[73] review of the available literature, points out the inability to consistently relate specific leader behaviors to effective group performance and group satisfaction. "Why these behaviors [consideration and initiating structure] do not predict or correlate with group performance represents a major theoretical problem. One clue that might assist us toward a satisfactory explanation is the finding that situational factors and certain personality attributes interact in determining leadership effectiveness. Could similar interactions determine leader behaviors?" Fiedler's response is a definite yes. Much of his energy, and that of the research community as well, has gone to supporting this contention.

In Chapter Six contingency variables were introduced as situational variables that influence the relationship between environmental demands and the organization's response to those demands. Writers in the area of leadership theory have also adopted contingency theory notions. Contingency theories of leadership treat contingency variables as those variables that influence the relationship between leadership styles and subordinate responses to those styles. For example, the success of a principal's style in mandating a change in classroom discipline procedures might be contingent upon the strength of the local teacher's union. By leadership style or personality style, Fiedler means "a transsituational mode of relating and interacting with others."[74] When building a contingency theory of leadership, the following interlocking factors must be accounted for:

A = some dimension of a leadership style (fastest draw in the West)

B = a situational variable (two broken thumbs)

C = a measure of effectiveness of leader behavior (first guy out of town)

The relationship between A and C, then is moderated in a predictable way by B. Perhaps one of the most important implications of the contingency theory of leadership is that in a large measure specific conditions within the organization are as responsible for the success or failure of the leader as the leader is himself or herself. According to this assumption, in the organization a variety of problematic situations confront the leadership setting. Leaders are in danger of floundering if they do not possess the appropriate leadership style to treat the situational character of the problem. Tannenbaum et al. provide a useful definition that emphasizes the situational nature of leadership. They define leadership as "interpersonal influence exercised in a situation and directed, through the communication process toward the attainment of a specified goal or goals."[75]

## *Task-Motivated/Relationship-Motivated*

Two basic assumptions are implicit in Fiedler's thinking. First, the contingency model maintains that personality attributes that are stable and enduring underlie the motivational system of the leader. The changes that do occur in personality are gradual and relatively small, barring major upsets in the leader's life. The leader has *either* a relationship-motivated or a task-motivated leadership style. Second, the three most important situational variables interacting with a leadership style are (1) leader-member relations, (2) the task structure, and (3) the formal power position. All three conditions have an impact on the degree of control of the leader.

*Relationship-motivated leaders* strive to maintain good interpersonal relationships with their subordinates. Under conditions of uncertainty and anxiety, they will seek support and closer relations with their subordinates. When leaders have the close support of subordinates and feel secure in the work situation, they will pursue the esteem and admiration of significant others. When task performance is essential to win the esteem and admiration of superiors, relationship-oriented leaders will strive in this direction—even if it sometimes detracts from the close interpersonal relationships with subordinates.

*Task-motivated leaders,* on the other hand, obtain personal satisfaction from accomplishing objectives effectively and efficiently. When they are placed in an uncertain and anxiety-provoking situation, they will place emphasis on giving structure and direction to events so that the task can be accomplished. Under other conditions, however, when conditions surrounding the task are under control and their influence is high, task-oriented leaders will relax and respond to the need for consideration of the subordinates' feelings. "In other words," Fiedler writes, "business before pleasure, but business *with* pleasure whenever possible."[76]

In short, the two leadership styles exist in a motivational hierarchy that reflects a set of personal priorities and goals. In each individual, one of these styles is dominant and the other is secondary. However, there are occasions when the secondary style may take the lead. "In order to accomplish a task," Fiedler writes, "one may need to be quite considerate and concerned with interpersonal relations under one set of conditions and fairly ruthless under others. To gain the support and loyalty of one's group, it may be first necessary to succeed."[77]

The two motivational systems are measured by an instrument called Esteem for Least Preferred Coworker, or simply the LPC. The instrument is given to a manager who is asked to consider all the people with whom he or she has ever worked. Then the manager is asked to rate the person he or she has been able to work with *least well* on 16 to 22 items, with an eight-point scale on each item. A semantic differential format is used.[78] As an illustration, two items from the LPC appear below.

Friendly:\_\_\_1:\_\_\_2:\_\_\_3:\_\_\_4:\_\_\_5:\_\_\_6:\_\_\_7:\_\_\_8:Unfriendly
Cooperative:\_\_\_1:\_\_\_2:\_\_\_3:\_\_\_4:\_\_\_5:\_\_\_6:\_\_\_7:\_\_\_8:Uncooperative[79]

Those who describe their Least Preferred Coworker in relatively *positive* terms are considered primarily relationship-motivated, whereas those who describe their LPC in relatively *unfavorable* terms are primarily task-motivated.

## Leadership Situations

In identifying the situations that moderate the potential of leadership effectiveness, Fiedler defines three variables that contribute directly to the leader's capacity to influence or control the group; these three variables result in "situational favorableness." In order of importance, the three major determinants to situational favorableness are:

1. *Leader-member relations:* The relationship between leaders and their group members is based on trust and loyalty. The members like the leaders and are willing to accept their guidance, or the opposite condition prevails.
2. *Task structure:* The task is clearly spelled out and programmed in terms of goals, procedures for obtaining goals, and progress measures, as applied to success criteria. Conversely, the task is ambiguous and the procedures for accomplishing the task are vaguely defined.
3. *Power position:* The formal organizational role lends to the leader certain powers of control, such as rewarding and punishing in varying degrees. The power of the formal role is tempered by such things as hierarchical level and length of appointment.[80]

The leadership setting is broken down into an eight-celled classification scheme, which is shown on the horizontal axis in Figure 7.2. In terms of the possession of power, these eight cells (or octants) are scaled from a "most favorable" leadership setting (octant 1) on the far left to a "least favorable" setting (octant 8) on the far right of Figure 7.2. On the basis of normative scores, or by dividing the scores at the median, groups can be categorized as being high or low on each of the three "favorableness" situations. When examining the mix of these situations, it becomes evident that exerting leadership is more possible when the leader is trusted, when the task is structured, and when the formal power is high. For example, a trusted airline pilot (octant 1) is in a much more favorable leadership position than a disliked chairperson of a volunteer committee (octant 8). It is important to note that as the "favorableness situation" changes, different types of leaders (high *versus* low LPC) tend to be more effective.

The vertical axis in Figure 7.2 shows the level—from poor to good—of group or organizational performance. The dotted line on the vertical axis indicates the good-poor level of performance for task-motivated (low-LPC) leaders across all eight octants. The solid line indicates the level of performance for relationship-motivated (high-LPC) leaders. Reflecting on the data from his numerous studies, Fiedler writes:

> The basic findings of the Contingency Model are that task-motivated leaders perform generally best in very "favorable" situations, i.e., either under conditions in which their power, control and influence are very high (or, conversely, where uncertainty is very low) or where the situation is unfavorable, where they have lower power, control and influence. Relationship-motivated leaders tend to perform best in situations in which they have moderate power, control and influence.[81]

Under situations of moderate favorableness, the relationship-motivated leader tends to be more effective in obtaining optimal group performance. This is because in

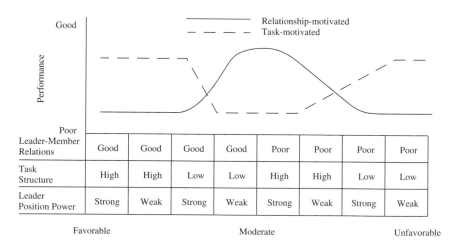

**FIGURE 7.2  Fiedler's Contingency Theory of Leadership**
From Fred E. Fiedler, "The Contingency Model: New Directions for Leadership Utilization," *Journal of Contemporary Business* (Autumn 1974): 71. Reprinted with permission.

these task situations the leader must be diplomatic and draw upon the creativity and cooperation of the members. When the task situation is very favorable (when the leader is well liked, the task structured, high formal power exists), nondirective behavior and an orientation toward consultation is neither appropriate nor beneficial; for example, an airline pilot would not ask the flight attendants if they think it is safe to land.

The task-motivated leader seems to perform best under conditions at both extremes (octant 1 and octant 8) of the horizontal axis. Although it is logical to expect the task-motivated leader to operate most effectively under conditions of situation favorableness, considering the same leadership style as the most effective at the other end of the continuum needs a word of explanation. Under unfavorable conditions (when the leader is not liked, the task unstructured, and low formal power exists), the group is quite likely to ignore completely the relationship-oriented leader. The leader might as well be forceful and directive under these conditions because something is better than nothing, and something just might emerge if specific direction is given. In other words, a General Patton-type leader would be more effective at both extremes of the favorableness continuum.

In terms of the model, it is not accurate to speak of a leader as being good or bad, because a leader may perform well under one set of conditions and not under another. For example, a skilled academic dean in a university would not necessarily make a proficient battlefield commander and vice versa.

## A Note of Caution

Like all new attempts to advance some dimension of the social sciences, Fred Fiedler's contingency theory of leadership is highly controversial. In the evolutionary process of a new theory, statistical gunfights inevitably break out between researchers who are trying to establish the validity of their theory and academicians who review the literature. Academicians police the research field to insure that the laws surrounding concepts, computations, and conclusions are not violated. To the interested third parties who try to discern the state of the art, the picture can indeed be confusing. (See, for example, the Schriesheim and Kerr challenge,[82] Fiedler's reply,[83] and the Schriesheim and Kerr response to Fiedler's reply.[84]) Such a situation brings to mind the counsel of William Foote Whyte. "We are often advised to 'let the facts speak for themselves.' Of course, the facts do not speak for themselves, but only through the people who present them."

Fiedler's contingency theory of leadership has received impressive support in the research literature.[85] Also, using a meta-analytic technique, Strube and Garcia tested significance in combined samples and concluded the model was extremely robust in predicting group performance.[86]

The model has also been vigorously challenged in terms of methodological rigor and theoretical adequacy.[87] Korman, for example, argues that personality measures, in which the LPC must be included, have shown little reliability over time and over different situations. "The question is a crucial one," Korman stresses, "since a measure that does not correlate with itself cannot possibly correlate with any other variable."[88] Thus, it seems hardly worthwhile, for example, to rotate a leader or change a job situation if the leader's LPC score does not hold steady over time.

Robbins summarizes weaknesses in the models that have been identified by several researchers.

> First, the contingency variables are complex and difficult to assess. It's often difficult in practice to determine how good the leader-member relations are, how structured the task is, and how much position power the leader has. Second, the model gives little attention to the characteristics of the subordinates. Third, no attention is given to varying technical competencies of the leader or the subordinates. The model assumes that both the leader and subordinates have adequate technical competence. Fourth, the correlations Fiedler presents in defense of the model are often low and statistically nonsignificant. Finally, the LPC instrument is open to question. The logic underlying the LPC is not well understood and studies have shown that respondent's LPC stores are not stable.[89]

Another difficulty with the contingency theory of leadership is suggested by Chemers and Rice, who point out that there are other situational variables (beyond the basic three) that can be important in determining the favorableness of the leadership situation; for example, stress, linguistic or cultural heterogeneity, organizational climate, and level of training.[90]

The point should also be emphasized that contingency theory concentrates its analysis on the internal environment of the organization and does not establish the important linkages between the internal and external environments. As such, a closed system bias exists in the model.

Finally, one of the strongest challenges to Fiedler's model is also recognized by him as an important point of debate; that is, whether or not a leader can switch leadership styles in the face of different types of problematic situations. Fiedler writes:

> The problem at issue is whether (a) the tendency to behave in a considerate, employee-centered manner is an attribute of the leader's personality, and therefore properly considered to be his leadership style; or (b) whether the leader's personality and the situation interact, and the person who is considerate under one condition tends to be relatively less considerate under other conditions. If the latter is the case, it will have major implications for current leadership theory.[91]

After a reanalysis of several LPC studies, Fiedler comments on why it appears that task-motivated and relations motivated people sometimes appear to reverse their leadership styles. When the job situation is under low or moderate control, the most effective leader is a relations-motivated leader. However, if a task-motivated leader is on that job, that manager will behave as indicated by giving orders, being punitive, and not showing great concern for feelings along the way. When situational control is established and job completion is virtually assured, "the task-motivated leader can focus on relationships and become nondirective and considerate. . . ."Task-motivated leaders do not have to change to a nondirective and considerate work style, but often do because the problems calling for their particular skills have been solved and light is at the end of the tunnel. The opposite condition fits relationship-motivated leaders. If they find themselves in control of a situation and the successful end of the task is in sight, "they can focus on the task and become more bossy and less considerate."[92]

Fiedler agrees that several other concerns critics raised about his contingency theory of leadership are valid. "The most important flaw in the contingency model is that the model has remained a 'black box' even after 25 years of intensive research."[93] One particular problem is the lack of an explanation for what causes some people to become task-motivated and others relations-motivated. In addition, even though the LPC is an internally consistent and stable measure, it lacks the comfort of face-validity, and it does not correlate well with other behavior observation scales or psychometric tests.

Whatever the final disposition of Fiedler's model becomes, his work has made it clear that an adequate analysis of leadership calls not only for a study of the leader, but also for a study of situations and organizations.

## *Cognitive Resource Theory*

The criticism that Fiedler's contingency theory of leadership did not provide an adequate explanation of how the interaction of personality and task situations lead to differentiated group performance led Fiedler to formulate his cognitive resource theory (CRT). With this theory, he attempts to explain how key variables such as intelligence, stress, and experience link to his contingency theory and influence the leadership process.

As noted in Figure 7.3, the most effective leadership style is determined in part by matching the leader's task- or relationship-motivated orientation (as measured by LPC score) with the degree of situational control.[94] Even when the most effective situational match is established, leaders perform differently.

Does the leader's intelligence level make a difference in group performance? The question has long been puzzling because literature reviews have consistently pointed out that cognitive variables are not strong predictors of leadership and organizational success.[95] Fiedler argues that intelligence does make a difference, but under those conditions where "the leader (1) directs the group, (2) works in a relatively stress-free environment, (3) has the support of the group, and (4) the task requires intellectual effort."[96]

The underlying assumption is that intelligent leaders can make and communicate more effective plans, decisions, and action strategies than less intelligent leaders.[97] However, personal stress resulting from the perceived inability to cope with environmental demands distracts the leader's attention from the task. Under conditions of stress, intelligence-guided actions tend to be impeded by worry or fear, which results in premature task closure, behavioral rigidity, and the inability to make clear observations, process information objectively and comprehensively, or make critical evaluations.[98]

Simply stated, under conditions of significant job stress, the more intelligent and creative leaders tend to lose the ability to use their heads, and babble—"talk much but say little of substance, and inhibit their group members from contributing meaningfully

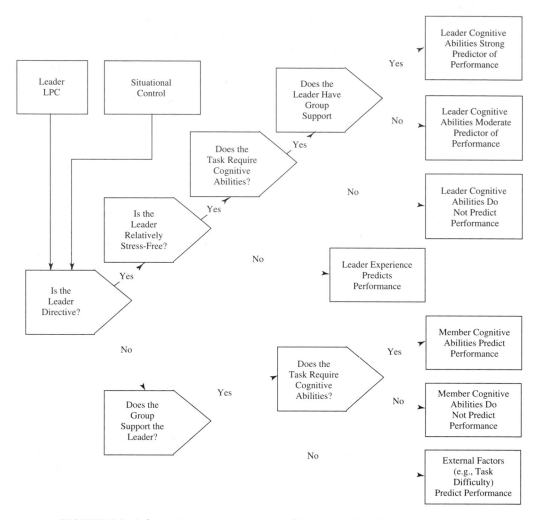

FIGURE 7.3  Schematic representation of the cognitive theory
From Fred Fiedler and Joseph Garcia, *New Approaches to Effective Leadership: Cognitive Resources and Organizational Performance* (New York: Wiley, 1987), p. 9. With permission.

to the group process."[99] Fiedler argues that stress is particularly debilitating to intelligent performance when the source of the stress is one's boss.

Under conditions of stress, where do leaders turn? When stress is low, leaders use their intelligence and not their experience; when stress is high, they use their experience but not their intelligence.[100] Thus, under stressful conditions, job experience pays off.

The cognitive resource theory is a relatively new development, yet to be tested extensively. The data used to develop Fiedler's CRT were mostly those from studies originally conducted to test his contingency theory model and later reanalyzed. Yukl points out that "most of the studies cited by Fiedler and Garcia (1987) were laboratory studies with temporary groups or studies of low-level military officers, and the results may not be applicable to executives and middle managers in large organizations."[101]

## Path–Goal Theory of Leadership: A Contingency Theory

Another contingency theory of leadership receiving widespread attention in the literature is called path-goal theory. As illustrated in Figure 7.4, subordinate and environmental characteristics are the contingency variables that mediate the relationship between leadership styles and subordinate outcomes (e.g., performance, motivation, satisfaction).

### Expectancy Theory of Motivation

Path-goal theory is rooted in an expectancy theory of motivation. As discussed in Chapter Eight, this theory argues that people are satisfied with their work and will work hard if they believe their work will lead to things that are highly valued (e.g., "I will get a raise in salary if my performance is good").[102] The implications for leadership is that subordinate behavior is motivated by leader behavior to the extent that the leader influences the expectations of subordinates in a positive way and is helpful in assisting subordinates in accomplishing goals. House and Mitchell write:

> From previous research on expectancy theory of motivation, it can be inferred that the strategic functions of the leader consist of: (1) recognizing and/or arousing subordinates' needs for outcomes over which the leader has some control, (2) increasing personal payoffs to subordinates for work-goal attainment, (3) making the path to those payoffs easier to travel by coaching and direction, (4) helping subordinates clarify expectancies, (5) reducing frustrating barriers and (6) increasing the opportunities for personal satisfaction contingent on effective performance.[103]

Contrary to Fiedler's orientation toward leadership, path-goal theory argues that the leadership style of an individual varies as situations within an organization change.[104] In other words, as a leader faces different problems or circumstances in the organization, that individual adjusts his or her leadership style accordingly (e.g., from directive to participative). House[105] and House and Dessler[106] have advanced the path-goal theory to the level that is shown in Figure 7.3. Four differing types of leadership styles are present in Figure 7.3.

1. *Directive leadership:* The leader gives structure to the work situation by establishing specific expectations for the subordinates, such as what, how, and when a task should be performed. Specific performance standards are maintained.
2. *Supportive leadership:* The leader has friendly relationships and shows concern for the well-being and needs of subordinates. The leader is approachable and exhibits trust.

| Leader Behavior | and | Contingency Factors | Cause | | Subordinate Attitudes and Behavior |
|---|---|---|---|---|---|
| 1. Directive | | 1. Subordinate characteristics: authoritarianism locus of control ability | Influence | Personal perceptions | 1. Job satisfaction job → rewards |
| 2. Supportive | | | | | 2. Acceptance of leader leader → rewards |
| 3. Achievement oriented | | 2. Environmental factors: the task formal authority system primary work group | Influence | Motivational stimuli Constraints Rewards | 3. Motivational behavior effort → performance performance → rewards |
| 4. Participative | | | | | |

FIGURE 7.4 Path-Goal Contingency Theory of Leadership

From Robert J. House and Terrence Mitchell, "Path-Goal Theory of Leadership," *Journal of Contemporary Business* (Autumn 1974): 89. Reprinted with permission.

3. *Achievement-oriented leadership:* The leader expects high levels of productivity from subordinates and exhibits the confidence that subordinates can
achieve these high levels. The leader sets challenging goals and emphasizes
excellence.
4. *Participative leadership:* The leader consults with subordinates and considers their views seriously before a decision is made.

## Subordinate Characteristics and Environmental Factors

Moderating the relationship between specific leadership styles and subordinate performance and attitudes are two contingent variables: (1) subordinate characteristics,
which shape their perceptions toward achieving goals; and (2) environmental factors,
which serve to stimulate, constrain, or reward the motivation of the workers. The contingent variables of subordinate characteristics are:

1. *Locus-of-control:* the degree to which individuals see themselves in control
of—or under the control of—events surrounding their own situation
2. *Ability:* the perception of the subordinates of their own ability to accomplish
an assigned task
3. *Authoritarianism:* the degree of authoritarianism in the subordinates influences their need for either a directive or a nondirective leadership style

The specific variables under environmental factors are outside the control of the subordinates, but are important to their ability to perform effectively.

1. *Task:* the level of task complexity and ambiguity
2. *Formal authority system:* the degree to which the formal authority system
facilitates or inhibits the work behavior of subordinates
3. *Primary work group:* the degree to which the primary work-group norms are
clear and supportive

Thus, the path-goal theory exists as another means of relating different types of
leadership behavior to differing attitudes and behavioral responses of subordinates. At
this point, it is unclear the extent to which it might be necessary to add additional contingency variables to the existing categories. However, the theory is stated in such a
way that additional variables can be added when the data suggest they are necessary.

## A Note of Caution

Reviews of the path-goal-theory literature by Schriesheim and Kerr,[107] Sheridan,
Downey, and Slocum,[108] and Bass[109] reveal mixed results. Enough underlying support
has been found, however, to maintain considerable interest in the theory.[110] A basic
advantage/disadvantage is that rooting the path-goal of leadership in the expectancy

theory of motivation (discussed in Chapter Eight) has created for the former all the strengths and weaknesses of the latter.

Yukl suggests that methodological limitations raise doubts about the findings. Because almost all the studies used only subordinate's questionnaires to measure leader behavior and considered only a few aspects of the model at a time, the theory has not been adequately tested.[111] In addition, the model implies that the leader has control over the rewards desired by the employees. In reality, those rewards are often controlled by the board of education, union contracts, or state law.

Path-goal theory also focuses on how leader behavior motivates subordinate behavior. Burack raises the issue of whether or not the theory *overemphasizes* the supposedly positive outcomes of the leader's influence on employee expectancies and paths of action. Burack writes, "What if the leader is too busy with his own 'pyramid climbing' to support the members of his task group? And what if, for example, evaluation is viewed as a threatening rather than a constructive discussion of goals or feedback to guide future actions?"[112] Also, while the path-goal theory has an environmental contingency, this really refers to an *internal* environment. The theory therefore has a closed-system bias.

In short, the path-goal theory of leadership has a great deal of potential in promoting an understanding of the intricacies of leader-subordinate behavior, but continued development of the model is important.

## *The Goose Theory of Leadership*

The popular perception of leadership often romanticizes the role. The popular imagery of the leader acting as a member of a team performing tasks is not unlike that of Joe DiMaggio playing center field—effortless, graceful, and strong. In the real world, however, the leader's role lacks the dash and glory of Joe Montana throwing the long bomb or Magic Johnson knitting his team together with ball-handling mastery.

Writing from the perspective of an educational administrator, Jerome Murphy, dean of the Harvard Graduate School of Education, believes that the real job of the leader tends to be resolving messes created by others. The role of the manager is perceived by employees to be that of chief problem solver. "Honking and hissing like geese, faculty and staff members will cruise into the boss' office, ruffle their feathers, poop on the rug, and leave. It then becomes the boss' job to clean up the mess."[113]

While the goose theory of leadership may not be the most comprehensively developed theory in the social sciences, it will no doubt be familiar to anyone who has held the job.

## *Toward A Contingency Theory of Educational Leadership*

Developing a contingency theory of leadership that applies specifically to the educational organization is an important step yet to be taken. Such a theory would necessarily have to entertain a variety of questions, such as the following:

1. What are the major contingency variables that moderate the relationship between leadership behavior and school outcomes?
2. How does the presence of a professional cadre of subordinates (i.e., teachers) enter into the make-up of situation-oriented contingency variables?
3. What is the nature of the relationship between degrees of turbulence in the external environment of a school system and effective leadership styles?
4. What is the range of leadership styles open to administrators as they deal with parents? teachers? students? immediate superiors? board of education members?
5. What part of the school's administrative and educational processes are structured? unstructured?
6. How do the structured and unstructured components differentially influence leadership styles of administrators?
7. What leadership styles of school administrators are most effective in which type of contingency situations?
8. What are the major outcomes of schooling and to what degree can they be legitimately related to administrator leadership?
9. Are the leadership styles of school administrators relatively stable across situations, or can they be systematically modified in the face of changing situations?
10. What type of measurement instruments could be designed that would delineate the relationship between leadership behavior, contingency variables, and school outcomes?

Somewhat related to the measurement issue is the context in which leadership has been studied since World War II. If research on leadership prior to World War II was constrained by a belief in the existence of key psychological traits, then research following World War II has been constrained by a focus on the human group (not the organization) as a leadership setting and on a relatively closed system perspective as a conceptual framework. As the next section will point out, the field of education has seemed unsatisfied with these closed system constraints and has been evolving toward a more expansive view of leadership.

## Open System Leadership Theory

### Expanding the View

The educational setting of the 1950s and early 1960s supported an intense interest in leadership research, as illustrated by the development and utilization of the LBDQ. The sociopolitical context of education changed rapidly during the late 1960s as schools were thrust into accelerating states of turmoil. Social scientists who might have continued the study of leadership in education turned their attention toward the issues of the times, such as teacher militancy, student activism, racial segregation, and bond-issue defeats. In fact, the entire thrust toward the contingency theory of leadership, which became such a core element in literature of the business and public sectors, was virtually ignored in the educational setting until the late 1970s.

With the publication of *A Nation at Risk*[114] in 1983 and its dramatic call for developmental change in American education, there was a renewed emphasis on analyzing and invigorating the leadership role in education.[115] The latter 1980s brought about a shift in focus as educational leaders found themselves trying to cope with *externally imposed* solutions for change, such as state-mandated career ladders for teachers, school-based management programs, merit pay, computer-based instruction, mentor teacher programs, differentiated staffing, and model curriculums. Earlier theories of leadership had proved to be conceptually inadequate to deal with the new focus.

## Conceptual Weaknesses

Just as had been the case with trait theories of earlier generations, situational leadership theories, as they were viewed in the 1980s and early 1990s, proved inadequate to deal with the external influences on the educational system. Situational theories, such as the LPC and path-goal models, function in a closed system perspective attending to day-to-day, micromanagement issues.[116]

These theories cast leadership as a *transactional* activity that, as Sergiovanni points out, functions almost as bartering. "Positive reinforcement is given for good work, merit pay for increased performance, promotion for increased persistence, a feeling of belonging for cooperation, and so on."[117] Leadership as bartering, such as seen in the negotiated order of the interacting spheres of influence model depicted in Chapter Four, is carried out almost in a cost-benefit exchange between the leaders and the led.

## Leadership in an Open System

As an open system, the school is sensitive and often vulnerable to shifts in its external environment, whether they be political, economic, demographic, ideological, or technical. Leadership theory has been late in developing a conceptual framework that effectively links the leadership requirements of the internal with the external environments of educational systems. That is, the field needs a solid theory of leadership that extends all the way from the teachers, who are in the trenches delivering the goods upward and outward, to those institutions and forces in the external environment that play influential roles in education.

Formulating such a theory is no easy task because, as Lipham writes, "the same behavior that may be viewed as leadership from an intraorganizational or sub-system point of view may be regarded as lack of leadership from an extra-organizational or supra-system point of view, and conversely."[118]

## Transformational Leadership Theory

A strong beginning toward the development of an open system theory of leadership has been formulated by James Burns who provides the concepts and language system that help us understand the parts and how they relate to the whole.[119]

Earlier situational versions of leadership are viewed as *transactional,* or establishing negotiated arrangements that satisfy participants who then agree to a course of action. *Transformational* leadership, on the other hand, works toward a higher order of change that establishes an integrative fit between the processes and products of the micro (internal) and macro (external) environments. Hunt and Osborn argue that the behavior of most productive leaders is influenced more by the macro- than the microvariables.[120]

"Transformational leadership takes the form of *leadership as building,*" Sergiovanni writes. "The focus is on arousing human potential, satisfying higher needs, and raising expectations of both leaders and followers to motivate them to higher levels of commitment and performance."[121]

To establish the best fit possible between the micro- and macroenvironments of the educational system, the transformational leader must be prepared to conduct strategic long-term planning, read the changing nature of external and internal situations, and manage organizational cultural variables to align them with action plans. The idea of transformation calls for energizing personnel to make a united response to a higher level of goals common to all those associated with the teaching-learning process. In the context of educational restructuring, transformational leadership skills can be particularly beneficial.[122]

## Leadership Training

### Contingency Theory: The Fiedler Orientation

Advocates of a contingency theory of leadership would require training programs that prepare leaders to function effectively in specific organizational situations. However, the Fiedler version of contingency theory and the path-goal version differ significantly with respect to their implications for the training and placement of leaders. Finch made the following observations:

> Leadership research seems to have evolved along two ends of a continuum: at one end is the supposition that leadership behavior is mainly a function of personality [Fiedler version] and at the other end is the supposition that leader behavior is extremely flexible [Path-Goal version] and that the leader can vary his behavior from situation to situation. Under the first of these suppositions, the appropriate strategy for management-development purposes would probably be to develop techniques to enhance personality assessment, to train leaders to make optimal use of what they have, and to place leaders in situations appropriate to their personality. Under the flexibility assumption, a leader would be trained in diagnostic skills and in being able to select and apply the appropriate behavior.[123]

Skillful managers are a scarce resource; not everyone has the training, aptitude, and motivation to qualify. As pointed out earlier, the leader's personality or style is relatively stable and is a major determinant of the type of situation in which he or she can perform effectively. With these two thoughts in mind (scarce resource and personality stability), Fiedler lays out a central theme of his leadership thesis: "If their leadership style does not fit the job, *we must learn how to engineer the job to fit their leadership style.*"[124]

Interestingly enough, once a match between the leader's style and the job situation has been established, extensive training and experience may serve to *disrupt* the match by increasing the leaders' power and influence or by leading them toward a more human-relations orientation. In other words, training may alter an already good match and therefore be dysfunctional. Precise thought about which leader will receive what type of training is critical when trying to establish or maintain the most effective match between a leader and a situation.[125]

However, organizations as well as jobs change.[126] Therefore, conditions of situational favorableness change over time, due to shifts in economic conditions, demographic composition, or political climate. Organizations go through stages, evolving through what Lippitt and Schmidt see as the developmental stages of birth, youth, and maturity.[127] The objectives, and the means established to obtain objectives, change significantly at each stage of the organization's life. In short, what might be a good personality-job match today might not be in one or two years, or even in six months. Fiedler comments on the possible consequences.

> Certain types of leaders will reach a "burn-out point" after they have stayed on the job for a given length of time. They will become bored, stale, disinterested and no longer challenged. A rational rotation policy obviously must be designed to rotate these leaders at the appropriate time to new and more challenging jobs.[128]

There are several implications in Fiedler's arguments for the selection, training, and placement of school administrators. If we accept Fiedler's arguments, an extensive review is called for of the criteria by which school administrators are now selected, of the logic used to keep them in a specific job-slot for a given length of time, and of the type of training given them. A comprehensive analysis of a vacant administrative position should be made when considering who should fill it. How turbulent is the environment surrounding the role? Is the position as currently constituted relatively structured or unstructured? Does the position have considerable formal power built into it? Is the position in an evolutionary state at the moment or is it relatively stable?

A relatively comprehensive personality analysis of each candidate for the position should be conducted. Does the candidate have a production-oriented or people-oriented leadership style? How psychologically secure is the candidate in unstructured as opposed to structured situations? Does the candidate exhibit risk-taking behavior in difficult situations or does he or she spread the risk among colleagues? Does the production-oriented leader have the sense to delegate a people-oriented problem to a people-oriented subordinate when the need arises?

Also, establishing an appropriately balanced mix of leadership styles among administrators of a school or district office is important. Administrators who handle people problems and others who can handle production problems effectively are needed. When a vacancy opens up in a key post such as a principalship or a superintendency, a promotion of the next person in line might not be appropriate. If the former occupant of the position was an effective production-oriented leader in a role calling for that orientation and the person next in line is people oriented, the leader-job match will be in jeopardy if a direct promotion takes place.

Matching specific inservice training programs to specific leadership styles is also an important activity. Attempts should be made to provide administrators with training that will help them perform even better the types of tasks that they now perform best. Fiedler argues that it would be a mistake, for example, to give effective task-oriented administrators extensive training in human relations tactics; their skill in supervising tasks may diminish and they may not gain a great deal of effectiveness in human relations.

If we accept the Fiedler view of personnel management, an important tool in establishing and maintaining effective leader-job matches is job rotation, both horizontal and vertical. The practice of horizontal rotation (also referred to as lateral transfer) of school administrators is becoming established in more and more school districts.

The point was made in Chapter Four that the effective-schools literature simultaneously calls for the school administrator to be a strong and involved structural leader while at the same time providing for teacher autonomy and shared governance. These conditions can lead to what Burlingame calls "leadership schizophrenia."[129]

Situational leadership theory resolves the dilemma by recommending that educational leaders with distinct styles and skills be rotated into positions with matching needs. As an illustration, Hallinger and Murphy write that "in effective low SES (socioeconomic status) schools, principals play a higher directive role in the selection, development and implementation of instructional programs."[130] In effective high-SES schools, on the other hand, principals tend to play an indirect-support role and allow much greater teacher autonomy. Teachers and parents tend to recognize the greater complexity of problems in the lower-SES schools and permit the principal a higher degree of authority to intervene in instructional activities.

In the past, a lateral transfer (e.g., the movement of a school principal from one school to another after a number of years of service) had negative overtones. The personnel being rotated often considered the transfer a negative comment on their skills and their futures in the district. The classical hierarchical perspective has much to do with this outlook, because it suggests any movement other than upward is a sign of failure. Contingency theory, however, suggests that horizontal rotation of administrative positions is simply sound management practice because it provides flexibility in placing school administrators with specific leadership skills in jobs that require those skills. The individual managers also benefit, because they are assigned to jobs that allow them to employ their strengths.

For similar reasons, contingency theory suggests that moving an administrator for given periods of time up or down the hierarchy to take on specific tasks (e.g., curricular reform, alleviation of racial tension) can be another effective management practice. Although this type of movement still tends to be looked upon as promotion or demotion in the public school setting, precedent exists in higher education for this type of movement. Professors, for example, move into the role of department chairperson and then back to a professorship as a matter of accepted routine.

## *Contingency Theory: Path-Goal Leadership Training*

If one accepts the path-goal orientation of contingency theory, the assumptions behind training programs and placement of school administrators change considerably. Unlike Fiedler's orientation toward leadership, path-goal leadership theory argues that a manager can vary his or her leadership style to *fit* specific situations. Following this basic assumption, leadership training for school administrators would invest heavily in (1) developing techniques for establishing reward-related goals; (2) developing organizational diagnostic techniques; and (3) building flexible leadership responses to differing problem situations. The objective of the leadership training program, therefore, is to provide the school administrator with the insight and skills to adopt a specific leadership style. The leadership style should be geared to helping subordinates achieve desired rewards (both psychological and material). A school superintendent, for example, can shape a process wherein the board of education and community groups will praise the efforts of school principals in the area of curricular reform. The superintendent can then diagnose the blockages to curricular reform and help clear away a path for the principals to accomplish their desired goal.

Placement and promotion within the path-goal context of leadership depends a great deal on the demonstrated ability of the school administrator to diagnose individual and group constraints to movement toward a goal. The proposed leader must be flexible enough to match a problem with an appropriate leadership style whether that be directive, supportive, participative, or achievement oriented.

## *Leadership Training in Open Systems*

Traditional approaches to leadership training try to change leader behavior or provide new skills. However, as Hunt and Osborn observe, if the leaders is in a setting where undiscretionary behavior is standard, traditional types of training are useless. Training must be directed toward behaviors that are going to be available to the trainee.[131]

Following the Hunt and Osborn micro-macro model of leadership, training would require an understanding of group and organizational processes within the context of changing economic, political, social, and legal environments.[132] In addition, the leader would need an accurate picture of his or her own personal make-up in areas such as: career expectations, risk-taking behavior strategic vision, people or task orientations, Machiavellian instincts, and so forth.

Providing training opportunities to match individual skills with organizational settings in which opportunities arise to develop and use alternate tactics of behavior is important. That is, opportunities should exist in which leaders can recognize different types of problem situations and adopt different patterns of leadership style in response to those situations.

Such open-system training is intended to be related to real-world conditions, as can be seen in a study of superintendents carried out by Pitner and Ogawa.

> Superintendents, rather than single-mindedly directing their organizations, are very responsive to both organizational and environmental influences. They monitor a broad

diversity of information sources to detect preferences to which schools need conform, issues which require attention, and opportunities to invoke their own agendas. Although superintendents do exert some influence, they are constrained by community values and socio-organizational structures, and they typically employ unobtrusive influence strategies.[133]

Hence, leadership training is the adapting of individual styles to changing needs and demands in the macro and micro environments.

## Conclusion

Leaders come in all sizes, shapes, sexes, colors, and qualities. Speaking before a distinguished audience in Washington, D.C., Rodney Dangerfield caught the spirit of the moment when he began by saying, "You can't imagine how happy I am to be here among all the greats, the near-greats, and the ingrates."

The "great man" theory of leadership has been with us a long time. During the first half of the twentieth century, researchers concentrated their efforts on trying to identify a set of psychological traits that would signify the presence of a leader. Leadership was viewed as an elitist concept; only a few were so endowed, and their good fortune was attributed to birth rather than training. The trait theory of leadership fit neatly with the classical organization theory of the time. Individuals who rose to the top positions in their respective hierarchies did so because of the superior psychological qualities they possessed, which other less fortunate people around them did not. The pronouncements of these leaders on what is good policy and procedure were attended to, not only because of the leaders' power in the hierarchy, but also because it was assumed that they had superior judgment on such things.

The idea that specific psychological traits were the source of leadership was fundamentally discredited by the 1950s. During the 1960s and 1970s, the search was on to match leadership styles to higher levels of employee production and satisfaction within the context of formal organizations. This form of situational leadership is usually categorized as contingency leadership theory.

Even though contingency leadership theory was alive and well in the 1980s, theory building continued in search of a leadership framework that produced added insight into processes of establishing an ever closer fit between the internal and external environments of educational organizations. Transformational leadership theory is now under development as a means to provide direction and movement in the complex conceptual arena of the open system.

Some of the leadership models presented were supported by empirical research and some were not. As pointed out earlier, some scholars are suspicious of theory that is not supported by empirical measurement. A "hawk" position on this matter is articulated by Korman when he writes, "Measurement and theory go hand-in-hand and the development of one without the other is a waste of time for all concerned."[134] A "dove" position argues that taking action on untested models is an essential part of management because organizational officials do not always have the luxury of waiting until all the data on an issue have been gathered. In other words, if it helps, use it.

To summarize, the various theories of leadership offer different advice about the roles of leaders. Trait theories admonish leaders to be kings, and reign firmly but fairly. Contingency theories advise leaders to be a lions and a foxes, and apply different strokes for different folks. Transformational theory presses leaders to think positively and convince people that together they can leap tall buildings with a single bound.

Regarding the overall field of leadership, Stogdill's observation of a few years ago still holds true.

> Each of these theories is concerned with a small subset of the total leadership problem. A complete theory of leadership should explain: (1) the emergence of leadership in initially unstructured groups, (2) the maintenance of leadership once a role structure has been developed and stabilized, (3) the relation of leader personality and behavior to follower and group response and (4) the conditions under which specific patterns of leader personality and behavior are effective. No such theory is presently available.[135]

In other words, if anyone is interested in conducting explorations in leadership theory in the field of education, he or she will not suffer for lack of a place to begin.

## *Notes*

1. Gary Yukl, *Leadership in Organizations,* 2nd ed. (Englewood Cliffs, NJ: Prentice-Hall, 1989), p. 267.

2. James Lipham, "Leadership: General Theory and Research," in *Leadership: The Science and the Art Today,* Luvern Cunningham and William Gephart, eds. (Itasca, IL: F. E. Peacock, 1973), p. 7.

3. Ernest Dale, *Management Theory and Practice* (New York: McGraw-Hill, 1969), p. 427.

4. F. Harbison and C. A. Myers, *Management in the Industrial World: An International Analysis* (New York: McGraw-Hill, 1959), pp. 15–16.

5. Henry Mintzberg, *The Nature of Managerial Work* (Englewood Cliffs, NJ: Prentice-Hall, 1980), p. 62.

6. Lee Bolman, Terrence Deal, "Looking for Leadership: Another Search Party's Report," *Educational Administration Quarterly,* 30 (1994): 78.

7. Thomas J. Sergiovanni, "Ten Principles of Quality Leadership," *Educational Leadership* 39 (1982): 330.

8. Edgar Schein, *Organizational Culture and Leadership* (San Francisco: Josey-Bass, 1985), p. 320.

9. Mintzberg, *The Nature of Managerial Work,* p. 62.

10. James G. Hunt and Richard N. Osborn, "A Multiple-Influence Approach to Leadership for Managers," in *Perspectives in Leader Effectiveness,* Paul Hersey and John Stinson, eds. (Athens: Ohio University, 1980), p. 49.

11. James J. Cribbin. *Strategies for Organizational Effectiveness* (New York: AMACOM, 1981), p. 35.

12. Ralph Stogdill, *Handbook of Leadership* (New York: The Free Press, 1974), pp. 7–16.

13. Yukl, p. 265.

14. Chester Barnard, *The Functions of the Executive* (Cambridge, MA: Harvard University Press, 1938), p. 283.

15. Martin Burlingame, "Images of Leadership in Effective Schools Literature," in *Instructional Leadership: Concepts, Issues and Controversies,* William Greenfield, ed. (Boston: Allyn and Bacon, 1987), p. 5.

16. Peter Blau and Richard Scott, *Formal Organizations* (San Francisco: Chandler Publishing Co., 1962), chapter 7.

17. Thomas Carlyle, *Lectures on Heroes, Hero-Worship, and the Heroic in History* (Oxford, England: Clarendon Press, 1910).

18. Daniel Katz and Robert L. Kahn, *The Social Psychology of Organizations,* 2nd ed. (New York: John Wiley, 1978), p. 527.

19. Reprinted with permission from *Organizational Behavior: An Existential-Systems Approach* by J. Kelly (Homewood, IL: Richard D. Irwin, Inc. 1974©), p. 494.

20. Ralph M. Stogdill, "Personal Factors Associated with Leadership: A Survey of the Literature," *Journal of Psychology* 25 (1948): 63.

21. Ibid., p. 64.

22. Stogdill, *Handbook of Leadership,* p. 72.

23. W. O. Jenkins, "A Review of Leadership Studies with Particular Reference to Military Problems," *Psychological Bulletin* 44 (1947).

24. Stogdill, "Personal Factors Associated with Leadership."

25. William Scott and Terence Mitchell, *Organizational Theory: A Structural and Behavioral Analysis* (Homewood, IL: Richard D. Irwin, 1976), p. 287.

26. Lipham, "Leadership: General Theory and Research," p. 2.

27. Alvin Gouldner, *Studies in Leadership* (New York: Harper and Bros., 1950), pp. 31–35.

28. James Lipham, "Leadership and Administration," in *Behavioral Science and Educational Administration* (Chicago: The University of Chicago Press, 1964), p. 130.

29. Daniel Katz and Robert Kahn, *The Social Psychology of Organizations,* p. 302. Copyright © 1966 by John Wiley & Sons, Inc. Reprinted by permission of John Wiley & Sons, Inc.

30. Lipham, "Leadership and Administration," p. 122,

31. Jacob Getzels, "Theory and Research on Leadership: Some Comments and Alternatives," in *Leadership: The Science and the Art Today,* Luvern Cunningham and William Gephart, eds. (Itasca, IL: F. E. Peacock, 1973), p. 16.

32. Jacob Getzels, James Lipham, and Roald Campbell, *Educational Administration as a Social Process* (New York: Harper & Row, 1968), pp. 135–136.

33. Kelly, *Organizational Behavior,* p. 365.

34. Harold Boles and James Davenport, *Introduction to Educational Leadership* (New York: Harper & Row, 1975), p. 153.

35. Willard Lane, Ronald Corwin, and William Monahan, *Foundations of Educational Administration: A Behavioral Analysis* (New York: Macmillan, 1966), pp. 301–302.

36. George Homans, *The Human Group* (New York: Harcourt, Brace and World, 1950), pp. 425–440.

37. Lane et al., *Foundations of Educational Administration,* p. 326.

38. Cribbin, *Strategies for Organizational Effectiveness,* p. 11.

39. Nancy J. Pitner and Rodney T. Ogawa, "Organizational Leadership: The Case of the School Superintendent," *Educational Administration Quarterly* 17 (1981): 61.

40. National Center for Educational Statistics, *Digest of Educational Statistics: 1993:* (Washington, DC: U.S. Government Printing Office, 1993), p. 79.

41. Charol Shakeshaft, "Women in Educational Management in the United States," in *Women in Educational Management,* ed. Janet Ouston (New York: Longman, 1993), p. 48.

42. Charol Shakeshaft, *Women in Educational Administration* (Beverly Hills, CA: 1987), p. 87.

43.  Catherine Marshall, "From Culturally Defined to Self-Defined: Career Stages of Women Administrators," *The Journal of Educational Thought* 19 (1985): 139.

44.  Marshall, p. 138.

45.  Shakeshaft, "Women in Educational Management," p. 50.

46.  Academic Senate, University of California, *Notice* 19 (October 1994), p. 1.

47.  Shakeshaft, "Women in Educational Management," p. 51.

48.  Charol Shakeshaft, "Women in Urban Administration: Introduction," *Urban Education* 4 (1994): 357–360.

49.  Marilyn Loden, *Feminine Leadership: Or How to Succeed in Business Without Being One of the Boys,* summarized by Stephen Ruben in *The Manager's Bookshelf,* J. L. Pierce and J. W. Newstrom, eds. (New York: Harper and Row, 1988).

50.  Gareth Morgan, *Images of Organization* (Beverly Hills, CA: Sage, 1986), pp. 182–83.

51.  Andrew Halpin and James Winer, "The Leadership Behavior of the Airplane Commander," mimeographed technical report (Columbus, OH: The Ohio State University Research Foundation, 1952).

52.  John Hemphill and Alvin Coons, "Development of the Leader Behavior Description Questionnaire," in *Leader Behavior: Its Description and Measurement,* Ralph Stogdill and Alvin Coons, eds. (Columbus: The Ohio State University Press, 1957).

53.  Andrew Halpin, *Theory and Research in Administration* (New York: Macmillan, 1966), p. 86.

54.  Ralph Stogdill, "Historical Trends in Leadership Theory and Research," *Journal of Contemporary Business* (Autumn 1974): 140.

55.  Andrew Halpin, *The Leader Behavior of School Superintendents* (Columbus: Ohio State University, College of Education, 1956).

56.  Stephen Hencley, "Situational Behavioral Approach to the Study of Educational Leadership," in *Leadership: The Science and the Art Today,* Luvern Cunningham and William Gephart, eds. (Itasca, IL: F. E. Peacock, 1973), chapter 4.

57.  Edwin Fleishman, "Twenty Years of Consideration and Structure," in *Current Developments in the Study of Leadership,* Edwin Fleishman and James Hunt, eds. (Carbondale, IL: Southern Illinois University Press, 1973), p. 37.

58.  Chester Barnard, *The Functions of the Executive* (Cambridge, MA: Harvard University Press, 1938).

59.  Chris Argyris, *Personality and Organization: The Conflict Between the System and the Individual* (New York: Harper & Row, 1957).

60.  Rensis Likert, *New Patterns of Management* (New York: McGraw-Hill, 1961).

61.  Getzels, Lipham, and Campbell, *Educational Administration as a Social Process.*

62.  Bernard M. Bass *Leadership, Psychology, and Organizational Behavior* (New York: Harper & Row, 1960).

63.  A. F. Brown, "Reactions to Leadership," *Educational Administration Quarterly* 3 (1967).

64.  Fred Fiedler, "Engineer the Job to Fit the Manager," *Harvard Business Review* (September–October 1965).

65.  Douglas McGregor, "On Leadership," *Antioch Notes* (May 1954): 2–3.

66.  T. B. Greenfield, "Research on the Behavior of Educational Leaders: Critique of a Tradition," *Alberta Journal of Educational Research* 14 (1968): 55.

67.  Ibid., p. 57.

68.  Abraham Korman, "Consideration, Initiating Structure, and Organizational Criteria—A Review," *Personnel Psychology* 19 (1966): 354.

69.  Ibid., p. 355.

70.  For important works see: Fred E. Fiedler, "Engineer the Job to Fit the Manager," *Harvard Business Review* (September–October 1965); idem. "Validation and Extension of the

Contingency Model of Leadership Effectiveness: A Review of Empirical Findings," *Psychological Bulletin* 76 (1971); idem, "The Contingency Model—New Directions for Leadership Utilization," *Journal of Contemporary Business* (Autumn 1974); and Fred E. Fiedler and Martin Chemers, *Leadership and Effective Management* (Glenview, IL: Scott, Foresman, 1974).

71. Fred E. Fiedler, "Recent Developments in Research on the Contingency Model," in *Group Processes,* Leonard Berkowitz, ed. (New York: Academic Press, 1978), p. 215.

72. Fred Fiedler, "Personality and Situational Determinants of Leader Behavior," in *Current Developments in the Study of Leadership,* Edwin Fleishman and James Hunt, eds. (Carbondale, IL: Southern Illinois University Press, 1973), p. 42.

73. Korman, "Consideration, Initiating Structure, and Organizational Criteria."

74. Fiedler, "Personality and Situational Determinants," p. 42.

75. Robert Tannenbaum, I. Weschler, and F. Massarik, *Leadership and Organization: A Behavioral Science Approach* (New York: McGraw-Hill, 1961), p. 24.

76. Fiedler, "The Contingency Model," p. 66.

77. Fiedler, "Recent Developments," p. 211.

78. For a discussion of this format see: C. E. Osgood, G. J. Suci, and P. H. Tannenbaum, *The Measurement of Meaning* (Urbana, IL: University of Illinois Press, 1957).

79. Fiedler, "The Contingency Model," p. 67.

80. Fiedler, "Engineer the Job to Fit the Manager."

81. Fiedler, "The Contingency Model," p. 68.

82. Chester A. Schriesheim and Steven Kerr, "Theories and Measures of Leadership: A Critical Appraisal of Current and Future Directions," *Leadership: The Cutting Edge,* James G. Hunt and Lars L. Larson, eds. (Carbondale and Edwardsville: Southern Illinois University Press, 1977), pp. 9–44; L. H. Peters, D. D. Hartke, and J. T. Pohlman, "Fiedler's Contingency Theory of Leadership: An Application of the Meta-Analysis Procedure of Schmidt and Hunter," *Psychological Bulletin,* 97 (1985): 274–85.

83. Fred E. Fiedler, "A Rejoiner to Schriesheim and Kerr's Premature Obituary of the Contingency Model," in *Leadership: The Cutting Edge,* pp. 45–51.

84. Chester A. Schriesheim and Steven Kerr, "R.I.P. LPC: A Response to Fiedler," in *Leadership: The Cutting Edge,* pp. 51–56.

85. Martin Chemers and Robert Rice, "A Theoretical and Empirical Examination of Fiedler's Contingency Model of Leadership Effectiveness," in *Contingency Approaches to Leadership,* James Hunt and Lars Larson, eds. (Carbondale: Southern Illinois University Press, 1974); and S. G. Green and D. M. Nebeker, "The Effects of Situational Factors and Leadership Style on Leader Behavior," *Organizational Behavior and Human Performance* 19 (1977); 368–377.

86. M. J. Strube and J. E. Garcia, "A Meta-analytic Investigation of Fiedler's Contingency Model of Leadership Effectiveness," paper presented at the American Psychological Assn. Annual Meeting, Montreal, Quebec, Canada, September, 1980.

87. G. Graen et al., "Contingency Model of Leadership Effectiveness: Antecedent and Evidential Results," *Psychological Bulletin* 74 (1970); and Abraham Korman, "Contingency Approach to Leadership: An Overview," in *Contingency Approaches to Leadership,* James Hunt and Lars Larson, eds. (Carbondale: Southern Illinois University Press, 1974).

88. Ibid., pp. 191–192.

89. Stephen P. Robbins. *Organizational Behavior: Concepts, Controversies, and Applications,* 2nd ed. (Englewood Cliffs, NJ: Prentice-Hall, 1983), p. 226.

90. Chemers and Rice, "A Theoretical and Empirical Examination," p. 107.

91. Fiedler, "Personality and Situational Determinants," p. 43.

92. Fred E. Fiedler, "The Leadership Situation and the Black Box in Contingency Theories," *Leadership Theory and Research: Perspectives and Directions* (Orlando, FL: Academic Press, 1993) pp. 6–7.

93.  Fiedler, "The Leadership Situation," p. 6.

94.  Fred Fiedler and Joseph Garcia, *New Approaches to Effective Leadership* (New York: Wesley, 1987), p. 9.

95.  Bernard Bass, *Leadership and Performance Beyond Expectations* (New York: The Free Press, 1985); R. M. Stogdill, *Handbook of Leadership: A Survey of the Literature* (New York: The Free Press, 1974).

96.  Fred Fiedler, "The Contribution of Cognitive Resources and Leader Behavior to Organizational Performance," *Journal of Applied Social Psychology* 16 (1986): 544.

97.  Fiedler and Garcia, p. 8.

98.  Fiedler and Garcia, p. 27.

99.  Frederick W. Gibson, Fred Fiedler, Kelley M. Barrett, "Stress, Babble, and the Utilization of the Leader's Intellectual Abilities," *Leadership Quarterly* 4 (1993), p. 204.

100. Fred E. Fiedler and Thomas G. Link, "Leader Intelligence, Interpersonal Stress, and Task Performance," in *Mind in Context: Interactionist Perspectives on Human Intelligence,* ed. R. J. Sternberg and R. K. Wagner (London: Cambridge University Press, 1994), p. 154.

101. Yukl, p. 200.

102. For a discussion of expectancy theory see: Victor Vroom, *Work and Motivation* (New York: John Wiley & Sons, 1964).

103. Robert House and Terence Mitchell, "Path-Goal Theory of Leadership," *Journal of Contemporary Business* (Autumn 1974): 84.

104. Cf. Walter Hill, "Leadership Style Flexibility, Satisfaction and Performance," in *Current Developments in the Study of Leadership,* Edwin Fleishman and James Hunt, eds. (Carbondale: Southern Illinois University Press, 1973); and M. G. Evans, "The Effects of Supervisory Behavior on the Path-goal Relationship," *Organizational Behavior and Human Performance* 55 (1970).

105. Robert House, "A Path-Goal Theory of Leader Effectiveness," *Administrative Science Quarterly* 16 (1971).

106. Robert House and Gary Dessler, "The Path-Goal Theory of Leadership: Some Post Hoc and A Priori Tests," in *Contingency Approaches to Leadership,* James Hunt and Lars Larson, eds. (Carbondale: Southern Illinois University Press, 1974).

107. Schriesheim and Kerr, "Theories and Measures."

108. John E. Sheridan, Kirk Downey, and John W. Slocum, Jr., "Testing Causal Relationships of House's Path-Goal Theory of Leadership Effectiveness," in *Leadership Frontiers,* James Hunt and Lars Larson, eds. (Kent, OH: Kent State University Press, 1975), pp. 61–80.

109. Bernard M. Bass, *Stogdill's Handbook of Leadership* (New York: The Free Press, 1981).

110. J. Indvik, "Path-Goal Theory of Leadership: A Meta-Analysis." (Proceedings of the Academy of Management Meetings, 1986), pp. 189–92.

111. Yukl, p. 103.

112. Elmer Burack, *Organizational Analysis: Theory and Applications* (Hinsdale, IL: Dryden Press, 1975), p. 320.

113. Jerome Murphy, "The Unheroic side of Leadership: Notes from the Swamp," *Phi Delta Kappan,* 69 (1988): 659.

114. The National Commission on Excellence in Education, *A Nation at Risk: The Imperative for Educational Reform* (Washington, DC: U.S. Government Printing Office, 1983).

115. Larry Cuban, *The Managerial Imperative: The Practice of Leadership in Schools* (Albany, NY: SUNY Press, 1988); Arthur Blumberg and William Greenfield, *The Effective Principal: Perspectives in School Leadership,* 2nd ed. (Boston: Allyn and Bacon, 1986).

116. Marshall Sashkin and Robert Fulmer, "Toward an Organizational Leadership Theory," in *Emerging Leadership Vistas,* James Hunt et al., eds. (Lexington, MA: Lexington Books, 1988), p. 57.

117. Thomas Sergiovanni, "The Leadership Needed for Quality Schooling," in *Schooling for Tomorrow*, T. Sergiovanni and J. Moore, eds. (Boston: Allyn and Bacon, 1989), p. 215.

118. James Lipham, "Leadership: General Theory and Research," In *Leadership: The Science and the Art Today*, Luvern Cunningham and William Gephart, eds. (Itasca, IL: F. E. Peacock, 1973), p. 8.

119. J. M. Burns, *Leadership* (New York: Harper and Row, 1978).

120. James G. Hunt and Richard N. Osborn, "Toward a Macro-Oriented Model of Leadership: An Odyssey," in *Leadership: Beyond Establishment Views*, J. G. Hunt, U. Sekaran, and C. Schriesheim, eds. (Carbondale: Southern Illinois University Press, 1982).

121. Sergiovanni, p. 215.

122. Kenneth Leithwood, "Leadership for School Restructuring," *Educational Administration Quarterly*, 30 (1994): 498–518.

123. Reported in Hill, "Leadership Style Flexibility, Satisfaction and Performance," p. 83.

124. Fiedler, "Engineer the Job to Fit the Manager," p. 115.

125. For a discussion of techniques of matching leaders to jobs see: Fred E. Fiedler and Martin Chemers, *Improving Leadership Effectiveness: The Leader Match Concept* (New York: Wiley, 1976).

126. B. R. Baliga and James Hunt, "An Organizational Life Cycle Approach to Leadership," in *Emerging Leadership Vistas*, James Hunt et al., eds. (Lexington, MA: Lexington Books, 1988).

127. Gordon Lippitt and Warren Schmidt, "Crisis in a Developing Organization," *Harvard Business Review* (November–December 1967).

128. Fiedler, "The Contingency Model," p. 76.

129. Burlingame, p. 9.

130. Philip Hallinger and Joseph Murphy, "Instructional Leadership in the School Context," in *Instructional Leadership: Concepts, Issues and Controversies*, William Greenfield, ed. (Boston: Allyn and Bacon, 1987), p. 194.

131. Hunt and Osborn, "A Multiple-Influence Approach," p. 59.

132. James G. Hunt and Richard N. Osborn, "Toward a Macro-Oriented Model of Leadership: An Odyssey," in Hunt, Sekaran, and Schriesheim, *Leadership*, pp. 201–206.

133. Pitner and Ogawa, "Organizational Leadership," p. 62.

134. Korman, "Contingency Approaches to Leadership: An Overview." p. 195.

135. Stogdill, "Historical Trends in Leadership Theory and Research," p. 4.

*C h a p t e r*  **8**

# *Motivation and Management*

A few years ago I was touring a central office with a district superintendent and we entered a large room with numerous desks in it. "How many people work here?" I asked. "About half of them," he replied. The superintendent, of course, was referring to motivation, a word that comes from the Latin *movere,* or to move. Like managers around the world, the superintendent obviously felt there was not enough *movere* in his people.

Aside from its Latin root, exactly what is motivation? In our own life experiences we have all encountered many people with different theories of motivation: a sweet old grandmother who offers you a cookie if you will play the piano; a teacher who will stamp a happy face on your wrist if you get a 100 on a spelling test; a marine drill instructor who threatens to kick your gluteus maximus from pillar to post unless you get in step; a school superintendent who offers a promotion if you acquire additional university credits.

Since the dawn of human history we have had a fascination with the varied kinds and qualities of motivation that seem to bring out the best, or perhaps the worst, in us. Important as the subject is, the essence of motivation still remains an enigma.

## *The Basis of Motivation*

Katz and Kahn write that motivational techniques must be responsive to three organizational needs. First, people must be attracted to and be retained by the organization. Second, people must be induced to conscientiously and effectively perform their tasks. Third, people must be spurred to engage in creative and innovative work-related actions that resolve problems in increasingly effective and efficient ways.[1]

Educational reformers of the 1980s tried hard to attract and retain bright, well-qualified college graduates into the teaching profession by increasing the extrinsic rewards of salaries and benefits. On paper, it looks like considerable financial gains were made over the years. From 1972–73 to 1992–93 the average elementary and secondary school teachers' salaries in *current* dollars increased from $10,174 to $35,334, or over $25,000. However, in *constant* dollars (1992–93) during the same twenty-year period, salaries increased from $33,873 to $35,334, or only about $1,500.[2] Such a low increment in real spending money does not afford educators the opportunity to significantly increase their standard of living.

Certainly, improved extrinsic rewards and benefits can attract good people to the profession, but using them to sustain conscientious and effective performance, as well as release creative energies over the duration of a career, is another matter. Mike Milstein writes of the stagnation and loss of job fulfillment that beset many educators. *Plateauing,* as this condition is called, usually comes with a long period of stability in a career during which the intellectual and work-related challenges become exhausted. A sense of being trapped can set in if the opportunities for career advancement or personal growth appear unlikely.[3]

Milstein points out that when educators reach a plateau, a period of reassessment and growth can begin, or dissatisfaction, coping behaviors, and personal stress can emerge. For educational leaders, the challenge is to recognize plateauing conditions and symptoms among their subordinates and respond with appropriate motivation strategy. But which strategy?

For most people, common sense explanations suffice as they link motivation to some culturally recognized goal. For example, Mr. Jones works hard to earn money. As a scientific explanation, however, this view is hardly satisfactory. As Edward Lawler points out, to be truly scientific it must explain "why money is the goal, why money is sought rather than some other goal, and why [Mr. Jones] pursues the goal in the manner he does."[4]

The guiding force behind motivation, Robbins writes, is "every person, consciously or unconsciously, asks himself, 'What's in it for me?' before engaging in any form of behavior. The principle that individuals are motivated by self-interest underlies . . . [almost every theory] of motivation." Robbins goes on to argue that the feelings of others do impinge on a person's self-interest actions. Many pursue self-interest through helping others, as did Albert Schweitzer, Joan of Arc, Florence Nightingale and "even the kamikaze pilots of World War II."[5]

Robbins, however, is only partially correct. In terms of scientific inquiry, the question, What's in it for me? only describes a *relatively recent* view of what is behind motivation. For most of this century another question has described the central force behind motivation: What turns me on? These questions suggest two different views of the nature of human beings. Lawler writes:

> One represents man as being driven by inherited, conflicting, unconscious drives that cause him to behave in instinctual and, at times, self-destructive ways. The second view represents man as rational and aware of his goals and as behaving in those ways that he feels will help him achieve his goals. The first view had its origin in the writing of Freud and the neo-Freudians and has continued to develop during the last fifty years.

The second view can be traced to the work of Plato and Aristotle and more recently to the work of Descartes, Hobbes, and Spinoza.[6]

The different views of motivation are important because, among other things, they suggest that alternate forms of organization and management are needed. One theory emphasizes an organization that stresses controlled, disciplined behavior as attempts are made to channel instinctual, impulsive actions along productive lines. The other theory suggests an organization that supports goal-oriented behaviors directly by enlightened self-interest and restrained by self-control.

This chapter explores motivation theory as it has evolved over this century. Special attention is given to the two major strands of thought that dominate the field: *content theory* and *process theory*. Implications for educational institutions are discussed and special problem areas pointed out.

## Content Theories of Motivation

Discovering the essence of motivation is not an easy task, because motivation is an academic concept that cannot be observed directly. Only the behavioral manifestations of motivation can be observed and inferences made about causes.

Motivation often is defined as "an inner state that energizes, activates or moves (hence 'motivation'), and that directs or channels behavior toward goals."[7] Hence, four sequential questions are involved: (1) What energizes human behavior? (2) What directs or channels that behavior? (3) How is that behavior sustained? and (4) How is that behavior terminated?

Content theories are based on the notion that things within us generate motivation. Content theories assume that (1) drives/needs initiate, channel, and sustain goal-directed behaviors, (2) the drives/needs behaviors are initiated when an equilibrium imbalance or a deprivation is felt, (3) the drives/needs are prioritized into higher and lower levels, (4) when the need is fulfilled it is no longer motivating, and (5) we all share basically the same prioritization of drives/needs.[8]

### Hedonism

The first known attempts to explain why we behave as we do go back more than 23 centuries to the Greek philosophers, and more recently to the English utilitarians of the eighteenth and nineteenth centuries, who believed that behavior is directed toward comfort and pleasure and away from discomfort and pain. This view is called *hedonism*. As a scientific explanation of motivation, however, hedonism is seriously lacking. Vroom writes, "There was in the document no clear-cut specification of the types of events which were pleasurable or painful, or even how these events could be determined for a particular individual, nor did it make clear how persons acquired their conceptions of ways of attaining pleasure and pain, or how the sources of pleasure and pain might be modified by experience."[9]

The first significant theories of motivation in this century focused on instincts.

## Instinct Theories of Motivation

Charles Darwin called the attention of the scientific world to the possibility that much of human and animal behavior is determined by instincts. To most theorists, instincts were thought to function in an almost automatic manner as the organisms of the body would pursue actions preprogrammed by heredity. William James in 1890 and Sigmund Freud in 1915 made significant contributions and gave considerable impetus to instinct theory, with the latter introducing important ideas about unconscious motivation.[10] In 1908, McDougall stated, "We may then define an instinct as an inherited or innate psychophysical disposition that determines the possessor to perceive and pay attention to objects of a certain class, to experience an emotional excitement of a particular quality on perceiving such an object, and to act in regard to it in a particular manner, or at least to experience an impulse to such action."[11]

During the early years of the century, instinct theory flourished as psychologists made up long lists attempting to account for more and more observable behaviors. Around World War I, instinct theory as the principal explanation of behavior came under heavy fire. Lawler writes that "by the 1920s the list of instincts totaled nearly 6,000 including the 'instinct to avoid eating apples in one's own orchard.' "[12] In a sense, instinct theory died of its own weight. As more and more instincts were stated, psychologists began to question the explanatory usefulness of the approach."[13]

With respect to the impact instinct theory had on the operation of schools, Ivan Russell writes that the influence could particularly be seen in the treatment of students. Behaviors that were viewed as favorable to education and society were considered as rooted in positive instincts or even learned behaviors (and thus not instincts). Problematic behaviors were seen as rooted only in instincts and had to be contained by punishment or some other form of suppression. "Thus, the focus of the school was very early given to punishment and thwarting, with little or no concern for creating conditions wherein students could learn to change their behavior so as to allow personal expression while, at the same time, meeting standards of acceptability. Unfortunately, this focus has been extremely resistant to change despite our willingness to discard instinct as a theory of behavior causation."[14]

## Drive/Need Theory

Drive theory emerged in part as a reaction to instinct theory. In 1918, Robert Woodworth formulated the notion of drive as a central force behind activating behavior. He used a model of a machine for thinking about human behavior. For the mechanisms of the machine to be set in motion, some source of energy had to be applied. Woodworth argued that conditions of deficiency or urges such as hunger and thirst were energizers or drives of behavior.[15]

The concept of drive replaced that of instinct in the language of psychology. Primary drives were associated with specific biological bases, such as hunger, thirst, avoidance of pain, sex, sleep, and care for the young.[16] As drives produce outcomes that respond to the inducement, the tension is reduced and a balance is once again established. Tension exists when a state of deprivation exists. Hull's work provided a classification of biologically based drives that are still in use and form the basis of other theories of motivation.[17] Hull felt that secondary or learned drives also existed, but ultimately were associated with fulfilling primary drives. For example, secondary rewards such as earning money and seeking social acceptance were related to the basic drives of food and comfort.

Notions about secondary or learned drives emerged during the 1930s.[18] Secondary drives were still generally thought to be linked to an individual's need to fulfill primary drives. In 1937, Allport took an important step when he suggested that secondary needs, or motives as he called them, acquired considerable autonomy from primary needs. "Each motive has a definite point of origin which may possibly lie in instincts, or, more likely, in the organic tension of infancy. Chronologically speaking, all adult purposes can be traced back to . . . infancy, but as the individual matures the tie is broken. Whatever bond remains is historical, not functional."[19] Also during the 1930s, the term *drive* was often substituted for by the word *need*. Laboratory psychologists doing animal experiments tended to use the concept of *drive* while social scientists who were interested in human behavior began to use the term *need*. Modern motivation theory begins with needs being placed in hierarchical order.

## Hierarchy of Needs

The work of Abraham Maslow in the 1950s significantly advanced our thinking about motivation; he was a leader among those who questioned whether animal experimentation in the laboratory was meaningful in the world of human beings. He also questioned the despairing, depraved, troubled, and constrained image of human beings that psychological theories of the time generally produced. Maslow's clinical experience led him to believe that "human life will never be understood unless its highest aspirations are taken into account. Growth, self-actualization, the striving toward health, the quest for identity and autonomy, the yearning for excellence (and other ways of phrasing the striving 'upward') must by now be accepted beyond question as a widespread and perhaps universal human tendency."[20]

Maslow argued that human motivation can be broken into five basic categories of needs: (1) physiological, (2) safety, (3) social, (4) esteem, and (5) self-actualization (see Figure 8.1). According to Maslow's theory, a satisfied need no longer operates as a motivator of behavior. For example, your need for air is not a motivator of behavior unless you are deprived of it. On the other hand, "man lives for bread alone, when there is no bread." Human needs for love, esteem, and self-actualization are significantly diminished in the face of a hungry stomach. The less satisfied a need, the more power it has to motivate.

The categories in Maslow's hierarchy are defined as follows:

> *Physiological needs:* This category consists of such basic survival needs as food, air, water, sex, shelter, and sleep.
> *Safety needs:* This category becomes important when the physiological needs have been satisfied. Safety needs include the protection of job security as well as protection from danger, illness, economic disaster, and the unexpected in general. Risk-taking behavior among managers and workers becomes possible after these needs have

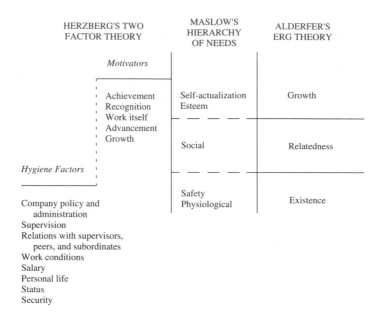

| HERZBERG'S TWO FACTOR THEORY | MASLOW'S HIERARCHY OF NEEDS | ALDERFER'S ERG THEORY |
|---|---|---|
| *Motivators* | | |
| Achievement Recognition Work itself Advancement Growth | Self-actualization Esteem | Growth |
| | Social | Relatedness |
| *Hygiene Factors* | | |
| Company policy and administration Supervision Relations with supervisors, peers, and subordinates Work conditions Salary Personal life Status Security | Safety Physiological | Existence |

FIGURE 8-1  Comparison of Three Content Theories of Motivation.

been treated satisfactorily. For example, teachers are much more willing to go out on strike after they have received tenure than before.

*Social needs:* Social needs are encompassed in a worker's desire for association, belonging, friendship, and approval from peers. When social needs are thwarted, maladjustment is the consequence.

*Esteem needs:* Esteem needs are divided into two types. The first is the need for self-esteem; that is, for self-confidence, achievement, knowledge, and independence. The second deals with one's reputation, for instance, the need for approval, prestige, and recognition of one's work. Teachers and administrators, for example, want to feel that the students and community they serve respect and appreciate their labors.

*Self-actualization needs:* At the uppermost level in the motivation hierarchy is the need for self-fulfillment. This is the need, Maslow states, behind the drive "to become everything one is capable of becoming."[21] These needs press for continued self-development and a release of creative energies. Whether a person is a university professor, a high school teacher, a corporate manager, or a parent, the drive to be effective, creative, and happy in that role is a manifestation of the need for self-actualization. Unlike motivation based on primary drives, where the need decreases with satisfaction, the need for self-actualization increases as more is obtained.

## ERG Theory

A more recent version of a needs hierarchy is Clayton Alderfer's ERG theory.[22] Alderfer postulated three core hierarchical needs: existence, relatedness, and growth (together called ERG), thus collapsing Maslow's five levels into three, as seen in Figure 8.1. The categories in Alderfer's hierarchy are defined as follows:

*Existence needs:* These include both physiological and safety needs essential to sustaining physical well-being.
*Relatedness needs:* These deal with a desire for meaningful and satisfying social relationships.
*Growth needs:* This category represents the highest level of needs and includes self-esteem and self-actualization, which represent an intrinsic desire for personal development.

ERG theory is more flexible than Maslow's in at least two important ways. ERG needs are less fixed to a hierarchical arrangement, as to some degree all three levels can be activated simultaneously. For example, a low-paid teacher who is worried about making the monthly house payment, or even having enough money to purchase food at the end of the month can still maintain high interest in friendship bonds with other teachers as well as pursuing new knowledge for intellectual stimulation.

Alderfer also recognizes a frustration-regression process. That is, if a higher-level need is thwarted, the individual will seek greater satisfaction at a lower level. For example, if intellectual growth needs are for some reason denied to an educator, that individual will seek to expand upon the satisfaction found in social relationships.

## Herzberg's Two-Factor Theory

Frederic Herzberg has made an important contribution to motivation theory by taking notions about need hierarchies and placing them in the workplace. In proposing his theory, he laments the limited genuine insight we have on this exceedingly complex subject, and warns that "the dismal ratio of knowledge to speculation has not dampened the enthusiasm for new forms of snake oil that are constantly coming on the market, many with academic testimonials."[23]

Herzberg discusses traditional forms of motivation in the workplace. He calls the first the negative *physical* KITA, or kick 'em in the you-know-what. There are, he muses, three disadvantages to this approach: "(1) it is inelegant; (2) it contradicts the precious image of benevolence that most organizations cherish; and (3) since it is a physical attack, it directly stimulates the autonomic nervous system, and this often results in negative feedback."

The negative *psychological* KITA is also popular at workplaces, and it has advantages over the physical version: "The cruelty is not visible; the bleeding is internal and comes much later." Also, it reduces the possibility of a physical backlash as the person administering the KITA can remain above it all and let the system do the dirty work. Finally, "if the employee does complain, he can always be accused of being paranoid."[24]

The author points out, however, that the KITA approach is more abuse than motivation because of the need to continually apply outside pressure. The "floggings will continue until morale improves" approach is inherently contradictory. To genuinely be motivation a "generator" must be created within the worker so he "needs no outside stimulation. He *wants* to do it."

Herzberg based his theory on the two different needs of humans (discussed earlier in this chapter)—the basic biological and physiological needs, and our unique human characteristic, the ability to achieve and experience psychological growth.

In developing his theory, Herzberg conducted a study in which he analyzed the responses of 200 accountants and engineers who were asked to describe the situations in which they felt exceptionally good and exceptionally bad about their jobs. The same methodology has since been used in a multitude of occupational settings and in numerous countries. An important supportive replication in the field of education was done by Thomas Sergiovanni.[25]

Herzberg found that when people talked about feeling good or *satisfied,* they identified factors intrinsic to the job itself. Herzberg called these factors *motivators,* and they included: achievement, recognition, the work itself, responsibility, advancement, and growth.

When employees talked about being *dissatisfied* with the work, they typically discussed factors extrinsic to the job but related to it. These sources of dissatisfaction were called *hygiene* factors because they form the outer environment of work and keep things from getting too disruptive. The hygiene factors included: company policy and administration, supervision, relationship with supervisors, work conditions, salary, relationship with peers, personal life, relationship with subordinates, status, and security.

It is important to note, as Figure 8.1 shows, that motivation factors and hygiene factors do not form a hierarchy; neither are they at opposite ends of a continuum. They are on two separate dimensions. Satisfaction on the job comes from motivators, and dissatisfaction comes from hygiene factors. This conclusion has important implications for any work environment, including schools, because it argues that educators cannot be motivated toward higher levels of productivity by improving hygiene factors such as increased salary, better working conditions, more lenient or restrictive school policies, and so forth. Manipulating those factors can only make educators respond on the range from dissatisfied to neutral. Only through the manipulation of motivators (improvement in the job itself) can improvement on a range from neutral to satisfaction be achieved.

Thus, according to Herzberg's theory, when teachers go to the bargaining table and argue that increased salaries or other hygiene factors are necessary to motivate or retain a high level of motivation, the observation is not accurate. Improved salaries and other hygiene factors will reduce the level of dissatisfaction, but they will not bring job satisfaction.

It should be noted, however, that the hygiene factors can have a severe impact on work effectiveness if not responded to conscientiously because of increased teacher absenteeism, turnover, frustration, or negative thinking in general.

## Theory X and Theory Y

Perhaps no theory captures the two separate views of the nature of humanity (instinctive and impulsive versus rational and goal-seeking) better than Douglas McGregor's Theory X and Theory Y.[26] These two orientations can play important roles in determining the particular strategy of motivation managers adopt. Theory X argues that the following are basic conditions of the worker:

1. Workers are indolent and work as little as possible.

2. Workers lack ambition, dislike responsibility, and prefer to be led.
3. Workers are indifferent to the needs of the organization and think only of themselves.
4. Workers are not very intelligent, are gullible, and are easily led by the demagogue.
5. Workers are resistant to change.[27]

When the needs of a student, teacher, or administrator are essentially social, esteem, or related to self-actualization, the coercion, threats, pressures, and sanctions associated with Theory X are essentially useless in motivating behavior.

McGregor's alternative to Theory X is called Theory Y. Theory Y exhibits a positive orientation toward the worker's interests and capabilities. The basic assumptions of Theory Y include the following:

1. The natural condition of humans is not to be passive or resistant to organizational needs. If they appear that way, it is only because their past experience in organizations has shaped this behavior.
2. The capacity for assuming responsibility, the ability to direct behavior toward the completion of organizational goals, and the potential for personal growth and development are present in all people. Management is responsible for designing a work environment that permits individuals to exploit their full range of motivations and hence be of greater use to the organization as well as to themselves. Subordinates thus assume some responsibility for their own destiny as well as that of the organization. Under these conditions "everybody wins."

Theory Y, of course, focuses on fulfilling those needs of the subordinate that are positioned near the top of Maslow's hierarchy of needs. If these conditions can be sustained, the essence of organizational control shifts from exterior pressures and manipulations (management to worker, or administrator to teacher, or teacher to student) to an interior sense (within the subordinate) of self-control and self-direction. This is the difference between treating people as children and treating them as mature adults. After generations of the former, we cannot expect to shift to the latter overnight.

At least three popular teaching-learning strategies have their ideological and conceptual roots in Theory Y and the hierarchy of needs: (1) learning contracts, (2) individualized instruction, and (3) behavioral objectives. In entering into a learning contract with a teacher, students give definition to what they want to learn, the methodology of learning (e.g., library, work books, visual aids), and how they want their level of learning to be evaluated (e.g., written exam, term paper, oral evaluation). Thus, students cast the learning experience at their own level of hierarchical need and focus it on specific areas of interest. Students exercise considerable control over their own work task, rate, level, and environment. Theory X tactics of control are not necessary. The role of the teacher is to facilitate the learning process as much as possible, but not to assume control over it.

Individualized instruction maintains many of the characteristics found in the learning contract. Students are intended to pursue knowledge at a rate determined by their own capabilities rather than by an artificially imposed rate such as a class average. The task of the teacher is to design the learning process so that as learners are ready, the work leads them into the higher levels of the needs hierarchy. The rate and level of learning are determined by a sequence of competencies, which students must master before moving on to the next stage of the academic process. As in the case of the learning contract, the procedures of control and discipline transfer from external sources (teachers) to internal sources of student self-discipline.

The use of behavioral objectives in the learning process tends to rest more in the hands of the teachers than with the students, although the students can participate in setting the objectives. A behavioral objective focuses on the percentage of students in the class who are going to learn a specific subject or acquire a skill within a defined time period as evaluated by a specific measuring instrument. In practice, the tendency has been to use behavioral objectives as a measure of teacher effectiveness in the classroom rather than as a way to promote student learning. This feature is a perversion of the intent (e.g., used by administrators as a Theory X tool rather than a Theory Y strategy). If used appropriately, however, the behavioral objective concept lends itself well to the Theory Y hierarchy of needs strategy.

A continuing problem in schools is a result of educators attempting to launch students into needs categories associated with *esteem* and *self-actualization* when the students are still trying to resolve their lower-level needs in the *social* category. During adolescence, students exhibit a considerable need for association, friendship, and approval from peers. However, in many instances students from poor families have powerful anxieties about the more basic needs of food, shelter, and protection from danger and illness.

If the hierarchy-of-needs framework can be accepted as rooted in reality, then educators' attempts to bypass systematically the lower categories of student needs for the higher-order categories can result in frustration, if not outright defensive reactions by students. The same holds true for teachers and school administrators who find themselves forced to work at higher levels when they have been unable to deal successfully with their lower-need levels.

When people are blocked in their attempts to satisfy needs or are pressured to work at a higher level than they are prepared for, they may employ one or more defensive mechanisms instead of constructive strategies to solve their problems. Some general patterns of defensive reactions to frustration are withdrawal, aggression, compensation, repression, regression, projection, and rationalization.

## The Achievement Motive

Numerous researchers have not tried to develop a theory based on categorization or hierarchy of needs, but have focused on a specific secondary need they feel is especially important in explaining special types of motivation in organizational settings.

Since shortly after World War II, David McClelland has been developing a profile of high achievers by studying corporation presidents, sales representatives, and numerous other roles found in highly competitive situations.[28] Four behavioral characteristics form central components in the profile of high achievers: (1) the willingness to take moderate, calculated risks; (2) a preference for activities that provide rapid and precise feedback on the nature of the problem as well as performance; (3) intrinsic satisfaction in getting a job done well over extrinsic rewards; and (4) a preoccupation with completing a task, often at the expense of interpersonal relationships.

In most societies high achievers are respected for their ability to produce results. Based on his years of experience studying high achievers, McClelland was once asked how he found them as personalities. He replied, "I find them bores. They are not artistically sensitive. They're entrepreneurs, kind of driven—always trying to improve themselves and find a shorter route to the office or a faster way of reading their mail."[29]

For several years McClelland has been attempting to promote entrepreneurial activity among adults through achievement motivation training. McClelland's achievement development course has four primary goals:

1. To teach participants how to think, talk, and act like a person with high achievement
2. To stimulate participants to set higher, but carefully planned and realistic, work goals for themselves over the next two years
3. To give the participants knowledge about themselves
4. To create a group esprit de corps from learning about each other's hopes and fears, successes and failures, and from going through an emotional experience together, away from everyday life, in a retreat setting.[30]

Based on his studies McClelland argues that training in achievment motivation can be successful. "Impressive evidence [exists] that achievement motivation training significantly improves small-business performance provided there is some minimum support from the economic infrastructure, in the form of available loans, market opportunities, and a labor force. . . .The type of business does not seem to matter: the training seems to be effective for manufacturing, retail, and service businesses."[31]

## *The Power Motive*

The notion of the acquisition of power as being a special need has long been noted in the literature. Many years ago Alfred Adler wrote, "Now I began to see clearly in every physical phenomenon the striving for superiority. . . .All our functions follow its direction; rightly or wrongly they strive for conquest, surety, increase. . . .Whatever premises all our philosophers and psychologists dream of—self-preservation, pleasure principle, equalization—all these are but vague representations, attempts to express the great upward drive . . . *the fundamental fact of our life.*"[32]

Over the years as McClelland studied need achievement, he continually ran into problems of leadership, power, and social influence that *n* Achievement alone did not prepare high achievers to cope with. "It is very clear," he writes, "that high *n* Achievement does not equip a man to deal effectively with managing human relations."[33]

McClelland concluded that stimulating achievement in others requires a different motive than wanting achievement satisfaction for oneself. "Studying the achievement motive led to a better understanding of business entrepreneurship. Analogously, studying the power motive may help us understand managerial, societal, or even political leadership better."[34]

The need to achieve is a personal characteristic and places no emphasis on interpersonal relationships. The power motive concerns the interest one holds in exercising some form of influence or power over the behavior of others. The desire to hold power, however, has two faces, one of which is a personal need for dominance as one seeks to win out over active adversaries. This individual can be as clever as Machiavelli and as ruthless as Atilla the Hun in extreme cases. This person normally doesn't get stress; he or she gives it. Only the strongest can survive in the management jungle is the guiding philosophy of this type of manager. At the other extreme the individual may be no more than a Dennis the Menace in pinstripes. J. Sterling Livingston writes:

> Power seekers can be counted on to strive hard to reach positions where they can exercise authority over large numbers of people. Individual performers who lack this drive are not likely to act in ways that will enable them to advance far up the managerial ladder. . . .
>
> The competitive battle to advance within an organization, as Levinson points out, is much like playing "King of the Hill."[35] Unless a person enjoys playing that game, he is likely to tire of it and give up the struggle for control of the top of the hill. The power game is a part of management, and it is played best by those who enjoy it most.[36]

On the other hand, the *positive* image of power is reflected in the individual who attempts to find and carry out group goals. The positive sense of power is more like that felt by the captain of a winning football team than that of the king of the jungle. The sense of personal satisfaction comes in shared success rather than personal domination.

## The Competence Motive

Reacting to the limits placed on human behavior by drive-reduction and psychoanalytic instinct theory, Robert White postulated the existence of a competence motive: a need to interact effectively with one's environment. "We need a different kind of motivational idea to account fully for the fact that man and the higher mammals develop a competence in dealing with the environment which they certainly do not have at birth and certainly do not arrive at simply through maturation. Such an idea, I believe, is essential for any biologically sound view of human nature."[37]

People gain competence slowly through the learning process in their desire to master challenges the environment presents. This motive is first seen in infants as they finger, poke, and push whatever they can reach. Later, exploring the local environment involves dropping, taking apart, and even throwing the objects around them. As one moves into adulthood one's sense of competence depends on the balance of successes and failures one has encountered during one's life experiences.

In organizational settings the competence motive is aroused when people are faced with new and challenging situations and diminished when a situation has already been explored. As problems become routinized, they become boring.

## *Implications of the Specialized Needs*

The intensity to which the specialized needs for achievement, competence, and power are present in us as individuals no doubt varies according to our own life experiences. However, more than most types of institutions, the educational organization requires large amounts of all three.

School systems value the competence motive as teachers and administrators are exhorted to pursue new challenges not only in the instructional process but also in dealing with parents and students. In a like manner, *n* achievement is valued especially among teachers as they carry out their tasks within which Dan Lortie calls the autonomy-equality pattern. The role is that of individual entrepreneur in the classroom.[38]

The power motive is perhaps the least understood and appreciated among educators. Many would argue, however, that individuals who are high in *positive* power motive are needed more than ever in education today. As a fact of life, school leaders must fight the good fight for a declining share of the public resource pie, mobilize an increasingly disenchanted community, promote supportive legislation, and combat the threat of tedium replacing spontaneity in the classroom. In other words, strong people must be around who can effectively promote on environment that is highly supportive of what goes on in classrooms. To do that difficult and trying job well, the individuals must both enjoy it and have the necessary skills.

## *A Note of Caution*

Three types of criticisms are often directed at the content theories of motivation, especially the general hierarchy-type theories that try to explain a full range of behaviors: (1) there are scant empirical data to support their conclusions; (2) they assume employees are basically alike in terms of what motivates them; and (3) they are not really theories of motivation at all, but theories of satisfaction.

The Maslow, Alderfer, and Herzberg models are the most prominent of the content theories and they attempt to identify specific content factors in the individual (Maslow and Alderfer) and in the job environment (Herzberg) that motivate people. The content approaches have an inherent logic that appeals to the practitioner world, but conceptual weaknesses have posed definite limitations. There is little research that supports the theoretical basis and predictability of the content models.

Regarding Maslow's hierarchy of need theory, Wahba and Bridwell conclude in a review of the literature that little consistent support for the theory can be found. Some of the basic propositions were totally rejected, although some evidence suggests that there may be low-order and high-order needs that form some kind of hierarchy.[39] Lawler and Suttle conclude from their research that there is little evidence to support a hierarchy of needs once one moves above the security level.[40]

The potential of Alderfer's ERG model has not yet been probed. As Luthans points out, other than Alderfer's own empirical works there has been no direct evaluation of his theory.[41] In examining Herzberg's two-factor theory, House and Wigdor identify four criticisms of the model from their literature review. First, they argue the model is

methodologically bound in identifying critical incidents of satisfaction and dissatisfaction, as people tend to take credit for things going well and blame the environment
when things go bad. Second, raters are required to evaluate behaviors of respondents,
which makes for possible rater contamination. Third, the research lacked a measure of
overall satisfaction, permitting workers to dislike part of their job but to be generally
satisfied with the job itself. Finally, situational variables were not treated in defining the
relationship between satisfaction and productivity.[42]

The point should be stressed that the need hierarchy theories have an intuitive logic
that has given them great societal popularity even though they have received little
empirical support.[43] The complications and unsettled nature of these theories stress caution in their application. Yet the theories have continued to stimulate new thinking in
researchers and managers alike, which is always a valuable asset in the social sciences.

If the lack of convincing empirical support is the first major criticism of content
theories of motivation, the second criticism is that they contain implicit erroneous
assumptions regarding sameness. Nadler and Lawler identify these erroneous assumptions as follows:

1. All Employees Are Alike: Different theories present different ways of looking at
   people, but each of them assumes that all employees are basically similar in their
   makeup: Employees all want economic gains, or all want a pleasant climate, or all
   aspire to be self-actualizing, etc.
2. All Situations Are Alike: Most theories assume that all managerial situations are
   alike, and that the managerial course of action for motivation (for example, participation, job enlargement, etc.) is applicable in all situations.
3. One Best Way: Out of the other two assumptions there emerges a basic principle
   that there is "one best way" to motivate employees. When these "one best way"
   approaches are applied in the "correct" situation they will work.[44]

Even the narrower need-theories focusing on the need to achieve, obtain power,
or realize competence carry an assumption that all of us one way or another respond
to these impulses. The degree to which we are capable of responding, however, is related to our life experiences.

The final major criticism of hierarchical content theories is that they really are not
theories of motivation at all but theories of satisfaction. Content theories implicitly
assume that satisfaction on the job leads to improved performance and dissatisfaction
detracts from job performance. Satisfaction is viewed as a feeling of psychological con-
tentedness associated with having received enough of a desired object. The assumption is made that the more a workers' needs are satisfied, the greater will be their loyalty and effective response to the tasks of the job.

The critical point is that satisfaction theories do not deal with the relationship
between satisfaction and performance beyond making a general assumption. Numerous studies and literature reviews have shown little relationship between satisfaction
and job performance.[45] Peter Drucker makes the point clear:

> What motivation is needed to obtain peak performance from the worker? The answer
> that is usually given today in American industry is "employee satisfaction." But this is

an almost meaningless concept. Even if it meant something, "employee satisfaction" would still not be sufficient motivation to fulfill the needs of the enterprise.

A man may be satisfied with his job because he really finds fulfillment in it. He may also be satisfied because the job permits him to "get by." A man may be dissatisfied because he is genuinely discontented. But he may also be dissatisfied because he wants to do a better job, wants to improve his work and that of his group, wants to do bigger and better things. And this dissatisfaction is the most valuable attitude any company can possess in its employees, and the most real expression of pride in job and work, and of responsibility. Yet, we have no way of telling satisfaction that is fulfillment, from satisfaction that is just apathy, dissatisfaction that is discontent from dissatisfaction that is the desire to do a better job.[46]

If content theories are really best described as theories of job satisfaction, then it is important to look further for true theories of motivation. Some people argue that process theories are the most promising.

## Process Theories of Motivation

During the 1960s an entirely different approach to explaining motivation emerged, called *process theory*. Process theory rejected the assumptions that human behavior was a response to some underlying instincts and drives, or that individuals possessed some common hierarchy of needs. Such thinking was considered overly simplistic, given the multitude of variables (e.g., economic, social, religious, cultural) that could influence motivation.

Process theories suggest that a greater understanding of motivation could be gained by attempting to identify the profile of a common psychological/behavioral process that people go through as they seek to achieve goals. The thing(s) that initiate motivation may be different for all people, but the process of initiating, channelling, sustaining, and finally terminating behavior fundamentally is common to all.

Generally, process theories are cognitive theories that assume: (1) people exert effort toward obtaining goal-related rewards as long as they expect that the rewards can be achieved; (2) people are autonomous beings who independently seek out solutions for achieving goals through the most effective alternate routes available; (3) effort is sustained while goal-directed actions are proving successful; and (4) effort is terminated when the goal is achieved or people realize that it will not be achieved.

The most important process theories today are called *expectancy theories,* but at least one less complex version, called *equity theory,* has received considerable attention.

### Equity Theory

*Equity theory* can best be understood as part of an exchange process, as in the social exchange discussed in Chapter Three. In that context one's membership and behavior in a social body (group or organization) in a large measure is determined by what he or she gives to and receives from that social body (e.g., friendship, loyalty, resources). Individuals have expectations about the outcomes that should result from their participation. If a satisfying ratio of giving to receiving (input to output) is received, a healthy participation in group activities is usually maintained. If the ratio gets out of balance in either direction, frustration, tension, and possibly even rejection can result.

Equity theory argues that the character of job performance is derived from the degree of equity or inequity workers perceives for themselves when compared with others in similar situations. Equity theory of motivation usually is attributed to Stacy Adams who postulates that workers consider their inputs to a job, such as experience, age, education, hard work, and so forth. Against this, they weigh intrinsic and extrinsic outcomes from their jobs such as promotion, pay, status, praise, or other benefits. If a worker perceives his or her ratio of outcomes to inputs is not equal to his or her comparison group, the worker will strive to restore the ratio of equity. This striving to restore equity is explained as the work motivation. The strength of the motivation is directly related to the degree of the perceived inequity.[47]

The motivation felt may take the form of increased or decreased effort. If under-rewarded, the worker may take positive steps by working harder, or may assume a less constructive stance by attempting to influence the productivity of comparison workers, cognitively distort the inputs or outcomes, change jobs, or even quit.

Being over-rewarded, as Jacques writes, also has its hazards. "Over-equity payment (more than the accepted norm) brings about disequilibrium in the form of an insecure non-reliance upon the continuance of earnings, provokes fear of rivalry in others who are not favoured, and stimulates an anxious and selfish desire further to improve the favoured position."[48]

It should be noted that an employee (worker or manager) makes horizontal comparisons with peers as well as vertical comparisons with subordinates and superordinates. Vertical comparisons can be quite motivational (e.g., cause for striving) if the gap between the perceived rewards of a superordinate and the subordinate is sufficiently large to initiate a high level of desire. The opposite, of course, can also be true.

Conclusions drawn from the research literature on specific components of equity theory are mixed, but the overall framework has received general support.[49]

While equity theory has been important in its own right, perhaps its greatest contribution came when it was incorporated as a component of expectancy theory.

## Expectancy Theory: The Vroom Model

*Expectancy theory,* which is attributed to Victor Vroom's work in the mid-1960s,[50] is based on four assumptions.

1. Behavior is determined by a combination of forces in the individual and forces in the environment.
2. People make decisions about their own behavior in organizations.
3. Different people have different types of needs, desires, and goals.
4. People make decisions among alternative plans of behavior based on their perceptions (expectancies) of the degree to which a given behavior will lead to desired outcomes.[51]

Before engaging in any goal-directed effort, expectancy theory argues that employees ask themselves a series of questions. For example, let us assume that Ms. Jones leans back from her desk one day and in her mind's eye looks longingly at the brass ring of her professional life. Being smarter than your average mule, Ms. Jones knows that nobody is going to walk in and hand that brass ring to her; she is going to have to go after it. Ms. Jones asks herself the same series of questions we all ask ourselves as we consider our own personal goals. How hard would I have to work to be awarded that brass ring? Can I work that hard? Do I have the ability? If I work that hard, would they (the awarders) really give me the brass ring? Do I really want it enough to put myself through all that would be required of me?

Expectancy theory contends that there is no commonly held set (or hierarchy) of brass rings in life that put people into motion. However, there is a common cognitive process we all go through that results in some level of personal motivation. All of us see an array of potential brass rings (personal rewards) hanging enticingly in our future (e.g., promotion, transfer, published book, class with the highest test scores, etc.). Some of them motivate behavior and others do not. The question is, why?

In response to this question, it is necessary to examine three of the critical components and their formulation of relationships as seen in Figure 8.2. The force of motivation equals the product of expectancy, instrumentality, and valence.

1. *Valence (goal attractiveness):* The motivation process begins with an employee's aspiration to achieve a *personal* goal or outcome. Valence is the strength of the

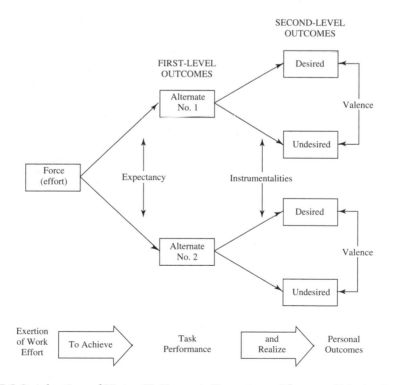

FIGURE 8.2  Adaption of Victor H. Vroom's Expectancy Theory of Motivation

desire for that particular reward. For example, I want a promotion. A valence can range from +1 (very desirable) to -1 (very undesirable).

2. *Expectancy (effort-performance linkage):* Expectancy is the strength of an employee's belief (from 0 to 100 percent) that he or she can perform the organizational tasks in a manner that will attract positive recognition for job performance. Thus, expectancy leads to a first-level outcome (task performance) and the recognition thereof. For example, if I work hard I can put on a quality performance, and it will be noted by the superintendent. At this stage of the motivation process an honest assessment of personal skills and experience is essential—preferably more introspective than the assessment Pete Rose once gave himself as, "I don't have no weaknesses."

3. *Instrumentality (performance-reward linkage):* Instrumentality is the perceived probability (from 0 to 100 percent) that a particular personal reward will be forthcoming as a consequence of the first-level outcome of task performance. "Expectancy is an action-outcome," Vroom writes. "Instrumentality is an outcome-outcome association."[52] For example, a vice principal might say, "If I work hard at my job, I can do the work extremely well" (action-outcome). "If I perform my tasks extremely well, I will get promoted" (outcome-outcome). "I very much want to get promoted" (valence).

As long as the vice principal retains high expectancy, instrumentality, and valence, his or her motivation toward work will remain high. However, if one of those three linkages is low from the beginning, an initial motivation toward task performance will not be present. Also, if one of the linkages declines sometime after an effort has begun, perhaps because now through experience the vice principal realizes his or her initial expectation was wrong, task motivation similarly will decline.

Two additional points should be made about the Vroom expectancy model of motivation. First, each employee studying his or her brass ring will explore various alternatives for acquiring it, as suggested in Figure 8.2. Second, along with the desired brass ring will come some undesired outcomes attached to each of the alternative paths, such as loss of time with the family, added expenses, loss of friends, job transfer, and so forth.

As an illustration, let us assume that the personal goal is still a promotion to the principalship. Mr. White, the vice principal, sees three possible avenues (alternatives) to obtaining that outcome. First, he could work hard and do better at his present job, and hope that the effort will be recognized by the superintendent. Second, he could go back to graduate school and obtain a master's degree and hope the newly acquired specialized knowledge will be recognized. Third, he could become the personal advocate in the district for all the superintendent's ideas. (The technical term for this is brown-nosing.) Mr. White then assesses each of the three alternatives in terms of the potential positive and negative outcomes associated with each and makes his choice.

A few years after the Vroom expectancy theory was published, an expanded version was developed, which will be discussed next.

## *Expectancy Theory: The Lawler-Porter Model*

The Lawler-Porter model extended and expanded Vroom's theory of motivation.[53] As Figure 8.3 shows, the Lawler-Porter version of expectancy theory is cyclical and contains

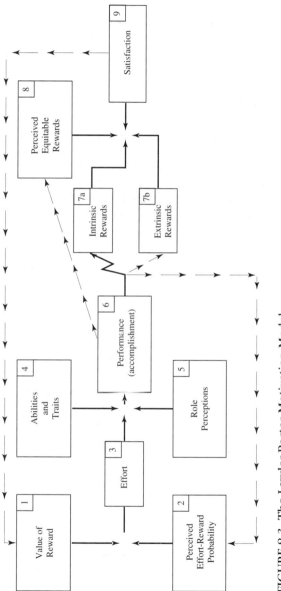

**FIGURE 8.3  The Lawler-Porter Motivation Model**

Lyman W. Porter and Edward E. Lawler, III, *Managerial Attitudes and Performance* (Homewood, IL: Richard D. Irwin, Inc., 1965), p. 165. Reprinted with permission.

explicit intervening variables. The component parts are as follows and numbered to their place in the model.

1. and 2. *Reward value/Reward probability:* This refers to the value an employee attaches to a particular *personal* reward, plus the perceived probability that the reward will come with a specified effort, will establish the intensity of the effort to be made.

3. and 6. *Effort to performance:* By effort it is meant how hard one tries or the amount of energy put into a given work situation. Performance is the degree of task accomplishment or productivity resulting from a specific level of effort. Additional outcomes are also recognized, such as enhanced cooperation and good working relationships. A general illustration of the effort-to-performance relationship is the amount of work given to preparing for an exam is effort, while the grade received is an indicator of performance.

4. *Abilities and traits:* These refer "to relatively stable, long-term individual characteristics—e.g., personality traits, intelligence, manual skills, etc.—that represent the individual's currently developed power to perform."[54]

5. *Role perceptions:* The effort to performance outcome is constrained or enhanced by the employee's role perception. For example, if one wants to play tackle for the Los Angeles Rams but weighs only 130 pounds dripping wet, something is wrong with the role perception. However, if his perceptions of his role correspond to those of his superiors in his organization, then he will be applying his effort where it will count most for successful performance as defined by the organization. Regarding abilities and role perceptions, a colleague of mine likes to point out, if you want to fly with the eagles be sure you are an eagle and not a turkey.

7A. and 7B. *Rewards:* Intrinsic (psychological) and extrinsic (material) rewards are a derivative of performance. These rewards represent the personal payoff (e.g., better job, pat on the back, higher status, etc.) an employee receives from the additional effort.

8. *Perceived equitable rewards:* This dimension of the motivation process is an outgrowth of equity theory, discussed earlier in the chapter. It refers to "the level or amount of rewards that an individual feels he *should* receive as a result of a given level of performance."[55]

9. *Satisfaction:* This variable is defined "as the extent to which the rewards actually received meet or exceed the perceived equitable level of rewards."[56] If the level of satisfaction does not meet expectations, the level of motivation drops accordingly. This occurs because the motivation process is a cycle of events and the employee knows that he or she was wrong in the original effort to performance probability estimation (numbers 3 through 6) or underestimated the abilities required. However, if the value of the reward remains high (number 1), then the employee might not give up but redouble his or her efforts.

It is important to note that satisfaction is treated differently in process theories of motivation as contrasted with content theories. In content theories, such as the need hierarchies, job satisfaction is assumed to lead to a quality performance. If one is satisfied on the job, one will perform better. Expectancy theories, on the other hand, argue that a quality performance leads to job satisfaction. If one performs well on the job then one will find satisfaction.

## Management Implications of Expectancy Theory

The Lawler-Porter model is more applications-oriented than Vroom's model, but it is still complex to put it into practice. As a starting point, traditional practices of measuring attitudes and aptitudes are not enough to insure motivation. Measurements on accuracies of role perceptions and reward expectations are also important. Job tasks must be defined clearly and performance expectations realistic. Ambiguous or "mission impossible" tasks will not stimulate much motivation.

This theory argues that it is more productive to adjust the reward structure than to try to change the individual. The link between the desired performance and the specified rewards must be clear. As pointed out in path-goal leadership theory discussed in Chapter Nine, the role of the manager is to remove as many obstacles as possible that impede employees from reaching their goals. Joe Kelly points out that in order to facilitate the efforts of employees, extensive task performance feedback is necessary, workers must feel they have extensive control over their work environments, the rewards must be the desired ones, and training must fit the designated tasks.[57]

## A Note of Caution

Steers and Porter report that over 50 studies have been conducted to test the validity of expectancy theory, and they tend to confirm that "the best performers in organizations tend to see a strong relationship between performing their jobs well and receiving rewards they value. In addition they have clear performance goals and feel they can perform well."[58]

There are, however, numerous important theoretical difficulties with the model. Expectancy theory, for example, applies only to those behaviors that are under the voluntary control of the employee. If the paths to goals as well as the performance rewards are prescribed by the organization, the predictive power of the theory diminishes. On this point Katz and Kahn emphasize that at the individual level, expectancy notions are useful in helping us understand how people evaluate rewards. However, "organizational life makes it difficult to apply such an individual model because rewards are group negotiated through union bargaining and because the interdependence of roles often does not permit ready identification of individual effort."[59]

The model also assumes rationality in decision making after a thorough exploration of all the alternatives. Steers and Porter find, however, that "people often stop considering alternative behavioral plans when they find one that is at least moderately satisfying, even though more rewarding plans remain to be examined."[60] In short, the model is more rational than people are.

In a major review of the literature, Mitchell found some support for the inference that expectations cause behavior, but the overall theory has proved to be too complex for researchers to test adequately. Writing from the perspective of the research community, Mitchell states, "Our empirical tests are inaccurate representations of the overall theory. Our measures do not reflect the underlying theoretical components. Our assumptions about the combinatorial properties of the theory are basically untested."[61]

Given the problems of testing the complexities of expectancy theory, to what extent is it useful? Porter, Lawler, and Hackman give us their answer to that question.

> It should be emphasized . . . that the expectancy model is just that: a model and no more. People rarely actually sit down and list their expected outcomes for a contemplated behavior, estimate expectancies and valences, multiply, and add up the total unless, of course, they are asked to do so by a researcher. Yet people do consider the likely outcomes of their actions, do weigh and evaluate the attractiveness of various alternatives, and do use these estimates in coming to a decision about what they will do. The expectancy model provides an analytic tool for mirroring that process and for predicting its outcome, but it does not purport to reflect the actual decision-making steps taken by an individual.[62]

In the final analysis, the same type of measurement problems that created uncertainty about the content theories of motivation also surround the process theories. For the research community, however, these latter theories hold a lot more promise than the former.

## Conclusion

### *Motivation and Classical Organization Theory*

Motivation of workers became the subject of systematic study following the industrial revolution during the era of scientific management. Early efforts to improve performance tended to deal with the simplification and standardization of the work environment, developing tests of aptitudes and abilities for improved personnel selection, and linking extrinsic rewards to improved productivity. Rule elaboration, disciplined compliance, close supervision, and centralized decision making were central features of organization and management. As discussed in Chapter Two, educational organizations did not escape this orientation.

This scientific management administrative model was closely supported by the then existing view of human motivation. Instincts, and later, biologically based primary drives or needs were seen as activating behavior in a manner almost programmed by heredity and physiological impulses. The heavy emphasis on organizational control, rules, close supervision, and the like, seemed necessary to channel and restrain the basic instincts and physiological drives of workers whereas extrinsic rewards were thought to be the principal stimulator of work behavior.

It was not until the 1930s that a new view toward worker motivation became popular.

### *Motivation and Social System Theory*

The Hawthorne studies conducted in the 1930s established human relations as the new approach to worker motivation (Chapter Three). Three important additive assumptions were made: (1) job satisfaction (e.g., high morale, positive work attitudes) is a derivative of good working conditions and satisfying economic rewards; (2) if an organization provides these rewards, the result will be a high level of job satisfaction; and (3) a high level of job satisfaction results in high productivity.

In addition, assumptions were made that if people had a voice in determining the nature, content, and climate of their work, this participative decision-making, along with the added challenges of the job, would stimulate higher levels of effort. Under conditions such as these, the human relations orientation stresses self-control and self-regulation rather than organizational control.

The social system approach to organizational thought emerged at the same time as an awareness of secondary or learned needs received acceptance from the academic community. Motivation increasingly was seen as a product of learned behaviors that released creative energies that were not tied to physiological needs or instincts. Need hierarchies provided popular understanding for worker behavior that seemed motivated toward fulfilling lower biological and social as well as higher intellectual needs.

In addition, the expectancy theories of motivation as currently defined also appear to best fit within the social system conceptual framework. Neither equity theory nor the Vroom or Porter-Lawler models directly involve external environmental variables in their formulations. However, the Porter-Lawler model of motivation comprises a cycle of events, which is a critical element of open system theory, as well as provides for situational variables influencing outcomes, which is an essential ingredient of contingency theory.

Given the number of motivation theories on the market, which can be confusing for us all, perhaps the best approach for the consumer is to be situationally selective. Steers and Porter write: "In recent years    the notion of a multiple strategy—using [different approaches to motivation] at one time or another depending upon the nature of the organization, its technology, its people, and its goals and priorities—has come to be labeled a 'contingency approach' to management."[63]

## A Burnout Case

Bill Heckman just finished walking around the campus of Liberty High School, poking his nose into various classrooms, the cafeteria, and the gymnasium, trying to get a better feel for how the school functioned. He had been appointed principal only three weeks ago, and as an outsider, he needed all the information he could get.

Finishing his walking tour, he pulled up a chair in the office of Vito Valencia, a long-term vice principal at Liberty High. The vice principal could see something was bothering his new boss. "Vito," the principal began, "every time I walk past Miss Grant's room, why do I get the feeling that there is a buffalo stampede going on inside?"

"You noticed the noise, huh?" Vito said, trying to stifle a smile as he signed a few letters going out to parents.

"Noticed the noise?" Heckman retorted. "It would drown out the San Diego Zoo at feeding time. Doesn't she care? Doesn't she know how to manage a class?"

Vito lit up his favorite brown briar pipe before contributing to the education of his new principal. "Miss Grant has been in this district for 26 years," he said slowly, wanting to be fair to the situation. "For 20 of those years she was generally acknowl-edged by everyone, even Mr. Brice, our long-standing but recently departed superin-tendent, as being the best damned teacher this district ever saw. For years she was here at school an hour before anyone else and left two or three hours after the school day ended. All those extra hours she devoted to helping kids catch up. Parents would do almost anything to get their kids in her class."

"So what happened?" the principal asked as signs of surprise crossed his face.

"Her dream in life," Vito continued, "was to be principal of this school. She did all the right things—she went back to the university and got a master's degree in educa-tional administration, and even held this vice principal's job for a few years. She was an excellent administrator. Unfortunately, those were the years when male superin-tendents generally didn't think women could handle the job of high school principal—especially Mr. Brice. He used to say in private that he would appoint a woman as a high school principal when he could find one that could walk on water. The school board was kind of wishy-washy and didn't get involved in personnel decisions.

"One day it all came to a head. Miss Grant, a number of women teachers, and sev-eral supporting parents went to a school board meeting and held up a few signs say-ing something about women's rights in education. Mr. Brice was furious and told the teachers to come to his office the next day. Miss Grant, in front of God and country, called him an ass. No, she called him a royal ass. The board chairman suspended the meeting at that point and everyone left. Only her outstanding reputation saved her job, but something went out of Miss Grant after that. She lost interest in her work. What had once been a vibrant, energetic, and creative teacher became a tired old lady hang-ing on for retirement. Even when Mr. Brice joined his ancestors, she didn't perk up.

"She has four more years to retirement. A lot of people are now saying you should try to get rid of her and set an example for some of the other burnout cases around here. Mr. Brice's replacement will never consider her for an administrative post, so a transfer in that direction is out. You'll have to do something soon because parents are really screaming and it's getting worse all the time."

The principal stood up and walked slowly out the door. He wasn't quite sure what to do.

## Notes

1.  Daniel Katz and Robert Kahn, *The Social Psychology of Organizations,* 2nd ed. (New York: Wiley, 1978).

2.  National Center for Educational Statistics, *Digest of Educational Statistics: 1993* (Wash-ington, DC: U.S. Government Printing Office, 1993), p. 84.

3.  Mike Milstein, "Plateauing: A Growing Problem for Educators and Educational Organi-zations," University of New Mexico, pre-publication manuscript.

4.  Edward E. Lawler, III, *Motivation in Work Organizations* (Monterey, CA: Brooks/Cole, 1973), p. 3.

5.  Stephen P. Robbins, *Organizational Behavior: Concepts, Controversies, and Applica-tions* (Englewood Cliffs, NJ: Prentice-Hall, 1983), p. 133.

6. Lawler III, *Motivation in Work Organizations,* p. 4.

7. Bernard Berelson and Gary Steiner, *Human Behavior* (New York: Harcourt, Brace & World, 1964), p. 240.

8. Fred Luthans, *Organizational Behavior* (New York: McGraw-Hill, 1981), p. 177.

9. Victor H. Vroom, *Work and Motivation* (New York: John Wiley, 1964), p. 10.

10. William James, *The Principles of Psychology* (New York: Holt, 1890); and Sigmund Freud, "The Unconscious," *Collected Papers of Sigmund Freud,* vol. iv, J. Riviere, trans. (London: Hogarth Press, 1949, original edition 1915).

11. William McDougall, *An Introduction to Social Psychology* (London: Methuen, 1908), p. 39.

12. E. J. Murray, *Motivation and Emotion* (Englewood Cliffs, NJ: Prentice-Hall, 1964), p. 6; cited in Lawler III, *Motivation in Work Organizations,* p. 13.

13. Lawler III, *Motivation in Work Organizations,* p. 13.

14. Ivan L. Russel, Motivation (Dubuque, IA: William C. Brown, 1971), p. 9.

15. Robert S. Woodworth, *Dynamic Psychology* (New York: Columbia University Press, 1918).

16. C. L. Hull, *Principles of Behavior* (New York: Appleton-Century-Crofts, 1943), pp. 59–60.

17. Ibid.

18. E. C. Tolman, *Purposive Behavior in Animals and Men* (New York: Appleton-Century-Crofts, 1932).

19. G. W. Allport, "The Functional Autonomy of Motives," *American Journal of Psychology* 50 (1937): 143.

20. Abraham H. Maslow, *Motivation and Personality* (New York: Harper and Row, 1954), p. xii.

21. Maslow, *Motivation and Personality,* p. 46.

22. Clayton P. Alderfer, "An Empirical Test of a New Theory of Human Needs," *Organizational Behavior and Human Performance* (May 1969): 142–175.

23. Frederick Herzberg, "One More Time: How Do You Motivate Employees?" *Harvard Business Review* 46 (1968): 53.

24. Ibid., p. 54.

25. Thomas J. Sergiovanni, "Factors Which Affect Satisfaction and Dissatisfaction of Teachers," *The Journal of Educational Administration* 5 (1967): 66–82.

26. Douglas McGregor, *The Human Side of Enterprise* (New York: McGraw-Hill, 1960).

27. Ibid., Chapter 3.

28. David McClelland, et al., *The Achievement Motive* (New York: Appleton-Century-Crofts, 1953); and David C. McClelland, *The Achieving Society* (Princeton, NJ: Van Nostrand, 1961.)

29. "To Know Why Men Do What They Do: A Conversation With David C. McClelland and T. George Harris," *Psychology Today* (January 1971): 36.

30. David C. McClelland, "That Urge to Achieve," *Think* (November-December 1966): 22.

31. David Miron and David C. McClelland, "The Impact of Achievement Motivation Training on Small Business," *California Management Review* (Summer 1979): 27.

32. Alfred Adler, "Individual Psychology," Susanne Langer, trans., in *Psychologies of 1930,* Carl Murchinson, ed. (Worcester, MA: Clark University Press, 1930), pp. 398–399.

33. David C. McClelland, "The Two Faces of Power," in *Organizational Behavior and the Practice of Management,* David Hampton, Charles Summer, and Ross Webber, eds. (Glenview, IL: Scott, Foresman, 1978), p. 30.

34. McClelland, "Two Faces of Power," p. 31.

35. H. Levinson, "On Becoming a Middle-Aged Manager," *Harvard Business Review* 47 (1969): 51–60.

36.  J. S. Livingston, "Myth of the Well-Educated Manager," *Harvard Business Review* 49 (1971): 87.

37.  Robert W. White, "Motivation Reconsidered: The Concept of Competence," *Psychological Review* 66 (1959): 297.

38.  Daniel Lortie, *Schoolteacher: A Sociological Study* (Chicago: The University of Chicago Press, 1975).

39.  Mahamoud A. Wahba and Lawrence G. Bridwell, "Maslow Reconsidered: A Review of Research on the Need Hierarchy Theory," *Organizational Behavior and Human Performance* 15 (1975): 212–240.

40.  Edward E. Lawler, III and J. L. Suttle, "A Causal Correlational Test of the Need Hierarchy Concept," *Organizational Behavior and Human Performance* 9 (1972): 265–287.

41.  Luthans, *Organizational Behavior,* p. 185.

42.  R. J. House and Lawrence Wigdor, "Herzberg's Dual-Factor Theory of Job Satisfaction and Motivation: A Review of Evidence and a Criticism," *Personnel Psychology* 20 (1967): 369–389. Also see; Donald Schwab and Larry Cummings, "Theories of Performance and Satisfaction: A Review," *Industrial Relations* 9 (1970): 408–430.

43.  Abraham Korman, Jeffrey Greenhaus, and Irwin Badin, "Personnel Attitudes and Motivation," in *Annual Review of Psychology,* Mark Rosenzweig and Lyman Porter, eds. (Palo Alto, CA: Annual Reviews, 1977), p. 178.

44.  David A. Nadler and Edward E. Lawler, III, "Motivation: A Diagnostic Approach," in *Motivation and Work Behavior,* Richard Steers and Lyman Porter, eds. (New York: McGraw-Hill, 1979), p. 216.

45.  A. H. Brayfield and W. H. Crockett, "Employee Attitudes and Employee Performance," *Psychological Bulletin* 52 (1955): 396–424; and Vroom, *Work and Motivation.*

46.  Peter F. Drucker, *The Practice of Management* (New York: Harper and Row, 1954), p. 302.

47.  J. Stacy Adams, "Toward an Understanding of Inequity," *Journal of Abnormal and Social Psychology* 67 (1963): 422–436; and J. Stacy Adams, "Inequity in Social Exchanges," in *Advances in Experimental Social Psychology,* L. Berkowitz, ed. (New York: Academic Press, 1965), pp. 267–299.

48.  E. Jaques, *Equitable Payment* (New York: John Wiley, 1961), pp. 142–143.

49.  Richard T. Mowday, "Equity Theory Predictions of Behavior in Organizations," in *Motivation and Work Behavior,* Richard M. Steers and Lyman W. Porter, eds. (New York: McGraw-Hill, 1979); and R. D. Prichard, "Equity Theory: A Review and Critique," *Organizational Behavior and Human Performance* 56 (1972): 75–94.

50.  Vroom, *Work and Motivation.*

51.  Nadler and Lawler III, "Motivation: A Diagnostic Approach," p. 217.

52.  Vroom, *Work and Motivation,* p. 18.

53.  Lyman W. Porter and Edward E. Lawler, III, *Managerial Attitudes and Performance* (Homewood, IL: Richard D. Irwin, 1968).

54.  Ibid., p. 22.

55.  Ibid., p. 29.

56.  Ibid., p. 30.

57.  Joe Kelly, *Organizational Behavior: Its Data, First Principles, and Applications* (Homewood, IL: Richard D. Irwin, 1980), p. 31.

58.  Steers and Porter, *Motivation and Work Behavior,* p. 220.

59.  Daniel Katz and Robert Kahn, *The Social Psychology of Organizations* (New York: John Wiley, 1978), p. 356.

60.  Steers and Porter, *Motivation and Work Behavior,* p. 221.

61.  Terence R. Mitchell, "Expectancy Models of Job Satisfaction, Occupational Preference and Effort: A Theoretical, Methodological, and Empirical Appraisal," *Psychological Bulletin* 81 (1974): 1074.

62.  Lyman W. Porter, Edward E. Lawler, III, and Richard Hackman, *Behavior in Organizations* (New York: McGraw-Hill, 1975), p. 58.

63.  Steers and Porter, *Motivation and Work Behavior,* p. 20.

$C\quad h\quad a\quad p\quad t\quad e\quad r\qquad 9$

# *Organizational Communication*

Albert Einstein once observed that our world of knowledge is like a small circle of light in a vast sea of darkness. The more we learn and expand that light, the greater the surrounding circumference of darkness becomes. Thus, the more we learn, the more we realize how little we really know.

Small or large, that circle of light creates our reality. Within that reality, however, we live in two worlds. "First, we live in the world of happenings about us which we know at first-hand. But this is an extremely small world. . . . So far as this world of personal experience is concerned, Africa, South America . . . New York, or Los Angeles do not exist if we have never been to these places."[1] For most of us, therefore, the reality of what we see, and think we understand, has been created for us through secondary sources of information. We see the world through a complex mix of books, television, newspapers, stories from parents, gossip, rumor, and a host of other assorted sources. The point is that our social reality is embedded in communication—the information we receive and the way we receive it—therefore, examining the act of communication and trying to improve upon it should play a central role in knowledge generation in the social sciences.

Many would argue that Einstein's "circle of light" is indeed small in the areas of organization and management. Over 30 years ago, anthropologist Alexander Leighton commented that administrators tend to use the social sciences "the way a drunk uses a lamppost, for support rather than illumination." Considerable progress has been made since that time, but, as Einstein predicted, the problems have only become more numerous and visible.

Some scholars, drawing upon a different perspective, argue that we are in an age of exploding knowledge and communication systems.[2] Through the mass media enveloping school-age children, an awareness of far off places and events has expanded their horizons, legions of new heroes (often with rather kinky value systems) have captured their imaginations, and a cultural fixation on material acquisition has shaped their life goals. The effect on the classroom has not been inconsequential.

Almost daily teachers are reminded that they must compete with television commentators for an interpretation of world events, with disc jockeys for establishing standards for the interpretation of music, and with movie stars for interpretations of Shakespeare. "In essence, among the chief changes in the circumstances of teaching brought about the rise of mass media has been a loss of the aura of authority."[3]

It should be remembered, however, that the image of reality the mass media creates is usually shallow and shaped to fit a particular format and age group. Even those who make their living in the communication business generally agree that, young or old, those who look to the mass media as their only window to the world will see little more than the shadows of substance. As Lane, Corwin, and Monahan write, "These functions—of interpretation, guidance in the formation of taste, critical analysis, and systematic and thorough study of a topic—remain the special province of the public school teacher. . . . The classroom is still one of the few antidotes to the narcotizing and escapist effects of the media."[4]

This chapter examines the communication process as it evolved through the periods of classical organization theory (scientific management and bureaucracy), human relations (later to become social systems or sociopolitical group theory), and open system theory. Particular issues associated with the intent, process, and consequences of communication are introduced. Within the context of the organizational hierarchy, vertical and horizontal information flows through formal and informal channels, and networks will be discussed as well as the blockages that must be overcome.

Many aspects of communication found in all three schools of thought can be found in what is frequently called the S-M-C-R communication model.

## S-M-C-R Communication Model

The S-M-C-R model, as illustrated in Figure 9.1, is composed of the following component parts: (1) the source (or the originator) of the message, who encodes it in written, oral, or some other form; (2) the message, which represents the ideas that are to be transmitted; (3) the channel (or the medium) by which the message travels; and (4) the receiver, who decodes the message. As the next sections will illustrate, each school of thought added a new dimension to the S-M-C-R communication model.

## Classical Theory and Communication

The classical theorists had definite ideas about how the communication process should operate, or, *who* should say *what* through *which channel* to *whom* toward *what effect.* Scientific management taught that communication existed to facilitate the leader's command and control over the organization through vertical, formal channels. As Rogers points out, "Communication was to be formal, hierarchical, and planned; its

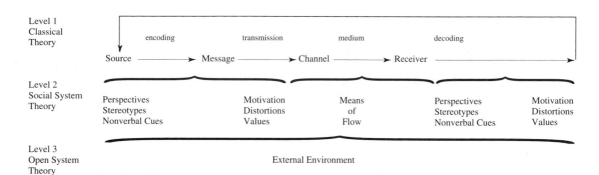

FIGURE 9.1  S-M-C-R Communication Model

purpose was to get the work done, to increase productivity and efficiency. In sum, Taylorism viewed communication as one-sided and vertical (top-down) and task-related."[5] The only concession to a need for feedback was a periodic progress report on the status of projects. In a sense, messages moved up the hierarchy through a series of whispers, but down the hierarchy through a series of loudspeakers.

Concerning classical theory orientation, communication is *the transmission of information.* The communication process is viewed as a bucket carrying messages from one person to another. The academic field of communication mainly dealt with issues involving skills in message production. Work in areas of speech, journalism, education, advertising, and broadcasting reflected that orientation until an awareness developed that message production and effective communication were not necessarily synonymous.

## The Human Relations School and Communication

Modern approaches to communication can be traced to the emergence of the human relations movement that took hold following the Hawthorne studies in the 1930s. With the human relations orientation, and especially when it evolved into sociopolitical group theory, concerns turned toward the less visible and informal aspects of the S-M-C-R model. Efforts were given to understanding why distortions and gaps frequently existed between the messages sent and those received. Not only were characteristics of senders and receivers studied, such as motivation, perspectives, nonverbal cues, and stereotypes, but also the way these informal characteristics influenced the behavior of both senders and receivers.

"Significantly, the words 'common,' 'commune,' and 'communication' have the same etymological root," Rogers observes. "Communication is not merely a matter of action and reaction; it is a transactional exchange between two or more individuals."[6] Within this context, communication can be defined as *the exchange of meaning.*

Such an exchange, however, requires that as much be known about the sociopsychological makeup of the receiver as the sender. The receiver (like the sender) is composed of a complex mix of hopes, expectations, biases, values, and preoccupations. The words exchanged are really symbols that stand for something else. "To communicate, a person must evolve a mental picture of something, give it a name, and develop a feeling about it," Goldhaber writes. The person on the other end must capture that name, concept, and feeling if the communication is to be effective. "In other words, you and I refer to the same thing when we talk. We share understanding."[7] S. I. Hayakawa put it this way: "The meanings of the words are not in the words; they are in us."[8]

## Open System Theory and Communication

The shift to systems theory, which can be defined as the science of wholeness, took place in the 1960s. Systems theory concerns the interconnectedness and subsequent functioning of subsystems within the organization. Open system theory expands that emphasis to include the complex mechanisms of exchanging (e.g., importing, analyzing, consuming, exporting) information with the organization's environment in order to cope with uncertainty.

In open systems, communication can be defined as *the exchange of messages and meaning between an organization and its environment as well as between its network of interdependent subsystems.* Communication is the glue that holds an organization together and harmonizes its parts.

Open system theory took on the orientation, as Katz and Kahn point out, that communication cannot be understood solely as a process of transmitting messages between senders and receivers. Communication can be understood only in relation to the social system in which it occurs.[9] Communication *within* a social system is difficult enough, but Lane, Corwin, and Monahan warn of the increased hazards of communicating *between* social systems. "People of different social classes not only learn different orientations to time and money, but they have a different language and use different child-rearing methods, manners, and morals. Free communication with other people is further impeded by the ethnocentrism of one's own social class."[10] Note how the following would take on added meaning when placed in different societal contexts: *pig, busing, justice, communist, boy, politician, unions, examination, power.* As stated earlier, communication is in us, it is not in the words.

In sum, the communication process in an organization must be examined, and hopefully understood, within the context of all three levels depicted in the S-M-C-R model, including the following: (1) the process of sending and receiving messages through specific channels; (2) the formal and informal impediments and facilitators of the process; and (3) the multivariate social, political, cultural, and economic environments that surround and permeate every aspect of the communication process. Such is the challenge of truly understanding how we communicate with one another.

The next section of the chapter introduces some specific complexities of communicating in a hierarchical setting.

## Hierarchical Settings

Everett Rogers defines an *organization* as "a stable system of individuals who work together to achieve, through a hierarchy of ranks and division of labor, common goals."[11] A key function of organizational structure is to define, channel, and give order to actions and events, thus providing stability and predictability. In a school setting the structure defines roles and responsibilities of teachers and administrators as well as insures that lines of coordination and control are in place.

In addition, the structure serves to restrict and stabilize the flow of communication, making possible an orderly distribution of information. "In terms of information theory," Katz and Kahn point out, "unrestricted communication produces noise in the system. Without patterning, without pauses, without precision, there is sound but there is no music. Without structure, without spacing, without specifications, there is a Babel of tongues but there is no meaning."[12]

In most types of organizations, including school systems, the information going down the line differs from that going up. Going down, one tends to find directives, such as faculty and student codes, program guidelines, state and district policy requirements, school board decisions, and new administrative procedures. Going up the hierarchy, one tends to find feedback-type information, such as summary reports, resource requests, evaluative information, explanations on the academic or disciplinary treatment of specific students, and curricular program documents.

The following sections will illustrate some of the types of problems that can distort the communication process in a hierarchical setting.

## Communication Filtering

This concept suggests that as information flows upward toward the center of authority, content of a derogatory or critical nature reflecting on the state of affairs at lower levels is *filtered out* (sanitized) at each level as it moves up the hierarchy. By the time a report on the state of morale of teachers or parents, for example, has gone through several filters from the bottom to the top of the hierarchy, the report may not reflect the true conditions at all. This situation is somewhat understandable, because no one wants to "look bad" in the eyes of his or her superiors.

Lewis argues that three interpersonal factors may be involved: (1) the trust subordinates have in their superiors (Will I get stuck with extra after-school duties because of this?); (2) the subordinates' perception of the control the superordinate has over their futures (The superintendent will read this and could get upset.); and (3) the mobility aspirations of the subordinate (This could affect my chances to get that principalship.).[13] Communication flows become even more distorted when the organization is operating under conditions of an arbitrary authority structure, vague or conflicting rules, strong rivalry between subunits, and high levels of anxiety or insecurity.

Downward communication must pass through filters also and thus also runs the risk of being distorted. Rogers provides a dramatic illustration of the operation of downward filtering.

> Newspaper reporters in Vietnam at the time observed that Army orders tended to be interpreted quite broadly, and frequently with distortion, as they passed from echelon to echelon down the chain of command. For instance, a war correspondent was present when a hamlet was burned down by the United States Army's First Air Cavalry

Division. Inquiry showed that the order from division headquarters to the brigade was: "On no occasion must hamlets be burned down."

The brigade radioed the batallion: "Do not burn down any hamlets unless you are absolutely convinced that the Vietcong are in them."

The battalion radioed the infantry company at the scene: "If you think there are any Vietcong in the hamlet, burn it down."

The company commander ordered his troops: "Burn down that hamlet."[14]

In sum, vertical communication distortions between superior and subordinates often result because their information requirements differ as well as because of the vulnerabilities they feel in their roles. The greater the constraints in the free flow of communication, the more likely the increase in lateral communication, as discussed in the next section.

## *Horizontal Communication—Rumors and the Grapevine*

Organizations tend to discourage the flow of communication along horizontal lines because the official channels are being evaded. Horizontal communication within the same hierarchical level is usually less subject to distortion because of a common sense of reference and a reduced sense of threat.

Generally speaking, the more homogeneous the groups, such as all the math teachers or all the elementary teachers, the more distortion-free the communication tends to be. In addition, information flowing through informal channels also tends to be faster than along formal channels because there is no verification mechanism to be dealt with.

Communication flows that respect neither horizontal nor vertical channels move along what is called *the grapevine*. The term allegedly comes from the early days of the telegraph when the wires were strung through trees, thus giving the impression of a grapevine.

Lewis writes that as information flows along the grapevine, it tends to undergo three types of changes. "The first change is *leveling;* leveling is the dropping of details, a simplifying of context and qualifications. The second change is *sharpening*, the preference for vivid and dramatic treatments of data. People work to make a story better and more entertaining. The third change information undergoes is *assimilation;* that is the tendency of people to adjust or modify rumor, to mold it to fit their needs."[15]

Rumors are the substance of great drama in organizations. Like incessant jungle drums, they keep the interested parties tuned into the mysteries of past and future events. Rumors can range from the vital (The board is leaning toward giving us a 12 percent increase) to the frivolous (The shop teacher has his eye on Miss Smith). A rumor, by definition, is an unconfirmed message traveling through informal channels.

Interestingly enough, studies of rumors in organizations tend to show that they turn out to be reasonably accurate. There is normally a kernel of truth around which the rumor is built.[16]

Some people are more prone to initiate or transmit rumors than others. Senior administrators will often initiate rumors as "trial balloons," just to measure the reaction and make a judgment whether or not the idea is a good one. Sometimes employees enjoy starting rumors because they obtain a certain satisfaction in manipulating the thoughts of large numbers of people, or they wish to influence a specific decision. I once had an associate who, whenever a job opened that was attractive to him, would start a rumor that he was a leading candidate. His voice was undoubtedly one of the great wind instruments of the English speaking world. Interestingly enough, his own rumors often worked well in his favor.

Another problem emerging in hierarchical settings occurs when too much paper flows to the top and congests the decision-making process, as discussed in the next section.

## Information Overload

The principle of centralized power in the hands of the chief executive, as well as his or her ultimate authority and responsibility, often generates the unintended consequence of flooding the executive office with paper—a condition known as *information overload.* Board of education members and district superintendents complain, and justly so, about the mountains of reports (national, state, and local), petitions, laws and proposed laws, school testing scores, building plans, letters from hostile parents, journal articles, and so on that arrive on their desks.

Miller points out seven possible outcomes of information overload: (1) *omission:* temporary failure to process some of the information; (2) *error:* processing incorrect information; (3) *queuing:* delaying responses during congested periods; (4) *filtering:* not processing certain types of information; (5) *generalizing:* reducing the levels of specificity; (6) *multiple channels:* processing information through other officials, as in decentralization; (7) *escape:* turning away from the task.[17]

An important function of the organizational structure is to restrict and condense information to the point that senior administrators do not drown in a sea of paper, but at the same time permit a sufficient enough flow so that they are well enough informed to make their decisions effectively.

The decisions that are finally made are frequently communicated through a *network,* which is the subject of the next section.

## Communication Networks

Information flowing within and between organizations or between an organization and individuals in the surrounding environment is channeled through a network. A network is composed of a specific body of individuals who are interconnected as links in the communication flow. Educational organizations generally have many such networks, and each normally is tailored to the specific information requirements of selected individuals with common information needs. The PTA and the State School Administrators Association, for example, form separate communication networks through which flow specific types of information of special interest to those groups.

Katz and Kahn define five important issues surrounding communication networks in organizations.

1. The size of the loop. Does the network include the entire organization or only a small subsystem, such as its officers?

2. The transmission process. Does the *same* message circulate unchanged to the network members, or can it be modified at select points in the system?
3. The feedback capacity. Is the network designed to cycle feedback to the initiator, or does it dead end somewhere down the line?
4. Efficiency. How fast and accurately can information be circulated through the network?
5. The network/organization fit. How close is the fit between the network delivery system and the organization's functional needs?[18]

Numerous researchers have designed experiments to determine the most effective and efficient configuration of networks. The experiments would usually call for individuals to try to solve problems (e.g., find a common characteristic in hands of cards) through different configurations of communication networks, such as those seen in Figure 9.2.

The dependent variables were such things as the amount of time required to solve the problem, the errors committed, the number of messages required, and member satisfaction. Networks such as the wheel were considered centralized because all information had to flow through a single point. The circle, all-channel, and similar variations were considered decentralized.

The following conclusions generally came from these small group communication network experiments.[19]

1. A centralized network, such as the wheel, tends to be faster, with fewer errors for the easier problems. As the message volume increases, a point of communication overload develops and the single central figure controlling the flow is no longer fast and efficient.

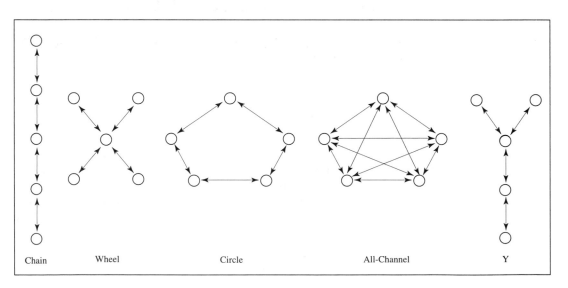

FIGURE 9.2 Common Communication Networks

2. For complex problems, the decentralized networks are the most efficient because all participants can explore for answers and more directly introduce possible solutions.
3. The decentralized networks are more effective when creative or adaptive thinking is required.
4. All networks become more efficient as the members discover how to organize themselves for a systematic distribution of information.
5. Participants in decentralized networks tend to be the most satisfied.
6. Individuals who are at the center of the information flows, and in a position to manage them, normally are identified as the leaders.

It should be noted that only with great caution can these laboratory studies be generalized to organizations. First, they were conducted on groups and not organizations. Second, the settings were artificial and usually did not allow for established personal relationships to apply.

As the next section will point out, understanding the configuration of networks is complemented by an understanding of the medium of communication that flows through them.

## Barriers to Communication

Communication barriers, from complete blockages to minor distortions, can emerge at almost any point in the process illustrated in Figure 9.1. In other contexts, various barriers or distortions, sometimes referred to as noise, have already been discussed, such as communication overload and filtering. A few additional barriers often found in educational organizations are discussed in the following sections.

### Organizational Size

Large, complex educational organizations have huge volumes of paper flowing through them at any given moment. Most people who take the time to count the different forms and messages that cross a teacher's or principal's desk in a week's time are amazed. In a large volume of paper flow, there is always the chance that a message will get lost, thrown away, or the recipient will be out of town. Also, the more hierarchical levels and separate units involved, the more difficult it is to compete for someone's attention.

In addition, in large organizations, reports frequently are several hundred pages long. To ensure they are read, executive summaries normally are prepared that synthesize the material down to a few pages. This synthesis significantly enhances the possibility of misunderstanding.

### Selective Perception

We cannot assimilate everything we see or hear; therefore we take in only bits and pieces. These bits and pieces are not chosen at random, but reflect our personal profile of special interests, biases, social class values, political affiliations, occupational orientations, and so forth. In other words, we tend to hear those things we are already attracted to or already believe in, which includes those things that threaten what we believe in. As Lane, Corwin, and Monahan write, "The school administrator who thinks in terms of efficiency perceives a different world from his teachers who may think in terms of educational objectives, student problems, and working conditions."[20]

## Coding and Decoding

The process of coding and decoding messages is always vulnerable to error. A school can code a message for parents, or others, incorrectly (e.g., calling a PTA meeting for the wrong day) or use the wrong channel for transmission (e.g., asking the students to remind their parents about the PTA meeting instead of sending a written message). In a similar manner, the receiver can decode the message incorrectly and attach the wrong meaning.

As illustrations of the kinds of coding and decoding problems that can sometimes emerge, *Life* magazine asked 1,165 translators to contribute their best examples of signs in fractured English that they had seen in their travels. Here are some of the winners of *English as she is spoke.*

- At an Acapulco hotel: "The manager has personally passed the water served here."
- At a Swiss restaurant: "Our wines leave you nothing to hope for."
- At a Bangkok dry cleaner: "Drop your pants here for best results."
- On a toy doll's package in Spain: "Laugh while you throw up."
- At a German campground: "It is strictly forbidden . . . that people of different sex, for instance men and women, live together in one tent, unless they are married with each other for that purpose."[21]

## Grin and Bear It

There are occasions when communication blockages are intentional and perhaps even essential. This is because for one reason or another it is better not to answer a question, or the answer we give must be less than complete. When we deal with confidential information about student psychological profiles or teacher personnel processes, for example, law and policy enter in. Or when we are working on sensitive contingency plans regarding such issues as school closings, good judgment must be used with regard to what is made public.

Sometimes the communication process must be tempered if the information will hurt feelings needlessly. For example, when someone asks our opinion about a new dress, and it appears better suited to the bride of Frankenstein, there is good reason to be less than candid.

There are particularly frustrating occasions that all school administrators frequently find themselves having to suffer through silently. When a taxpayer accuses you at a board meeting of wasting public money, when a parent berates you because his or her son didn't make the honor society, or when a pompous city councilman tells a meeting of the PTA that "your kids are getting cheated by lazy and underworked teachers," you may want to explode—but you can't. More often than not, you have to formulate a calm and rational response to an emotional and irrational accusation—or you simply grin and bear it while the accusor lets off steam. The catharsis of the situation is often the right medicine for the moment.

Under difficult circumstances as those described, we rarely can communicate what we really think, and the frustration builds within us. Once in a great while, however, we encounter a situation in the communication process where true feelings override conventional common sense. Such a situation was described in a newspaper article on the Associated Press (AP) wire not long ago to the applause of many who would love to do the same, if only once in a lifetime. The article is as follows.

*SORRY?*

> SIGNAL HILL (AP)—When a Signal Hill Telegram editorial compared City Councilman George [Papadopolis] to a "Greek orator," the target took offense at the "racial slur" and demanded an apology.
>
> So editor Ken Mills gave it to him.
>
> "The Tribune apologizes, George," the next column generously began. "What we intended to call you is a loquacious asshole, a bore without peer. (The public is to understand, however, that is just the opinion of Trib management and is not intended to be taken as fact.)
>
> "We reported your councilmanic doings accurately and without malice," the editorial concluded, "so stuff it. . . ."[22]

The article ends by saying that George did not demand a second apology.

Verbal communication is often supplemented (or contradicted) by nonverbal communication, which is the subject of the next section.

## Nonverbal Communication

William Shakespeare never set foot in a singles' bar, but he certainly knew the name of the game.

> *There's a language in her eye, her cheek, her lip,*
> *Nay her foot speaks.*
> *Her Wanton spirit looks out*
> *At every joint and motive of her body.*

The academic study of body movement is called *kinesics.* As Julius Fast writes, "Rarely do we send our [nonverbal] messages consciously. We act out our state of being with nonverbal body language. We lift one eyebrow for disbelief. We rub our noses for puzzlement. We clasp our arms to isolate ourselves or to protect ourselves. We shrug our shoulders for indifference, wink one eye for intimacy, tap our fingers for impatience, slap our forehead for forgetfulness."[23]

We send nonverbal messages through many media, such as the following.

1. *Distance:* How far we stand from someone suggests something about our relationship to them. Distance may reflect status or intimacy. If a physical object such as a desk stands between the individuals, an authority relationship is heightened.
2. *Dress:* Our clothes say much about how we want to represent ourselves—conservative, rich, laid-back, mellow, unconcerned. Our manner of dress alone can create tensions. A male teacher who wears a black leather jacket in class at an elitist prep school may create tension, just as someone who wears a three-piece suit in a slum classroom.
3. *Physical contact:* Shaking hands, clasping both hands, kissing on the cheek, and embracing all reflect varying degrees of friendship.
4. *Facial expressions:* The frown, yawn, smile, and raised eyebrow all have almost universally recognized meanings.
5. *Gestures:* Although some gestures have almost universally recognized meanings, such as shaking the head for yes or no, others are tied to a particular culture or are even unique to an individual. The emotion of our thoughts can often be read in our hand gestures just as they can in our eyes.

Nonverbal cues play an important role in our everyday conversations. Perhaps the point when we most recognize how important nonverbal cues are is when we are learning a foreign language. With only the rudiments of a new language, we can often communicate effectively on a face-to-face basis. However, on the telephone where we can't read the visual cues, our ability to communicate can collapse quickly.

Verbal speech and nonverbal cues may often conflict. When they do, as the saying goes, actions speak louder than words.[24] A teacher, for example, who says that a student report is creative and interesting, but yawns and looks periodically at the clock on the wall is sending conflicting messages. A superintendent who announces that his or her door is always open, but at the same time keeps a secretary out front guarding against access is also sending contradictory messages.

When verbal or nonverbal signals reinforce each other, the message can be particularly strong. For example, when a superintendent tells a newly assigned principal that he or she has complete confidence that the job will be done well, and puts a hand on the principal's shoulder at the same time, the combined affect can be inspiring.

When studying the communication process, and trying to determine how it can be improved, it is important to develop the skills of communication analysis.

## Communication Analysis

When the sheriff of that unnamed southern county looked down at the battered and beaten yet still angry and resentful body of Cool Hand Luke (in the movie of the same name), he issued his famous line, "What we have here is a failure to communicate." Rogers tells us that there are three types of communication consequences: changes in a receiver's knowledge, a receiver's attitudes, and a receiver's overt behavior.[25] Certainly Cool Hand Luke (played by actor Paul Newman) knew what the sheriff wanted of him, so new knowledge was not involved. Also, the sheriff knew he could never make Luke enjoy his condition on the road gang, so a change in attitude was not the anticipated consequence of the beatings. What the sheriff wanted was a change in overt behavior, something Luke was unwilling or perhaps unable to give.

When analyzing the communication process, problems cannot simply be blamed on a failure to communicate. Usually the problems have nothing to do with one side not knowing what the other wants. More often, one side is unwilling to give what the other is asking, such as in Cool Hand Luke's case. In education, for example, if the teachers are asking for a 12 percent salary increase and the board of education is holding firm at 4 percent, blaming the problem on a failure to communicate is inappropriate. The problem is not one of communication but of agreement.

When analyzing the communication process, at least four major questions must be posed: (1) What are the situations of communication? (2) What are the intentions? (3) What are the logistics? and (4) What are the consequences?

The *situations* in which we communicate usually fall into patterns. Most of the situations are routine with relatively standardized and predictable messages, such as calling meetings or sending home report cards. Other occasions are episodic, reflecting some special need of the school, such as a special request for parent volunteers to help with a new reading program or the crisis communiques surrounding a teachers' strike. Mitchell writes, "The more important, uncertain, and unexpected the event is, the more we tend to communicate with others."[26]

By examining the flow of paper, phone calls, and other communication modes within an educational system, as well as with its environment, emerging patterns suggest something about the periods of normality and storms that flow through the communication process. Too many storms or too much normality can suggest something about the organization that is being examined.

Closely meshing with the situations of communication is the *intent* of communications. When we initiate communication we usually do so for a purpose, such as to inform, change opinion, sell an idea, refine an accusation, or simply to feed our or someone else's ego. Thus, the analysis can match patterns of the purpose of communication with situations. What is the educational system generally trying to do when episodic communication patterns exist? Is it usually selling an idea? Refuting an accusation? Making urgent resource requests?

The *logistics* of communication also must be analyzed. Logistical issues involve questions of the channels and networks used, expansiveness and completeness of the networks, costs involved, barriers encountered or overcome, and time required. Logistical issues are easy to overlook in school settings because we tend to depend on traditional methods such as sending letters home. Unfortunately, we typically receive little or no feedback with which to make a judgment about the effectiveness of the channel selected or the special types of barriers encountered. More often than not, the same method of communication will be used the next time around.

Because educational systems tend to function with limited feedback, especially from parents whose children need the most help, it is difficult to evaluate the consequences of the communication process. More analysis evaluating the techniques used in the intention to communicate (e.g., selling an idea or warning about a concern) with the consequences would undoubtedly strengthen the communication process in education.

Another way to strengthen the process is to conduct an analysis of the communication network. The following activities can be helpful in conducting a network analysis.

1. Conduct a communication sociogram that maps out *who* gets *what* message *when* through *which channel* by what *medium.*
2. How long does it take for a message to get through the network, and how accurate is it at journey's end?
3. What are the quality and character of feedback that returns to the message senders?
4. Are any communication barriers visible in the network?
5. Can any unique communication roles be identified in the network, such as opinion leaders, bridges, liaisons, or isolates?
6. What type of messages flow through the network the fastest?

In short, whether considering formal or informal, verbal or nonverbal communications, a systematic analysis of the communication process usually is essential to improve its effectiveness.

## Conclusion

A foreign-born plumber in New York once wrote to the Bureau of Standards that he found hydrochloric acid fine for cleaning drains, and he asked if they agreed. Washington replied: "The efficacy of hydrochloric acid is indisputable, but the chlorine residue is incompatible with metallic permanence."

The plumber wrote back that he was mighty glad the Bureau agreed with him.

Considerably alarmed, the Bureau replied a second time: "We cannot assume responsibility for the production of toxic and noxious residues with hydrochloric acid, and suggest that you use an alternative procedure." The plumber was happy to learn that the Bureau still agreed with him.

Whereupon, Washington wrote: "Don't use hydrochloric acid; it eats hell out of pipes."[27]

Communicating easily and clearly is no simple task. There are, however, various orientations toward how it can be carried out most effectively. Classical theory, social system theory, and open system theory all incorporate a perspective toward the communication process; or, *who* should say *what* through *which channel* to *whom* toward *what effect.* Classical theory stresses that the communication process exists to facilitate the manager's command and control over the employees in a formal, hierarchical, and downwardly directed manner. The purpose is to increase efficiency and productivity.

The social system (human relations) orientation suggests that to be effective, communication has to be two-way, and that the meaning of the message is as much to be found in the psychological makeup of the receiver as it is the sender. The channels can be informal as well as formal and include anyone who has an interest in a particular subject.

The open system orientation emphasizes the communication process working toward drawing the various subsystems of an organization into a collaborating whole. Also, drawing the organization's actions into a close fit with the needs of its environment is an essential outcome of the process. This orientation emphasizes that between senders and receivers, the communication process must penetrate social class differences, cultural values, time orientations, and ethnocentrism of all types.

None of the conceptual frameworks introduced in the chapter escape barriers to communication. The story of the plumber illustrates the problems of message coding, decoding, and officialese. Other barriers such as filtering, overload, and hidden agendas can also disrupt the communication process.

The communication barriers existing at the micro (social unit) level also exist at the macro (national) level. At the macro level a great deal of filtering, overload, and selective perception exist. Perhaps one of the biggest barriers to communication at this macro level is indifference—a general lack of concern about what is going on around us. Attempts to alert our society, for example, about the crumbling economic conditions of our schools usually seems to spread like rain through limestone rather than like the weight of water breaking through a dam.

In any case, whether discussing the possibilities or problems of communication at the micro or the macro level, much work remains to be done to determine how the process can be improved.

## *Notes*

1. S. I. Hayakawa, *Language in Thought and Action* (New York: Harcourt, Brace, Jovanovich, 1949), p. 292.

2. Alvin Toffler, *Future Shock* (New York: Bantam, 1970).

3. Educational Policies Commission, *Mass Communication and Education* (Washington, DC: National Education Association, 1958), p. 76.

4. Willard R. Lane, Ronald C. Corwin, and William G. Monahan, *Foundations of Educational Administration: A Behavioral Analysis* (New York: Macmillan, 1967), p. 113.

5. Everett M. Rogers and Rekha Agarwala-Rogers, *Communication in Organizations* (New York: The Free Press, 1976), p. 34.

6. Ibid., p. 18.

7. Gerald M. Goldhaber, *Organizational Communication* (Dubuque, IA: William C. Brown, 1979), pp. 16–17.

8. Hayakawa, *Language in Thought,* p. 292.

9. Daniel Katz and Robert Kahn, *The Social Psychology of Organizations,* 2nd ed. (New York: John Wiley, 1978), p. 429.

10. Lane, Corwin, and Monahan, *Foundations of Educational Administration,* p. 88.

11. Rogers and Agarwala-Rogers, *Communication in Organizations,* p. 6.

12. Katz and Kahn, *The Social Psychology of Organizations,* p. 430.

13. Phillip V. Lewis, *Organizational Communication: The Essence of Effective Management* (Columbus, OH: Grid Publishing Co., 1980), p. 65.

14. Rogers and Agarwala-Rogers, *Communication in Organizations,* p. 93.

15. Lewis, *Organizational Communication,* pp. 69–70.

16. Ithiel de Sola Pool, "Communication Systems," in *Handbook of Communication,* Ithiel de Sola Pool and Wilbur Schramm, eds. (Chicago: Rand-McNally, 1973), p. 13.

17. James G. Miller, "Information Input: Overload, and Psychopathology," *American Journal of Psychiatry* 116 (1960): 697.

18. Katz and Kahn, *The Social Psychology of Organizations,* p. 472.

19. For a discussion of this research see Harold J. Leavitt, "Some Effects of Certain Communication Patterns on Group Performance," *Journal of Abnormal and Social Psychology* 46 (1951): 38–50; and M. E. Shaw, "Communication Networks," in *Advances in Experimental Psychology,* Leonard Berkowitz, ed. (New York: Academic Press, 1964), pp. 111–147.

20. Lane, Corwin, and Monahan, *Foundations of Educational Administration,* pp. 65–66.

21. From *Life* magazine (reproduced in *Parade Magazine,* Jan 2, 1994, p. 6.

22. Clipped from the *Press-Enterprise,* 23 December 1980. The last name of the councilman has been changed by the author.

23. Julius Fast, *Body Language* (Philadelphia: M. Evans, 1970), p. 7.

24. For a discussion of conflicting verbal and nonverbal cues see: John Keltner, *Interpersonal Speech Communication* (Belmont, CA: Wadsworth, 1970); and A. Mehrabian, *Silent Messages* (Belmont, CA: Wadsworth, 1971).

25. Rogers and Agarwala-Rogers, *Communication in Organizations,* p. 13.

26. T. R. Mitchell, *People in Organizations: Understanding Their Behavior* (New York: McGraw-Hill, 1978), p. 207.

27. Stewart Chase, *Roads to Agreement* (New York: Harper and Brothers, 1951), p. 206.

# Chapter *10*

# *Educational Marketing and the Public Schools*

For school people, marketing is all too often associated with the black art of hard sell as practiced by Joe Isuzu, Elmer Gantry, or Professor Howard Hill (of trombone fame). Undeniably, this form of selling mentality exists, but it plays a minor role on a very large stage.[1]

If public schools are to produce an increasingly educated citizenry, then "building and maintaining confidence in education is the most important single task we face."[2] In any organization, consumer confidence is neither accidental nor automatic, but the product of careful attention to the needs and expectations of the marketplace—whether that be private sector customers, public sector clients, or school district parents.

Schools cannot assume they can communicate the information that builds public confidence to those whose voices and votes make a difference (e.g., legislators, parents, business officials, retired residents) by osmosis or inspired revelation. Especially in today's turbulent social, political and economic times, providing clear and convincing exchanges of information between school systems and communities and marking directions for future development are critical undertakings.

The public school should not apologize for using sophisticated marketing techniques, because it must resolve most of the same types of problems as private sector organizations, such as: reputation building, resource mobilization, personnel employment, program development, client satisfaction, community good will, and public political support. However, because schools in the public sector have a guaranteed clientele, and thus can operate as a local monopoly, they do not face the life and death significance of marketing in a customer-dependent environment. Consequently, to their peril, public school systems can and typically do ignore the marketing process.[3]

Private schools, on the other hand, must actively build a clientele if they are to survive in a competitive environment. Survival requires marketing. A national association of private schools recently adopted a marketing slogan with an unsubtle message: "Private schools—schools you can trust."

The objectives of this chapter are to analyze the marketing concept and illustrate how it can be applied to public school systems. Drawing upon the research literature, this chapter addresses the following questions:

1. What is marketing, and how does it differ from public relations?
2. Why apply marketing techniques to schools?
3. What market forces exist in education that create bridges or barriers between schools and their communities?
4. How would school "choice" strategies change the current configuration of market forces?
5. How do marketers contact the various community segments?
6. How can strategic marketing be conducted in an educational system?

## Educational Marketing and How It Differs from Public Relations

When interacting with their surrounding communities, schools commonly develop public relations programs. Serious public relations programs go far beyond simply spreading liberal applications of industrial-strength good cheer. Public relations can be defined as "a planned and systematic two-way process of communications between an educational organization and its internal and external publics designed to build morale, goodwill, understanding and support for that organization."[4] Intended outcomes are usually goodwill, positive attitudes, respect, understanding and basic support.[5]

Although a good PR program is an important foundation (or perhaps a launching pad) for a marketing program, they are not the same. Public relations is a broad-based, multifaceted approach to building public understanding of the full range of activities going on within an institution such as a school system.[6]

Institutional marketing, on the other hand, can be defined as "the analysis, planning, implementation, and control of carefully formulated programs designed to bring about voluntary exchanges of values with target markets to achieve institutional objectives."[7] Educational marketing involves developing or refining *specific* school programs in response to the needs and desires of specific target-markets (e.g., "at risk" families, parents of pre-school children, voters) and using effective means of communication to understand those needs and inform and motivate those markets. Educational marketing can be short-term, but strategic educational marketing takes the long view.

With its long-term focus, strategic educational marketing is often linked with *strategic planning*. Strategic planning involves defining the organization's mission and developing methods and strategies to achieve that mission in the most effective way possible.[8] If strategic planning enables an educational system to envision its future, then strategic marketing is the communication technology the managers use to link the realities of the present to the expectations of the future.

Perhaps the most practiced form of educational marketing is short-term and not necessarily tied to a strategic plan. *Project marketing* involves drawing the community, or a segment thereof, into a special school activity such as joining the PTA, attending a lecture on earthquake safety, or donating to the purchase of new musical instruments. It can also involve providing a special program in response to the needs of a particular market segment, such as classes in English as a second language or honors science.

An effective marketing strategy does not emerge out of some inherent organizational instinct. A market strategy must be shaped consciously as part of an educational policy. Central to establishing this working relationship is the concept of an *exchange* of valued goods and services between schools and their communities. Introducing a marketing process is the means by which all types of organizations, including schools, create a satisfactory exchange process.[9]

In helping to establish the exchange, a marketing strategy initiates a cyclical process that not only gathers and distributes information, but also changes educational programs in response to that information. In marketing language, educational change really is *product design* in the face of shifting consumer demands.

## Why Apply Marketing Techniques to Schools?

There are many reasons why educational systems and communities can benefit by seriously applying marketing techniques. Three such reasons especially critical at this moment are: (1) developing truer images of what goes on in schools, (2) obtaining additional resources available only through resource-generating methods such as passing bond issues or tax levy referendums, and (3) addressing the potential for increased student learning.

### Public Perceptions and Image Modification

Within and around the school, information from a multitude of sources (e.g., newspapers, television, research reports, "grapevine") regarding the existing quantity and quality of educational services shapes perceptions and images. Unfortunately, these sources often trawl only the darker institutional currents for their information, and thus present ugly and unrepresentative images of the day-to-day life in schools. These images, as Stough writes, "often become crystallized into attitudes and behaviors which positively or adversely affect their support of school policies, programs, and very importantly—budgets."[10]

What image do Americans hold of their public schools? The 1993 Gallup Poll asked people to grade the quality of schools nationally. Twenty percent of adults with no children in school (the group which makes up the largest electoral voting block) gave grades of (A) and (B), while 67 percent gave them a (C), (D) or (F) (the rest marked "don't know"). Nineteen percent of adults with children in public schools gave (A) & (B) grades to schools nationally, while 70 percent gave (C), (D), or (F) grades.[11]

As an interesting aside with respect to images, the Gallup organization conducted a national survey that rated 26 institutions with respect to the public's level of confidence. Private and public schools were rated in seventh and eighth places respectively. Political parties and Congress, which have rarely resisted the temptation to skewer the schools at every opportunity, came in dead last.[12]

Because the popular images community members hold count for so much in education, school people must face a version of the same need that private organizations face—image modification. Image modification is important in the business sector because the outcome of an excellent image (e.g., reputation for quality, respected brand name, durability, time saving features) leads to *sales,* and thereby profits. In education, the outcome of an excellent image (e.g., quality teaching, effective programs, sound discipline) leads to local *political support* and thereby both the capacity to make difficult changes and to raise revenues.[13]

## Educational Marketing and Increased Resources

For numerous observers, the main fallout from the perception of a growing isolation between communities and the ever-increasing complexities of schools (and declining confidence in them) is failed bond issues and tax levies.[14]

Bond issues, and other forms of local tax levy referendums for educational projects (normally, construction of new school facilities) usually are proposed only at irregular times every few years. Thus, these *special* needs to raise revenues are not constantly before voters, and so do not constitute a natural, continuous market force. All too often school people market their system in a communitywide effort only before bond referendums.

The outcome of referendums for educational funding has been increasingly disconcerting in recent years. In California, for example, from 1983 to November, 1993 only 61 of 164 (37 percent) of the parcel tax initiatives were passed in contrast to general obligation bond referendums, in which, since 1986, 263 were held and 120 (46 percent) were successful.[15]

States around the nation have had significant problems in raising educational revenues. When state aid declines, local communities are asked to pick up the slack, usually through increased property taxes. In New Jersey and Ohio, for example, voters rejected approximately half the proposed school district budget proposals, largely because they would have increased local taxes or simply in an anti-tax revolt.[16]

Typically, communication practices associated with special revenue-generating elections for education do not go beyond the local school district communities. However, as a percentage of total public school revenues across the nation, only slightly more than 46 percent come from local sources. In California, only 25.6 percent is generated locally, with 66 percent coming from the state government.[17] The implication is that if education is to be funded adequately, not to mention comprehensively, educational marketing should not be limited to the school community but must be carried out aggressively statewide.

And how well is education marketed nationally in America? At the "educational summit" in September of 1989, President Bush characterized educational expenditures in the United States as *lavish,* and said that the focus should be not on resources, but on results. The Bush administration, exhibiting its own marketing strategy, then offered international comparison data as proof that Americans are getting less for more.

Using UNESCO and U.S. Department of Education data, 16 industrialized nations, which included the United States, most of western Europe, Australia, and Japan, were compared. When comparing expenditures as a percentage of gross domestic product (GDP), the United States' 6.8 percent expenditure places us in an impressive three-way tie for second place (with Canada and the Netherlands, but behind Sweden's 7.6 percent).

The numbers that the Bush administration used are indeed impressive but unfortunately are deceptive, because they include expenditures for higher education. How lavish is our K-12 educational effort? When comparing expenditures as a percentage of GDP for K-12 public schools only, the 4.1 percent the United States spent ranks a low fourteenth out of the 16, with only Australia and Ireland spending less. When comparing our K-12 per-pupil expenditures as a percentage of per capita income, the United States again ranks fourteenth (20 percent), with Sweden spending the most (35.3 percent), Austria second (29.7 percent), and Japan seventh (24.1 percent)[18]

The main point is that politicians, generally in response to public sentiment, establish policies setting the levels of educational funding. To provide educational funding commensurate with available resources, effective marketing practices by educators must function in the macroenvironment of the state and nation as a whole, not just in the microenvironment of the community.[19]

In educational affairs at any level on any subject, ignorance, to a large degree, is a consequence of poor marketing. And how well informed do Americans feel about their schools? In a Gallup Poll, only 15 percent of the public without children in school felt well-informed about public schools in America. In contrast, 55 percent of that same population said they were not well-informed or simply "didn't know." The figures were slightly worse when the same groups were asked about how well-informed they feel about their local schools and what is being taught in them.[20]

Does this lack of information impact on resource generation? Probably so, as a 1993 Gallup Poll points out. The poll reports that in 1993, for the first time in its 25-year history, the "lack of proper financial support has clearly emerged as the number one public school problem. Twenty-one percent of poll respondents named it, while 16 percent cited drug abuse and 15 percent mentioned lack of discipline." In addition, 68 percent of all adults would be willing to pay more taxes to improve the quality of the public schools in the poorer states and communities.[21]

An important implication is that educators at the grassroots and national levels are not making an effective case that additional resources (e.g., more buildings, better paid teachers, new technology, reduced teacher-student ratios, etc.) will improve the quality of education. Developing and convincingly communicating that case is, of course, a principal purpose of educational marketing.

## *Educational Marketing and Increased Learning*

The second major benefit of effective educational marketing involves increasing parent participation, with its potential for increasing student achievement. But does parent participation translate into increased student achievement? Responses to that question range from one extreme to the other. For example, Anne Henderson reviewed 49 studies and concludes that ". . . parent involvement improves student achievement. When parents are involved, children do better in school, and they go to better schools."[22] On the other hand, the Clark, Lotto, and McCarthy examination concludes that "On its own, parental involvement is likely to influence parental attitudes toward school, but is unlikely to affect student achievement, unless other school variables are also manipulated."[23]

An important task in educational marketing is sorting out where to invest limited time and energy in pursuit of increased learning. The literature often is categorized into four forms of parent involvement, and there is some evidence (albeit inconclusive) that in hierarchical order they have differing impacts on student learning.[24]

1. *Parents involved in the classroom* (e.g., volunteers, aides). When parents volunteer or work as paid aides in their students' classrooms, they learn about teaching methods, textbooks, daily homework assignments, and the school culture. The information and skills parents obtain from this experience impact positively on both the learning environment and the level of learning.[25]

2. *Learning in the home.* The learning environment at home is the sum of the quality and quantity of educationally stimulating experiences the home provides. Because children and young adults spend much more time at home than in school, anything educators can do to stimulate the educational enrichment of home learning can have an impact on student learning.[26]

3. *Parents involved in school decision making.* There is little evidence that parent participation in school governance activities, such as leadership role in the PTA, booster club, or school advisory committee, translates into increased learning for their own children.[27]

4. *School visitation* (e.g., attending PTA meetings, participating in back-to-school orientations, cheering at sporting activities). Educators place considerable emphasis on school visitation, but there is little evidence that such activities contribute to increased learning.

However, parent involvement apparently does have another kind of impact. In a study of the reasons new teachers (two years or less) leave or consider leaving the profession, the clear leader, at 40 percent, was lack of support or help from parents. This led financial considerations by 11 percentage points.[28]

In short, it may be that if the goal of a marketing program is to make an *impact on student achievement,* it probably must do so by directing its energies toward stimulating increased parent attention to (and participation in) the home learning environment first, and school governance and visitation activities last. However, if the marketing goal is to *increase political support* of school policies and programs, quite probably the exact opposite is true in terms of the priority of activities.

One might think that the obvious requirements of school–community exchanges for educational development would create natural linkages and result in effective information transfer. As the research literature shows, usually such is not the case.

## Market Forces that Create Bridges or Barriers

### Consumer Demand as a Market Force

Market forces in the private sector drive producers and consumers into an interdependent exchange process. To survive, producers must seek out clients and offer products that are responsive to their demands. Through consumer demand, therefore, clients decisively shape producers decision-making processes. Similarly, market forces motivate the clients. Requiring goods and services they cannot produce themselves, clients seek out producers who offer high quality at reasonable prices.[29] Do market forces operate that way between public schools and their communities?

As will be noted soon, although the natural market forces that drive consumers and producers together in the private sector also exist between families and schools, they do so only at a much reduced level. Sara Lightfoot is a principal proponent of an argument that sheds light on this issue. The emotionally charged family-child relationship and the more impartial school-student relationship produce forces that both restrict and enhance the working relationship between families and schools.[30] At the center of the issue is the question, who should control the child's education? Because the response to this question has always been unclear, fully collaborative efforts on both sides are never completely possible.

Norms of professionalism and expertise combined with building configuration converge to permit teachers to work relatively unimpeded within their sphere of influence behind closed classroom doors. In contrast, large numbers of parents armed with a constant parade of demands push to get their students out of one teacher's classroom and into another's, insist on a different set of biology textbooks, and complain to the board of education that the curriculum should include English as a second language rather than bilingual education.

To cope with the seemingly incompatible needs and expectations of teachers and parents, Lightfoot argues, schools organize ritualistic encounters with families. "Parent-Teacher Association meetings and open-house rituals at the beginning of the school year are contrived occasions that symbolically reaffirm the idealized parent-school relationship but rarely provide the chance for authentic interaction."[31]

If there is something in education that could be called a natural market force based on consumer demand, it results from parents seeking to monitor or influence their children's education and schools recognizing services and benefits that can be derived from such participation.[32] In fact, the force often can be so strong that teachers feel the need to be protected from "pushy" parents of high achieving students.[33]

The emphasis of this primary market force, however, tends to be unevenly distributed across socioeconomic lines, and decreases from the elementary through the high school years. Parents from higher socioeconomic levels tend to be significantly more involved than those at lower levels.[34] In fact, many states are passing *parent responsibility legislation* that would not be necessary if the market force for family–school interaction were evenly distributed.[35]

In short, public school systems can be very effective in educational marketing with the assertive and politically influential body of ethnic-majority, middle-class parents who closely monitor the educational process. These parents *inform* and *are informed*. On the other hand, due to the lack of significant market forces, public school systems easily can lose contact with the upper socioeconomic classes (their children go to private schools), the uninvolved middle and lower socioeconomic classes, and the culturally different.

In marketing and in the consumer-demand market force just discussed, there often comes the powerful market force of competition.

## *Competition as a Market Force*

"What do we think of when we think of competition?" Rados asks. "We may think of Darwin or of amateur sports; or we may think of business, which immediately calls to mind professional sports; but we do not think of a library, a housing authority, or the United States Olympic Committee."[36] Or even the public school, he might have added.

Richard Carlson identifies private-sector organizations as "wild" because they must compete and struggle for resources to survive. Public schools, on the other hand, receive almost all their funding through average daily student attendance. Carlson writes that

> They do not compete with other organizations for clients; in fact a steady flow of clients is assured. There is no struggle for survival for this type of organization—existence is guaranteed. Though this type of organization does compete in a restricted area for funds, funds are not closely tied to quality of performance. These organizations are domesticated in the sense that they are protected by the society they serve.[37]

As a "domesticated" organization, the school does not yet have to "forage for its fodder." That is, the most powerful market force that exists in the private sector, economic survival, does not work to any significant extent for schools. Consequently, the public school, with its captive complement of students and guaranteed economic support, can function as a local monopoly and exist relatively independent of community expectations.

Many public-sector organizations, including schools, when faced with the uncertainties of a changing world, and "unable to use standard measures of performance, like sales or market share . . . are prone to sanctify policies that have worked well in the past."[38] These policies often are geared more to pacification (e.g., accepting teacher salary demands, improvements to the landscaping, a tougher discipline program) than significant changes in classroom teaching-learning processes.

The important point of this section is not that schools and communities are failing to operate at a healthy level of interactive exchange, because many schools across America do just that. The point is that the powerful, natural market forces that tend to drive the private sector exist only marginally in the public schools.

Without natural market forces pressing for and shaping producer–client exchanges, the organization tends to develop what market researchers call *product* and *production* orientations. An educational organization with a "*product orientation* presumes that the school's major task is to offer programs that it believes are 'good for' its clients."[39] They deal in "impression management" with the objective of making parents feel good about schooling activities independent of whether or not the popular impressions accurately reflect realities.[40]

An organization with a *production orientation* seeks efficiency based on its own terms and is prone to view clients as objects to be treated, not customers to be served. In contrast, an organization with a *customer orientation* operates to service the needs and wants of target markets through communication, product design, proper pricing and the timely delivery of services.[41]

Whether a school system adopts a product and production orientation or a customer orientation can have major consequences for the student. When considering the issue of dropouts, for example, schools with a product and production orientation focus on what is taught, whereas those with customer orientations are concerned with what is learned.

Searching for ways to pull down one of the major barriers to educational reform, serious attention has been focused on the program called "choice."

## How Would "Choice" Change Current Market Forces?

The Bush administration's "America 2000" and the Clinton administration's "Goals 2000" plans both advocate giving parents the opportunity to choose the school where they want to enroll their children. There are numerous versions of the "choice" initiatives, such as: within and between district open-enrollment plans; vouchers for students from low-income families; vouchers for all students regardless of family income; vouchers to use at either public or private schools; charter schools, and magnet school (e.g., bilingual, artistic). By introducing this powerful free market force into public education, in theory good schools will drive out bad schools as parents take their children to those places where a higher quality of education can be found. As the bad schools see themselves losing students, and the large amounts of money that go with them, they will change their ways or wither away.

If this version of a free market force were introduced massively into the educational system, the implications would be enormous for the practice of educational marketing. In theory, schools would have to constantly improve the quality of their product to retain or even build their share of the market.

The potential negatives of "choice" have many people concerned. As in institutions of higher education, the process of "choice" will introduce incentives for schools, as well as students, to become selective. Schools with good test scores undoubtedly will feel pressures to obtain even better test scores. Unfortunately, one way of doing this is to deny admission to low-achieving students, poor discipline risks, or children with special learning handicaps.

If high quality schools run out of space, or are enrolled to capacity to begin with, they cannot expand quickly. Constructing new facilities typically takes years of lead time and millions of dollars; dollars that local tax payers have been increasingly reluctant to offer in local revenue elections.

Certainly, the danger of resegregating the schools through "choice" has not gone unnoticed.[42] The potential for utilizing marketing techniques to attract student scholars, leaders, and athletes from one school to another becomes a real possibility if the business approach to "choice" becomes the educational model.

Because the many potential negative consequences of applying the business model of "choice" to education, controls no doubt will have to be introduced. Nevertheless, if educational choice models truly open up the possibility of shifting the flow of students, and the funding that goes with them, from one type of school (public or private) to another, as a natural consequence the practice of educational marketing techniques undoubtedly will increase.

## How Marketers Contact Segments of the Community

"Marketing is not a peripheral activity of modern organizations," Kotler and Andreasen stress, "but one that grows out of the essential quest of modern organizations to effectively serve some area of human need. To survive and succeed, organizations must know their markets."[43] When educators are asked to identify their market, a common response is, "the community."

The concept of community, however, is ambiguous. It can, for example, refer to a specific location, as the Palm Springs community; or an ethnic body with a cultural identity, as the Hispanic community; or a body of people with a technological identity, as the scientific community.[44] Within each of these "communities" are subsets of other communities (e.g., Hispanics within the scientific community) thus complicating the concept even further.

When considering the field of education, there are so many communities that the concept is rendered almost useless. Rather, it is more productive to speak of markets, market segments, and target markets. In the field of education, just as in the private sector, clearly identifying target markets to be served is central to any marketing activity.[45]

### Market Segmentation and Target Marketing

Organizations can respond to their markets in two ways: ignore the differences in consumer needs and preferences and use a *mass marketing* approach; or, adapt to the differences and use *market segmentation* followed by *target marketing*.[46] The first approach assumes a "homogenized" view of the families, is less expensive, and easier to deliver than the second. Mass marketing is convenient when the clients, no matter how different their tastes and needs, have nowhere else to turn. While mass marketing is the dominant model in education, market segmentation and target marketing are best suited to contacting specific populations.

The underlying premise behind market segmentation is simple; that is, different people have different needs, and organizations must respond to them as such. In its most basic form, a market segment is a grouping of people with a similar characteristic that may be important to the serving organization, such as age, economic status, educational level, social status, number of children, or political power.

Kotler and Andreasen point out that the process of market segmentation involves three tasks.[47]

1. Identifying the bases for segmenting the market. That is, what are the those special characteristics in people that might have some special importance for the school? At risk families? Exceptional children? Limited English speakers? Community leaders? High/low socioeconomic status of families?
2. Developing profiles of resulting segments. That is, what are the characteristics of those individuals who fall in a specific market segment.
3. Developing measures of segment attractiveness. That is, how great is the need for specific programs for specific groups, and how accessible are the groups?

Following market segmentation comes *target marketing,* a task that is essential in education because, unlike psychologists, educators cannot customize their product to the specific needs of each individual. Educational targets are conceptualized as parents, students (as extensions of their parents) or members of other market segments. Target marketing also comes in three stages.[48]

1. *Selecting the target markets.* Magmer and Russell stress that because resources are limited, educators must choose among *priority publics* based on specific marketing goals.[49]
2. *Positioning a program for each priority target market.* Positioning calls for shaping existing programs, or developing new ones, to meet the requirements of target markets.
3. *Developing marketing mix for each target market.* A marketing mix involves the final menu to be offered which involves: program or project (e.g., a new language laboratory, land purchase for a new school); cost (e.g., per item expenditure); distribution (e.g., which market segment is to get what); and promotion (e.g., communication messages and channels).

A significant but unanswered question in the research literature is, how much market segmentation and target marketing go on in education? While the private school literature pays considerable attention to these processes, the public school literature is nearly silent on the topics.[50] Perhaps that in itself is an answer of sorts. However in some specific areas, especially where state or federal laws are in effect, market segmentation and target marketing can be found, such as with parents of the handicapped or Chapter One children.

As demonstrated in the national surveys, the American public generally is willing and prepared to support the social and economic requirements of schools, but clear and convincing reasons to do so have not yet been forthcoming. What do come forth are stuttering and confusing messages that do not match the information needs of specific audiences.

There is no reason why educators should not look toward adopting policies with proven marketing technologies and procedures that can strengthen the exchange processes between schools and their communities. To do less is to deny the schools access to valuable tools for shifting away from the problematic status quo in education. A good place to begin would be for school districts to develop strategic marketing plans.

## Strategic Marketing Plans

Strategic marketing must be conceived as a system with a beginning, middle, and end, and a new beginning. As a system it is composed of parts which fit into a whole, not an *ad hoc* collection of programs and actions. Morrow Stough, following his extensive analysis of the San Diego school system, concludes that "there has been little evidence that schools in general have sought to organize their home–school communication systems into a purposeful, coordinated thrust."[51]

As an ongoing system with yearly or multiyear cycles, it does not operate only when something special is needed from the public at a given moment, such as passing a bond issue under crisis conditions. As Figure 10.1 indicates, a strategic marketing program should be linked to a strategic planning program to insure that, speaking metaphorically, as the ship leaves the pier it knows where it is going and specifically trained people are assigned to get it there. The trip must be planned in advance and must take into account as many contingencies as possible.

In strategic marketing this process involves a sequence of coordinated *research steps* and *operational steps.*[52]

### Market Analysis: Research Step

Market analysis is simply gaining an understanding of a community's needs and expectations. The NSPRA argues that such an understanding is not common.

> School board and administrators may think they know how their community feels, but rarely do they know. Usually only two small segments of the community take the time to make their thoughts known at the board or administrative level. These are the critics, who waste little time complaining about almost anything, and the backslappers, who smile and praise you and tell you how wonderful everything is.[53]

Difficult as it is to understand the needs of the current community segments, the shifting demographic currents running through the nation complicate matters significantly. In terms of ethnicity alone, for example, "between [1990] and 2030, the Latino youth population will grow by almost 80 percent—to 10 million in number—and the black youth population by 14 percent, while the white youth population will decline by 10 percent."[54] Also, specific industries considering relocation (in or out of the area) have their own sets of educational expectations.

Market analysis also incorporates the task of understanding the current images (perceptions) the community segments hold of the school system, its coverage, and the quality of its programs. The images may range from perceived excellence in the science program to a math program that couldn't teach Albert Einstein to add. Then

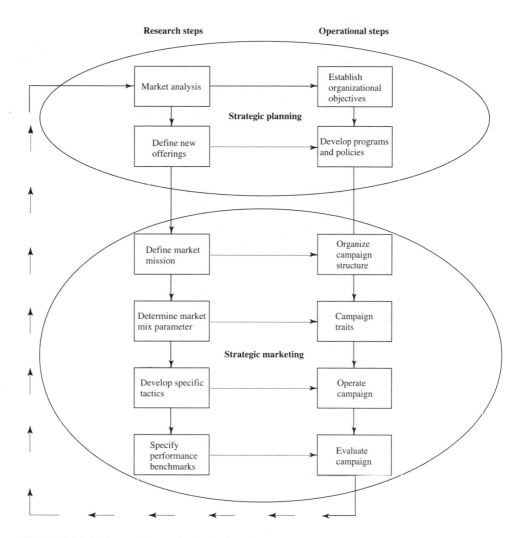

FIGURE 10.1  Strategic marketing\planning process

there is the disconcerting position of school principals who suddenly realize that their schools have no reputation at all, good or bad.

In education, performing a *needs assessment* fulfills many of the requirements of a market analysis. However, a needs assessment must move beyond gathering information on need identification and into taking into account the complexities of problem evaluation and priority setting.

Most needs assessment research is based on some type of discrepancy view that identifies gaps between a given condition (what is) and a desired condition (what should be). A critical issue is who makes the decision on which gaps to fill, based on what criteria? The criteria employed reflect a system of values.

Research and practice reflect at least three needs assessment models: (1) The *expert model,* which holds that schools gather a team of experts to evaluate the gaps and propose solutions that reflect their collective wisdom based on expertise and experience; (2) the *decision-maker model,* based on the notion that the organization has a chief executive officer who bears the responsibility of making choices and ultimately must be accountable for those choices; (3) the *marketing model,* which reflects the perception that the schools belongs to the community and choices should be made in response to popular perceptions of need.[55]

There are many ways to gather information for a market analysis. Utilization of a *focus group* is a data-gathering method marketers in the private sector use, and it is now starting to see some use in the field of education. A relatively homogeneous group (e.g., socioeconomic status, ethnicity, occupation) of 7 to 10 people is gathered for a group interview by a trained moderator with the expectation that their views are representative of the larger community segment to which they belong.

Krueger defines a focus group as a small body of people participating in a "carefully planned discussion designed to obtain perceptions on a defined area of interest in a permissive, nonthreatening environment. . . . The discussion is relaxed, comfortable, and often enjoyable for participants as they share their ideas and perceptions."[56] Patterned insights emanating from focus groups representing distinct segments of the community often are shaped into a sequence of questions that form the basis for a survey questionnaire (either in writing or by telephone) issued to a representative sample of the larger community.

The survey provides at least two types of data: *demographic* and *opinion.* The demographic (e.g., age, sex, occupation) helps classify the opinions according to their respective community segments. Surveys should be conducted regularly, such as once a year, to enable the school system to identify shifts in historical patterns.

## *Establish Organizational Objectives: Operational Step*

After the market analysis identifies the needs and expectations of the segments of the community, the school system must evaluate them in terms of its current programmatic offerings (e.g., science, student discipline, language arts). Once the gaps are identified, two questions must be addressed: (1) To what extent are the community images of unmet needs real or imagined? and (2) What new organizational objectives can be established to treat those *real* needs judged to be unmet?

If the community's needs and expectations are unrealistic or are already met, then an educational marketing program must be put in place to reduce these gaps between the real and the imagined. No educational leaders want to be caught unaware as did the managers of Du Pont industries a few years when they woke up to realize that the public viewed their company as a merchant of death.[57]

## *Define New Offerings: Research Step*

Based on the newly established objectives, the next step in a strategic marketing program, as illustrated in Figure 10.1, calls for identifying new programs or activities (or modifying existing ones) in response to newly defined community needs. If community members participate extensively in this process, the outcomes can contribute greatly to the marketing program. The educational system must also evaluate what marketers call SWAT. That is, its strengths and weaknesses, opportunities and threats. This evaluation is necessary to determine the degree to which it can respond (e.g., economically, politically, academically) to challenges raised by by programmatic changes.[58] For example, the school may be able to afford a new set of textbooks, but not a parent demand for computers on every desk in mathematics classes.

It is not easy to decide on new program offerings or changes in existing programs, because, as Stufflebeam, et al. point out, "many needs are worthy and defensible and hence are in competition for limited resources."[59] Priorities must be established, and, again, community participation aids the marketing program when the priorities become public information.

## Develop Programs and Policies: Operational Step

Once the new programs and program modifications are identified, new policies and activity guidelines must established to set the framework for this operational stage. While such program changes are never easy, they are essential components in any strategic plan and strategic marketing program.

## Define the Marketing Mission: Research Step

Just as the newly developed educational activities were based on educational objectives, the marketing mission must have its objectives outlined clearly. The planning at this stage typically is broad and directional, with the specific tactics left to the next stage, as identified in Figure 10.1.

Questions of short- versus long-range focus of activities, gathering support for new programs, reducing the gap between the desired and current image, "positioning," and desired outcomes dominate the planning at this stage of the strategic marketing planning process. *Positioning* is a marketing concept that involves placing your "product" (e.g., school, activity, program) in the minds of your consumer relative to the perception of the product of similar institutions. In education it involves an attempt to shift where

> your community has already placed your school or district in a pecking order with other schools and districts, both public and private. It may be as simple a notion as "private schools are better than public," or "the suburban district across the line is better than our urban district."[60]

In a strategic marketing plan, more than one educational marketing program can be run at the same time. Individual schools as well as the district office can be running various programs simultaneously.

## *Organize the Campaign Leadership Structure: Operational Step*

A strategic marketing program is carried out in a series of well planned, coordinated, ongoing campaigns. Because they have been thought out and prepared for in advance, ideally they can become almost routine in nature rather than crisis undertakings by people under intense pressure.

Key to organizing the strategic marketing program is the leadership structure to run the individual campaigns. Often a team is selected that includes a combination of school-system members and authority and community members who represent its various segments: There should be members with expertise in politics, fund raising, advertising, volunteerism, and demographics. Sometimes the team runs all the marketing campaigns and at other times subcommittees are created to direct specific campaigns.

The leadership structure defines who should do what, when, how, at what cost, with what objective in mind. In addition, it is essential that the leaders provide coordination within and between the various marketing campaigns.

## *Campaign Planning and Marketing Mix: Research Step*

After the marketing objectives and leadership structure is identified, a strategic marketing program requires the creation of a *marketing mix.* Kotler and Fox define a marketing mix as "the particular blend of controllable marketing variables that the institution uses to achieve its objectives in the target market."[61]

Private-sector marketers frequently break down these controllable variables by using the classification scheme called the "four P's" formulated by E. Jerome McCarthy: product, price, place, and promotion.[62] With respect to *product,* in marketing there is a significant phrase called "primacy of the product." As Pfeiffer and Dunlap write, it:

> relates to the basic worth of whatever is being described to the public. Even highly promoted consumer products such as automobiles or toothpastes cannot be successfully marketed unless they are intrinsically good (i.e., the autos really *do drive* easily—if the ads say so; the toothpastes really *do prevent cavities*—if the ads say so). And, by the same token, if a school system is to be described in glowing terms, the school had better glow![63]

In educational strategic marketing, honesty and integrity count. Because strategic marketing is a cyclical process, going back to a public wounded by an earlier experience for obvious reasons is often unproductive.

The *price* of the new programs (e.g., buildings, personnel, technology) should be clear as well as the per-capita impact on each of those community members who will be required to share in the financial burden. Also, the price of *not* supporting the request for new programs should be equally clear (e.g., more dropouts, declining neighborhoods, loss of local industry, increased class sizes).

*Place* involves the means of delivering the messages, such as the channels used. Certainly, a wide variety of channels is available at varying costs with differing audiences. Commonly used communication vehicles are, for example, radio spots, local cable television, speakers bureau, key communicators (e.g., barbers, bartenders, clergymen, ethnic leaders), newspapers, school newsletters, and public information flyers.

"In seeking audiences," Bagin writes, "don't aim at that general public. Identify specific audiences or segments of an audience."[64] Good *promotion* is based on target marketing.

Target marketing is important because each community segment examines any proposal with the thought in mind: "What's in it for me?"[65] For example, in a school bond issue the retired community may respond to messages about improved security, home owners about property values, and the business community about improved quality in the labor force.

Marketers stress that each message should approach the interests of each market segments using a formula such as AIDA;[66] that is:

1. A—(get) Attention
2. I—(arouse) Interest
3. D—(generate) Desire
4. A—(ask for) Action

Applying target marketing does not violate the principle of "primacy of the product" in any way.

## Campaign Trials: Operational Step

It is always wise and necessary to pretest the campaign components on market segments. The trials examine those entities upon which the entire campaign was premised: the market analysis, the proposed new offerings, the composition and foresight of the leadership structure, the campaign channels, materials, and messages, and so forth. As a rule, if it doesn't work on representative small samples, it won't work on the parent populations.

## Define Specific Tactics: Research Step

While strategic marketing in education may have a broad, long-term focus, at some point specific tasks have to be carried out by specific individuals. Planning, therefore, shifts from the macro- to the micro-level as the tactics and details of who does what, when, and how are scripted.

## Carry out the Campaign: Operational Step

The coordinated components of the strategic plan are executed. The initiative is carried forward as a team effort rather than a collection of isolated actions by individuals.

## Determine Performance Benchmarks: Research Step

Performance benchmarks are important because they indicate how the marketing campaign is unfolding. Bench marks at various points in the campaign may include, for example, the number of radio spots broadcast, brochures distributed, community meetings held, and so forth. Benchmarks are also important in guiding any called for mid-course corrections in the campaign.

## Evaluate the Plan and the Campaign: Operational Step

The evaluation stage in strategic marketing must go beyond examining the *final* outcome of any specific campaign. Baskin and Aronoff stress that an *impact analysis* is important; this includes audience coverage, audience response, campaign impact, and environmental mediation.[67]

*Audience coverage* involves an understanding of the extent to which the intended community segments were exposed to the messages targeted for them, which unintended audiences received the messages, and why? For example, was the retired community exposed to the information intended for parents with young children?

Measures on *audience response* are important because they give the marketers insight on whether specific messages interested or were understood by the intended audiences. With respect to *campaign impact,* Baskin and Aronoff stress that

> the whole is not equal to the sum of the parts. If a campaign is correctly researched and polled, its elements will interact to produce an effect that is much greater than the sum of the response to the individual messages. If the mix is not right, however, the elements of the campaign combined, no matter how individually excellent, may fall far short of the goal.[68]

*Environmental mediation* refers to the fact that campaigns exist in a social environment that can have as much or more effect on the goals of the effort as the prepared messages. Therefore, the results must be interpreted in the light of the various unanticipated positive and negative forces that played a role in the campaign. A series of newspaper articles during a campaign about a proposed, but unrelated, state tax increase is an example of what could be an unintended negative force.

In addition to conducting an impact analysis, marketers evaluate all of the research and operational steps carried out within the strategic marketing framework, as seen in Figure 10.1. Such an evaluation is essential for preparing the next cycle of events in the continuing process.

# Conclusion

Strategic marketing in education is an idea whose time has come. Strategies and marketing tools developed primarily for the private sector in most cases are applicable to the education sector. Passing new revenue-raising measures, gathering community support for a new job training program, introducing and supporting school "choice," or any of the multitude of changes associated with the restructuring movement in America can benefit by strategic marketing.

It is important to note that many, if not most, of the component parts of strategic marketing are already used in educational systems. Anyone who has been associated with public schools for long is familiar with activities-identified in the various strategic marketing steps such as needs assessment, community surveys, goal setting, program development, campaign planning, performance measurement, and so forth. Unfortunately, these tasks typically are carried out sporadically and reactively using a mass-marketing approach.

Thus, educators interested in introducing strategic marketing into their school systems probably have many of the component activities already in place. The challenge is to shape them into ongoing cycles of events where the separate parts reinforce the functioning of the whole.

## *Notes*

1. David Rados, *Marketing for Non-Profit Organizations* (Boston: Auburn House, 1981), p. 246.

2. National School Public Relations Association, *Marketing Your Schools* (Arlington, VA: NSPRA, 1987), p. 14.

3. Michael Fullan, *The Meaning of Educational Change* (New York: Teachers College Press, 1982).

4. National School Public Relations Association, p. 27–28.

5. Chris Barnes, *Practical Marketing for Schools* (Oxford, UK: Blackwell), 1993), pp. 72–78.

6. Don Bagin, Donald Gallagher, Leslie Kindred, *The School and Community Relations,* 5th ed. (Boston: Allyn and Bacon, 1994).

7. Philip Kotler and Karen Fox, *Strategic Marketing for Educational Institutions* (Englewood Cliffs, NJ: Prentice-Hall, 1985), p. 7.

8. Peter Obrien, "Strategic Planning and Management for Organizations," in *Educational Planning: Concepts, Strategies, Practices,* eds., Robert Carlson and Gary Ackerman (New York: Longman), p. 164.

9. John Holcomb, *Educational Marketing: A Business Approach to School-Community Relations* (New York: University Press of America, 1993), p. 13.

10. Morrow Stough, *Lowering Barriers to Home-School Communications* (San Diego, CA: San Diego State University, 1982), p. 7.

11. Stanley Elam, Lowell Rose and Alec Gallup, "The 25th Annual Gallup Poll of the Public's Attitudes Toward the Public Schools," *Phi Delta Kappan* 75 (1993): 138.

12. National Center for Educational Statistics, *Digest of Education Statistics: 1993* (Washington, D.C.: U.S. Department of Education, 1993), p. 34.

13. Frederick Wirt and Michael Kirst, *The Politics of Education: Schools in Conflict* (Berkeley, CA: McCutchan, 1989).

14. Michael Newman, "New Jersey Voters Resoundingly Reject Property-Tax Hikes," *Education Week,* May 9, 1990.

15. Bruce Munro, "Parcel and Facility Tax Elections" (Sacramento, CA: School Services of California, 1993, unpublished report).

16. Newman.

17. National Center for Educational Statistics, p. 151.

18. Edith Rasell and Lawrence Mishel, "Shortchanging Education: How U.S. Spending on Grades K-12 Lags Behind Other Industrial Nations," *Briefing Paper* (Washington, D.C.: Economic Policy Institute, 1990), pp. 11–14.

19. The goal of the Bush Administration, "America 2000," and Clinton Administration's, "Goals 2000," that our K-12 students will be first in the world in mathematics and science by the year 2000, seems rather curious in view of the comparative level of international educational expenditures. The degree of challenge is underscored by the fact that American 13-year-olds in a recent International Assessment of Educational Progress test placed thirteenth in math and twelfth in science when compared with similar populations in 14 developed and developing nations. National Center for Educational Statistics, pp. 414 and 417.

20. Alec Gallup and David Clark, "The 19th Annual Gallup Poll of the Public's Attitudes Toward the Public Schools," *Phi Delta Kappan* 68 (1987): 29.

21. Elam, Rose and Gallup, pp. 139 and 143.

22. Anne Henderson, ed., *The Evidence Continues to Grow: Parent Involvement Improves Student Achievement* (Columbia, MD.: National Committee for Citizens in Education, 1987), p. 1.

23. David Clark, Linda Lotto and Martha McCarthy, "Factors Associated with Success in Urban Elementary Schools," *Phi Delta Kappan* (March 1980): 467–480.

24. M. Fantini, "Community Participation: Alternative Patterns and their Consequences on Educational Achievement" (Paper presented at the American Educational Research Association, 1980).

25. Henry Becker and Joyce Epstein, "Parent Involvement: A Survey of Teacher Practices," *The Elementary School Journal* 83 (1982): 85–102; Patricia Olmsted and Roberta Rubin, "Linking Parent Behaviors to Child Achievement," *Studies in Educational Evaluation* 8 (1982): 317–325.

26. Charles Benson, "Household Production of Human Capital: Time Uses of Parents and Children as Inputs," in *Financing Education: Overcoming Inefficiency and Inequity,* eds., W. W. McMahon and T. G. Geske (Urbana, IL: University of Illinois Press, 1982); Concha Delgado-Gaitan, *Literacy for Empowerment: The Role of Parents in Children's Education* (New York: The Falmer Press, 1990).

27. Edward Gotts and Richard Purness, "Communications: Key to School-Home Relations," in *Child Rearing in the Home and Schools,* eds., R. J. Griffore and R. P. Boger (New York: Plenum, 1986).

28. National Center for Educational Statistics, p. 83

29. Douglas Dalrymple and Leonard Parsons, *Marketing Management: Strategy and Cases,* 5th ed. (New York: Falmer, 1990).

30. Sara Lightfoot, "Toward Conflict and Resolution: Relationships Between Families and Schools," *Theory Into Practice* 20 (1981): 97–104.

31. Sara Lightfoot, *Worlds Apart: Relationships Between Families and Schools* (New York: Basic Books, 1978), p. 28.

32. Joyce Epstein, "Parents' Reactions to Teacher Practices of Parent Involvement," *The Elementary School Journal* 86 (1986): 277–294.

33. Sanford Dornbush and Philip Ritter, "Parents of High School Students: A Neglected Resource," 66 *Educational Horizons* (1988): 77.

34. Don Davies, "Parent Involvement in the Public Schools: Opportunities for Administrators," *Education and Urban Society* 19 (1987): 147–163.

35. Lisa Jennings, "Tough State and Local Measures Seeking to Force Parental Control," *Education Week*, August 1, 1990.

36. Rados, p. 234.

37. Richard Carlson, "Household Production of Human Capital: Time Uses of Parents and Children as Inputs," in *Change Processes in the Public Schools*, eds. Richard CArlson, et al., (Eugene Oregon: University of Oregon, 1965), p. 6.

38. Rados, p. 15.

39. Kotler and Fox, p. 11.

40. Lightfoot, 1981.

41. Philip Kotler and Alan Andreasen, *Strategic Marketing for Nonprofit Organizations*, 3d ed. (Englewood Cliffs, NJ: Prentice-Hall, 1987), p. 41.

42. Julie Miller, "Bush Strategy Launches "Crusade" for Education" *Education Week*, April 24, 1991, p. 26.

43. Kotler and Andreasen, p. 36.

44. J. W. Getzels, "The Communities of Education," in *Families and Communities as Educators*, ed., H. J. Leichter (New York: Teachers College Press, 1979), p. 101.

45. Gordon Wise, Glenn Graham, and Duane Bachman, *Marketing Levies and Bond Issues for Public Schools* (Dayton, OH: Wright State University, 1986), p. 5

46. Rados, p. 2.

47. Kotler and Andreasen, p. 120.

48. Kotler and Andreasen, p. 120.

49. Jeanne Magmer and Ronald Russell, eds., *Building-Level PR Programs* (Arlington, VA: National School Public Relations Association, 1980), p. 6.

50. Lynne Stamoulis, "Market Segmentation and the Private School" (Dissertation, University of Washington, 1988).

51. Stough, p. 14.

52. James Swinehart, "Evaluating Public Relations," *Public Relations Journal* 25 (1979): 17.

53. National School Public Relations Association, p. 17.

54. Children's Defense Fund, *Latino Youths at a Crossroads* (Washington, D.C.: CDF, 1990), p. 3.

55. Jack McKillip, *Need Analysis: Tools for the Human Services and Education* (Newbury Park, CA: Sage, 1987).

56. Richard Krueger, *Focus Groups: A Practical Guide for Applied Research* (Newbury Park, CA: Sage, 1988), p. 18.

57. Mark McElreath, "Public Relations Evaluation Research: Summary Statement," *Public Relations Review*, 3 (1977): 130.

58. Kotler and Andreasen, p. 161.

59. D. L. Stufflebeam, C. H. McCormic, R. O. Brinkerhoff, and C. O. Nelson, *Conducting Educational Needs Assessments* (Boston: Kluwer-Nijhoff, 1984), p. 3.

60. National School Public Relations Association, p. 18.

61. Kotler and Fox, p. 153.

62. Jerome McCarthy, *Basic Marketing: A Managerial Approach* (Homewood, IL, Irwin, 1960).

63. Isobel Pfeiffer and Jane Dunlap, "Advertising Practice to Improve School-Community Relations," *NASSP Bulletin* 72 (1988): 15.

64. Don Bagin, "Marketing Your Program," *Community Eduction Journal* (April 1981): 14.

65. National School Public Relations Association, p. 23.

66.  Kotler and Fox, p. 280.

67.  O. W. Baskin and C. E. Aronoff, *Public Relations: The Profession and the Practice,* 2d ed. (Dubuque, IA: Brown, 1983), pp. 174–175.

68.  Baskin and Arnoff, p. 177.

Parts of this chapter were adapted from the following publications: E. Mark Hanson, "Educational Marketing and the Public Schools: Policies, Practices, and Problems," *Educational Policy,* Vol. 6, No. 1 (1992): 19–34. With permission of Corwin Press; E. Mark Hanson and Walter Henry, "Strategic Marketing and Educational Systems," *National Association for Secondary School Principals Bulletin,* Vol. 77, No. 556 (1993): 79–88. With permission of the NASSP; also, excerpts from *School Organisation,* Vol. 12, No. 3 (1992): 255–267. With permission of Carfax Publishing Co., Abingdon, Oxfordshire OX143UE, United Kingdom.

# Chapter 11

# Conflict and Stress in Education

For many educators who spend their days in schools—facing the challenges of everything from intellectual inelasticity to kids with "industrial strength" mouths—riding the tiger is by no means satisfying or easy. Yet there are those who respond to those same situations with poise, talent, and the requisite élan. How is this possible?

As is the case with all complex organizations, educational systems manufacture the ingredients of conflict and stress. An analysis of this manufacturing process is the focus of this chapter. The chapter objectives are to respond to the following questions: First, what are the types, causes, and consequences of conflict and stress? Second, how can conflict and stress in educational systems be managed effectively?

The natural ingredients that comprise the educational system carry with them the characteristics of a pressure-packed environment. For school administrators the hours are long, approximately 53 hours per week for secondary school principals and 50 hours for elementary principals. The job is characterized by "a high volume of work completed at an unrelenting pace, variety, brevity, and fragmentation of tasks."[1]

The work experiences can range from intense challenges featuring traumatic adrenaline rushes to mindless rituals and syncopated drudgery. The problems associated with stress can be found at both ends of the scale. At the lower end, Cedoline points out that the administrator's job has been increasingly encumbered by "paper mountaineering." That is, filling out enormous numbers of forms and reports that are frequently complex, confusing, and often contradictory. "It has been estimated that paperwork has increased by 400–600 percent since 1970."[2]

At the other end of the scale, outright violence in recent years has cast a frightening chill over the profession. Gangs, drugs, and even classroom shootings have injected outright fear in schools of numerous distressed regions of the country. Administrators and teachers frequently express feelings of serious concern. Almost one-third of elementary and secondary school teachers stated in a 1990–91 survey that "if I had the chance to exchange my job as a teacher for another kind of job, I would."[3]

The degree of concern the public feels is also an issue. When asked to grade their *local* public schools as part of a Gallup Poll survey, 56 percent of the parents *with children* in school gave generally favorable ratings of A or B. Forty-four percent of adults *without children in local schools* graded them A or B. However, the bottom seemed to drop out as only 19 percent of public school parents graded the *nation's* public schools at A or B. Adults without children in school graded them only marginally better at 20 percent A or B.[4]

Defining conflict and stress is a useful place at which to begin a discussion of the issues involved. "Conflict is defined as an 'interactive state' manifested in incompatibility, disagreement, or difference within or between social entities" such as individuals, groups, or organizations.[5] The sources of the conflict usually are rooted in incompatible goals, cognitions (e.g., different viewpoints), or emotions (e.g., differing loyalties).[6]

Is conflict real? Allport has pointed out that "the way a [person] defines his [or her] situation constitutes for him [or her] its reality."[7] Conflict, therefore, like power or communication, is not a tangible or objective entity. Conflict is subject to the interpretation of the minds of those who are party to it. However, the outcomes of conflict, such as anger and fighting or creative planning and relationship building, are objective and real. "More and more social scientists are coming to realize—and to demonstrate—that conflict itself is no evil, but rather a phenomenon that can have constructive or destructive effects depending upon its management."[8]

While *conflict* can occur within and between groups and organizations, *stress* occurs within the individual. *Stress* can be defined as a lack of harmony between workers and their work environment. Stress can be a healthy stimulus to creative acts, or can become a burden with harmful effects. Litt and Turk define *teacher stress* as "the experience by teachers of unpleasant, negative emotions and distress that exist when the problems confronting teachers threaten their well-being, and surpass their ability to resolve these problems."[9]

The harmful types of stress often are referred to as *distress* or *strain* because of their negative psychological and physiological responses. Studying the links between the state of mind and the state of body has become an increasingly important interdisciplinary research effort, bringing together social scientists and medical researchers who usually do not meet. A new discipline called *psychoneuroimmunology (PNI)* is the emergent leader in this research domain.

It is important to note that conflict and stress are not constants but have variable thresholds depending on the circumstances and the social units involved. For example, up to a certain point, an annoying critic might be passed off as just stupid. After all, being stupid has never been against the law in America. However, the growing tension may reach a point where open conflict appears unavoidable. That conflict threshold varies with people, situations, and perceptions of situations.

## Levels and Sources of Conflict

Conflict arises whenever perceived or real interests collide. The collision can result from a divergence in organizational goals, personal ambitions, group loyalties, departmental budget demands on scarce resources, ethnic expectations and demands, and so forth. Conflict, therefore, comes from a multitude of sources and is found at personal and organizational levels.[10]

### Conflict Characteristics

Figure 11.1 illustrates that conflict and stress can result from (1) interactions within and between *formal* organizational levels, (2) interactions within and between *informal* organizational levels, and (3) interaction between *formal and informal* organizational levels.

1. *Intrarole conflict:* An organization establishes understandable and predictable behavior by structuring itself into roles, each with a set of activities. Each role, such as that of principal, interacts with a cluster of other roles, or a role set. "Principals, as middle managers, must simultaneously manage at least four sets of relationships: upward with their superiors, downward with subordinates, laterally with other principals, and externally with parents and other community and business groups."[11] The greater the complexity and specialization, the greater the degree of interdependence and need for role conformity. Teachers, for example, must predictably abide by the rules governing standardized testing procedures if valid comparative results are to be produced. *Role expectations* are the prescriptions for actions that members of a role set hold for one another.[12]

Intrarole conflict results when various members in a role set simultaneously and legitimately make differing demands on a single role. For example, a school district curriculum coordinator feels intrarole conflict when the teachers claim that instructional materials are too difficult for grade level, some board of education members argue those same materials are too easy, minority-group parents campaign that they ignore the accomplishments of distinct ethnic groups, and coaches pressure for retesting policies for athletes who could earn college scholarships and improve their situations in life.

The principal cause of intrarole conflict is *role ambiguity,* or "the focal person's perception of a lack of clear, consistent information about the job's required activities and tasks."[13] Also, unrealistic job expectations leading to *role overload,* or too much work, are major contributors.[14]

2. *Interrole conflict:* This type of conflict is defined as "the simultaneous occurrence of two (or more) sets of pressures such that compliance with one would make more difficult compliance with the other."[15] It typically occurs when one individual holds several different roles that make competing demands. For example, a school district superintendent on a given Thursday evening may look at his calendar and realize that as a member of the mayor's bowling team he should be bowling, as a tenor in the

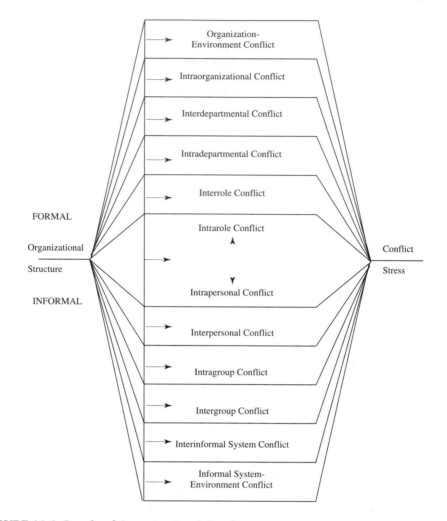

FIGURE 11.1  Levels of Organizational Conflict

church choir he should be at practice, as a father he should attend his son's Boy Scout award ceremony, and as a superintendent he should give a speech at a party for a retiring teacher.

3. *Intradepartmental conflict:* When members of the same formal specialty unit cannot agree on an important issue, intradepartmental conflict often results. For example, when the mathematics teachers cannot agree on whether to introduce computers into the classroom instructional process, the outcome can be considerable turbulence. The situation is complicated by the fact that both positions are correct, as seen from differing viewpoints.

4. *Interdepartmental conflict:* I witnessed this kind of conflict when on several occasions the football coach and the band leader both scheduled (and attempted

to use) the football field at the same time. Interestingly enough, the groundskeeper often had the sprinklers going at the times in question. The essence of the conflicts involved each of two formal units attempting to place its own goals and interests ahead of those of the other.

5. *Intraorganizational conflict:* This form of conflict is often characterized by clashes that transcend hierarchical levels, such as teachers complaining to the superintendent about unrealistic demands on their time or principals getting upset by the central office's "pull-out" policy for students in special programs. Perceived unfair work distribution and unfair deadlines are also major sources of this type of conflict.

6. *Organization-environment conflict:* Demands, pressures, or expectations emanating from outside the educational system in an attempt to influence policy or outcome typically cause this form of conflict. It can range from unannounced visitors wandering the school grounds to an attempt by a national organization to distribute birth control information to students.

7. *Intrapersonal conflict:* "Trouble is caused by troublemakers" is a view held by many generations of educators. Troublemakers are increasingly being seen as disturbed people who have not developed satisfying and healthy interaction patterns with society.[16] In other words, their person-environment fit is not satisfactory and the behavioral outcomes spell trouble for themselves and others.

In the context of school administrators, intrapersonal conflict often is caused by such things as poor time management, underestimation or overestimation of skills, and assigned tasks that do not match goals, interests, values, or abilities.[17] Additional causes are the inability to say no to requests, a lack of self-confidence, and the perception of "lack of control (locus of control) and limited requisite authority (powerlessness) to handle assigned organizational responsibilities."[18] All of these issues are complicated by doubts about how others evaluate us.

8. *Interpersonal conflict:* This form of conflict involves some form of clash stemming from the personal motives of those involved. Douglas Yates writes about famous conflict situations, such as the interpersonal conflict between Eisenhower's generals during World War II.[19]

> [Eisenhower knew] that his key subordinates were locked in one kind or other of personal and bureaucratic rivalry. In particular, he knew that the infantryman Bradley tended to distrust the cavalryman Patton for reasons of institutional bias and pride. Patton, who liked to do things fast, viewed Bradley as an indecisive plodder, referring to him as Omar "the tent maker." And both shared varying degrees of animosity for Montgomery, whom they viewed as intolerably arrogant and so concerned with chalking up personal victories, as the hero of El Alamein, that he would not move ahead until the enemy had virtually shown a white flag in advance. It was clear to Eisenhower throughout that "doing something to satisfy Montgomery might make Patton angry; a decision that pleased Marshall would leave Brook unhappy; bowing to the President's wishes could mean opposing the Prime Minister."[20]

9. *Intragroup conflict:* Perhaps the classic situation of intragroup conflict in education develops when two members, perhaps normally good friends, find themselves seeking promotion to a single job. The relationship of these two individuals can often

become troubled and perhaps embittered. The group itself can become conflictual if and when the various members begin to join the ranks in support of one candidate or the other.

10. *Intergroup conflict:* This form of conflict is witnessed at all levels of the educational system. On the school grounds, the "hawks" challenge the "choppers"; during faculty meetings, the "old guard" goes head-to-head with the "young Turks"; and in the central office, the management bargaining team lines up against the union team.

11. *Interinformal system conflict:* General Eisenhower always seemed embroiled in problems of this type. Yates writes that the general always attempted to maintain a spirit of Allied cooperation and "insisted that Yank-baiting and Limey-baiting would not be tolerated at his headquarters."[21] The Allied commander was completely serious. On one occasion when "he heard an officer refer to another staff officer as 'that British sonofabitch' he ordered the man sent home, not for the noun but for the adjective."[22] In education, school rivalries and struggles between districts over proposed unification plans and adjustments to school boundaries can result in this form of conflict.

12. *Informal system—environmental conflict:* All informal levels can conflict with the pressures from the external environment, although the most predominant come at the intrapersonal level. Virtually all administrators struggle with pressure from their families for more quality time at home; overcommitment to community service; or the rising cost of living.

In sum, there are numerous levels that can and do support the introduction of conflict into the educational system. As will be pointed out later, there are both advantages and disadvantages to having numerous points of entry.

## Structure and Process Conflict Models

In examining the research literature, Thomas identified two ways that researchers typically try to understand the conflict phenomena. He identifies them as structural and process models.[23]

The *process model* "focuses upon the *sequence of events* which transpire within a conflict episode, and is particularly useful when one is faced with the need to understand and intervene directly into the stream of events of an ongoing episode."[24] It involves tracing the internal dynamics of the events by plotting and recording the impacts in kind and degree that each event has on those succeeding.

For example, there is the case when teachers protest to their principal that a new vice principal is being overly assertive in classroom supervision and breaching a long-standing value of teacher autonomy. The vice principal strikes back, saying that classroom supervision is his proper role and that the teachers' performances do not meet his standards. The teachers retort, in exchanges that become more heated, that his standards were set at another school and are inconsistent with traditions of academic freedom in this school. And so it goes until the entire episode reaches the desk of the superintendent, or perhaps the newspapers, a few weeks later.

The *structural model* "focuses upon the *conditions* which shape conflict behavior in a relationship, and is useful in restructuring a situation to facilitate desired kinds of behavior patterns."[25] The parameters that energize conflict situations usually are fixed or slow to change, such as the characteristics of formal organizational roles or informal group membership.

The triggers of the conflict typically are built right into the structure, such as restrictive rules, social pressures, biased promotion procedures, and unbalanced incentives. Many structural conflicts are almost natural to the system, such as union and management, the simultaneous demands for classroom discipline and intellectual creativity, the coaches who want sixth-period athletes excused for extra practice and the teachers who want those students in class, and so on.

The outcome and conflict aftermath are also important to study and understand. When the degree of conflict finally is reduced to a level no longer considered disruptive or perhaps is resolved, the outcome often includes residual baggage. A sense of success and hopeful expectation can be a foundation upon which future understandings can be based, while a sense of frustration and mistrust can be the stuff of new conflicts later down the line.

Boulding calls lingering, unresolved, and long-hidden problems, *conflict traps.*[26] These traps can be triggered by insignificant issues seemingly unrelated to anything, but they can bring forth strong, even explosive reactions. The decision to add another section of a history class, for example, may trigger long-hidden resentment in the vocational education area that favoritism plays an important part in the school's decision-making process.

## Reactions to Conflict and Stress

Out of conflict comes stress, a condition that in some circumstances can be particularly debilitating. Kahn et al. point out that from the beginning of our lives, our self-identity is shaped by the manner in which people in our environment interact with us. The process of self-identity is continual: Each new life experience is somehow integrated into the established sense of self. "Conditions of conflict and ambiguity, therefore, are not merely irritating; in persistent and extreme form they are identity destroying."[27]

In rank order, Cedoline identifies major stressors cited by administrators.[28] (Very similar lists of stressors were found by Gordon[29] and Gmelch[30] in their studies of educational leaders.) Generic categorical descriptors are identified in parentheses.

1. Lack of sufficient resources, such as supplies, fiscal aid, help with evaluation, personnel, inservice funding, and so forth (control over one's destiny; training deficits).
2. Lack of support from superiors and the public (communication/feedback).
3. Quantity of work (work overload).
4. Paperwork (work overload).
5. Collective bargaining (communication/feedback; work overload).

6. Lack of clear direction of role from school board and superintendent (role conflict/ambiguity).
7. Federal and state laws (control over one's destiny).
8. Lacking control of students, teachers, and schools (control over one's destiny).
9. Responsibility for child's total needs and assumption of many parental roles (work overload; contact overload; role conflict/ambiguity).
10. Parent and community relationships and pressures (contact overload).

Our reactions to stressors have a direct impact on performance, as the next section will point out.

## Stress and Performance

Figure 11.2 illustrates a bell-shaped stress and performance curve developed by Gmelch.[31] Low to high ranges relate to stress on the horizontal axis and performance on the vertical axis. The performance curve runs through zones: understimulation, optimum stimulation, and overstimulation. The point is that too much stress or not enough stress detract from the psychological and physiological balance is essential to enjoying our work and performing at peak levels. High-quality performance can be conceived of as a finely tuned violin string. Too loose and it groans; too tight and it screeches; just the right stretch and it sings.

As illustrated in the model, death can be found at both extremes of the horizontal lifeline. Death from stress, or lack of such, need not come in the physical variety, as in giving up your immortal soul (although dying for your job is now almost as popular as dying for your country once was). Being physically alive but professionally dead is not altogether uncommon these days. This condition is described in a variety of ways, such as "retired in place" or "institutionally comatose."

Those toiling in the *understimulation zone* are inflicted with the "trauma of uneventfulness," as Gmelch puts it.

> People resting here are underchallenged and suffer from boredom, fatigue, frustration, and dissatisfaction. Educators resting here too long literally rust out from sitting in the same job without periods of variety, change, or stimulation to keep their motivation high. Either their skills or jobs have become obsolete or routine, leaving them with little or nothing to do that requires excitement or challenge.[32]

At the other end of the bell curve is the *overstimulation zone* where people are daily hammered by the demands of work. It becomes a less and less meaningful aspect of their lives. The consequence of continuous and excessive stress is *burnout*. Spaniol and Caputo view burnout as a three-state phenomena, not unlike the trauma of a burn.[33]

First-degree burnout is usually a mild, short-lived bout with anxiety, fatigue, worry, and frustration. A new day, a bit of reflective thought, or perhaps an afternoon of fishing (a good antidote for almost anything) will reinvigorate body and soul. The second-degree bout is longer and more intense, accompanied by mood changes; an increasingly

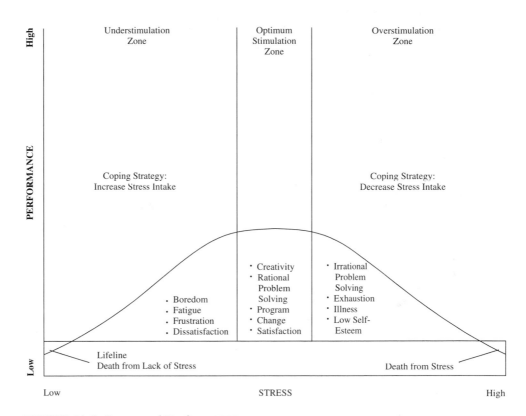

FIGURE 11.2  Stress and Performance
From Walter Gmelch, *Beyond Stress in Effective Management* (New York: Wiley, 1982), p. 29. Reprinted with permission.

cynical attitude toward the job, subordinates, and superiors; difficulty in achieving restful sleep; and persistent irritability.

Third-degree burnout is continuous, physically and psychologically debilitating, compounded by depression, a low sense of self-esteem, negative feelings, and often withdrawal from work and social contact in personal relationships. Burnout has physical, intellectual, and social manifestations. Glicken and Janka write:

> The burned-out individual is smoldering in place, riddled with stress and dissatisfaction and responding with an ever-intensifying loss of energy and interest. The burned-up individual has progressed to such a degree of lethargy and immobilization that he or she is generally destined for a radical event, such as mental or physical illness, sudden resignation, or involuntary termination.[34]

The conditions creating a stressful environment are present in most school systems, certainly some more than others. The long hours, overcrowded space, upset parents, limited resources, potential for physical violence, and so forth go with the job for most educators. The tragedy is that like most formal organizations, educational systems typically ignore the impact that stress has on administrators and teachers, even when it reaches the second- and third-degree ranges.

The sad fact is that dysfunctional stress usually is considered a personal problem for which those suffering must find their own way out. Few provisions are made other than an allotment of sick days, transfers, and discussions with untrained colleagues or supervisors (a talk with the principal or superintendent perhaps). The situation is complicated by the fact that many educators with years of training and experience behind them, do not have the option to quit. As they look around, they see no place to go.[35] Consequently, they must suffer in place.

The *optimum stimulation zone* illustrated in Figure 11.2 represents the violin string finely tuned to produce at its best. Sufficient stress is present to heighten awareness, clear the senses, focus the mind, and make the adrenalin flow. Work tends to be challenging and satisfying. Problems are viewed as obstacles that can be overcome while providing opportunities to strengthen, perhaps even change, the educational system. The optimum stimulation zone maintains neither too much stress (so as to be debilitating) nor insufficient stress (so as to be unmotivating). Like an athlete in training, the trick is to know where you are on the performance curve and what you have to do to maintain yourself at peak levels through differing situations over extended periods of time.

Organizational conflict and performance functions in a similar fashion to individual stress and performance. "Organizational conflict as it stands now," Rahim writes, "is considered as legitimate, inevitable, and even a positive indicator of effective organizational management. It is now recognized that conflict within certain limits is essential to productivity."[36] Conflict and attempts toward its resolution are seen as perhaps the most powerful force for bringing about changes in patterns of organizational behavior, a subject of the next section.

## Conflict Analysis

Conflict, in varying degrees and situations, is present in all organizations. When decisions must be made to the satisfaction of some and not to others, conflict will be present or perhaps lurking around the corner. Neither a natural enemy nor inherently bad, conflict should not be repressed or fueled. Rather, it should be managed.

Conflict *anticipation* and *detection* are the first two phases of good conflict management. By anticipating a probability of conflict, such as upheaval over the necessary but last-minute shifting of teaching assignments, actions can be taken to keep tensions from expanding to other areas of the school and its programs. Anticipation, *proaction* rather than *reaction,* is the intended strategy.

Searching for and analyzing the underlying dynamics of conflict are essential because the causes might not be what they seem on the surface. A probing analysis would try to determine if contributing causes were structural or episodic. Structural causes, such as management and union or line and staff, suggest that natural tensions have surfaced among any of the formal and/or informal systems seen in Figure 11.2. Episodic conflict is unique to a specific situation, as when various people compete for the same job or promote competing alternatives.

Nonroutinized, episodic conflict that has political overtones and comes from the surrounding community (e.g., special interests of developers) can be disruptive, especially at the top, because as Zeigler, Kehoe, and Reisman point out:

> Superintendents rely on expertise rather than more traditional political skills, the power base of the superintendent is destroyed when this resource is declared inapplicable. It is no surprise that issues of episodic conflict unresolvable by technical skills (such as busing and school closures made necessary by declining enrollments) are troublesome to superintendents.[37]

An effective diagnosis can determine and place in perspective a number of underlying issues that compound the problem and must affect the strategy selected. Such complicating, underlying issues are, for example, when stakes are perceived as high, jobs are on the line, the issue is a matter of principle, emotions are high, many people are involved, it is a zero-sum game, leadership is weak, the parties are fractionalized or amorphous, or loyalty to the organization is questionable.[38]

## Conflict Management

Conflict is managed when it no longer interferes with the ongoing activities of the parties involved. "Conflict management is the process of removing cognitive barriers to agreement."[39] Such agreement does not suggest that the pressures creating the conflict have gone away. However, sufficient commitment to a course of action has allowed the positive aspects of *collaboration* to overcome the restraining aspects of *conflict.*

Depending on the findings of the diagnosis, conflict management techniques often focus on changing structure, changing process, or both. Milstein, Lusthaus, and Lusthaus point out that educators often attempt to change structures by, for example, inviting leaders of the teacher union to join in policy decisions, establishing parent advisory committees on important topics, decentralizing decision making, or creating a limited enrollment, nontraditional academic program within a traditional school.[40]

Sometimes structural modifications are not very creative, and the response to conflict is simply more rules and hardening of the role structure. Such efforts can improve the situation outwardly (a school can become a prison) but not without consequences. Sanford writes that "the hardening of the role structure which is an organization's best defense against the inroads of individual irrationality gives equal protection against failure and against success."[41]

### Tactics of Conflict Management

*Expanding Resources*     The tactics selected to manage conflict depend on the force driving the conflict. One of the most common forces is scarce resources. The skillful management of scarce resources and the ability to *expand the resource base* whenever possible are important to management. Yates reports on General Eisenhower's skill at managing the delicate resource-balancing act.

Throughout the war, Bradley, Patton, and Montgomery constantly badgered the supreme commander with demands for resources or, as in the case of Patton, for permission to head east to Berlin. Eisenhower handled his warring lieutenants in somewhat the fashion of a manager making salary increases. He sought to take advantage of opportunities where added resources could spur further military success, at the same time honoring the tacit constraint that he could not let any commander feel that he was receiving no support or what were subjectively perceived as intolerable low levels of support.[42]

*Appeals System*    Establishing an appeals system that provides the right of formal redress to a superior in the organization is an important method of treating conflict associated with disputes at lower hierarchical levels. The higher authority studies the situation and enforces a solution—something the disputants cannot do on their own. Sometimes the bureaucratic constraints of the hierarchy or perceived favoritism can get in the way of formal appeals, so some institutions adopt an ombudsman approach—a trained, impartial specialist to arbitrate differences or find a solution in some other manner.

*Changing Interaction Patterns*    Sometimes the most appropriate tactic involves the degree of interaction between the conflicting parties. If the basis of the conflict is lack of trust or suspicion of motives, an effective approach is often to bring the parties together and let them get to know each other. If, on the other hand, the conflict is rooted in differences in values or principles, increased interaction will most likely exacerbate the situation. In this instance, separating the parties, such as not appointing them to the same committees, can be helpful.

*Modifying Reward Systems*    If inequity in the intrinsic or extrinsic reward system is at the foundation of conflict, adjustments in the reward structure should make a difference. Whenever possible, eliminate zero-sum rewards (for every winner, there is a loser), reward performance as well as rank, and establish evaluations that reward "preventive contributions" rather than "success in finding errors."[43]

*Mergers*    When units (e.g., departments, special programs) conflict because of struggles for policy control or resources, most likely they are operating in their own self-interest. If merged, they may identify with the enlarged unit and struggle for the common good. Breaking up a unit that has intense internal conflicts may at times be the answer to facilitating smoother working relationships.

*Role Clarification*    In order to decrease task ambiguity, there are various role clarification procedures, such as the job expectation technique (JET) and the role analysis technique (RAT). Both approaches emphasize gathering the people who interact with a particular role and defining their responsibilities and duties through dialogue and debate.[44]

*Third-Party Consultation*    A neutral third party can often establish the confidence, atmosphere of goodwill, and emotional support to bring a sense of rationality that is otherwise missing in the decision-making process. The third party must establish that all parties have reasons to resolve the conflict, that the power controlling the situation is essentially equal on all parts, and that everyone must be prepared to compromise.

*Conflict "Sponge"*     At times, for the good of order, managers will attempt to redirect the tensions and conflictive behaviors toward themselves, thus clearing the atmosphere and enabling more productive actions to take place at lower levels. When managers assume responsibility for a troublesome event that took place somewhere in the system, the outcome redirects the heat in their own direction.

Becoming a conflict "sponge" is not easy on body and soul. Yates writes that "in terms of burdens and frustrations, there is no doubt that Eisenhower had to absorb a great deal of punishment in the course of managing his competitive policy debate and keeping all his players functional. Sheer physical fatigue became a serious problem for Eisenhower and led Marshall to order his general home for a rest shortly before the invasion."[45]

## *A Model of Conflict Management*

Approaches to conflict management are often portrayed on a continuum with *flight* ("I'm catching the first bus out of town!") and *fight* ("Fire the bastard!") at the

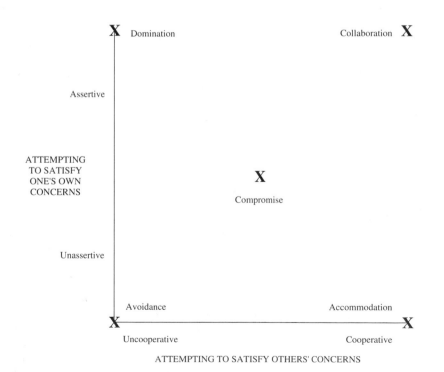

FIGURE 11.3  Conflict Management Strategies
Adapted from Kenneth Thomas, "Conflict and Conflict Management," in *Handbook of Industrial and Organizational Psychology,* Marvin Dunnette, ed. (New York: Wiley, 1976), p. 900. Reprinted with permission.

extremes. Figure 11.3 represents a seminal work by Kenneth Thomas that illustrates a greater, more balanced range of conflict responses. The model represents the degree to which managers desire to satisfy their own concerns and the degree to which they desire to satisfy the concerns of others.

> *Avoidance* often is a form of flight that can suggest indifference, evasion, withdrawal, or isolation. Being unassertive and uncooperative can also represent a delay tactic, hoping that time and events will treat the problem.
> *Domination* frequently means a desire to win at the other's expense. In this context, it is a win-lose power struggle. The opinions and interests of others are of little interest.
> *Accommodation* can be appeasement or submission to others at one's own expense. Under some conditions, it can also represent generosity. Under others, it might mean conserving energy and resources by giving up a few battles in order to win the war.
> *Compromise* reflects splitting the difference or giving up something to get something. When there is not enough to go around, half a loaf usually is better than none.
> *Collaboration* represents a desire to integrate and fully satisfy the interests of both parties. Neither party desires to acquire the advantage over the other. Thus, it is a mutually beneficial stance based on trust and problem solving so that everyone wins.

When examining various approaches to conflict management, situational *contingency theory* becomes applicable. Derr reminds us that it is essential for managers to be selective in matching the characteristics of specific situations with the various strategies available.[46] As situations change, the most appropriate strategy changes. None is appropriate for every situation, even collaboration. Collaboration often represents an ideal condition not reflected in the bull pit where we sometimes find ourselves. Some critical conditions affecting strategy choices include time available, existence of emergency conditions, emotional and ego involvement, resources already invested, linkages with other external systems, frequency with which the choices arise, and the need to work with other parties after a choice is made.

## Stress Management

Albrecht writes that his general hypothesis about stress and behavior is:"A person will act in ways that help reduce the unpleasant and uncomfortable physical feelings caused by stress, within the constraints of his [or her] value system and . . . beliefs."[47] My own corollary to this hypothesis is that negative stress, like greed, has a way of stretching value systems.

People react to personal stress in many ways: Some tie on their jogging shoes and run through the neighborhood, others blur out the world through drink or pharmaceutical elixirs, and still others watch "Rush Limbaugh" on TV. From self-development to self-destruction, the range of behaviors in reaction to stress appears almost limitless.

The place to begin in stress management is diagnosing the situation. Unfortunately, we are not very objective about ourselves, thus making accurate self-diagnosis difficult. Making the effort, however, is unavoidable. The diagnosis should attempt to establish the perspective that helps shape countermeasures. For example:

1. Does the source of the stress stem from a past, present, or future situation or event?
2. Does the stress source fit into a category, such as medical, job-related, financial, or social?
3. Who is involved? self? family? friends? colleagues? the IRS?
4. Have other people I know faced similar situations? How did they come out? What actions did they take?
5. What is the worst-case scenario? life threatening? lose your job? family break-up? ego tweaked?
6. What is the best-case scenario? never happen?
7. Is there any preparation that can be made now to reduce the likelihood of a worst-case outcome?

Reality testing the conclusions with someone trusted is important as a means to critique the personal assessment. All this assumes that the entire context of concerns and pressures is within the scope of coping behavior. If not, seeking professional help is certainly warranted and should never be considered a sign of weakness. Rather, it is a sign of strength.

Understanding the conditions generating the stress facilitates developing a stress management program. At the organizational level, Koff et al. argue that the best way to be proactive is to develop effective and efficient organizational and planning procedures that reduce the chances of stressful situations taking hold.[48] Planning for the unknown is always difficult. Plugging all the leaks possible in advance, however, does enhance the chances of survival if the big wave hits.

Reducing the level of stress can be achieved by seeking the optimal fit between the characteristics of the individual, the requirements of the job, and the type of organizational structure. The tighter the fit, the less chance for dysfunctional stress.[49] When additional adjustments in the person-job fit are no longer possible, defensive coping mechanisms must be developed. When the person-job fit is not good and extensive coping mechanisms are required for an extended time, the consequences can be damaging to physical and psychological health.

At the personal level, stress often is transmitted by Typhoid Mary-type carriers. (She was the noted New York waitress who at the turn of the century unknowingly infected many patrons with typhoid at a restaurant.) All organizations, including educational systems, have stress carriers—perhaps a vice principal who is always handing out time-consuming papers to fill out, a superintendent who constantly criticizes teachers, a group of parents that publicly demands that the football coach be fired, or board members that incessantly insist that *McGuffey Readers* be reintroduced into the curriculum. Then there is the famous Massachusetts case where a stress-carrying principal scares the teachers once a month during the full moon when he shows up either as a vampire, a werewolf, or a Republican.

One important behavior in learning to deal with stress carriers is learning to say no. Turning down a superior or anyone who wants a piece of your time is not always easy. However, pointing out the nature of the workload, the availability of time, and what will necessarily have to be put aside frequently makes a convincing argument.

Teachers who are looking for a way to deal with stress carriers might consider approaching their local zoo. As reported in *The Cincinnati Post:*

> The folks in the Cincinnati Zoo are giving workers a chance to celebrate Boss' Day by likening their boss to an animal for a $5 nomination fee. "It struck me one day reading through the list of animals at the zoo that they reminded me incredibly of some of the bosses I've known and loved," said . . . the zoo's associate director for annual giving.
>
> Disgruntled employees can choose from the following: striped skunk, bearded pig, red-necked ostrich, blood-sucking assassin bug, spiny toad, cock-of-the-rock, or hissing cockroach. Those feeling magnanimous can opt for a golden eagle or a king cheetah. The boss with the most nominations will be recognized publicly with a certificate naming him or her as the appropriate zoo animal—signed only by the people at the zoo.
>
> "The blood-sucking assassin bug is clearly the favorite at this point," said (the zoo official), "followed closely by the striped skunk." (Actually, everyone in the office likes the big ape.)[50]

For those feeling tensions and pressures, Albrecht argues that "a great deal of today's stress is avoidable," and that "most stress is self-induced." He proposed the development of three antistress skills: physical relaxation, self-management, and life-style management.[51]

1. *Physical relaxation* enables the individual to deactivate the body's response to stressful conditions and substitute a physiologically calming response. A jog around the park, a switch in tasks from people contact to paper work, or using deep-relaxing, biofeedback techniques often can help. Positive self-indulgence, such as going to the opera or eating a meal at a terrific restaurant, can often change a negative mood.

2. *Self-management* is a slightly longer timeframe and involves the daily monitoring of stress levels and learning to respond calmly to provocative situations. Breaking routines, perhaps by switching classes or committees for a time, will introduce different types of stimulation. It may also remove one from constant contact with a stress carrier.

3. *Lifestyle management* requires effort toward balancing stresses and rewards through life decisions about priorities, time utilization, and long-range goals. Taking time out from a career, such as going back to school or taking a year's leave of absence to work at another job, can help balance life forces.

## A Note of Caution

Is the educational institution really stressed to the point of near exhaustion? Are most administrators barely coping in roles filled with ambiguity and out of control? A small but growing body of literature suggests not. These studies argue that typically the administrator role is robust, challenging, meaningful, and action packed.[52] The image of frustration, anxiety, and burnout is derived from the folklore of anecdotal literature and wire service stories that spread around the country through an efficient communication system. Much of the negative anecdotal literature was produced by disaffected educators who attempted to generalize their personal experiences.[53] When comparing superintendents to city managers, Zeigler, Kehoe and Reisman write that

> the data seem to refute the beleaguered superintendent hypothesis. Superintendents spend significantly less time overall managing conflict than do city managers. Superintendents also spend substantially less time resolving conflict with their legislative bodies than do city managers. Likewise, superintendents report low levels of disagreement among the public significantly more often than do city managers. Also, when the public does get involved in conflicts regarding school matters, they tend to participate as individuals rather than as members of groups. The opposite is true for municipal matters.[54]

In their study of 129 elementary and secondary school principals, Eisenhauer, Willower, and Licata found that they reported the role as robust, challenging, and exciting. They generally like their jobs.[55]

Using Mintzberg's[56] structured observation approach to studying administrator work behavior, Kmetz and Willower[57] studied five elementary school principals and Martin and Willower studied five high school principals.[58] At both levels, it was concluded that although the principalship was fast paced and complex, involved periodic crises and conflicts, and featured long hours, those holding the job could not be considered beleaguered. Typically, they enjoyed their work, were able to cope with the turbulence, and took obvious pride in their schools. Rather than being burned out, they appeared enthusiastic.

Farkas found in his study of 302 elementary and secondary principals that as a group they perceived a low level of stress, a high locus of control, and were fundamentally in control of future events. Also, they possess sufficient decision-making authority to carry out the responsibilities of their jobs. Gender also made a difference. As a group, female principals felt lower levels of stress than their male counterparts.[59]

Concluding a review of this "doing just fine, thank you" literature, Milstein and Farkas write:

> The profession more closely approximates a low level occupational stress group than a high level occupational stress group. Role clarity, authority, and the ability to plan do not seem to be issues for educators. Further, while teachers and administrators may not always see themselves as being at the center of the information network, they do perceive that they can obtain information required to do their jobs. Finally, educators many of whom have been teaching and/or administering for more than a decade, do not seem to feel blocked in their careers. They may not see much room for advancement, but most appear to have made peace with themselves about the status of their professional lives.[60]

Thus, there is a strand of literature that casts encouraging light over the less-than-encouraging diagnosis often associated with the job of school administrator. Hopefully, additional research will bring insight into how the role can be strengthened even further.

### Conflict and the Conceptual Models

Classical organization theorists believed that conflict produced inefficiency and therefore was undesirable, detrimental to the organization, and should be eliminated, or at least minimized to the extent possible.

Conflict was seen as created by troublemakers and prima donnas who refused to go through channels or insisted on rocking the boat. When conflict existed, the leadership was viewed as weak and at fault.

The prescription for eliminating conflict was enhanced control through, for example, stronger leadership, firing the malcontents, tighter rules, clearer role definitions, heightened rewards and punishments, and more precise division of authority. Stress, to the extent that it was understood, was seen as a personal problem and not the proper concern of the organization. Individual workers had to learn to handle their own stress.

Views toward conflict changed with the emergence of social systems and open system theory. Rahim observes that

> organizational conflict as it stands now is considered as legitimate, inevitable, and even a positive indicator of effective organizational management. It is now recognized that conflict within certain limits is essential to productivity. However, conflict can be functional to the extent to which it results in the creative solution to problems or the effective attainment of subsystem or organizational objectives which otherwise would not have been possible.[61]

Thus, organizational conflict and personal stress in educational systems are by no means the antitheses of the makings of quality education. Rather, when properly understood and managed, conflict and stress often are the vitality behind growth and innovation, balanced coalition formation, enhanced communication feedback, expanded participative decision making, and cooperative problem solving.

## Conclusion

I once heard the story of a school district superintendent who, while attending an American Association of School Administrators meeting in Atlantic City, ate "mystery meat" containing a gastronomic surprise that put him in the hospital for a short time. While there, he received numerous phone calls and bouquets of flowers from well wishers. A telegram also arrived from the president of his board of education: "The board wishes you good health and a speedy recovery. The vote was four to three."

Certainly, the study of conflict is pertinent to the field of education. Interestingly enough, there is growing conflict regarding how much conflict surrounds the role of educational administrator. There are two schools of thought regarding this issue. The traditional view holds that the role is the target of intense conflict and that the occupants operate under such stress that all too often they leave the field altogether or try to cope on the thin edge of physical and psychological exhaustion.

The newly developing school of thought suggests that the role of school administrator is robust and that the occupants are typically on top of the job, genuinely enjoying the work and all the benefits that come with it. Unfortunately, we do not yet have the research to reconcile these two viewpoints. What can be said, however, is that at some time all educational administrators become involved in conflict situations and feel the resultant stress. So, whether the administrative posts are robust or fragile, conflict and stress still must be managed.

The objective of management is balance—neither too much nor too little. Too much conflict and stress can lead to organizational turbulence and intense personal anxieties followed by dysfunctional coping mechanisms. Too little conflict and stress can lead to boredom, apathy, and dissatisfaction. The right amount of conflict and stress can be the seeds of innovation, creativity, improved interpersonal relations, and higher levels of productivity.

## *We are Not Amused*

Before the meeting began, everyone had expected some high-octane grousing, but no one had expected anything like this. "The food is great if you come from Russia!" a barely controlled shout rang through the room. Sylvia Miller, principal of Green Acres High School, looked briefly at the rebellious agriculture teacher and replied with that "we are not amused" expression of hers.

The principal had been at the school five years, and her tenure corresponded with the rapid changes that were taking place in the region. Bedroom communities and shopping malls were springing up like mushrooms where once only cornfields existed as far as the eye could see. Mrs. Miller was part of the new movement that saw dramatic changes in the curriculum that now emphasized urban skills and opportunities. She found strong support in the newly hired young and vigorous teachers that now represented 40 percent of the staff.

The new health food program was only one of many changes that had been introduced to Green Acres High by the recently hired staff members. In the beginning, the program seemed to have faculty support from all sectors of the school.

The trouble started with the sign. Three weeks ago when the health food program for the faculty cafeteria began, a placard was unveiled over the door that read, "YOU ARE WHAT YOU EAT." Yesterday someone had covered the placard with a homemade sign which read, "ALL YOU CAN KEEP DOWN FOR $1.95."

No one could remember exactly how it started, but 10 minutes into lunch, the fishsticks, boiled cabbage, and raw carrots were flying. If the president of the board of education hadn't walked in at just the wrong time, probably nothing would have come of it. Now, Mrs. Miller was trying to chair a meeting that was generating a great deal more heat than she believed the situation warranted. At the moment, she wasn't sure what to do or how to do it.

## *Notes*

1. John Kmetz and Donald Willower, "Elementary School Principals' Work Behavior," *Educational Administration Quarterly* 18 (1982): 65.

2. Anthony Cedoline, *Job Burnout in Public Education: Symptoms, Causes and Survival Skills* (New York: Teachers College Press, 1982), p. 84.

3. National Center for Educational Statistics, *Digest of Educational Statistics: 1993* (Washington, DC: U.S. Government Printing Office, 1993), p. 33.

4. Stanley Elam, Lowell Rose, and Alec Gallup, "The 25th Annual Gallup Poll of the Public's Attitudes Toward the Public Schools," *Phi Delta Kappan* 75 (1993): 139–140.

5. Afzalur Rahim, *Managing Conflict in Organizations* (New York: Praeger, 1986), p. 13.

6. Don Hellriegel, John Slocum, and Richard Woodman, *Organizational Behavior,* 4th ed. (New York: West, 1986), p. 487.

7. G. W. Allport, *Becoming* (New Haven: Yale University Press, 1955), p. 84.

8. Kenneth Thomas, "Conflict and Conflict Management," in *Handbook of Industrial and Organizational Psychology,* Marvin Dunnette, ed. (Chicago: Rand McNally, 1976), p. 889.

9. Mark Litt and Dennis Turk, "Sources of Stress and Dissatisfaction in Experienced High School Teachers," *Journal of Educational Research* 78 (1985): 178–185.

10. Garreth Morgan, *Images of Organizations* (Beverly Hills: Sage, 1985), p. 155.

11. Ellen Goldring, "Principals, Parents, and Administrative Superiors," *Educational Administration Quarterly* 29 (1993): 95.

12. Robert Kahn, D. M. Wolfe, R. P. Quinn, J. S. Snock, and R. A. Rosenthal, *Organizational Stress: Studies in Role Conflict and Ambiguity* (New York: Wiley, 1964), p. 14.

13. Hellriegel, Slocum, and Woodman, p. 499.

14. Mike Milstein and James Farkas, "The Over-Stated Case of Educator Stress," *The Journal of Educational Administration* 26 (July, 1988): 4.

15. Kahn et al., p. 19.

16. Elise Boulding, "Further Reflections on Conflict Management," in *Power and Conflict in Organizations,* Robert Kahn and Elise Boulding, eds. (London: Tavistock, 1964), pp. 146–150.

17. Rahim, p. 16.

18. Milstein and Farkas, p. 3.

19. Douglas Yates, Jr., *The Politics of Management* (San Francisco: Jossey-Bass, 1985), p. 169.

20. S. E. Ambrose, *Supreme Commander: The War Years of Dwight D. Eisenhower* (New York: Doubleday, 1970), p. 323.

21. Yates, p. 172.

22. D. Irving, *The War Between the Generals* (New York: St. Martin's Press, 1981), p. 14.

23. Thomas, pp. 892–893.

24. Thomas, p. 926.

25. Thomas, p. 927.

26. Boulding, p. 146.

27. Kahn et al., p. 6.

28. Cedoline, p. 76.

29. Dick Gordon, "Administrator Stress: Some Surprising Research Findings," *Planning and Changing* 12 (1982): 195–199.

30. Walter Gmelch, *Beyond Stress to Effective Management* (New York: Wiley, 1982), p. 163.

31. Gmelch, p. 29.

32. Walter Gmelch, "Stress for Success: How to Optimize Your Performance," *Theory Into Practice* 22 (1985): 10.

33. L. Spaniol and J. Caputo, *Professional Burn-out: A Personal Survival Kit for How to Help Others Without Burning Yourself Out* (Lexington, MA: Human Services Associates, 1978).

34. Morley Glicken and Katherine Janka, "Executives Under Fire: The Burnout Syndrome," in *Organizational Behavior: Readings and Exercises,* Keith Davis and John Newstrom, eds. (New York: McGraw-Hill, 1985), p. 410.

35. Robert Sutton, "Job Stress Among Primary and Secondary Schoolteachers," *World and Occupations,* 11 (1984).

36. Rahim, p. 7.

37. Harmon Zeigler, Ellen Kehoe, and Jane Reisman, *City Managers and School Superintendents: Response to Community Conflict* (New York: Praeger, 1985), p. 23.

38. Leonard Greenhalgh, "SMR Forum: Managing Conflict," *Sloan Management Review,* 27 (Summer 1986): 45-51.

39. Greenhalgh, p. 50.

40. Mike Milstein, Charles Lusthaus, and Evelyn Lusthaus, "Conflict in Education," in *Schools, Conflict and Change,* Mike Milstein, ed. (New York: Teachers College Press, 1980), p. 13.

41. Nevitt Sanford, "Individual Conflict and Organizational Interaction," in *Power and Conflict in Organizations,* Robert Kahn and Elise Boulding, eds. (London: Tavistock, 1964), p. 100.

42. Yates, p. 176.

43. Stephen Robbins, *Organization Theory: Structure, Design and Applications,* 2nd ed. (Englewood Cliffs, NJ: Prentice-Hall, 1987), p. 350.

44. Edgar Huse and Thomas Cummings, *Organizational Change and Development,* 3rd ed. (New York: West, 1985), p. 329.

45. Yates, p. 192.

46. C. Brooklyn Derr, "Managing Organizational Conflicts: A Contingency Theory with a Collaborative Bias," in *School, Conflict and Change,* Mike Milstein, ed. (New York: Teachers College Press, 1980), p., 260.

47. Karl Albrecht, *Stress and the Manager* (Englewood Cliffs, NJ: Prentice-Hall, 1979), p. 125.

48. Robert Koff, James Laffey, Gary Olsen, and Donald Cichon, "Stress and the School Administrator," *Administrator's Notebook* 28 (1979-1980): 4.

49. Glicken and Janka, p. 412.

50. From *The Cincinnati Post* (reproduced in *Parade Magazine,* January 2, 1994), p. 11.

51. Albrecht, p. 175.

52. John Eisenhauer, Donald Willower and Joseph Licata, "Role Conflict, Role Ambiguity, and School Principals' Job Robustness," *The Journal of Experimental Research,* 53 (Winter 1984-85): 86.

53. Milstein and Farkas, p. 12.

54. Zeigler, Kehoe, and Reisman, p. 156.

55. Eisenhauer, Willower, and Licata, pp. 86-90.

56. Henry Mintzberg, *The Nature of Managerial Work* (New York: Harper and Row, 1973).

57. Kmetz and Willower, pp. 62-78.

58. W.J. Martin and Donald Willower, "The Managerial Behavior of High School Principals," *Educational Administration Quarterly* 17 (1981): 69-90.

59. James Farkas, "Stress and the School Principal: Old Myths and New Findings," *Administrator's Notebook* 30 (1983): 1-4.

60. Milstein and Farkas, p. 14.

61. Rahim, p. 13.

# Chapter *12*

# *Educational Change*

In our society a certain magic surrounds the word *change*. For many, the force of that word seems to tap a well of hope—that events, conditions, and people will somehow be better than they are now. For others, the contrary is true as they argue that the complexities, confusion, and pace of this technologically oriented society have separated us from the intangible qualities of life that we once knew in the old family values, the tradition of self-help, and the security of solid institutions under local control. For these individuals, change means going back to what was good in the past and not going forward toward what they see as the plastic society of a synthetic generation. However, let us not forget those who defend the status quo; they too have needs that must be fed.

Whatever one thinks about educational change, the concrete reality that schools have changed exists. Schools have changed in almost all aspects of their historical composition, including curricular programs, physical designs, instructional methodologies, and procedures of policy formation.[1] In some instances, the path toward change has been long and difficult, such as the case of school integration. In other cases, change has come so rapidly that it seems to have arrived unannounced, such as the introduction of transistorized calculators. For those who have grown up in the modern school with its learning resource centers, computer registration, and instructional media, a brief look at a teacher's contract in force early in the twentieth century provides a startling contrast to current practices.

> I promise to take a vital interest in all phases of Sunday-school work, donating of my time, service, and money without stint for the uplift of the community. I promise to abstain from all dancing, immodest dressing, and other conduct unbecoming a teacher and a lady. I promise not to go out with any young men except insofar as it may be

necessary to stimulate Sunday-school work. I promise not to fall in love, to become engaged, or secretly married. I promise to remain in the dormitory or on the school grounds when not actively engaged in school or church work elsewhere. I promise not to encourage or tolerate the least familiarity on the part of my boy pupils. I promise to sleep at least eight hours a night, to eat carefully, and to take every precaution to keep in the best of health and spirits in order that I may better be able to render efficient service to my pupils. I promise to remember that I owe respect to the school board and the superintendent that hired me, and that I shall consider myself at all times the willing servant of the school board and the townspeople and that I shall co-operate with them to the limit of my ability in any movement aimed at the betterment of the town, the pupils, or the schools.[2]

Granting that schools have changed, this chapter will attempt to respond to the basic question, How does change take place? Unfortunately, there is no answer to this question. Rather, there are many answers, and that is part of the problem. The literature is strewn with manuscripts that address the subject of change, ranging from rigorous designs lending enlightened insight to loose subjective accounts lending maximum possible misunderstanding. This chapter is organized to establish a meaningful framework to help sort out the complexities of the process of change.

The objective of this chapter is to examine major elements of a *planned* change process. This involves analyzing the major characteristics of the school's internal and external environments that will ultimately reject, support, or render impotent the thrust of a change initiative. The analysis can best be carried out by determining exactly what it is that is going to be changed (e.g., people, technology, tasks, structure). This process of identifying what is to be changed in an organization's environment is referred to as *targeting* and includes such elements as the *focus, level, potency,* and *impetus* of change efforts.

Within the discussion of the organizational environment in this chapter, the forces that are resistant to change at the individual, group, and organization levels will be identified. These resistance forces include vested interests, mobility expectations, incentive systems, bureaucratic constraints, and so forth. The creation of a force-field analysis is next discussed. A force-field analysis amounts to an identification of *forces supporting* and *forces resisting* a change initiative.

Following a discussion of the environment of an organization, *planned change strategies* will be examined. Change-agent strategies will be discussed, including individual "good guy" and "bad guy" variants as well as the role of the federal government as an agent of change. This discussion will be supplemented by an examination of the relatively new and rapidly growing field of organization development. This subject incorporates activies such as organization training, team building, quality circles, temporary systems, and others.

The third major element in the change formula, the *technology of a specific innovation* (e.g., programmed reading or mastery learning) will not be discussed, because the technology of innovations is better suited for discussion in a curriculum text rather than a text on administration. This chapter will conclude with a discussion of how the change process is viewed differently through the conceptual lenses of classical theory, sociopolitical group theory, and open system theory.

This chapter will not provide prescriptive, "how to do it" steps of planned change. Because people, problems, and settings are so different, prescriptive approaches rarely work with difficult problems in complex environments. Rather, this chapter offers what to consider in attempting change; that is, a discussion of organizational concepts, processes, models, and strategies that can be useful in diagnosing a problem and mounting a change effort that fits the conditions of a specific situation.

Because of the size and complexity of the literature on change, before beginning a discussion of the organizational environment it might be helpful to first clarify terms, then briefly discuss types of change, and finally enumerate the major cornerstones of the change process.

## Clarification of Terms

When dealing with definitions, no one can stand up and say, as did the caterpillar in *Alice in Wonderland,* "A word means exactly what I want it to say; nothing more and nothing less." The literature is overrun with interpretations and definitions focusing on the concept of change. Some common features do emerge, however. Distinguishing the concept of *change* from the concepts of *invention* and *innovation* is important.

*Invention*    This refers to the *process* of developing new technologies, projects, or procedures for an organization. Umans reminds us that inventors are usually classified by the category of their invention. "If the object is a bolt of cloth, he might be called a designer; if it is a poem, he is a dreamer; if it is a building, an architect. If, however, the object is a person and the purpose is to design a system whereby the person will most fully interact with his environment, then one becomes an engineer of human behavior."[3]

*Innovation*    This term refers to "deliberate, novel, specific change, which is thought to be more efficacious in accomplishing the goals of a system."[4] An innovation, therefore, is a *product,* such as an idea, a technology, or perhaps a new instructional methodology proposed for use in a school or a recently implemented one. *Invention* is the process of developing an *innovation* that is intended to resolve a problem or improve performance in an educational system.

*Organizational Change*    This is the *process* of altering the behavior, structures, procedures, purposes, or output of some unit within an organization. Hence, change is the process of implementing an innovation in an organization. It is important to note that many writers interchange the concepts of change and innovation; therefore, the concepts occasionally will be used interchangeably in this chapter.

## Types of Change

At least three types of organizational change can be distinguished in the literature: planned change, spontaneous change, and evolutionary change.

*Planned Change*    This is a conscious and deliberate attempt to manage events so that the outcome is redirected by design to some predetermined end. In an educational setting, for example, planned change takes place when an effort is made to initiate the use of behavioral objectives as a significant component in the teaching-learning process. Anyone can initiate a program of planned change, whether or not he or she is formally charged with the responsibility of directing an organization.

*Spontaneous Change*    This type of change is an alteration that emerges in a short time frame as a result of natural circumstances and random occurrences.[5] No deliberate attempt is made to bring about this form of change; it just happens. For example, a guidance counselor might find that one day the vice principal leaves to accept a position in another district, two days later the principal dies, and five days later the counselor is elevated to the principalship. Due to the pressures continually converging inside and outside the school, spontaneous changes often are a result of coping reaction to the turbulence of events. In other words, no grand design directs the course of events.

*Evolutionary Change*    This refers to the long-range, cumulative consequences of major and minor alterations in the organization. The cumulative consequences of limited change initiatives can be seen in every aspect of school life today. For example, the movement from the educationally depressed classroom settings that historically have befallen Mexican-American children to the enriched bilingual, bicultural setting that are now present in numerous schools did not come about by benevolent local initiative. The change resulted from a series of court cases, intense racial tension, the passage of new state laws, the revocation of old policies, federal grants to areas of high Mexican-American concentration, and so forth.

While many practitioners and scholars are great believers in planned change to redirect the course of organizational events, others think of genuine planned change as no less than an illusion beyond the reach of mortals. Kaufman speaks for this latter group:

> I have the impression that most literature on management, not to mention the literature on planning and policy analysis and public affairs, stresses mankind's ability to will the direction of social development. The fact that the historical record is full of events and trends that large numbers of people—even large majorities—deplore does not seem to discourage this view. The evidence of mankind caught up in complexes of forces that sweep us along, often in directions many or most of us may be unhappy about, are regarded simply as proof of failure to think and act rationally, or of the machinations of a few evil leaders, or of both, but not of inherent incapability to manipulate these forces. The tone, if not the explicit argument, implies a view of mankind as currently possessing the capacity to exercise full control over the evolution of all our institutions. It perpetuates a myth of managerial omnipotence.[6]

The idea of evolutionary change is often associated with the idea that as organizations evolve through time, people, conditions, and events improve. In response to this assertion of faith, a colleague of mine likes to observe that "at the birth of this nation we had a population of around four million people, and the presidency was surrounded by men like George Washington, Thomas Jefferson, Benjamin Franklin, John Adams, and Alexander Hamilton. Two hundred years later we had a population of over 200 million people and the presidency was surrounded by men like Richard Nixon, Spiro Agnew, John Mitchell, and Bob Haldeman. This all goes to show that Darwin was wrong."

Returning to the process of planned change, the major emphasis of this chapter, there are at least three major cornerstones that need to be discussed.

## Cornerstones of Planned Change

Shepard suggests, "Perhaps the most general formula for effective innovation is:'an idea; initiative; and a few friends.' "[7] As he set out to right the wrongs of the world, Don Quixote had similar notions. However, despite his jousting at the forces of evil, things remained pretty much as they were. Something is missing in this particular formula of change.

When attempting to bring about planned change, there are at least three basic cornerstones that must be built into the foundation of a change design: (1) a full understanding of the technology of an innovation; (2) a comprehensive knowledge of the environmental constraints operating within and around a school; and (3) a strategy of change. The trick is to identify a *specific strategy* for implementing a *specific innovation* in a *specific organizational environment*. All this goes toward the end of accomplishing *specifically defined objectives*.

Each of these three cornerstones of the change process has numerous variations, making it essential that time and energy go into determining the most effective combination, given the constraints facing the situation. As sophomoric as that last bit of wisdom might sound, the rest of the chapter will bear witness to the fact that in school settings change is rarely carried out in this manner. Wayland observes:

> When proposals for innovations such as team teaching, programmed instruction, or ungraded schools are made, the advocates' assumptions about the structure of the schools are not usually made explicit. Attention is usually focused on the attributes of the proposed innovation and the points at which the innovation differs from those aspects of the existing system which are being modified or supplemented. Implicit in this approach is the assumption that parts of an on-going system can be modified without giving attention to the possible impact on the other parts of the system. However, this assumption has proved incorrect in many efforts at innovation, with predictable consequences: the innovation is ultimately rejected, or new problems are created which were not anticipated by those favoring the innovation.[8]

In reviewing the research literature, Levine and Cooper identify what they call *prerequisites to successful planned change*. The change efforts should have a *site-level emphasis* involving *continuing training and staff development*. Participation should not be assumed but provided through *incentives* and the avoidance of too much additional work and *change overload*. Clear *goals and means* supported by modifications in procedures and routines, and backed by *strong leadership,* are keys to generating energy and direction for change.[9]

## Counsel to the Fainthearted from an Old Master

The subject of organizational change in educational systems is complex and confusing. Nonetheless, some still search for Merlin's wand with which they can make one magical sweep and exorcise the demons of rigidity, waste, and inefficiency. The history of educational change, however, will bear witness to the fact that there are no easy solutions.

To those fainthearted who contemplate entering the ring, the old master himself, Niccolo Machiavelli, offers some sage advice in *The Prince,* written about 1513.

> It must be considered that there is nothing more difficult to carry out, nor more doubtful of success, nor more dangerous to handle, than to initiate a new order of things. For the reformer has enemies in all those who profit by the old order, and only lukewarm defenders in all those who would profit by the new order, this lukewarmness arising partly from fear of their adversaries, who have the laws in their favor; and partly from the incredulity of mankind, who do not truly believe in anything new until they have had actual experience of it. Thus it arises that on every opportunity for attacking the reformer, his opponents do so with the zeal of partisans, the others only defend him halfheartedly, so that between them he runs greater danger.[10]

However, another distinguished philosopher of sorts, Zorba the Greek, would have us reject caution and advises us to take any and all risks necessary. Conscious of the danger, said he, "A man needs a little bit of madness or he never cuts the rope to be free."

Quite possibly one of the problems reformers have is that they believe that they understand more than they actually do.

## The Organizational Environment: The Target of Change

Kurt Lewin has written that if one really wants to learn how an organization works, one should try to change it. In attempting such a change, one of the early steps in diagnosing the organizational environment (internal and external) is the *targeting process.* Unless some precision based on serious diagnosis is achieved in targeting, the wrong clients may be approached by a manager using the wrong strategy, which results in the wrong outcomes. Under conditions of poor or improper targeting, either nothing at all happens or unanticipated consequences develop, such as increased faculty turnover or parental protest.

The next sections will treat key elements of the targeting process, which include the focus, level, potency, and impetus for change.

### Focus of Change

When determining the focus of change, the following variables in an organization should be considered, along with the proposed changes: (1) its *tasks,* such as a modification of goals to emphasize individualized instruction and deemphasize traditional forms of instruction; (2) its *structure,* such as decentralization, departmentalization, workflow, communication channels, or role definitions; (3) its *technology,* such as introducing computer-assisted instruction or new accounting procedures; and (4) its *people,* such as changing the composition or constitution of its members so that new skills, values, loyalties, or motivations emerge.[11] These four focuses of change are *interdependent;* a change in one of them probably will bring alterations in others. For example, adopting computer-assisted instruction will probably require the addition of new teachers with different skills or new role training for present teachers.

In a slightly different context, Katz and Kahn speak of the need to distinguish between targets at the *individual level* and those at the *organization level.*[12] Managers frequently confuse individual change with organizational change. Commonly, someone is pulled out of a job for special training in human relations techniques, for example, and then returned to the same job with the expectation that he or she can operate within the original set of organizational constraints. Unveiling and sustaining "the new me" is no easy task.

The major difference between individual and organization change, as Katz and Kahn point out, is that the former is determined largely by personality needs and values while that latter is determined by the more formal, structured characteristics of a system. Katz and Kahn firmly stress the importance of simultaneously changing the organizational variables along with the individuals. "Yet we persist in attempting to change organizations by working on individuals without redefining their roles in the system, without changing the sanctions of the system, and without changing the expectations of other role incumbents in the organization about appropriate role behavior."[13] Ideally, the readiness skills and attitudes necessary for genuine change to take place will be present at the individual and the organizational levels.[14]

Along with giving attention to the focus of change, thought must to be given to the *level* at which change is to take place in the organizational environment.

## Level of Change

An interesting facet of our creative arts is that they have different levels of meaning to trained and untrained enthusiasts. For example, as any student of literature is aware, *Moby Dick* is not about a demented sea captain possessed with chasing a white whale across the Seven Seas, nor is *Walden Pond* about a recluse camping out by a lake. Both works have realities that go far beyond their story lines. In a way, the same is true of forms of social organization; they have different levels of reality.

For example, a group of anthropologists once set out to discover why the Hopi Indian rain dance has continued to play a central role in the life of that tribe for several hundred years. The anthropologists were aware that if a social act is not reinforced in some way, it withers away and dies.

As far as anyone could tell, there was no correlation between the dance and the abundance or occurrence of rainfall, although the ceremonials persisted for centuries. In discussing the matter with individual Hopi Indians, however, the anthropologists were told that the rain dances were held to assure an abundance of rain. After diligent study, another explanation for this continued behavior began to emerge. They noted that the rain ceremonial was the one time during the year that the far-flung Hopi tribe would gather together from across a geographical expanse that spanned many states. During this period the youth of the tribe would become acquainted, eventually resulting in marriages. Therefore, the true significance of the rain dance was not to bring rain, but to serve as a social instrument to preserve the life of the tribe. If young Hopi Indians had routinely married outside the tribe because of a lack of local marriage partners, the tribe probably would have perished.

Just as the Hopi Indians did not recognize the deeper level of reality associated with their yearly rain dance, those who set out to initiate change in an organization often are unaware that various levels may be involved. Wilfred Brown has identified four levels of an organization, three of which are not officially recognized:[15]

1. *Manifest organization:* The level is portrayed by the line-and-staff charts that represent the *formal structure* as the leadership would like it represented to the world.

2. *Assumed organization:* This level of organization is revealed in the *conventional wisdom* about how the system actually works. For example, most people might believe that the organization charts misrepresent the situation slightly or even considerably. A general feeling may be that the superintendent has gained control of the board of education members and manages them rather than the other way around (as the line-and-staff charts indicate).

3. *Extant organization:* If a systematic study were undertaken by researchers to determine how a system *actually* functions, it would reveal the extant organization. For example, such a study might reveal that neither the board of education nor the superintendent controls the system directly—they actually are reacting in anticipation of demands that are brewing in the teachers' union.

4. *Requisite organization:* An "organization as it would have to be to accord with the real properties of the field in which it exists." In a sense, this is an *ideal* type organization, representing the way an organization *should* function for maximal effectiveness and efficiency. In the real world it no doubt would have to be put together by an Olympian sage acting through divine inspiration, so we don't encounter requisite organizations. Requisite organizations act as conceptual models, which are very useful as backdrops against which to compare real organizations.

In targeting change, one not only must know the focus of change but also the *level* at which the change is to be consummated. Probably we all have seen change initiatives that are heralded with much fanfare, followed by reorganizing departments, rewriting job descriptions, upgrading titles, and redefining goals. But in the end nothing really happened that had not been going on before, causing a condition to emerge known as "creative status quo." When change does not result, it often is because the *focus* and the *level* of change were misunderstood. Or it may be because the proposed changes were only tactics designed to diffuse outside pressures for change by proclaiming a reform but keeping everything but the facade in place. James Boren refers to this behavior as "capturing the bold spirit of irresolution."

Along with the important issues of focus and level in the targeting process is the issue of the *potency* of a particular change.

## *Potency of Change*

Potency refers to the degree to which a change requires a significant departure from existing conditions. If the change is simply a redrafting of the organization chart, which nobody believes in anyway, then a limited potency is involved. If the projected change is simply adding a few courses to the curricular program, then a limited change potency also is involved. However, if the projected change is requiring all teachers to adopt a team-teaching mode of instruction, then a high level of change potency necessarily would be involved.

The level of potency suggests the degree to which resources, time, energy, power, and goodwill are involved in a change initiative. Targeting a change initiative, therefore, calls for thought regarding whether a match exists between the degree of change required and the energies and resources available to do battle.

As the next section will point out, the targeting process also is related to the impetus behind the change initiative.

## *Impetus for Change*

Getzels argues that change can be categorized into three types according to the origin of the impetus for change: enforced change, expedient change, and essential change.[16] *Enforced change* results when the cultural dimension outside the organization brings external pressures on the system to which it must respond. The mechanism of change in this case is *accommodation.* The Supreme Court decision eliminating prayer in the public school is a case of enforced change; the teachers' altering their opening-day rituals in the classroom represents accommodation to that change.

The second category is *expedient change;* its mechanism of change is *reaction.* As external pressures build up around an organization, counter pressures against change may develop within the system. To diffuse the external pressures, expedient changes may be made. Getzels writes, "Changes are introduced for the paradoxical reason of avoiding change, or at least more fundamental change."[17] Fads can be a result of the need to defuse intensive pressures for change. Fads come and go so quickly that nothing fundamental in the system actually changes, except perhaps its terminology.

The third category is *essential change;* its mechanism of change is *voluntarism.* This type of change is not just an accommodation to external pressures or a reaction of internal counter-pressures "but instead had its origin in the will and imagination of human beings striving for self-actualization." The result is neither faddism nor enforced change but an authentic response to the clear recognition that a problem should be solved in as genuine and creative a manner as possible.

The targeting process, therefore, cannot be carried out independent of the impetus behind the change. Targets usually differ, depending on whether the prime mover is enforced, expedient, or essential change. For example, if the impetus for change is the imminent arrival of an accreditation team, the target might be the creation of a paperwork facade rather than a deeply rooted organizational modification.

However, the question of targeting cannot be settled without identifying and exploring the forces that resist change in the educational organization. The next section of the chapter will address this topic.

## Resistance to Change at the Organization Level

After reviewing the literature on forces resistant to change, one is left with the impression that they can indeed be formidable. These forces range from the simple ignorance of an individual—"what I'm not up on I'm down on"—to the complex vested interests of our own organizations' members. As the comic-strip character Pogo so eloquently phrased it, "We have met the enemy and they is us."

The forces that can contribute to slowing down or even blocking the change process are important parts of an organization's environment. They must be diagnosed, understood, and taken into account in the targeting process and the selection of a change strategy. The environment harboring the forces of resistance (and support) is typically not social or technical but actually sociotechnical. A sociotechnical interpretation of the environment refers to the behavior of individuals as the environment shaped by the interaction of technical characteristics (such as instructional equipment, physical layout of the school, activity schedules) and social characteristics (such as norms, informal groups, power centers, and the like). As Chin and Benne point out, "The problem-solving structures and processes of a human system must be developed to deal with a range of sociotechnical difficulties, converting them into problems and organizing the relevant processes of data collection, planning, invention, and tryout of solutions, evaluation and feedback of results, replanning, and so forth, which are required for soluting the problem."[18]

Resistance to change occurs at the organization level and at the individual level. There is a high level of interaction between the two, and they cannot be completely separated. Resistance forces also differ among schools in terms of source, strength, and makeup. The forces that are presented here are not an exhaustive list, but simply represent some of the major blockages. The first blockage discussed suggests that established linkages within and between educational systems serve to inhibit better ways of treating old and familiar problems.

### A National Educational System

Americans tend to believe that schools are autonomous units that determine financing, organization, and programs. But Wayland argues that "we have, in fact, developed a national educational system, with the consequence that serious innovation at the local level is extremely difficult to introduce and to maintain."[19] We have created an interlocking network of schools and supporting organizations that has resulted in a type of standardized system with a high degree of "sameness" about it. The interlocking nature of the network between schools and support systems makes the process of change difficult, because change in one unit requires reciprocal change in supporting units.

Wayland offers the following arguments to suggest the existence of a national educational system.

1. We have national recruitment of teachers.
2. Students transfer successfully from school to school across state lines with minimal problems.
3. Textbook companies tend to set the content and structure of curricular programs in this country, and there is a national market for their instructional materials.
4. National examination systems, such as the National Merit Scholarship system, the College Entrance Examination, the Iowa or Stanford Achievement Tests, and the Graduate Record Examination, establish the standards for excellence and entry into higher education.
5. Accreditation associations force unifying standards upon schools, as do courts by case law and state legislatures by statutory law.

In short, this argument goes, the interlocking characteristics of the national educational system severely reduce the possibility of educational change. However, these same interlocking features can foster the processes of change, for better or worse. In the area of textbook adoptions, for example, of the 22 states that adopt textbooks at the state level, Texas and California hold the largest markets by a considerable margin. Books those two states adopt usually are sold nationwide.

The potential national impact of this market-driven adoption process can be seen, for example, in the decision by the Texas state board of education to require more than 300 changes in five high school health textbooks. The battleground involved health-related issues, particularly sex education. The combatants dueling over control of the instructional content were old enemies—the Christian Right, and health and family-planning advocates. Some of the changes in the texts involved the deletion of AIDS hot lines, some illustrations of human sexual organs, information about sexually transmitted diseases, and condoms. Information added included material on the penal code involving sexual activity involving minors as well as the laws against sodomy. In short, the final product of the textbook struggle in Texas almost assuredly will be carried into many other states whether or not they endorse the outcome.[20]

Also consistent with the notion of a national education system, when producers of standardized tests come out with a new series stressing new orientations and skills, schools across the country begin adjusting their instructional programs to enhance the chances of higher scores for their students (a process that always seemed to me to be in reverse order). In a similar manner, when major colleges upgrade their admission requirements, high schools fall in line with program modifications because they want their graduates to gain admission to the best schools.

## Bureaucratic Organization

Remarks from an administrator such as "Please stand up when your number is called," or "I should be able to see you in about two weeks" are indicative of an impersonal and rigid educational system. Many organizational scholars have detailed the ways in which formal bureaucratic structure can become resistant to change because of emphasis on hierarchical levels, role relationships, standardized procedures, control from the top, values of disciplined compliance, and the like.[21]

Abbott, for example, stresses that superordinates tend to have "rights," and subordinates "obligations."[22] Superordinates have the right to veto or affirm. When a teacher or lower-level administrator has a good idea for change, it must pass through the hands of three or four superiors—all of whom have the right to veto it. Abbott also points out that superordinates have the right to control communication, initiate activities, set the goals for subunits, call meetings and set the agenda, invade the work space of teachers, and settle conflicts. All these characteristics can result in severe consequences for an organization that needs to be original and creative.

However, asserting that change in a buearucracy spreads like rain water through limestone can be a serious overstatement, according to one interesting school of thought. Lloyd Bishop, in his study of 21 school systems, found that bureaucratic organizations are capable of making significant changes because they possess internal stability, stress conformity to norms, and form a tightly coupled system. When enthusiasm for an innovation exists, the stable and cohesive organizational framework can provide a sound basis for the changes to be brought about.[23]

The same can also be true for governing boards of education. Muth and Azumi write about what can happen with boards that lack those elements that make up the core of a bureaucracy: *stability, unity,* and *knowledge.*

> Boards that are constantly in flux, disunited, continually bombarded by competing demands, unsure of the issues, or indecisive will not be hampered in reaching workable agreements but also will have difficulty following through on implementation and appraisal functions. Board stability and unity depends in turn, on autonomy from governmental and community influence—particularly if that influence is itself factionalized. Similarly, administrative stability is critical. Constant change in administrative leadership leads to district dependence on part-time laypersons for program change, implementation, and assessment.[24]

The view that organizational bureaucracy in education isn't always a bad thing is supported by a much cited study of Moeller and Charters who examined the sense of power of teachers in 20 school systems.[25] Contrary to their hypotheses, they found that from the standpoint of being able to influence the organizational forces acting upon and within the school, teachers in highly bureaucratic systems had significantly higher, not lower, senses of power than those in less bureaucratic schools. In a system promoting rationality, structure, and rules, teachers know where they stand and consequently can take a stand. In an ambiguous, ill-defined environment, going one-on-one with a formidable foe can be disconcerting when you are not sure of your rights, authority, and back-up.

In sum, the bureaucratic, mechanistic form of organization and management may not always be detrimental to the process of change. As the contingency theorists are fond of saying, it all depends on the situation.

## *Accountability*

Accountability undeniably is as important in education as it is in any other type of insti-tution. It can and often is applied with the simplistic subtlety of a sledgehammer on stone, or it can be used as an insightful tool to build rather than crush. All too often, accountability is driven by the easiest and most visible tool available—student test scores. If scores are low, the educators are blamed. This tends to be true even though we have known for a long time that test scores are correlated more with the socioe-conomic conditions students bring with them into the classroom than what takes place in that classroom. If accountability is to have genuine meaning, the focus should not fall on one, but on all four bodies of participants who should play forceful roles in the educational process: legislators, parents, citizens of the community who already have their education, and educators.

This is not to say that school administrators are off the accountability hook, only that test scores do not stand alone as a good measure. As Darling-Hammond and Asch-er point out, accountability should encompass

> how a school or school system hires, evaluates, and supports its staff; how it relates to students and parents; how it ensures that the best available knowledge will be acquired and used; how it evaluates it own functioning; and how it corrects its problems and provides incentives for continual improvement. Thus, performance indicators do not themselves create accountability. At best, test scores may provide data for accountability systems that enable schools to improve and correct problems. At worst, they may deflect attention from needed school changes. In fact, properly designed performance indicators can undermine accountability by creating incorrect assumptions.[26]

## *Goal Displacement*

Most people have encountered bureaucratic functionaries who seem to adhere rabid-ly to the rules, no matter how insensitive, inappropriate, or just plain stupid the rules seem to be. Robert Merton states that when following the rules becomes the goal of the individual functionary or perhaps even of the organization itself, we have a situa-tion referred to as *goal displacement*.[27]

The presence of goal displacement is very often attributed to routinized practice over an extended time. Blau disagrees with the "ingrained habit" notion because in his research he found that rigid conformity to rules and resistance to change were not typ-ical of all bureaucrats in all situations.[28] To Blau the pivotal concept is the *security* of the official. He writes, "Social insecurity breeds rigidity, and this finds varied expres-sion. When officials were afraid of possible negative reactions of superiors, overcon-formity ensued."[29] As long as officials follow the rules, no matter how inappropriate, they cannot be censured by superiors; and if a program fails or the clients become angry, the officials cannot be touched. Such might be the case in a team-teaching sit-uation, where, because the interests and styles of the teachers do not mesh, they go through the motions only to comply with district policy and thus avoid censure.

Blau also found that higher level administrators at times objected to an innovation not because they opposed a change in general, but because it might reveal or highlight weaknesses in their departmental operations. In this context, for example, school administrators might object to a differentiated staffing program because they think teacher turnover is already dangerously high and thus fears such an innovation might accelerate it.

In short, those teachers and administrators who feel psychologically secure in their world of work and believe they have mastered their job will be much more willing to promote change because it represents an attractive challenge as well as something new to learn.

## The School as a Domesticated Organization

Another major organizational feature that contributes to resistance to change is the domestication of public schools, a concept introduced in Chapter Five in relation to the management-information system. A domesticated organization has many of the properties of a local monopoly: it is not compelled to compete for resources, except in a very limited area; it has a steady flow of clients; and its survival is guaranteed.[30]

Because public schools are domesticated organizations, they do not face the problems of private organizations that make it necessary to build major change mechanisms into their structures. Change capability permits private organizations to continually make the necessary modifications in production and product to hold their share of the market and expand it if possible. The domestication of the school builds in layers of protective insulation—insulation that can be penetrated, although not easily.

An interesting example of behavior that could only be found in a domesticated organization was that part of California's omnibus educational reform bill S.B. 813 (1983), which was intended to increase instructional time. A California Business Round-table study found that the state's students received fewer days and instructional minutes per day than students in comparison states. At the high school level alone, California's students received 2.5 months' less instructional time than the average pupil, nationally. The response of S.B. 813 was to offer financial incentives to districts to meet the target of 180 days per year and 240 minutes per day at a cost of $250 million annually for the first three years and $450 annually thereafter beginning 1984–1985. The average high school needed to add four days to its school year and six minutes per day to qualify for the incentive award of $75 per pupil. The average elementary school needed to add four days for a $55-per-pupil-per-day bonus.

In the face of potential labor conflict because teachers resisted increased instructional time without compensation, districts found creative ways to lengthen the school day and year without increasing instructional time. Some districts added one minute to each passing period between classes, which could add up to 900 minutes or about eighteen 50-minute classes. Other schools extended homeroom periods by five minutes each day, totaling 900 minutes per year. Others added an extra recess to the school day. Some schools did add one or two minutes of instructional time to each class.[31] When considering educational change in a domesticated organization, the desired outcome of "more for less" is not always the result. Sometimes, "less for more" is a distinct possibility.

## *Costs: Time, Energy, Money*

One of the basic problems associated with adopting innovations in educational organizations is the difficulty of obtaining accurate measures of benefits as they relate to
costs. Typically, the educational goals of specific schools are as diverse as they are controversial, and they seldom emerge as a single package behind which all interested parties can line up. They also are often vague in meaning, general in scope, and intangible
in substance, thus avoiding measurement. Miles writes, "In the absence of good measures of output, educational organizations tend to stress cost reduction."[32]

When there is an appropriate match between resources and responsibilities,
Bacharach, Scott, and Shedd observe, there are at least four consequences that miti-
gate against change. Teachers must become "scavengers," using *make-shift techniques*
as they attempt to scratch out resources in a deprofessionalized organizational setting
that undervalues their contributions and limits their ability to accomplish assigned
tasks.[33]

Sunk costs (money already spent on programs and equipment) also act as forces
resistant to change. If a school district, for example, has recently invested thousands
of dollars in a language laboratory with special features or in an open-space classroom
complex, no one will seriously entertain proposals that would render obsolete or even
modify significantly these costly items.

The costs of change that involve traditions or sacred cows of a school will be unacceptable to many and thus provocative of resistance. Many impassioned old-timers
would rather see their school burned to the ground than to see an alteration in its tradition as a college preparatory institution. In a similar vein, only a masochistic administrator would try to deemphasize football in a community that is insatiable for local
athletics.

## *Resistance Cycle*

Goodwin Watson argues that during the life of an innovation, perceived resistance
moves through a four-stage cycle. He describes the arrival of an innovation or a change-
enterprise almost as one would describe the scenario of a revolutionary movement
with bandits coming out of the mountains. "In the early stage, when only a few pioneer thinkers take the reform seriously, resistance appears massive and undifferenti-
ated. 'Everyone' knows better; 'No one in his right mind' could advocate the change.
Proponents are labeled crack-pots and visionaries."[34]

In the second stage some support becomes evident, the pro and con forces
become visible, and the lines of battle are drawn. In the third stage the battle is engaged
"as resistance becomes mobilized to crush the upstart proposal."[35] The supporters of
the change are often surprised and frequently overwhelmed by the tenacity of the
opposition. Survival of the innovation is dependent upon developing a base of power
to overcome the opposition.

If the supporters of change are victorious in the third stage, the fourth stage will
be characterized by support flowing to the newly arrived innovation. "The persisting
resistance is, at this stage, seen as a stubborn, hide-bound, cantankerous nuisance. For

at times, the danger of a counter-swing of the pendulum remains real."[36] The cycle begins anew when another effort toward innovation begins.

In the next section the individual is the unit of analysis, and resistance to change is explored in terms of personal costs.

## Resistance to Change at the Individual Level

Although no attempt is made here to catalog all the forces of resistance that derive from impulses at the individual level, some that stand out as particularly deadly in the educational setting are discussed.

### Vested Interests

Any school manager who attempts to change (significantly modify or eliminate) a major educational program usually encounters the vested interests that Halpin describes.

> Once a program has been funded, the personnel who operate the program immediately acquire a strong vested interest in the perpetuation of the program. Their jobs are at stake. No matter how stupid or pointless the program may be, once a man accepts a job with it, he must proceed to bolster and defend his own personal decision; so he uses rhetoric to tell himself that his decision was, indeed, a wise decision.[37]

The sort of individual described above will also use rhetoric to tell others that the program is a wise one, which will prove itself given more time, more money, and more staff to provide the necessary momentum the program deserves.

Educators may be highly resistant because a change may be a threat to their personal status; dissolve an informal group that is a source of personal satisfaction; be interpreted as a criticism of their personal performance; increase their work load or responsibilities; or have been proposed by someone they dislike or distrust.[38] Vested interests, in other words, come in social, political, economic, and psychological varieties.

### Mobility Expectations

Along with personal vested interests, teachers and administrators often have positive or negative motivations toward change, and these motivations are dependent on their own mobility expectations within the system. Presthus has identified three career motivational patterns that can influence the process of change: upward-mobile, indifferent, and ambivalent. "While the upward-mobile finds the organization congenial, and the indifferent refuses to become engaged, the ambivalent can neither reject its promise of success and power, nor can he play the roles required to compete for them."[39]

The *upward-mobile* person aspires to a leadership role and adapts his or her behavior to conform to the school's philosophy, goals, norms, and rewards. This individual will promote or resist change initiatives according to the expectations of the organizational leadership.

The *indifferent* person is another type entirely. Often people will regard the indifferent administrator as a burnt-out case—one who has nothing old to restore and nothing new to suggest. This may be true only insofar as the school system is concerned. Indifferent people finds their rewards *outside* the school system in the family, the bowling team, Monday night football, or the Lions Club. In any case, the indifferents choose not to compete for the higher rewards that motivate the upward-mobile, and therefore, are frequently more resistant to change. To them, the burdens that often come with change are not worth bearing.

The *ambivalents* aspire to all the rewards of achievements and success that motivate the upward-mobile, but they cannot make themselves conform to the conditions expected of them. The ambivalents are often seen as troublemakers with limited loyalty who want to disrupt a well-ordered system. Ambivalents may see the "well-ordered system" as irrelevant and repressive to the needs of minorities, such as youth groups, racial groups, or some teacher groups. Ambivalents often initiate attempts to bring about major changes in an organization, changes that are directed against the vested interests of the majority.

Interestingly enough, the preparedness of superintendents to move on can significantly motivate them to take risks in initiating a program of change. Maginnis and Willower, in a study of 37 school superintendents who moved from one district to another, found that most of them began to think about leaving in their fourth year. "The possibility of moving on appears to function as a safety valve for chief executives. About the time their position may begin to weaken, the legitimacy of a job search has been enhanced by length of service. This means the superintendents can fight their battles knowing they can cut their losses and leave the field if defeat seems inevitable."[40]

In sum, when discussing resistance to change or support for change, a basic ingredient must be the mobility aspirations of those who are to carry out the change. Whether or not they are upward-mobile, indifferent, ambivalent, or just ready for a new job can make a significant difference.

## Search Behavior

Modern mythology has it that organizational officials, teachers, and administrators in this case, are constantly searching for new and better ways to perform their tasks. March and Simon argue, however, that ongoing search behavior is not representative of most people. People begin to seek out new strategies only when they become dissatisfied with the present course of affairs. March and Simon write:

> Individuals and organizations give preferred treatment to alternatives that represent continuation of present programs over those that represent change. But this preference is not derived by calculating explicitly the costs of innovation or weighing these costs. Instead, persistence comes about primarily because the individual or organization does not search for or consider alternatives to the present course of action unless that present course is in some sense "unsatisfactory." The amount of *search* decreases as *satisfaction* increases.[41]

This argument implies that educators will not start a search for improvement unless some sort of feedback mechanism convinces them that present procedures are not working well and the resulting anxiety compels them to look for a better way. Outsiders or insiders trying to initiate change cannot simply convince a school of a better innovation based solely on its merits. They must also present data that suggest that an aspect of a current program needs improvement. Only then will concerned attention be adequately focused.

## Psychological Systems

Goodwin Watson argues that many forms of resistance have their roots in the psychological systems of the individual. Some of the psychological forces that generate tendencies toward resisting change are:[42]

1. *Habit:* A habit becomes established because the repetition of a specific behavior is satisfying. An administrator, for example, may continually act autocratically because the sense of power derived from this behavior is highly satisfying. The behavior thus becomes routinized.

2. *Primary:* When an individual first copes successfully with a task or problem, a persistent pattern of behavior often is established.

3. *Selective Perception and Retention:* Once a belief has been established in an individual, a type of information screening takes place, which tends to reinforce the attitude. In-service teachers who go to graduate school, for example, often hear lectures on new instructional approaches, but conclude that it is just theory and will not work in practice.

4. *Dependence:* Educators tend to have dependent relationships, as do all human beings. Whether they stem from parental attitudes, colleague expectations, or early reference groups, dependent relationships tend to constrain independent thought.

5. *Insecurity and Regression:* "The reaction of insecure teachers, administrators and parents is too often to try to hold fast to the familiar or even to return to some tried-and-true fundamentals that typify the schools of the past."[43]

## Rejection Stages

Just as many researchers argue that there are stages in adopting innovations (e.g., awareness, interest, evaluation, trial, and adoption), Eichholz argues that there are stages through which an individual goes in rejecting or resisting an innovation.[44] He argues that an individual may go through each stage in sequence or several of them at once. At each stage, Eichholz identifies (1) the form of rejection, (2) the cause of rejection, and (3) the anticipated response.

| Form of Rejection/ Cause of Rejection | Anticipated Response |
|---|---|
| 1. Ignorance/Lack of dissemination | "The information is not easily available." |

2. Suspended judgement/Data not logically compelling

"I want to wait and see how good it is before I try."

3. Situational/Data not materially compelling

"Other things are equally as good."
"The school regulations will not permit it."
"It costs too much to use in time and money."

4. Personal/Data not psychologically compelling

"I don't know if I can operate the equipment."
"I know I should use them, but I don't have the time."
"These gadgets will never replace a teacher."

5. Experimental/Present or past trials

"I tried them once and they aren't any good."

Through the recognition of the type of response an innovator receives, appropriate adjustments can be made to the strategy for bringing about the change.

## Resistance from the Lowerarchy

With the publication of the findings of the Hawthorne studies, social scientists and practitioners began to understand the nature and source of power that subordinates command.[45] From their positions of power in the lowerarchy, in many instances subordinates can assume control of the organization's productive efforts by slowing down, speeding up, or striking. They also can become highly resistant to change.

As pointed out in Chapter Four, teachers often use their power to control events as well as to resist attempts at change. They may try to control change by subtle use of the pocket veto (refusing to take action) or by unsubtle demands shouted out at a meeting of the board of education. Through the use of their power in the lowerarchy, teachers can strongly support change initiatives as well as resist them.

In a related context, Huse points out that behaviors in subordinates may have no direct, visible relationship to resistance to change, although these behaviors can be just as devastating. "The individual may not openly manifest his resistance by such methods as insubordination, grousing, and griping. Instead, other signs of opposition may become much more evident, e.g., 'nervousness,' resignations, increased errors, increased learning time, absenteeism, etc."[46] Whatever form it takes, the power in the lowerarchy of an organization can generate significant forces that resist change.

## Lack of Experimental Ethic

Bridges believes that one reason teachers and administrators often are resistant to change is because norms of experimentation do not exist in which *instructive failure* is a possible outcome. A prevailing belief that good teachers and administors do not fail causes many to "demand proof that the innovation fits perfectly the local circumstances of the school—a condition which is not likely to be met."[47] In other words, risk-taking behavior, an essential ingredient in the change process, is not reinforced by the normative structure of the school. For an administrator, a failure could result in censure by parents or the end of a promising career. Along with the lack of an experimental ethic, Bridges argues that teachers often are not interested in supporting change initiatives because the incentive system in most schools does not reward such involvement.[48]

## Post-Initiation Resistance

Gross, Giacquinta, and Bernstein have seriously challenged the notion that forces resisting change come into play *prior* to the time a basic decision on the adoption of an innovation is made.[49] The authors also argue that at the time change is actually initiated there might be complete and enthusiastic support behind what is about to take place. In their major study of educational change, Smith and Keith also found this to be the case.[50]

However, Gross, Giacquinta, and Bernstein found that the obstacles and frustrations leading to the abandonment of efforts to adopt an innovation developed *after* the teachers found they could not carry out in practice what had looked interesting and attractive on paper. When students did not behave in the way they were supposed to and events began to get out of hand, the insecurity of the situation propelled teachers to beat a quick retreat back to the old and familiar ways. In other words, teachers who are initially favorable to an innovation may later develop a negative orientation. The ultimate consequence of this shift in attitude may be the end of the change effort.[51]

## The Good Side of Resistance

To suggest that resistance to change is inherently bad is to suggest that all efforts toward change are good. Such, however, is not the case. Earlier views of teacher resistance suggested an almost irrational reaction to change initiatives based on such characteristics as habit, fear of the unknown, or unwillingness to take risks.[52] However, as Rossman, Corbett, and Firestone point out, resistance often is a "rational defense against poorly planned and executed innovations."[53] Resistance is often a rational message communicated upwardly that the intended change is attacking the wrong problem, has not been adequately thought out, or perhaps has insensitively overloaded the staff with too much additional work.

Take, for example, the introduction of a continuous writing program into the high school curriculum. A proposal that requires all students to write something every day sounds reasonable, even desirable. However, Albert Shanker points out the potential dangers of not thinking these things out.

> The average high school teacher has five classes a day with 30 to 35 students in each—a total of at least 150 papers to read and grade for each writing assignment. If he or she spends just five minutes reading each paper and another five minutes making comments, the total time expended adds up to at least 25 hours of work—for one

assignment! Added to the enormous amount of normal preparation time needed for daily lessons, an effective, continuing writing program is simply impossible.[54]

For school administrators, the study of resistance to change should be viewed as a learning experience. It focuses on and clarifies the informal goals, priorities, and motives of many individuals close to the students.

## Planned Change

Throughout the history of American education, schools have been attractive lightning rods. Lortie observes:

> In less than twenty years the schools have been damned successively (and sometimes concurrently) as soft on subject matter, as unjust to members of minority groups, as tools of international communism, as pathologically bureaucratic and unresponsive to the public will, as destructive of the human spirit, as perpetrators of class privilege and as conducted in a mindless fashion.[55]

Granting that a good deal of criticism of the school is partially true, as it is of all institutions, the solution many academicians and practitioners propose is the pursuit of *planned change.* Planned change is often seen as a tool for adopting an exciting new innovation, resolving a conflict, clearing communication channels, upgrading instructional quality, and so forth. These are all important targets of change, but taken as singular efforts they are limited in scope. A more expansive approach to planned change does not simply facilitate the dissemination or adoption of an innovation, but seeks to establish built-in problem-solving capabilities that provide for creative experimentation in educational organizations.

### Total Quality Educational Management

The relatively recent appearance of total quality educational management (TQEM) is a good example of planned change. TQEM is an educational adaptation of the total quality management (TQM) approach to improving industrial and manufacturing processes initially shaped by Walter A. Shewhart in the 1920s but more specifically by Edward Deming beginning in the 1930s.[56]

TQEM is based on a management-worker philosophy that actively challenges organizational structures, processes and cultures that accept anything less than absolute excellence. TQEM embodies a total, unrelenting, forceful, client-centered commitment to improving the quality of education. Drawing on the industrial example, Schmoker and Wilson relate that in 1983 a Japanese company bought a Firestone tire plant in Tennessee. "Until that time, Firestone manufactured and sold three grades of tires: excellent, average, and inferior. Under the new management, they now produce only one kind of tire—excellent." Schmoker and Wilson draw the forceful analogy that in American schools three types of students are produced: "Well-educated, not so well-educated, and poorly educated."[57]

The TQM work Shewhart and Deming pioneered before and during World War II was ignored by American industry after the war as the nation's retooling emphasized quantity over quality. The Japanese, however, invited Deming to Japan for a series of lectures following the war and, as the saying goes, the rest is history.

Not unlike the scientific management experts of an earlier period, Deming taught management and workers to keep statistics on the processes and product of their work and seek ways to adjust for greater efficiency. "He taught them that the more quality you build into anything, the less it costs. In other words, you design quality in. . . ."[58]

Unlike the scientific management experts, however, Deming taught that one must think of any organization as a system made up of interacting, interdependent managers and workers. Managers *and* workers have the capacity to think and improve the product, and no one can be considered as the mere extension of a machine.

Any organization will improve by, for example, strengthening its culture and capacity to communicate internally and externally, building trust and loyalty, taking risks without fear of failure, and looking to the people closest to the problems for ideas about how to solve problems.[59]

First, last, and always, Deming taught that TQM must be client centered. Quality is judged by the consumer, not the producer. Quality is based on what is needed rather than what is delivered. In the educational setting, quality can be judged only by what is learned, not what is taught.

Joseph Fields adapts Demming's famous 14 points to the educational field.

1. Knowing your business, how and what satisfies customers, and sticking to that business.
2. Realizing that the world is changing and we must change our leadership style to tap into everyone's potential.
3. Designing quality into home and educational environments, ensuring a fitting condition for excellence at the beginning.
4. Maintaining high expectations of loyalty and trust of all inputs to the schooling process; expecting and demanding the best of parents and others.
5. Constantly improving everything we do—personally, in our families, socially, and at work.
6. Training in TQ for everyone in the school community.
7. Sharing leadership based on knowledge and competence first and authority second.
8. Taking risks without fear and making constructive efforts to improve education.
9. Breaking down whatever barriers exist between people that prevent school quality improvement.
10. Allowing people to determine their own goals, targets, and quotas, and giving people the latitude to use their own judgment.
11. Eliminating administration, teaching, or learning by [the] numbers.
12. Eliminating artificial reasons for mandates, fostering instead ownership and involvement for accountability.
13. Seeking, gaining, and using new information continually.
14. Attacking poor quality education. Everyone in the educational community must work together.[60]

At the request of the Committee on Education and Labor in the U.S. House of Representatives, the General Accounting Office (GAO) conducted a study of the use of TQM principals in elementary and secondary schools. The GAO found that in 1994 there appeared to be approximately 75 ongoing TQM programs at the school or school district level. There were, however, many more educational systems using bits and pieces of the TQM framework under the guise of a school improvement or reform program.

Where TQM has been introduced in the schools, often it is under the influence of corporate enterprises (e.g., Xerox, Corning, Bellcore) who sponsor schools in their community outreach programs. Thus far the federal government has played little or no role.

The GAO identified several barriers to the successful implementation of TQM. Convincing the "keepers of the purse" to invest scarce resources in staff training has been difficult during these hard times of fiscal conservatism. In addition,

> one of the biggest barriers is cynicism on the part of school management and staff toward implementing "yet another" school reform or educational restructuring effort. Another hurdle is the reluctance of school board and school district officials to change their traditional approaches to managing operations.[61]

My own view is that TQEM is going to be the buzz word in the field of education in the immediate future. It remains to be seen, however, whether TQEM becomes one more innovation that washes up on the beach and floats out again into the sea, or takes root and grows.

## Categories of Change Strategies

As previously mentioned, the process of planned change involves at least three elements: *an innovation,* or a specific change with unique features and technology; *an organizational environment* with sociotechnical characteristics and blockages and supports to change; and *a specific strategy* to implement the innovation in the organization's internal or external environment. Strategies of change often are categorized around their common traits.

One of the more popular categorization schemes was proposed by Chin and Benne who identify empirical-rational strategies, normative-reeducative strategies, and power-coercive strategies.[62]

*Empirical-rational strategies* assume that individuals or groups are rational, that they act when data reveal that a change is reasonable and justified, and when it can be shown that they will gain by a change. These strategies are closely associated with classical organization theory. Empirical-rational strategies are similar to what Giacquinta calls the "show and tell" approach to change.[63] Included are such activities as demonstration projects, in-service workshops, pilot projects, visitation days, survey data analysis, management by objectives (MBO), brainstorming, and quality circles. The principal weakness of these strategies is that they assume people act in a rational manner, or at least share a singular conception of rationality with the leaders of the organization.

*Normative-reeducative strategies* assume the rationality and intelligence of people, but they also assume that motivation and action are not based on logic alone. Because patterns of activity are supported by sociocultural norms, change involves modifications in attitudes, values, interpersonal relationships, loyalties, and skills. In other words, normative-reeducative strategies deal not only with objective elements, but also with feelings and values. This category of strategies is similar to what Giacquinta calls the "lock arms, forward together,"[64] or "a kind word goes a long way." In schools this approach often is manifested by team building, consensus decision making, feedback procedures, human relations practices, stress management programs, process consultation (study of the dynamics of a group), and advancements in the quality of work life (QWL). The principal weakness of these strategies is that as emotional attachments, loyalties, or informal group memberships shift, the strategies often break down.

*Power-coercive strategies* emphasize political or economic sanctions (both positive and negative) and rule enforcement as the means of bringing about change. The essence of this approach to change was captured by that noted social critic John Dillinger, when he once said, "A kind word will go a long way, but a kind word along with a gun in your hand will go a lot farther."

These strategies may be legitimate, such as offering a promotion to a vice principal because he or she will take strong steps to curb a discipline problem or threatening to demote an administrator for poor performance. The strategies can also be illegitimate, such as overstating the benefits of an innovation in order to obtain additional funding, or making a less-than-accurate performance evaluation to coerce someone into changing. Besides categories of change strategies, other elements in the process of planned change, such a timing, should not be overlooked.

## Timing

In the business of change, timing counts. Whether an administrator is trying to pass a tax-rate increase to support local schools, obtain new recreational facilities, or change a curricular program, certain time periods in which to make a move are more favorable than others. For instance, seeking a school-related tax increase shortly after income-tax filing time is not very sensible, but going after expanded recreational facilities following a racial conflict is. The time to encourage support for a major curricular change is not just after teachers have spent long hours writing behavioral objectives for the old program, but rather the months prior to an accreditation visit.

There are occasions, however, when the timing of events is controlled by outside circumstances, such as desegregation orders laid down by the courts or curricular changes legislated by the state. In this context, I once asked a superintendent known to have a subtle sense of timing what he did when he found himself cornered by events ruled by someone else's timetable. "Well," he replied, "I guess I do what all superintendents are paid to do and that is take the bull by the tail and look a bad situation in the face." In other words, it is better to be the timer than the timed.

Also important to consider in the planned change process is a fad, which is often mistaken for genuine change.

## Faddism

Fads in schools seem to arrive like ocean waves striking a beach. They crash on shore with great ferocity and strength, but then they somehow sink back into the depths from whence they came. The arrival and departure of flexible scheduling, planning-programming-budgeting system (PPBS), performance contracting, and programmed reading are familiar cases in point.

Numerous writers have commented on the seemingly simultaneous honoring of change and dedication to the traditional and routine.[65] An interesting question is, Why do we seem to walk on both sides of this street at the same time? Although we have no firm answers to this question, a view is developing that is rooted in the seemingly contradictory characteristics of the school administrator's role. As Havelock observes, "The executive leadership of an organization has two responsibilities: one is *maintenance* of the system the way it is, and the other is *changing* the system so that it performs better. In other words, the leader is both a change agent and a resister of change.[66] The built-in dilemma in this role might have found its release in faddism—in other words, in creating the appearance or image of change without actually generating substantive change.

How do fads gain such widespread currency so quickly? Again, no one can say for sure, but contributing to the spread no doubt are teacher-training programs, national and state conferences, educational journals, and state departments of education. Smith and Keith, in their excellent field study of an elementary school, suggest the importance of the "traveling salesperson" in the spread of fads. They write:

> During the August teachers' meeting, the Milford School District followed the standard ritual of having a program with an out-of-town speaker who trades glowing epithets with the superintendent. Spanman introduced the speaker as an educational statesman of "ideas and integrity." The speaker, in turn, lauded the superintendent and the bright spots of Milford. He talked of the significance of teaching, "a job to build a dream on." The observer, who had attended opening night and had seen the play before, suggested an hypothesis which, although a bit cynical, still extends the nonconceptualization of issues in true belief and innovation.
>
> Field Notes
>
> "As I listen to him I get some feeling for the reasons that fads develop in education. These characters need something new and different to talk about as they journey around. They reach so many people that a 'new' idea can spread rapidly. Superintendents and others looking for fame can grab hold and offer their school a case in point."[67]

Although faddism is very prevalent, substantive change does at times take place. When planning for change, considerable debate still exists as to whether the "earthquake" or the "incremental" variety is more appropriate as a general strategy.

## Earthquake and Incremental Change

When contemplating change, questions of degree are critical. Earthquake change, just as the name suggests, responds to a felt need of the organizational leadership that a change should be comprehensive and rapid, impacting on structures, people, programs, and technologies. An earthquake change strategy is such a high risk that you must hit it just right or you come up sucking swamp water.

Smith and Keith conducted a case analysis of earthquake change, which they call the "alternative of grandeur." Responding to the district superintendent's mandate to "go build a school," the newly hired administrators and bright but inexperienced teachers set about to do just that. They planned for a new physical plant and for an academic program to include such innovations as team teaching, ungradedness, totally democratic teacher-administrator decision making, daily demand instructional schedules, absence of curriculum guides, individualized learning programs, and so forth. Smith and Keith write, "One makes the big gambit, by capitalizing on the high degree of system interdependence. If the pieces are finely honed and the machinery smoothly interlocked, the system takes off; if not, then the problems are momentous."[68]

And indeed the problems were momentous in the new elementary school. Because of the interconnectedness of the various parts of the school, the errors multiplied rapidly, resulting finally in the resignations of many educational personnel and the virtual collapse of the program.

Many valuable insights on the trails of educational change come from the Smith and Keith study, but one of the most interesting is the cloaking of organizational realities through the generation of a facade. They use the term *facade* to refer to the image of reality (not reality itself) presented by the school to the several interested publics (i.e., the press, parents, taxpayers). As the upwardly mobile administrators did a successful selling job of the innovative physical plant and academic format to the community and the media, pressure began to grow for demonstrations of success in student achievement. Consequently, a "public face" began to emerge, which focused on intentions—on "what we want to do," rather than on the realities of "what we are doing." The cloaking of organizational realities was carried on as the school personnel desperately tried to get their act together. When they began to realize that they had greatly overextended themselves, the "abandon ship" drill began. The administrators left quickly for better jobs at higher pay and most of the teachers went to other schools. No mention is made, however, of what happened to the students who could not leave.

In contrast to earthquake change, many academicians and practitioners argue that incremental change, with its series of small steps forward, is the most efficacious form of change.[69] This argument suggests that although incrementalism is not as glamorous as earthquake change, it has better, surer, results. Smith and Keith write:

> We hypothesize that a gradualist strategy which applies an alteration of a few components involves (1) lower levels of uncertainty and fewer unintended outcomes, (2) decreased time pressure, (3) an increased interval for major change, (4) limited decisions related to the changes, and (5) decreased demand on resources will have as a concomitant the increased likelihood of success in initial goals. In turn, this increases the opportunity to create a position of strength.[70]

Subjects such as faddism, earthquake change, and incremental change raise the question of when one can say that change actually has taken place. This issue is the subject of the next section.

## Basic Lessons of the Process of Change

Michael Fullan emphasizes the point that as educators we often respond to complex problems with simplistic solutions that only make matters worse. To harness the forces of change, he argues that there are eight basic lessons we should learn to live by.

1. You can't mandate what matters. (The more complex the change the less you can force it.)
2. Change is a journey not a blueprint. (Change is nonlinear, loaded with uncertainty and excitement, and sometimes perverse.)
3. Problems are our friends. (Problems are inevitable and you can't learn without them.)
4. Vision and strategic planning come later. (Premature visions and planning blind.)
5. Individualism and collectivism must have equal power. (There are no one-sided solutions to isolation and group-think.)
6. Neither centralization nor decentralization works. (Both top-down and bottom-up strategies are necessary.)
7. Connection with the wider environment is critical for success. (The best organizations learn externally as well as internally).
8. Every person is a change agent. (Change is too important to leave to the experts; personal mind-set and mastery is the ultimate protection.)[71]

The next section points out that while everyone is a change agent, there are different types of change agents.

## The Change Agent

By definition, "a *change agent* is a professional whose role it is to influence his clients' behavior in a desired direction."[72] The roles and responsibilities of the change agent vary from complex to simplistic and tough to permissive, depending on the demands of the situation and the orientation of the individuals involved.

After an analysis of the internal and external organizational environment early in the planned change process, the special characteristics of the change agent can be identified. Based on this analysis, the roots of the blockages to change that the change agent must overcome can be identified; for example, lack of information, focused power, political support, fresh ideas, incentives, coordination, communication linkages, or perhaps all of the above. Given the nature of the problem or problems, the type of change agent needed can be selected. He or she can serve such functions as catalyst, solution giver, process helper, or resource linker.[73]

At least three of four types of change agents have been identified in the literature: white hats, Machiavellians, guerrillas, the hatchet men. The hatchet man is not developed in the literature, although most of us will have some personal knowledge of the type.

### "White-Hat" Change Agents

Most of the literature on agents of change falls into the "white-hat" category. This orientation assumes the change agent has an engaging personality, maintains close bonds based on trust with the client system, and practices democratic procedures at all times. Reflecting the white-hat tradition, Morin states what a change agent should be.

1. The change agent must enjoy high professional esteem.
2. The change agent must be a stimulator, an inspiring person.
3. The change agent must be (a) open to changing his point of view, (b) prudent, and (c) well aware of social implications.
4. The change agent must be capable of working with others.
5. The change agent must have leadership qualities and must be influential.[74]

Havelock identifies the sequence of steps by which a change agent of this ilk works.

1. *Relationship:* Establishes a viable relationship with the client system.
2. *Diagnosis:* Determines whether or not the client is aware of his or her problems and can articulate them in problem statements.
3. *Resources:* Once the problem has been defined, identifies and obtains relevant resources.
4. *Solution:* Generates a range of alternatives and makes a choice.
5. *Acceptance:* Through the process of describing, detailing, discussing, and demonstrating, the change agent helps the client system to develop awareness and interest and finally to adopt the innovation.
6. *Stabilization:* Develops within the client system the internal capability to sustain the innovation without the continued presence of the change agent.[75]

In schools, white-hat change agents often are experts on curricular matters, human relations-oriented inservice-training experts, and planning consultants.

## The Machiavellian Change Agent

The basic assumptions underlying the Machiavellian change agent tactics differ considerably from those underlying the white-hat tactics, although both are equally dedicated to accomplishing objectives. The Machiavellian types have no bias toward the use of democratic procedures, nor do they cultivate highly visible and close relationships with the client system. They might choose to be quite invisible, engineering events from behind the scenes while carrying on a public role of a different nature altogether.

Baldridge has identified rules for the Machiavellian change agent.[76]

1. *Concentrate your efforts:* Don't squander your energy and efforts by chasing too many rainbows. Pick a few key targets and go for them.

2. *Know when to fight:* Don't go into a fight if you know ahead of time you cannot win. The issue will return again and the circumstances may be more favorable the second time. If possible, do not fight if it is not necessary, but if it becomes necessary, fight to win.

3. *Learn the history:* Seek out the history of an important issue. How long has it been around? Who favored it and who opposed it last time around? What was the outcome of the last struggle over the issue? What tactics were employed?

4. *Build a coalition:* Build a political base that can support your efforts when push comes to shove.

5. *Join external constituencies:* Develop bonds with external constituents of the organization, such as parent and alumni groups or the chamber of commerce. These groups can bring strong pressures to bear on the internal processes of an educational organization.

6. *Use committees effectively:* Get on the right committees and stick with them long after others have dropped off. Do your homework and try to become the expert on the issue. Also, try to become the secretary or chairperson of the committee. The chairperson sets the agenda and the secretary acts as the "memory" of the committee and brings to the attention of the committee selected information from the past at opportune times.

> Finally, a major tactical procedure in committees is to "fill in the garbage can." Since decision issues, like garbage cans, attract various irrelevant material, they can be used to the change agent's advantage. Dump new garbage into the can, and then compromise readily on the unimportant issues. Helping to load the garbage can leaves plenty to bargain over when the deadlines are close and allows you the chance to insist stubbornly about retaining key issues.[77]

7. *Use the formal system:* Often an important but overlooked tactic is to simply ask for what you want. Frequently you will receive it.

8. *Follow through to push the decision flow:*

> We have said that the concept of "decision making" is a delusion. Decisions are not really made; instead, they come unstuck, are reversed, get unmade during the execution, or lose their impact as powerful political groups fight them. In real life decisions go round and round in circles, and the best one can hope for in the political battle is a temporary win.[78]

Therefore, the seasoned veteran will follow events as the decision goes downstream and through the turbulent rapids on its way to full implementation.

9. *Glance backward when the change is completed:* Try to be as objective as possible and if the change doesn't satisfactorily treat the problem, go back and do it over again. Perhaps most difficult of all, be prepared to step in and kill your project when it has outlived its usefulness. Ego-investments are nice and often harmless when the innovation is on the rise, but when the decline sets in the ego can prove to be a problem.

Adopting a Machiavellian change agent style *should not* be construed as "playing dirty," although certainly there is potential for that if carried to the extreme. Many forms of American life have institutionalized this strategy, such as football (fake to the left side and screen pass to the right), politics ("and if I am elected I promise that") and school administration ("if we offer them 4 percent to start out"). In the real world the strategies and tactics of administration are important skills to be learned. Unfortunately, management-training programs have not taken this point into account. Training still tends to concentrate on rational change strategies using democratic processes and smiling change agents. Rational strategies and democratic processes are important and very useful, but in our complex organizational environments they are often simply not enough.

### *"Hatchet Men" Change Agents*

"Hatchet men" change agents are not among nature's noblemen. Their arrival on the scene usually is a clear signal that major organizational surgery has been called for and the surgeon is now on hand. In the educational setting at times they come as ideological warriors who are elected to school boards with a pledge to burn the dirty books in the library or return the schools to the basic fundamentals of the three R's. At other times they might be employed as vice principals with mandates to clean up the discipline problems in high schools. Frequently, an outside hatchet man may be assigned to a school to provide a plan for drastically overhauling some aspect of the curricular program that has been blamed for poor achievement scores.

Encounters with white-hat and Machiavellian change agents are common experiences in the natural flow of organizational life. An encounter with a hatchet man, however, is neither common nor easily forgotten. My own baptism into this strategy of change came a number of years ago when I was employed as a training officer in a large federal government educational mission. In the Washington-based parent agency there was a turnover in directors, and a new philosophy of training emerged from the new leadership. Shortly thereafter a new man of known reputation (called Jack the Ripper by his friends) rode into our regional training site with two assistants. We all knew a skirmish was imminent; we just didn't know how bad it would be.

The first whiffs of grapeshot came early as basic parts of the traditional program were cut out. Soon new people began to arrive to instruct in the new program, and on one final day most of the old staff was terminated (myself included).

Although at the time I thought otherwise, the lessons I learned through that experience served as part of my education about the process of educational and organizational change. My teachings at the knee of the hatchet man prompted me to define a set of rules of change as he might have written them himself.

1. *Needs of the organization:* Respond only to the needs of the organization as defined by the sponsors who send you in to do a job. You must ignore the needs of the employees, which serve only to confuse matters.
2. *Power base:* Remember that in the game of political hardball, power wins. You can be successful only as long as you retain and continually reinforce your power base.
3. *Loyalty:* Be loyal to your sponsors and no one else. If your sponsors detect a divided loyalty, they can easily throw you away.
4. *Program first:* Chop the program and then the people. Once the program has been cut, the people in the old areas become highly visible as having little to do. Cutting them out then can be sold as an obvious measure of efficiency.

5. *Divide and conquer:* Break up coalitions that have natural power bases of their own.
6. *Meetings:* Don't hold or attend meetings where you must respond to questions in public.
7. *Trust:* Don't trust anyone. Trust is a sign of weakness and can only serve as an eventual instrument of your own downfall.
8. *Friendship:* Don't make friends. Friends are really the enemy in disguise.
9. *Timing:* Strike quickly and go for the throat. Do it all at once and with finality because if the unpleasantness continues for an extended period of time your sponsors might turn on you.
10. *Controversy:* Do your job and divert the heat away from your sponsors because that is what you are getting paid for.
11. *Departure:* Get out quickly. After the deed is done, don't hang around because the organization needs to stabilize around its new programs, personnel, and structures. With you present it can't be done effectively. Take with you the heat, the frustration, and the trauma that have been generated because they can only serve to enhance your reputation for your next assignment.

Hopefully, in the field of education we won't see many hatchet men change agents operating in our schools. However, as frustrations build in communities over the inability of some school systems to change, the call is being heard more and more for a hatchet-man response.

## *The Organizational "Guerrilla"*

The organizational "guerrilla" is a "true believer" in the Eric Hoffer sense of the term.[79] Guerrilla change agents work from inside the organization, usually as an employee. After building cells of support, the guerrillas expand their network by drawing in diverse elements. Gregg and Maanen write, "The organization guerrilla is purposeful in his acts. He enters the organization committed to effecting changes which correspond with his own value system. Working across and up the organization rather than down, the guerrilla engages in consciousness raising and social networking."[80]

The guerrilla works against the formal leadership in an attempt to bring about change and win concessions. Especially in the beginning, these actions often must be covert in nature. Once the movement is strong enough and has been legitimated by the various populations in and around the organization, it usually can become less secretive and attempt to appeal to a broader segment of the organization. In the early days of the movement to organize teachers in unions, guerrilla-type operations were mounted frequently. In many ways the informal groups of teachers or staff personnel that characterize any organization also promote their own versions of change through "guerrilla-like" movements. Of all forms of change agents, the guerrilla is probably the least understood.

The adoption of a change-agent strategy is only one of many possible approaches available in the relatively new and rapidly growing field of organizational development, the subject of the next section.

## Organizational Development

Like human beings, educational organizations get sick, suffer from paralysis, under-nourishment, fatigue, growing pains, and from time to time die. In many instances organizational "doctors" must be called in to put these systems back into shape. These "doctors" are called *organization development specialists*.[81]

In defining the subject Beckhard writes, "Organizational development is an effort (1) *planned*, (2) *organizationwide*, and (3) *managed* from the *top* to (4) increase *organization effectiveness* and *health* through (5) *planned interventions* in the organization's 'processes,' using *behavioral science* knowledge."[82] After World War II various social science training techniques emerged from academic institutions and from private industry. These have served as the foundations of organization development (OD). Kurt Lewin was a pioneer in the field of interpersonal dynamics and was instrumental in the founding of the Research Center for Group Dynamics and the National Training Laboratories following World War II.[83] His work and influence were instrumental in developing the orientation toward interpersonal dynamics in laboratory training sessions.

Another emergent orientation in OD is the development of survey research and feedback techniques (e.g., attitude surveys and feedback in workshops). Significant efforts also came out of private companies such as Esso Standard Oil and Union Carbide, as attempts were made to improve behavior and performance in such areas as leadership training and intergroup conflict resolution. Training in OD techniques has now become a standard part of many graduate academic programs in educational administration and is expanding rapidly.[84]

Typical objectives of an OD training program are identified by French as:

1. To increase the level of trust and support among organizational members.
2. To increase the incidence of confrontation of organizational problems, both within groups and among groups, in contrast to "sweeping problems under the rug."
3. To create an environment in which authority of assigned role is augmented by authority based on knowledge and skill.
4. To increase the openness of communication laterally, vertically, and diagonally.
5. To increase the level of personal enthusiasm and satisfaction in the organization.
6. To find synergistic solutions to problems with greater frequency. (Synergistic solutions are creative solutions in which 2 + 2 equals more than 4, and through which all parties gain more through cooperation than through conflict.)
7. To increase the level of self and group responsibility in planning and implementation.[85]

In working toward objectives such as those listed above, organization development training sessions often are organized around such topics as team building, intergroup conflict resolution, conducting interesting meetings, effective interpersonal communication, processes of personal growth, job enrichment, goal setting, role-playing, power equalization, sensitivity training, and unblocking communication channels.

Matt Miles, a modern guru of organizational development research and training, argues that the key variable driving OD is *data feedback*. "Data feedback and clearer communication help to align perceptions with privately held attitudes and provide support (in this instance) for innovativeness as a stance; the old, incorrectly perceived norm loses its force. Other important norms we studied dealt with openness, trust, collaboration, inquiry, conflict, and expression of strong emotion."[86]

## *Structural versus Process-Oriented OD Specialists*

A basic premise or assumption behind OD intervention theory is that the client system contains within itself the resources are well as the capability to change. The role of the OD specialist is to facilitate this change process by helping to identify areas that require change and to remove obstacles blocking change.

Typically two types of OD specialists are in the field: those who are structurally oriented and those who are process oriented. OD specialists with a *structural orientation* tend to hold a formal organization perspective toward change that is rooted in classical theory. When approaching a change task, this type of specialist is likely to involve himself or herself in activities that suggest modification of activities relating to goal setting, departmentalization, centralization and decentralization of decision-making activities and functions, policy and rules, the division of labor, and the reward and penalty system, for example. In other words, the structural specialist focuses on changing the characteristics of the *formal* organization.

The *process-oriented OD specialists* are much more likely to hold a sociopolitical group perspective of organizational behavior and to involve themselves in such activities as team building, interpersonal dynamics, T-groups, conflict management, and the like.

Some OD specialists are able to vary their responses, depending on specific needs at specific times (the contingency theory approach). They work toward facilitating a solution by shifting the power distribution and the framework within which decisions are made, for example. Barnes,[87] reporting on the work of Greiner,[88] identifies seven approaches to change that illustrate differing concentrations of power. These concentrations of power range from unilateral-autocratic at one extreme to participative-democratic at the other.

1.  *The decree approach:* Unilateral decisions are made by top officials who pass rules down through the hierarchy for disciplined compliance.
2.  *The replacement approach:* Individuals in key roles are replaced by others more supportive of or knowledgeable about a projected system change.
3.  *The structural approach:* Changes in the relationships of personnel through reorganization will cause organizational behavior to change.
4.  *The group decision approach:* The support of group members is obtained after a decision has been made by others higher up in the organization.
5.  *The data discussion approach:* Organizational members are encouraged to analyze the feedback of relevant data (e.g., case materials, survey findings), which are supplied to them by the OD specialists or superordinates.
6.  *The group problem-solving approach:* The group, itself, identifies the problem, gathers the data on alternative solutions, and makes the final choice with the help of an outsider.

7. *The T-group approach:* Training in sensitivity will change work patterns and improve interpersonal work relationships.

A favorite of OD specialists is the organizational training approach, the subject of the next section.

## Organizational Training

Organizational training seeks to increase the effectiveness of groups as they set out to accomplish specific tasks. No attempt is made to change the personalities of members, as is often the case with T-groups; rather, organizational training tries to provide individuals with more open and effective interpersonal skills.

Schmuck et al. state the four basic features of organizational training: (1) its unit of focus is the working group rather than the individual; (2) communication skills are emphasized; (3) improvement in group problem-solving capability is an end objective; and (4) the training is developmental and sequential, moving from simulations to problem solving of real issues in the actual work setting. Schmuck et al. write:

> The technique typically begins with clarifying the problem areas and desirable goals, goes on to analyzing the forces that keep problems from moving toward solution, sets priorities on the forces to be increased or decreased, makes plans for action, and finally evaluates the effects of the action taken. To prepare for such problem-solving, the training sequence begins with practice in methods of increasing the face-to-face flow of valid information. The skills we have emphasized are paraphrasing (making sure that you understand the other person's message), describing behavior (avoiding interference), describing feelings (not simply venting them), and checking one's perception of another's feelings (describing to another how you think he is feeling, so that he can verify or deny your perception).[89]

Another approach to training, which is intended to have an impact is the temporary system.

## Temporary Systems

The creation of a temporary system with unique features is often a technique employed by OD specialists. A temporary system is not only a powerful learning environment for the participants, but also a tool to bring about change and innovation in permanent educational systems. Miles writes:

> For many reasons, permanent systems—whether persons, groups, or organizations—find it difficult to change themselves. The major portion of available energy goes to (1) carrying out routine goal-directed operations and (2) maintenance of existing relationships within the system. Thus the fraction of energy left over for matters of diagnosis, planning innovation, deliberate change, and growth is ordinarily very small.[90]

Temporary systems, then, do not carry with them all the historical freight that permanent systems do, so energy for change can be focused with lesser levels of constraint.

Miles identifies the special characteristics of a temporary system that make it a powerful tool of change.[91]

1. *Time limit:* A confronting deadline serves to focus attention and energy.
2. *Isolation:* Physical and social isolation free the minds of inhibiting symbols of the "permanent system" as well as filter out distractions, such as a ringing telephone.
3. *Self-examination:* Each participant finds it easier to examine his or her own behavior in a setting in which the "old" rules do not apply.
4. *Role experimentation:* Each participant can experiment more easily with new role behavior as well as with new ideas.
5. *Status equalization:* In a temporary system the old rules of deference to hierarchy are reduced in emphasis (especially if the members are strangers).
6. *Norms:* The norms of conduct surround completing the task confronting the group rather than supporting a hierarchical framework.

Miles writes, "Bounded by time and often by physical isolation, temporary systems could bypass the status quo of permanent systems, mobilize high energy, open up communication, devise creative alternatives, and flatten the power structure."[92] Changes produced by a temporary system can be seen in people, in relationships, and in decisions. Problems also result. A group may take a superficial, unrealistic, or utopian approach to tasks. Group members also may lack the necessary skill, information, or power to carry out new ideas once they return to their permanent systems.

## A Note of Caution

In short, the OD specialist has available a rather comprehensive inventory of tools, ranging from the rather simple show and tell exercises of staff meetings to team-building exercises for work groups to sensitivity training for staff members. The selection of a specific tool should be based on an analysis of the nature of the forces blocking the change efforts, such as a lack of precise information, a low level of motivation, or insecurity in interpersonal relationships.

One important criticism suggests that OD specialists typically tend to skip over any genuine diagnosis of the organization's environment in search of the roots of the problem; instead, they jump right into some form of training for the clients. "As a result," Greiner writes, "there is an insensitive application of a nicely packaged program, based on general theories or misleading past experiences. The organization is asked to fit itself to the package, not vice versa."[93] Often these packages are so general that they can be used to cover almost any need, from curricular development to industrial espionage.

Additionally, as Baldridge and Deal point out, the use of a "black bag of tricks" approach to problem solving often discourages experimentation because *simple* solutions are promised.[94] Furthermore, the conceptual thought processes of school managers are neglected; the ways in which they analyze or think about their problems are not explored. If a pill is handy, one does not have to know much about the cause of the illness, the reasoning goes.

Warner Burke sums up the thoughts of many interested but concerned observers.

> The OD practitioner is asked to mend fences, not build new ones—and, it may be, heaven forbid, that in some cases, no team or teamwork is needed at all. OD practitioners seem to be useful in times of crisis for "putting out fires" and for conducting organizational surveys (this last activity is sometimes euphemistically called "diagnosis"). But, when it comes to considering, if not planning, on the basis of a behavioral science theory, a major organizational change, such as designing the organizational structure of a major corporate division or building a new system for rewarding employees for their work, the OD practitioners are rarely involved.[95]

In sum, on the scale of things OD might be considered a lightweight technology, but in many ways it is very important, because as of now it is one of the few games in town.

## School Culture and Situational Conditions of Change

Why do schools take different paths toward change? Rossman, Corbett, and Firestone state that a principal reason is that "teachers will evaluate an innovation according to how well it meshes with [thc] existing culture. Innovations that further already established purposes will be welcomed, but others will be resisted."[96]

*Culture,* as defined by Wilson, is "socially shared and transmitted in act and artifact."[97] Culture is a human invention that establishes meaning for us by integrating our knowledge, and perception of that knowledge, into the immediate world we can understand and feel comfortable within.

Various idiosyncratic elements help shape a school's culture, such as early history, community expectations, leadership, traditions involving standards of excellence, and rates of teacher turnover. Hence, schools are different because their cultures are different. Cultures emphasize different aspects of the social dynamics in making a school function. Some schools emphasize a hierarchical culture and spend "considerable organizational energy in the care and feeding of status and role differentiation."[98] Others stress quantitative measurement (frequently ignoring quality) and focus on the numbers: test scores, instructional minutes per day, per week, and class credits, and parents attending PTA meetings. Still others emphasize sports. In these schools, winning is not everything, unless you are losing.

The cultural fabric of a school has the loose and tight properties of woven threads. "At some points it is porous and easily loses shape; at others it is impenetrable and retains its integrity."[99] At the University of California campus where I teach, the chancellor dropped the football program a few years ago. This decision came as a surprise to almost everyone, especially because the team had won the league championship the previous year. Interestingly enough, the local culture hardly spoke; only a few voices were raised in protest (except for those of a few members of the business community who were somewhat bent out of shape). I suspect that if the presidents of

Michigan State University and the University of Alabama were to make similar moves, their institutional cultures to be not nearly so understanding.

It is an organization's cultural norms, in other words, that establish what it is legitimate to change. In those areas of locally recognized legitimate change, such as promoting more women to the high school principalship or promoting literature-based reading texts, new initiatives are supported and risk taking is rewarded. When a proposed change threatens vested interests, a sense of identity, or perhaps a view of what is right and wrong, a school's culture can be very resistant.

Fullan and Miles give us their views on avoiding resistance to change.[100] They identify seven orientations of thought and action that must be present if successful change is to take place:

1. Change is a learning process that is loaded with uncertainty. No one should ever be fooled into thinking that the change process works the way it is supposed to. "Anxiety, difficulties, and uncertainty are *intrinsic to all successful change.*"[101]

2. There are no blueprints for the change process. Rational planning models don't work as intended for complex social change. Change is a journey where learning and adjusting must take place.

3. Problems along the journey should be embraced rather than avoided. Educational change is a problem-solving process and only by seeking out problems and resolving them through "deep coping" can we confidently continue the journey.

4. Change requires resources, because efforts to shift from the status quo require energy (e.g., new space, training, materials, personnel).

5. Educational change is not self-directing, but requires an integrated source of power to direct it. "The management of change goes best when it is carried out by a *cross-role group* (say, teachers, department heads, administrators, and—often—students and parents). In such a group different worlds collide, more learning occurs, and change is realistically managed."[102]

6. Successful change is a systemic rather than a segmented process. That is, any reform must not concentrate on just the formal components of the organization, such as policy and regulations, but also on less visible but highly potent elements of the organizational culture. Also, the reform must consider and focus on the system's interrelationships, of such as curriculum, teaching, community, student support, and so forth.

7. Change must be implemented locally and not from afar. That is, people on the scene who are most familiar with the needs and problems are in the best position to do something about them.

In sum, this view holds that there is no one best path to planned change; on the contrary, there are many ways to get there from here. Perhaps the best advice is that proffered by Professor Howard Hill, that enthusiastic and successful seller of trombones in *The Music Man.* Said the professor, "You gotta know the territory."

## Three Perspectives Toward Planned Change

As previously stated, there are three conceptual models in the literature, which contribute to what managers see and how they act in problem-solving situations: the classical theory model, the social system model, and the open system theory model. The approaches toward planned change in educational organizations differ with respect to which model happens to operate at a given time.

### The Classical Theory Model of Change

Rational models of planned change have long been popular because they suggest a way out of a problem—a way that is conceptually neat and definitive. The field of education is continually generating rational responses to complex problems, and the promises held forth to potential adopters are enticing.

When considering the formula of change—that of embedding a specific innovation in a specific organizational environment using a specific strategy—the rational approaches all too often ignore the special characteristics of the environment. Rational approaches also stress directive and mandate-type strategies of change as opposed to collaborative strategies. In their significant study of an attempt at innovation in an elementary school, Gross, Giacquinta, and Bernstein capture the rational person approach school administrators use:

> Another critical problem that the administrators at [the school] overlooked was the need for the teachers to be resocialized. Teachers were asked to conform to a new role model but were not provided with the skills and knowledge they needed. It was assumed by the innovator that any professional teacher "worth his salt" could read a document describing the innovation and then, on his own, radically change his behavior in ways that were congruent with the new role model. The teachers were exposed to a host of difficulties when they tried to do just that, and these difficulties were not recognized by their superiors or resolved. As noted, teachers tried to behave in accord with the [innovation] but immediately found themselves exposed to new and unanticipated responses from their pupils. Neither prepared for this new pupil behavior nor equipped to deal with it effectively, they quickly reverted to the security of their previous role behavior.[103]

Rational strategies of change are dependent on people acting in a similarly rational way, and that is the rub. As a graduate student of mine once so graphically wrote on an examination, "It is the human dimension that has the capacity to screw up the grand design."

When individual academicians or educational observers superimpose rational models on the operations of a living organization and compare the difference between what *should* happen and what *does* happen, they are often quick to blame the teachers and administrators for performing ineffectively. Actually, the school personnel might be performing heroically, above and beyond the call of duty. They might be seen as such when viewed as working within an outrageously irrational environment that is the product of economic, social, and political forces far outside their control.

Attempts to understand the processes of planned change as they take place in a real world context often shift the conceptual framework from classical bureaucratic theory to social system theory.

## The Social System Model of Change

Chapter Three established the framework for understanding the processes of change as they take place in the social system model (or the sociopolitical group model, as it is sometimes called). This model of educational organization is made up of numerous social systems. These social systems must be brought into a collaborative effort if a program of directed change is to be carried out successfully. The task is complicated because the various social systems often have their own informal goals, power sources, norms governing behavior, and incentive systems.

Given the existence of various semiautonomous subgroups in the organization (e.g., the teachers' union or the curriculum council), the possibility of change taking place *independent of the formal leadership* always exists. Direct or indirect resistance to change initiatives on the part of the social systems also is a possibility. The task of the formal leadership in the educational system is to try to coordinate and control as much as possible the various subgroups so that they more or less move together as a coalition in a preestablished direction of change.

Expanding on this notion, Chapter Four drew together elements of the bureaucratic model and the social system model and merged them in a single conceptual framework. In Chapter Four the school was described as being composed of spheres of influence—rational, bureaucratic, and spontaneous or creative environments. Administrators as bureaucrats and teachers as professionals control specific types of decisions.

The model in Chapter Four proposed that change initiatives tend to be more successful when administrators are cognizant of the composition and strength of the various social systems and take them into account. That is, if a change initiative involves only the administrator's own sphere of influence (e.g., legal requirements for the school), then unilateral decisions are most efficient and expedient. However, if a desired change falls across another sphere of influence in the school system, that calls for strategies and tactics. These strategies (what to do) and tactics (how to do it) might call for varying the decision-making process along a unilateral-participative continuum. Or they may call for manipulating various social system variables discussed in Chapter Three, such as rank, stress-strain, reward sanction, and the like.

When confronted with the complexities of an irrational organizational environment, a planned change strategy often calls for the use of an organization development specialist. The OD specialist may personally assume an intervention role. He or she thereby becomes a change agent, attempting to direct the course of events. Or the OD specialist may establish some sort of training sessions to facilitate more effective action on the part of others. In any case, the course of change is uncertain, although movement is anticipated.

In terms of planned change, the social system perspective does not consider to any significant extent the important role the *external* environment plays in the change process. For an understanding of the planned change process that takes into account the external and internal environments of a school system, one might turn to the open system model.

## *The Open System Model of Change*

The open system model as applied to change in educational organizations suggests an understanding of the relationships between three bodies of theory: open system theory, contingency theory, and management-information theory. Open system theory, discussed in Chapter Four, emphasizes the dependency relationship of the school and its surrounding environment. When the needs and demands of the environment shift, the output of the school (and therefore of the teaching-learning process) must also change, if the school is to be an engine of development rather than a contributor to the problems of society.

An open system approach to change is necessary for what is sometimes referred to as *systemic educational change;* that is, an integrated effort toward change that encompasses the major dimensions of schooling, such as enhancing student expectations, introducing sophisticated curriculum frameworks, promoting creative teaching methods, and providing for enabling rather than restrictive school governance processes.[104]

Katz and Kahn argue that major changes are the exception rather than the rule, but when changes do come usually they can be attributed to two sources: (1) new inputs from the external environment (e.g., new tax laws, demographic shifts, new inventions, economic cycles, etc.), and (2) internal system strain or imbalance, such as conflict or uneven growth patterns or budget support.[105]

Contingency theory, a derivative of open system theory, says that variable environmental demands require variable organizational responses. For example, as a greater number of parents want more basic education for their children, the school must be able to respond to that need. The more turbulent the environment, the more differentiated and integrated the subsystems must be to maintain the flexibility to respond with diversity of output.

The management-information system, discussed in Chapter Five, has five information loops that are the mechanisms that gather precise information and link the external environment needs with internal structures. In theory, changes in the needs of the environment are reported through the MIS and result in corresponding changes in the educational process.

However, theory is not practice, so change initiatives all too frequently fail. In education, numerous organizational forces contribute to a breakdown in the creation of a close bond between the school and its environment. Some of these organizational forces are: the domesticated character of the school, the vagueness of educational goals, the separation between departments, the lack of integration and differentiation between subsystems, and the limited resources devoted to information gathering. However, those who find themselves discouraged by the trials of attempting to attain the fruits of planned change need only look at the staggering problems other nations face to realize that our lot is not nearly as bad as we might think.[106]

## Conclusion

Always interested in the processes of school improvement, I once asked the superintendent of a large, urban school district, "How does change come around here?"

He thought for a moment. "Well," he replied, "there is the normal way and the miraculous way. The normal way," he continued, "is where the heavens part and the angels come down and do the change for us. The miraculous way is when we do it ourselves."

Change obviously does not come easily. Until we develop more insightful conceptual tools to diagnose the reasons why and then create alternative organizational forms, we will have to live with the all-too-familiar consequences of falling somewhat short of our expectations. The relationship between open system theory, contingency theory, and management-information system theory provides a promising avenue for greater understanding of the organizational problems in the field of education. Given this greater understanding, there is potential for generating more successful change in our schools.

This is not to say that the bureaucratic model and the sociopolitical group model are not important, because indeed they are. Each contributes to an understanding of organizational life and suggests important strategies for change. But it must be remembered, nevertheless, that any model holds potential traps for mindless devotees. A central theme of this book is that the most successful administrators probably will be those with an understanding of all three models and with the capability to go with one at any moment, given the demands of the specific conditions faced.

## The Case of the Dusty Computers

You are an experienced change agent who recently received a call from Ms. Wilma Trombone, Superintendent of Highland Unified School District. Ms. Trombone is somewhat depressed because six months ago she purchased 43 Dasher microcomputers for the district that were supposed to speed up communication and decision-making processes.

"For the most part, these Dasher machines just sit around gathering dust," Ms. Trombone said. "People who work in this district are very busy, but for some reason they just haven't realized how much time and energy they could save if they used the new computers." Ms. Trombone then asked you to look into the matter and assume the role of change agent. She will back your efforts.

1. You decide to start by developing a plan of action. Identify the series of stages that would make up your plan. In each of the stages, be sure to point out *what* you would do, *how* you would do it, and *why*. Be sure to include a discussion of what you would need to find about the district, the innovation, and the employees.
2. What criteria would you employ to decide on an appropriate strategy of change?

## *Notes*

1.  *Cf.* Raymond Callahan, *Education and the Cult of Efficiency* (Chicago: University of Chicago Press, 1962); L.A. Cremin, *The Transformation of the School* (New York: Alfred A. Knopf, 1961); and Dan Lortie, *Schoolteacher* (Chicago: University of Chicago Press, 1975).

2.  Reported in Arthur Coladarchi and Jacob Getzels, *The Use of Theory in Educational Administration,* Monograph no. 5 in Educational Administration (Stanford, CA: Stanford University Press, 1955), pp. 20–21.

3.  Shelley Umans, *The Management of Education* (Garden City, NY: Doubleday, 1971), p. 34.

4.  Matthew Miles, "Educational Innovation: The Nature of the Problem," in *Innovation in Education,* Matthew Miles, ed. (New York: Teachers College Press, 1964), p. 14.

5.  Everett Rogers and Lynne Svenning, *Managing Change* (San Mateo, CA: San Mateo County Superintendent of Schools, 1969), p. 16.

6.  Herbert Kaufman, "The Direction of Organizational Evolution," *Public Administration Review* 33 (1973): 307.

7.  Herbert Shepard, "Innovation-Resisting and Innovation-Producing Organizations," in *The Planning of Change,* Warren Bennis et al., eds. (New York: Holt, Rinehart and Winston, 1969), pp. 520–521.

8.  Sloan Wayland, "Structural Features of American Education as Basic Factors in Innovation," in *Innovation in Education,* Matthew Miles, ed. (New York: Teachers College Press, 1964), p. 588.

9.  Daniel Levine and Eric Cooper, "The Change Process and Its Implications in Teaching Thinking," *Dimensions of Thinking and Cognitive Instruction* (Hillsdale, NJ: Erlbaum, 1989).

10.  Niccolo Machiavelli, *The Prince,* Luigi Ricci, trans., revised by E. R. P. Vincent (New York: New American Library of World Literature, 1952), p. 55.

11.  Harold Leavitt, "Applied Organizational Change in Industry: Structural, Technological, and Humanistic Approaches," in *Handbook of Organizations,* J. G. March, ed. (Chicago: Rand McNally, 1965).

12.  Daniel Katz and Robert Kahn, *The Social Psychology of Organizations,* Copyright © 1966, John Wiley & Sons, Inc. Reprinted by permission of John Wiley & Sons, Inc.

13.  Ibid., p. 391.

14.  Kathleen Anderson, Mike Milstein and Nancy Greenbert, "Change and Restructuring: What About Staff Development Readiness?" *People and Education,* 1 (1993): 303–313; Fred Newmann, "Beyond Common Sense in Educational Restructuring: The Issues of Content and Linkage," *Educational Researcher* 22 (1993), p. 11.

15.  Wilfred Brown, *Organization* (London: Heinemann Educational Books, 1971), p. 25.

16.  Jacob Getzels, "Theory and Research on Leadership: Some Comments and Alternatives," in *Leadership: The Science and the Art Today,* Luvern Cunningham and William Gephart, eds. (Itasca, IL: F. E. Peacock, 1973), pp. 22–23.

17.  Ibid., p. 22.

18.  Robert Chin and Kenneth Benne, "General Strategies for Effecting Changes in Human Systems," in *The Planning of Change,* Warren Bennis et al., eds. (New York: Holt, Rinehart and Winston, 1969), p. 47.

19.  Wayland, "Structural Features of American Education," p. 599.

20.  Debra Viadero, "Health Textbooks In Texas Attacked From Both Sides," *Education Week,* XII (February 23, 1994), pp. 1, 15.

21. *Cf.* Warren Bennis, *Changing Organizations* (New York: McGraw-Hill, 1966); and James G. March and Herbert A. Simon, *Organizations* (New York: John Wiley & Sons, 1958).

22. Max Abbott, "Hierarchical Impediments to Innovation in Educational Organization," in *Organizations and Human Behavior: Focus on Schools,* Fred Carver and Thomas Sergiovanni, eds. (New York: McGraw-Hill, 1969).

23. Lloyd Bishop, "Bureaucracy and Educational Change," *The Clearing House* 44 (1970):305–309.

24. Rodney Muth and Jann Azumi, "School Reform: Whither Boards of Educations?" *Metropolitan Education* 5 (1987):52.

25. Gerald Moeller and W. W. Charters, "Relations of Bureaucratization to Sense of Power Among Teachers," *Administrative Science Quarterly* 10 (1966):444–465.

26. Linda Darling-Hammond and Carol Ascher, "Accountability Mechanisms in Big City School Systems," *ERIC Digest,* 71 (1991), p. 2.

27. Robert Merton, *Social Theory and Social Structure* (New York: The Free Press, 1957), pp. 199–200.

28. Peter Blau, *The Dynamics of Bureaucracy* (Chicago: The University of Chicago Press, 1963).

29. Ibid., p. 247.

30. Richard Carlson, "Barriers to Change in Public Schools," in *Change Processes in Public Schools,* Richard Carlson et al., eds. (University of Oregon, Eugene, OR: Center for the Advanced Study of Educational Administration, 1965).

31. Thomas Timar and David Kirp, *Managing Educational Excellence* (New York: Falmer, 1988), pp. 85–95.

32. Matthew Miles, "Innovations in Education: Some Generalizations," in *Innovations in Education,* Matthew Miles, ed. (New York: Teachers College Press, 1964), p. 635.

33. Samuel Bacharach, Bauer Scott, and Joseph Shedd, "The Work Environment and School Reform," *Teachers College Record* 88 (1986):248.

34. Goodwin Watson, "Resistance to Change," in *The Planning of Change,* Warren Bennis et al., eds. (New York: Holt, Rinehart and Winston, 1969), p. 488.

35. Ibid.

36. Ibid., p. 489.

37. Halpin, "Change: The Mythology," p. 4.

38. William Savage, *Interpersonal and Group Relations in Educational Administration* (Glenview, IL: Scott, Foresman, 1968), p. 190.

39. Robert Presthus, *The Organizational Society* (New York: Vintage Books, 1962), p. 257.

40. Joseph P. Maginnis and Donald J. Willower, "The School Superintendent and the Decision to Move On," *Administrator's Notebook* 35 (1991-92): p. 4.

41. March and Simon, *Organizations,* pp. 173–174.

42. Watson, "Resistance to Change," pp. 487–496.

43. Ibid., p. 493.

44. Gerhard Eichholz, "Why Do Teachers Reject Change?" *Theory into Practice* 2 (1963): 266.

45. F. J. Roethlisberger and W. J. Dickson, *Management and the Worker* (Cambridge, MA: Harvard University Press, 1938).

46. Edgar Huse, *Organizational Development and Change* (New York: West, 1975), pp. 112–113.

47. Edwin Bridges, "The Principal and the Teachers: The Problem of Organizational Change," in *Perspectives on the Changing Role of the Principal,* Richard Saxe, ed. (Springfield, IL: Charles C. Thomas, 1968), p. 63.

48. Ibid., pp. 64–65.

49. Neal Gross, Joseph Giacquinta, and Marilyn Bernstein, *Implementing Organizational Innovations* (New York: Basic Books, 1971).

50. Louis Smith and Pat Keith, *Anatomy of Educational Innovation: An Organizational Analysis of an Elementary School* (New York: John Wiley & Sons, 1971).

51. Gross, Giacquinta, and Bernstein, *Implementing Organizational Innovations.*

52. Joseph Giacquinta, "The Process of Organizational Change in Schools," in *Review of Research in Education,* Fred Kerlinger, ed. (Itasca, IL: F. E. Peacock, 1973).

53. Gretchen Rossman, H. Dickson Corbett, and William Firestone, *Change and Effectiveness in Schools: A Cultural Perspective* (New York: SUNY, 1988).

54. Albert Shanker, "Reforming the Reform Movement," *Educational Administration Quarterly* 24 (1988):370.

55. Dan Lortie, "Observations on Teaching as Work," in *Second Handbook of Research on Teaching,* Robert Travers, ed. (Chicago: Rand McNally, 1973), p. 474.

56. W. Edward Deming, *Out of the Crisis* (Cambridge, MA: MIT Press, 1986).

57. Michael J. Schmoker and Richard B. Wilson, *Total Quality Education* (Bloomington, IN: Phi Delta Kappan Educational Foundation, 1993), p. 1.

58. Joseph C. Fields, *Total Quality for Schools: A Suggestion for American Schools* (Milwaukee, WI: ASQC Quality Press, 1993), p. 47. With permission of ASQC Quality Press.

59. Mary Walton, *Deming Management at Work* (New York: Perigee, 1990).

60. Fields, p. 66. With permission of ASQC Quality Press.

61. Human Resources Division, "Total Quality Management," General Accounting Office, GAO/HEHS-94-76R, Washington, D.C., 1994, p. 2.

62. Chin and Benne, "General Strategies for Effecting Changes," p. 34.

63. Joseph Giacquinta, "The Process of Organizational Change in Schools," p. 184.

64. Ibid.

65. Donald Willower, "Educational Change and Functional Equivalents," *Education and Urban Society* 2 (1970): 390; and Getzels, "Theory and Research on Leadership," p. 21.

66. Ronald Havelock, *The Change Agent's Guide to Innovation in Education* (Englewood Cliffs, NJ: Educational Technology Publications, 1973), p. ix.

67. Smith and Keith, *Anatomy of Educational Innovation,* pp. 118-119.

68. Ibid., p. 368.

69. Charles Lindblom, "The Science of Muddling Through," *Public Administration Review* 19 (1959); and Burton Nygren, "How to Survive Those 'Innovations' That Nearly Ruined the Schools in the Sixties," *The American School Board Journal* 163 (1976).

70. Smith and Keith, *Anatomy of Educational Innovation,* p. 373.

71. Michael Fullan, *Change Forces: Probing the Depths of Educational Reform* (New York: Filmier, 1993), pp. 21-22.

72. Rogers and Svenning, *Managing Change,* p. 86.

73. Havelock, *The Change Agent's Guide,* p. 7.

74. Andre Morin, "An Innovator's Odyssey: How to Become a Thoughtful Change Agent," *Educational Technology* 15 (1975): 43.

75. Havelock, *The Change Agent's Guide,* pp. 13-14.

76. Victor Baldrige, "Rules for a Machiavellian Change Agent: Transforming the Entrenched Professional Organization," in *Managing Change in Educational Organizations,* Victor Baldridge and Terrence Deal, eds. (Berkeley, CA: McCutchan, 1975), pp. 383-384.

77. Ibid., p. 386.

78. Ibid.

79. Eric Hoffer, *The True Believer* (New York: Harper and Bros., 1951).

80. Roy Gregg and John Van Maanen, "The Realities of Education as a Prescription for Organizational Change," *Public Administration Review* 33 (1973): 529.

81. Richard Schmuck, "Organizational Development in Schools: Contemporary Concepts and Practices," in *Handbook of School Psychology,* 2nd ed., T. Gutkin and C. Reynolds, eds. (New York: Wiley, 1989).

82. R. Beckhard, *Organization Development: Strategies and Models* (Reading, MA: Addison-Wesley, 1969), p. 9.

83. Kurt Lewin, "Frontiers in Group Dynamics," *Human Relations* 1 (1947); idem, *Field Theory in Social Science* (New York: Harper & Row, 1951).

84. Richard Schmuck et al., *Handbook of Organizational Development in Schools* (Palo Alto, CA: National Press Books, 1972).

85. Wendell French, "Organizational Development: Objectives, Assumptions, and Strategies," in *Tomorrow's Organizations: Challenges and Strategies,* Jong Jun and William Storm, eds. (Glenview, IL: Scott, Foresman, 1973), p. 380.

86. Matthew Miles, "40 Years of Change in Schools: Some Personal Reflections," *Educational Administration Quarterly* 29 (1993), p. 224.

87. Louis Barnes, "Approaches to Organizational Change," in *The Planning of Change,* Bennis et al., eds. (New York: Holt, Rinehart and Winston, 1969), pp. 82–83.

88. Larry Greiner, "Organizational Change and Development," Ph.D. dissertation, Harvard University, 1965.

89. Schmuck et al., *Handbook of Organization Development in Schools,* pp. 15–16.

90. Matthew Miles, "On Temporary Systems," in *Innovation in Education,* Matthew Miles, ed. (New York: Teachers College Press, 1964), p. 443.

91. Ibid., chapter 19.

92. Matthew Miles, "40 Years of Change in Schools," p. 221.

93. Larry Greiner, "Red Flags in Organization Development," in *Readings in Organizations: Behavior, Structure, Processes,* James Gibson, John Ivancevich, and James Donnelly, Jr., eds. (Dallas: Business Publications, 1976), p. 366.

94. Victor Baldridge and Terrence Deal, "Overview of Change Processes in Educational Organizations," in *Managing Change in Educational Organizations,* Victor Baldridge and Terrence Deal, eds. (Berkeley, CA: McCutchan, 1975), p. 7.

95. Warner Burke, "The Demise of Organization Development," *Journal of Contemporary Business* 1 (1972): 58.

96. Rossman, Corbett, and Firestone, p. 20.

97. Wilson, as reported in Rossman, Corbett, and Firestone, p. 5.

98. Thomas Timar, "The Politics of Restructuring" (Paper presented at the Coalition of Essential Schools Seminar at Brown University, April 14, 1989), p. 10

99. Rossman, Corbett, and Firestone, p. 9.

100. Michael Fullan and Matthew Miles, "Getting Reform Right: What Works and What Doesn't," *Phi Delta Kappan* (June 1992): 745–752.

101. Fullan and Miles, p. 749.

102. Fullan and Miles, P. 751.

103. Gross, Giacquinta, and Bernstein, *Implementing Organizational Innovations,* p. 211.

104. Susan Fuhrman, "Politics and Systemic Education Reform," *CPRE Policy Briefs* (New Brunswick, NJ: Rutgers University, 1994), pp. 1–8.

105. Katz and Kahn, *Social Psychology of Organizations,* p. 446.

106. E. Mark Hanson, *Educational Reform and Administrative Development: The Cases of Colombia and Venezuela* (Stanford, CA: Stanford University, Hoover Institution Press, 1986).

# Chapter 13

# Educational Management in Developing Countries

Consistent with the popular theme of the globalization of nearly everything, several reviewers have suggested that the fourth edition of this textbook should include a chapter on international educational management. In response to that idea, this chapter will be made up of two parts. The *first* part will examine critical organization and management problems associated with educational development in Third World nations. I focus on Third World nations because the waves of immigration coming to the United States are from these countries. Also, most American educators know little about the types of management problems their Third World educational colleagues face.

The *second* will identify, examine, and contrast various types of national governance structures (e.g., unitary versus federal, autocratic versus democratic) and explain how they often influence educational policy.

## Bangladesh: A Quick Look

In the summer of 1994 I traveled by small boat up the Meghna River to visit three rural, island schools; islands not untypical of the many hundreds in Bangladesh formed by meandering tributaries of the Ganges and Brahmaputra rivers. The country, a low-lying delta flatland, is the geographical size of Wisconsin. However, unlike Wisconsin, which has a population of under five million, with 4.7 people per square mile, Bangladesh has a population of 114 million, with a density of 2,087 people per square mile. The education problem, not to mention the social and economic problems, becomes evident when you consider what it would be like to put almost half the population of the United States into a geographical area the size of Wisconsin.[1]

The river islands had no electricity or telephones, and thus the three-classroom elementary schools were bare of everything but overflowing students, a collection of ancient desks, a teacher, and a square patch of black paint on the wall which served as a blackboard. Each school had a monthly budget of US$30 dollars per academic year with which to purchase all school supplies. Happily, the students had books, the by-product of a World Bank loan. Except for the presence of the books, these schools were not unlike several hundred others I have visited in other developing nations around the world as a consultant for the World Bank, UNESCO, UNDP, or USAID.

The numbers reveal the depth of the educational problem. In Bangladesh, elementary schooling is a five-year cycle with an average teacher-student ratio of 56 to 1, although it can exceed 100 to 1. Primary schools operate two shifts, the first two grades for two hours and the next three for three-and-a-half hours. The proportion of boys to girls in these predominantly Moslem schools is 55 to 45.

Only 35 percent of the children that enroll in grade one actually finish primary school, and of that number only a little more than one-third will have achieved basic competencies in reading, writing, and numerical skills. The schooling outcome showed up in the adult literacy rate (age 15+) of approximately 31 percent in 1990.[2]

In departing the last island school I visited that day, I asked the headmaster whether the boys or the girls had the higher attendance rate. His answer was a first for me. "The boys," he replied without even having to consider his response, "because they can swim to school." Apparently, the girls are at a disadvantage because of the long dresses they must wear in keeping with their Islamic faith.

As I returned down the sprawling river, all around I could see young children, no more than six or seven years of age, poling longboats across the reeds, throwing fish nets into the muddy waters or stooped over planting rice in the never-ending fields. The sad truth is that those children probably will be laboring at those same tasks the rest of their lives. Like millions of children in developing countries around the world, they will never have the chance to be bankers, teachers, or poets.

## The Context of Education in the Third World

The purpose of discussing the Bangladesh case is to give a thumbnail sketch of the difficult conditions educators must face in a poor country struggling with all the problems of underdevelopment. The next section will expand the exploration of education and underdevelopment to include the contextual variables of many Third World nations.

### Social and Economic Deprivation and Wealth

Development requires resources, and the wealth of the world is by no means evenly divided among countries or within countries. For example, the richest 20 percent of the nations account for 84.7 percent of the world's gross national product (GNP), 84.2 percent of the world trade, and 85 percent of domestic investment. The poorest 20 percent of the nations account for 1.4 percent of the world's GNP, 0.9 percent of world trade, and 0.9 percent of domestic investment (1991 data).[3]

The same gap between rich and poor that exists *between* countries also exists *within* countries. If one examines the country comparisons in Table 13.1, it becomes clear that in most countries of the world the poorest 20 percent of the population share only marginally in whatever wealth the nation possesses.[4] The magnitude of the uphill battle, especially for the poorer countries, can be seen in the per-capita annual income comparisons (1991 dollars). The average per-capita income for the World Bank's listing of the 40 low-income countries is $350; in the 43 middle-income countries is $2,480; in the 22 upper-middle-income countries is $3,530; and in the 22 high-income countries is $21,050. Certainly, if any progress is to be made toward closing the massive income gap, economic growth and education must play considerably greater roles than they do currently.[5]

However, since the early 1980s, foreign debt has been a major constraint to economic development and the investment in human resources. From 1970 to 1992 the total external debt in Third World countries grew from $100 billion to $1,500 billion. Service charges are the cost of borrowing, and during the 1983–1992 decade the financial flow reversed, with developed countries receiving net transfers of $147 billion from developing countries as payment of service charges on long-term loans. Consequently,

TABLE 13.1    Income Distribution Within Nations

|  | Poorest 20% | Richest 20% |
|---|---|---|
| *Low-Income Countries* |  |  |
| Tanzania | 2.4 | 62.7 |
| Bangladesh | 9.5 | 38.6 |
| India | 8.8 | 41.3 |
| China | 6.4 | 41.8 |
| Honduras | 2.7 | 63.5 |
| *Middle-Income Countries* |  |  |
| Peru | 4.9 | 54.5 |
| Colombia | 4.0 | 53 |
| Thailand | 6.1 | 50.7 |
| Panama | 2.0 | 59.8 |
| *Upper-Middle Income* |  |  |
| Venezuela | 4.8 | 49.5 |
| Mexico | 4.1 | 55.9 |
| Botswana | 1.4 | 66.4 |
| *High Income* |  |  |
| Spain | 6.9 | 40 |
| Italy | 6.8 | 41 |
| Canada | 5.7 | 40.2 |
| United States | 4.7 | 41.9 |
| Japan | 8.7 | 37.5 |

Note: Selected country illustrations.
Selected statistics from: The World Bank, *World Development Report 1993* (New York: Oxford University Press, 1993), pp. 294–297. Used with permission of the World Bank and Oxford University Press.

for over a decade the poorest nations of the world have been subsidizing development in the world's richest nations.[6]

Economic and educational investment in many developing countries have been hostage to political conflict and the appetites of military budgets. Most armed conflicts today are *within* rather than *between* countries. From 1989 to 1992, of the 82 armed conflicts, only three were between countries. Many of these internal conflicts are governments repressing their own people, *coup d'états* or civil wars. In 1993, there were 79 countries with major conflicts or political violence, and 65 of them were in the developing world.

Consequently, scarce resources that could go into nation building actually go into nation destruction. The total cost of military expenditures around the world is enormous. In 1992 the collective world military spending was $815 billion, a sum that equals the combined income of nearly 50 percent of the world's people.[7]

From 1960 to 1987 (the peak year in military spending), military expenditures in developing countries increased from US$24 billion to $145 billion, with $95 billion of that spent by some of the world's poorest countries. The opportunity cost of money spent on weapons of war instead of human development is enormous. For example, only 4 percent of the $125 billion spent in developing nations on military expenditures in 1992 "would reduce adult illiteracy by half, provide universal primary education and educate women to the same level as men."[8] A few of these countries spent more on their military than their combined expenditures on education and health—for example, Angola, Ethiopia, Mozambique, Myanmar, Pakistan, Somalia and Yemen.[9]

The industrialized nations of the world must share a large measure of blame for the developing countries eating up large portions of their scarce resources on military expenditures. When profits are to be made, or a poor nation can be used to fight a proxy war, the rich nations of the world have exhibited little moral restraint. It is interesting to note that the top five arms exporters in the world are all permanent members of the United Nations Security Council: the United States of America, the former USSR, France, Germany, China and the United Kingdom.

Between 1988 and 1992, the United States was the world's top arms merchant, with exports of nearly $55 billion (1990 U.S. dollars). Interestingly enough, between 1980 and 1990 the USA supplied approximately 57 percent of the weapons sales that went to Iraq and 67 percent that went to Somalia.[10]

## Foreign Aid and Human Development Assistance

Foreign aid is a contentious subject at home and abroad. After all, why should we spend money on the world's poor when we have our own poor at home? Well, to put the situation in perspective, the 15 most industrialized nations of the world spend 15 percent of their combined GNPs (1992 data) to provide for their own social safety nets while allocating 0.3 percent to foreign assistance safety nets. While it is true that the USA's nearly $11 billion in AID (1992) is second only to Japan's $11 billion (plus), of 15 industrialized countries allocating bilateral aid the USA is dead last, with only 0.18 percent of its GNP going to these foreign development programs. The next three lowest are

Austria (0.29%), Japan (0.30%), and the United Kingdom (0.30%). The Scandinavian countries of Norway, Sweden, and Denmark give more than one percent of their GNPs to foreign AID, more than any other industrialized country.[11]

Is international AID money targeted for the world's poor? In a word, no. Nearly two-thirds of the world's poor reside in 10 countries, but less than one-third of the development AID goes to those nations. Of the 10 nations, in Bangladesh 93.2 million people, or 78 percent of the total population, live in poverty. It received 3.8 percent of the world's total development assistance. In China, 105 million people, or 9 percent of the total population, live in poverty, and it received 6.5 percent of the total international AID.[12]

How much of the bilateral AID goes toward human development projects (e.g., education, primary health care, nutrition programs, sanitation, rural water supplies)? An average of only 7 percent of the AID from the 15 industrialized countries goes to human development projects. This varies, of course, from country to country. The highest is Denmark which gives 25 percent of its AID to human development projects. The USA, Japan, and Germany give 11.3 percent, 3.4 percent, and 2.1 percent, respectively. Interestingly enough, within the human development priorities, higher education gets preference over primary education, which gets less than 20 percent of the total education expenditure.[13]

How are AID priorities set? Typically, AID follows the donor nations' commercial and geopolitical interests. Commercially, AID from a donor nation must be (or is encouraged to be) spent back in the donor's home markets on equipment, foodstuffs, or even consultants. Also, for political reasons donors like their AID to be highly visible. Thus, physical infrastructure such as bridges and buildings often get high priority.

Then there are the proxy conflicts, because international AID is used to stabilize or destabilize governments or balances of power between regions of the world. The USA, for example, has concentrated its AID (1990–91 data) on Israel, El Salvador, Bolivia and Egypt. The military priority is clear when one sees that El Salvador received 16 times more AID per poor person than did Bangladesh even though the per capita GNP in El Salvador is five times higher.[14]

In sum, as the old saying goes, God truly must have loved the poor because he made so many of them. With the world's riches so unevenly distributed, there is little wonder that one of the great movements of the latter part of the twentieth century has been migration—both legal and illegal. Efforts in Third World nations to stimulate their own development have more often than not been thwarted by overpopulated land, untrained labor, and unavailable capital. The next section will illustrate the consequences of improving the quality of education.

## Education and Development

In discussing the linkages between education and Third World modernization, a report from the World Bank states that education, technology, and openness enable economic systems to respond not only to price signals but also to new ideas. "Openness encourages the flow of technologies from industrialized countries to developing countries; education encourages the adoption, adaptation, and diffusion of technology. Differences in the rate of technology adoption and economic growth among countries are in large part the result of differences in education."[15]

How important is education in a poor country? The World Bank reports that ". . . the evidence that eduction promotes economic growth, and thus puts other goals of development within reach, is firm. A one-year increase in schooling can augment an individual's wages by more than 10 percent . . . ," or even increase farm output between two and five percent. In addition, during the first three years of schooling, "increasing the average amount of education of the labor force by one year raises GDP by 9 percent."[16]

A classic illustration of the interaction between new technology and education is the spread of the green revolution in agriculture. With the development of new, high-yield varieties of wheat and rice, diffusing a body of information that provided farmers with the capability to make use of the new knowledge was the absolute key to success.

However, simply setting new educational policies and allocating more money to schools is insufficient. Critical to educational development are enabling policies and programs such as providing for clean water, waste disposal, child nutrition, primary health care, family planning, and incentives for parents to keep their children in schools and out of the fields.

## *Comparative Indicators of Educational Development*

The United Nations Development Program (UNDP) has identified a series of characteristics that reflect the level of educational development in 127 Third World countries. Comparison indicators of 47 *least* developed countries are extracted from the full list and presented in Table 13.2.

A sharp contrast can be seen between developed and developing nations, with the developed countries' literacy rate exceeding 97 percent and the number of mean years of schooling at 10. The two nations with the highest mean years of schooling are the United States (12.4) and Canada (12.2). The two lowest are Niger (0.2) and Burkina Faso (0.2). (Author's note. If you know where that last one is, your geography is better than mine.)

The "net primary enrollment" indicates the percentage of primary school-age children who actually are in school. The degree of human loss can be readily understood when one realizes that in the least developed countries, only 53 percent of the elementary school-age children actually are enrolled in school. In terms of geographical regions, the East Asian nations (excluding China) approach 100 percent, while for the Sub-Sahara African nations the figure is 43 percent.[17] Looking at the enrollment figures for secondary schools, one might ask what type of development opportunity exists in countries where only 15 percent of the secondary school-age adolescents attend school.

In terms of gender differences, the percentage of females enrolled in school in some countries is extraordinarily low, although worldwide significant improvements were made between 1970 and 1990.

It should be noted that for all the developing countries (1990 data), at the primary school level females have only 72 percent the enrollment rate of males and at the secondary level 51 percent. In the *least* developed countries, the gender gap is considerably greater, with the number of females enrolled at only 60 percent that of males at the

TABLE 13.2　Educational Development Indexes

| | Least developed countries (n = 47) | All developing countries (n = 127) | Industrial countries (n = 28) |
|---|---|---|---|
| Adult literacy rate | | | |
| 1970 | 29.0% | 46.0% | .. |
| 1992 | 46.0% | 69.0% | 97.3% |
| Mean years of schooling | | | |
| total | 1.6 | 3.9 | 10.0 |
| female | 0.9 | 3.0 | |
| male | 2.2 | 4.9 | |
| Access to safe water | 45.0% | 70.0% | |
| Access to sanitation | 32.0% | 56.0% | |
| % enrolled, ages 6–23 | 32.0% | 46.0% | |
| Primary net enrollment | 53.0% | 86.0% | |
| Secondary net enrollment | 15.0% | 33.0% | |
| First-grade intake | 75.0% | 92.0% | |
| Primary completers | 51.0% | 71.0% | |
| Transition to secondary | 39.0% | 65.0% | |
| Tertiary enrollment | 2.2% | 6.8% | |
| People below poverty line | | | |
| total | 64.0% | 31.0% | |
| rural | 71.0% | 37.0% | |
| urban | 31.0% | 28.0% | |

Note: (. .) means data unavailable.
Selected statistics from: UNDP, *Human Development Report 1994* (Delhi: Oxford University Press, 1994), pp. 129, 207, 209, 210. Used with permission of UNDP and Oxford University Press.

primary school level and 30 percent at the secondary level.[18] Regional data for women along with some country examples are seen in Table 13.3.[19]

Aside from the gender equity issue, the World Bank reports that "the status of women is by far the most important variable explaining changes in infant mortality and secondary school enrollments. An extra year of education for women is associated with a drop of 2 percentage points in the rate of infant mortality. Household-level studies have reported even larger reductions of 5–10 percentage points."[20]

## *Haves and Have Nots in Educational Finance*

As discussed earlier, the wealth of the world is by no means evenly distributed among nations. The annual per capita income of the 40 poorest countries averages US$350 per year (1991 dollars) while the 22 wealthiest nations average US$21,050. The extremes of the range finds Mozambique at US$80 and Switzerland at US$33,610. (Bangladesh is twelfth poorest at US$220 and the United States is eighth richest at $22,240.)[21]

In the percent of GNP spent on education, the least developed nations average 3.0 percent, the developing nations average 3.9 percent, and the industrialized nations

TABLE 13.3   Percentage of Female School Enrollment

| | Female Primary | | Female Secondary | |
|---|---|---|---|---|
| | 1970 | 1990 | 1970 | 1990 |
| Low-Income Economies | | | | |
| Tanzania | 27 | 63 | 2 | 4 |
| Ethiopia | 10 | 30 | 2 | 12 |
| Bangladesh | 35 | 68 | . . | 11 |
| India | 56 | 83 | 15 | 33 |
| China | . . | 129 | . . | 41 |
| Egypt | 57 | 90 | 23 | 71 |
| | | | | |
| Middle-Income Economies | | | | |
| Bolivia | 62 | 78 | 20 | 31 |
| Colombia | 110 | 111 | 24 | 57 |
| Thailand | 79 | 85 | 15 | 32 |
| Poland | 98 | 99 | 65 | 84 |
| | | | | |
| Upper-Middle Income Economies | | | | |
| Venezuela | 94 | 94 | 34 | 41 |
| Mexico | 101 | 110 | 17 | 53 |
| Greece | 106 | 101 | 55 | 97 |
| | | | | |
| World Regions With | | | | |
| Low- & Middle-Incomes | | | | |
| Sub-Saharan Africa | 36 | 61 | 4 | 16 |
| East Asia & Pacific | 77 | 123 | 16 | 44 |
| South Asia | 50 | 75 | 14 | 29 |
| Europe & Central Asia | 100 | 100 | 44 | 70 |
| Middle East & N. Africa | 50 | 90 | 15 | 50 |
| Latin America & Caribbean | 94 | 106 | 26 | 57 |

Note: ( . .) means data unavailable.
   Gross enrollment figures may exceed 100 percent because of enrollment above or
      below standard school age.
   Twenty-two high-income economies not included in data.
Selected statistics from: The World Bank, World Development Report 1993 (New York: Oxford University Press, 1993), pp. 294–295. Used with permission of UNDP and Oxford University Press.

average 4.9 percent (1990 data).[22] The relative wealth of nations can be seen in the public recurrent per-pupil expenditures in pre-primary, primary and secondary education, with the developing countries averaging nearly US$100 and the developed countries $2,000 (1988 data and dollars).[23]

The poorer countries tend to underinvest in education, and the reasons no doubt vary with the country. Some countries, for example, still are trying to solve infrastructure problems of roads, clean water, electrical power, and communication that other countries solved early in the twentieth century. Other poor countries have virtually no natural resources, or even the capacity to feed themselves. Consequently, they must use scarce resources to purchase everything from petroleum to wheat simply to survive.

Military spending is one high priority item in the developing world. In the *least developed* countries, military spending accounts for 65 percent of the combined education and health expenditures. In *all developing* countries it is 60 percent of the combined expenditures, and 33 percent in the *industrialized* countries (1991 data).[24] When a military government or an elitist oligarchy control the treasury, education for the masses typically suffers at the extreme.

Argentina is an interesting illustration. The last civilian government (1973–75) prior to the military regime in Argentina (1976–1983) was spending approximately 3.98 percent of the GNP on education. Under the military, this figure was cut to a yearly average of 3.22 percent. With the return of democracy in 1984, the percent of GNP going to education almost immediately advanced to 4.84.[25] In Spain, when General Franco died in 1975 the nation was spending 1.8 percent of its GNP on education, the lowest in all of western Europe by a considerable margin. Within 10 years the educational expenditure had risen to 3.3 percent of GNP.[26]

Military governments and civilian oligarchic elites, both of which are abundant in the Third World, typically are unwilling to spend much money on public education.[27] Education tends to be viewed as an expense rather than an investment. Military governments are aware that riotous student demonstrations protesting the abuses of government usually are at the vanguard of movements that eventually throw the generals out of power. For the oligarchies, the educated masses become threats to their traditional prominence as an elitist ruling class.

## Government Structures and Educational Policy

Making choices based on goals and directing the system toward accomplishing them is the essence of governance. Around the world, the processes of educational governance and policy formation are shaped, in part, by: (1) the political institutions holding the reigns of power, such as democratic or authoritarian systems of government; (2) the territorial distributions of authority, such as a unitary, federal or confederation frameworks; and (3) powerful societal forces emanating from inside or outside the nation, such as rapid urbanization, shifts in sources of revenue, ideological orientations, judicial interpretations, bureaucratic structures, and the International Monetary Fund. This section points out that although reasonably well-defined models of governance and educational policy making can be found in the world of theory, in the real world the complex combinations of national cultures, political systems, socioeconomic structures, and historical traditions tend to erase the contours of the idealized theoretical frameworks.

## Governance Frameworks: Concept and Theory

Public and private educational systems around the world operate within frameworks established by the political systems of the nations to which they belong. Political systems are concerned with the exercise of power to make choices among competing alternatives.[28] Making choices based on goals and directing the system toward their accomplishment is the essence of governance.

In making choices, no political system, democratic or autocratic, can operate without some distribution of tasks and accompanying authority. This happens because, as Duchacek[29] reminds us, "political rulers can focus on some problems some of the time but cannot focus on all the problems all of the time and in all localities." Insight into the dynamic relationships of governance, intergovernmental relations, and educational policy indicates that the national distribution of authority and the locus of political control should be examined.

## *Unitary Framework of Government*

Unitary government systems typically were formed by powerful monarchies or colonial powers that once dominated the political structures of nations, such as in France, England, Russia, Spain (before 1987), and almost all Third World nations. "The state, it is claimed, is the guardian of efficiency and effectiveness, and it alone can ensure high and equitable standards of social and economic services. . . ."[30]

France is the classic example of a country where the uniformity of the educational system is derived from the supremacy of the state. The Ministry of Education in Paris, for example, establishes a uniform curriculum for the entire nation, employs and places all teachers, determines new school locations, allocates resources, and administers examinations. Regional and local educational agencies exist only to carry out the directives of the ministry of education.

## *Federal Framework of Government*

Federal systems of government often were formed as smaller autonomous polities joined together for the mutual benefit of the whole. The distribution of powers, as safeguarded by a constitution, provides for the coexistence of regional diversity and national unity. The United States, Switzerland, Germany, Canada and Australia typify the federal system.[31]

In a federal system, power in the hands of regional governments is not delegated or devolved from the central government,[32] but is "residual" power. That is, power reserved by the constitution for regional governments so that it is autonomous and cannot be revoked or returned to the national level. In many federal systems, as in the United States, education is a residual power reserved for the states.

## *Confederation Framework of Government*

A confederation is a collectivity of nations that share certain institutions or functions of government, such as import duties, foreign policy, or perhaps an army. A powerful confederation of immense proportions is now taking shape in the European Community. Begun with the Treaty of Rome in 1958 and amended in 1987 in the "Single European Act," the confederation is incrementally on the way to becoming the world's largest economic block.[33] Significantly, the barriers surrounding national systems of education are not being torn down. National identity and culture are held dear by each participant in the evolving European Community, and the educational system in each country is being sheltered as the keeper of the flame.

## Theory versus Practice

Theory, of course, is not practice. In the real world, with respect to educational policy frequently one finds unitary systems operating as federal or even confederate systems, and vice versa. When this happens there are often significant ramifications for the processes of educational governance and policy formation. One of the most important contributing forces to this phenomenon is a nation's locus of control—a locus that can shift periodically.

### Locus of Control

At the fulcrum of any governance framework are the forces of accountability and control. If the government is accountable directly to the people, then the structure of control is democratic. If the government is accountable only to itself, such as in many military-type governments, then the structure of control is autocratic. The implications for intergovernmental relations and the impact on educational policy are enormous.

### Democratic Forms of Government

In the democratic model of governance theory, the relationships between society and state are driven by the concepts of *consent, control,* and *accountability.* Through the electoral process, society gives its consent to be controlled by the rules of the state, which in turn must be accountable to society for its actions. Under theoretical conditions as these, the relations among levels of government tend to function as federal, unitary, or confederate systems were intended. However, as the following examples illustrate, in practice there are numerous intervening forces that impact on the formation of educational policy.

*Shifts in Source of Revenue*    In a federal system public schools typically receive funding from local, state, and federal governments. When the established contribution percentages shift, educational policy problems can develop. In the United States, for example, between 1960 and 1991 the contribution of the states to public education increased from 39 percent to 50 percent.[34] The consequence has been that local school districts often legitimately attempted to set policy on issues involving personnel employment, salary increases, and building construction that the state governments were unable or unwilling to fund.

*Judicial Interpretation*    In federal systems, the high court frequently interprets the national constitution in such a way that policy-making power shifts from one level of government to another. In the United States, for example, the Supreme Court frequently intervenes in state and local educational policy-making on issues involving the rights of minorities, and public funding for private school education.

*Political Ideological Orientations*    The United Kingdom is a unitary state with a parliamentary democracy that historically has decentralized extensive decision-making authority to the local educational agencies (LEAs). With the Conservative party defeat over Labour in 1979, an ideological shift to the political right brought about a decade of struggles and tensions with the LEAs as the central government strengthened its policy control over, among other things, the curriculum, student evaluation, financial expenditures and multicultural education.[35]

*Urbanization*    The population migration from rural to urban areas has been extensive in recent years, especially in Third World nations. For example, from 1970 to 1991 urbanization increased significantly in Mexico (59% to 73%), Brazil (56% to 76%), China (18% to 60%), Bangladesh (10% to 19%), South Korea (34% to 73%), and Nicaragua (47% to 60%).[36] Significant population shifts generally are followed by increased power and resources flowing to the major cities and a significant weakening of the smaller local educational agencies and their capacity to make and implement educational policies.

*Resource Generation at the Top*    The so-called "one crop" countries typically accumulate a large measure of their national income in the central government. In Venezuela, for example, 95 percent of its export income and 30 percent of its GNP come from petroleum exports. Because of this concentrated wealth, the 20 state governments are extremely weak financially. Thus, even though the country is a federal system, its educational institution is dominated by the center and is governed basically as a unitary system.[37]

*Resource Distribution*    Unitary systems of government usually provide a more equitable geographical distribution of resources for education than do federal systems. Consequently, shaping common educational policy for the entire nation is facilitated considerably. In France, for example, there is a single salary system for public schools and per-pupil expenditures, basically equivalent throughout the country. In federal systems, equity in resource distribution can be a serious problem. In the United States, for example, almost every school district has its own salary scale. In the early 1990s at the elementary and secondary school levels, per-pupil expenditures in Utah were $2,906; Alabama $3,627; Arizona, $4,309; Michigan, $5,883; and New York, $8,565. Such expenditures in the U.S. Virgin Islands were $6,002 as compared to $1,913 next door in Puerto Rico.[38]

*Local-Level Influence*    In a federal system the capacity of individuals and groups (e.g., business, minority, religious, wealthy) to influence the direction of local level educational policy is much greater than in a unitary system, such as France, where policy decisions are made at the top.

## Authoritarian Forms of Government

In an authoritarian form of government the command structure is controlled by a political elite, which neither requires consent of the people nor is accountable to them. Recent examples of authoritarian governments illustrate that they may be purely military in makeup, as in Argentina and Bolivia; military and civilian coalitions, as in Brazil and Uruguay; general turned president, as Chile under Pinochet and Spain under Franco; or political party, as in China and North Korea. Whether the structure of government is unitary or federal is usually irrelevant, because central power must dominate the processes of governance in order to retain control.

Authoritarian governments typically attempt to use the educational systems to indoctrinate the nation regarding its legitimacy to rule as well as bind it together through a singular interpretation of historical events as represented in textbooks. The former Soviet Union is a classic case, and when it began to break up educators in Russia and the various republics were faced with the enormous problem of sorting fact from fiction and discovering the reality of their own national history.[39]

The impact on educational governance and policy is considerable, depending on whether the type of authoritarian government is conservative or radical.

*Conservative Authoritarian Governments*    The political elites in a conservative authoritarian state are dedicated to maintaining the status quo, particularly the class structure. Political alliances often emerge between societal power blocks as the military, the upper-class oligarchy, and religious/cultural institutions. Educational policy and governance are shaped to reinforce the nation's existing social, political, and economic structure, such as occurred in many Latin American nations, colonial African nations, and dynastic monarchies in the Middle East.[40]

*Radical Authoritarian Governments*    This form of government usually emerges when a political group dedicated to changing the status quo seizes power. The educational system strives to serve the needs of the social classes that supported its rise to power, usually the middle or lower socioeconomic classes. Nations with Marxist orientations often fit into this framework, such as Cuba; or those recently freed from colonial rule, such as Zimbabwe;[41] or those driven by the principles of Islamic fundamentalism, such as Iran. Adopting new textbooks that introduce a new version of the national history, its values, oppression under past regimes, and faith in the new leadership is one of the first acts of a newly arrived radical authoritarian government.

## Institutional Power Centers

a. Educational governance often is influenced significantly by external centers of power. For example, the *Catholic Church* has established strong church-state alliances with the conservative governments of Hispanic nations, even negotiating concordats that give it extensive control over the value, moral, and religious content of the educational curriculum.[42]

b. Large donor organizations such as the International Monetary Fund or the World Bank commonly place restrictions on borrowing nations as conditions for loans. In education, these restrictions often limit a nation's ability to make policy choices, such as whether to use the funds for training more doctors or more teachers, or to construct vocational secondary schools or elementary schools.[43]

c. The large *bureaucratic structure* internal to the educational system also acts as an important center of power. It typically develops the regulations for any new educational laws and executes education policies. Bureaucrats with long tenure generally know how to shape the course of events by slowing down reforms that are not in their interests and speeding up those that are.[44]

## Conclusion

The first part of this chapter emphasized the point that the world's poor are not poor by choice. Just as water covers 70.8 percent of the earth's surface, so does relative poverty. The circumstances of life (e.g., weak national economies, barren lands, political turbulence, social stratification) have seemingly conspired against poor nations. Unfortunately, we tend to forget that the poor are just as intelligent as the rest of us. They simply were born in a thatched hut near a rice field in India, or a mud shelter on the high plains of Bolivia, or a stone shack in central Africa, or an urban slum in Honduras.

The countries where large numbers of poor are found typically do not have the human or material resources to build schools, train effective teachers, and expand the quality and quantity of schooling. These countries have to run hard simply to keep up with the pace of their exploding population growth.

Donor countries do give assistance, but only a tiny portion of their GNP. As pointed out, even that assistance tends to go to countries of special commercial or geopolitical interest to the donors. Only a small part of the international aid that finally reaches the poorest of the poor nations, actually goes to human development sectors such as health and education.

It is no wonder that, in ever-greater numbers, families seek to immigrate, either legally or illegally, to the developed nations of the world. Which of us wouldn't try to do the same for our own family?

The second part of this chapter stressed that outside the world of theory, government structure (federal or unitary), educational policy formation, and governance are not consistently related. Educational policy is shaped by centers of power that can be located; for example, inside or outside the educational institution, such as the ministry of education or a political party; inside or outside of the government, such as the legislature or a group of elite families; or inside or outside the country, such as the presidential palace or the International Monetary Fund.

Whether there exists a democratic or autocratic form of government is also important in understanding the governance process. A nation with a democratic government, whether unitary or federal, must be accountable for its actions to the electorate. Thus, the natural tendency is to shape educational policy in the best interests of the electorate. However, a nation with an authoritarian government will focus educational policy on reinforcing the special interests of the body in power, such as legitimizing its rule, reinforcing the social class structure, or imposing behavioral standards as defined by a body of religious beliefs.

Given the inexact and shifting relationships among governmental, cultural, political, economic, social, and educational institutions, how is educational policy formed in the international context? Considering what has thus far been said, perhaps Delany and Paine put their finger on the point as they discuss the shifting patterns of authority in Chinese schools.[45]

> We need to recognize that policy is the result of mutually conditioned interplay between the schools and the state. Rather than viewing the relationship between the state and society as strictly top-down . . . policy generation is an interactive and iterative process—described, at times, as a stumbling, "groping" affair.

In short, even though all nations have centers of power and geographical distributions of authority, only in the broadest context can common patterns linking types of government structures to policy formation be found. While in some ways this lack of international consistency might be viewed as detracting from development potential, in other ways this uniqueness of nations can be seen as a quality to be celebrated.

## Notes

1. *The 1994 Information Please Almanac,* 47th ed. (Boston: Houghton Mifflin, 1994), pp. 150, 883.

2. UNICEF, *Primary Education in Bangladesh: Selected Facts, Goals and Strategies* (Dhaka: UNICEF, 1993), pp. 1–26.

3. UNDP (United Nations Development Program), *Human Development Report: 1994* (Delhi: Oxford University Press, 1994), p. 63. Reproduced with permission.

4. World Bank, *World Development Report: 1993* (New York: Oxford University Press, 1993), p. 297. It should be noted that the World Bank qualifies its numbers with various assumptions, and its figures range from the late 1970s to the early 1990s. Reproduced with permission.

5. World Bank, 1993, pp. 238–239.

6. UNDP, 1994, p. 63.

7. UNDP, 1994, p. 48.

8. UNDP, 1994, p. 50.

9. UNDP, 1994, p. 171.

10. UNDP, 1994, pp. 55, 52.

11. UNDP, 1994, pp. 71, 74.

12. UNDP, 1994, p. 73.

13. UNDP, 1994, p. 74.

14. UNDP, 1994, p. 75.

15. World Bank, *World Development Report, 1991: The Challenges of Development* (New York: Oxford University Press, 1991), p. 35.

16. World Bank, 1991, pp. 43, 56, 57.

17. UNDP, 1991, p. 208.

18. UNDP, 1994, p. 208.

19. World Bank, 1993, pp. 294–295

20. World Bank, 1991, p. 49.

21. World Bank, 1993, pp. 238–239.

22. UNDP, 1994, p. 209.

23. UNESCO, *World Education Report, 1991* (Paris: UNESCO, 1991), p. 98.

24. UNDP, 1994, pp. 170–171.

25. Pablo Hensel and Mónica Levcovich, *Análisis del gasto Público en educación* (Buenos Aires: Universidad de Buenos Aires, 1989), p 11; Ministerio de Educación y Justicia, *El proyecto principal de educación en Argentina* (Buenos Aires: República de Argentina, 1991), table 24.

26. E. Mark Hanson, "Education, Administrative Development and Democracy in Spain," *International Journal of Educational Development* 9 (1989): 133.

27. E. Mark Hanson, *Educational Reform and Administrative Development: The Cases of Colombia and Venezuela* (Stanford, CA: Hoover Institution Press of Stanford University, 1986).

28. A. J. Heidenheimer, H. Heclo, and C. T. Adams, *Comparative Public Policy,* 3rd ed. (New York: St. Martin's Press, 1990), p. 12.

29. I. D. Duchacek, *Comparative Federalism: The Territorial Dimension of Politics* (New York: Holt, Rinehart and Winston, 1970), p. 4.

30. V. Bogdanor, ed., *The Blackwell Encyclopaedia of Political Institutions* (Oxford: Blackwell, 1987) p. 82.

31. M. T. Magstadt, *Nations and Governments: Comparative Politics in Regional Perspective,* 2nd ed. (New York: HarperCollins, 1991).

32. D. A. Rondinelli, *Decentralizing Urban Development Programs: A Framework for Analyzing Policy* (Washington, D.C.: U.S. Agency for International Development, 1990).

33. J. Havemann, "A Divided Continent Sees Shared Destiny," *Los Angeles Times,* February 4.

34. National Center for Educational Statistics, *Digest of Educational Statistics: 1993* (Washington, D.C.: U.S. Department of Education, 1993), p. 151.

35. D. R. Miller and M. B. Ginsburg, "Restructuring Education and the State in England," in *Understanding Educational Reform in Global Context,* ed. M. B. Ginsburg (New York: Garland, 1991), pp. 49–84.

36. World Bank, 1991, p. 264.

37. E. Mark Hanson, *Educational Reform.*

38. National Center for Educational Statistics, 1993, p. 162.

39. W. B. Husband, "Administrative *Perestroika* and Rewriting History: The Dilemma of *Glasnost* in Soviet Education," *Journal of Educational Administration* 29 (1991): 7–16.

40. R. C. Macridis and S. L. Burg, *Introduction to Comparative Politics: Regimes and Change,* 2nd ed. (New York: HarperCollins, 1991), pp. 115–120; Ernesto Schiefelbein, "Restructuring Education Through Economic Competition: The Case of Chile," *Journal of Educational Administration* 29 (1991): 17–29.

41. B. J. Dorsey, "Educational Development and Reform in Zimbabwe," *Comparative Education Review* 33 (1989): 40–58.

42. V. W. Leonard, *Politics, Pupils, and Priests: Argentine Education Since 1943* (New York: Peter Lang, 1989).

43. Dennis A. Rondinelli, *Decentralizing Urban Development Programs;* World Bank, 1991.

44.  E. Mark Hanson, "Democratization and Decentralization in Colombian Education," *Comparative Education Review* 39 (1995): 101–119; Guillermina Tiramonti, *Hacia dónde va la burocracia educativa?* (Buenos Aires: CEFYL, 1990).

45.  B. Delany and L. W. Paine, "Shifting Patterns of Authority in Chinese Schools," *Comparative Education Review* 35 (1991): 26.

# Subject Index

# Name Index

351